WHO IS BURIED IN CHAUCER'S TOMB?

THE

POETICAL WORKS

OF

GEOFFREY CHAUCER.

LONDON.
EDWARD MOXON, DOVER STREET.
1843.

The Poetical Works of Geoffrey Chaucer (Moxon, 1843)

WHO IS BURIED IN CHAUCER'S TOMB?

STUDIES IN THE RECEPTION OF CHAUCER'S BOOK

Joseph A. Dane

Michigan State University Press
East Lansing

All Michigan State University Press books are produced on paper which meets the requirements of American National Standard of Information Sciences—Permanence of paper for printed materials ANSI Z39.48-1984.

Michigan State University Press
East Lansing, Michigan 48823-5202

05 04 03 02 01 00 99 98   1 2 3 4 5 6 7 8

Library of Congress Cataloging-in-Publication Data

Dane, Joseph A.
    Who is buried in Chaucer's tomb? : studies in the reception of
Chaucer's book / Joseph A. Dane.
      p.   cm.
    Includes bibliographical references and index.
    ISBN 0-87013-432-9 (alk. paper)
    1. Chaucer, Geoffrey, d. 1400—Criticism, Textual. 2. Chaucer, Geoffrey,
d. 1400—Bibliography. 3. Chaucer, Geoffrey, d. 1400—Authorship. 4.
Chaucer, Geoffrey, d. 1400—Editors. 5. Literature publishing—Great
Britain—History—18th century. 6. Manuscripts, Medieval—England—
Editing. 7. Manuscripts, English (Middle)—Editing. 8. Paleography,
English. I. Title.
PR1939.D36 1998
821'.1—dc21   98-2718
                                                                       CIP

CONTENTS

Selbst in der Sprache der älteren Tragödie war ihm vieles anstössig, mindestens rätselhaft; besonders fand er zu viel Pomp für einfache Verhältnisse, zu viel Tropen und Ungeheurlichkeiten für die Schlichtheit der Charaktere. So sass er, unruhig grübelnd, im Theater, und er, der Zuschauer, gestand sich, dass er seine grossen Vorgänger nicht verstehe.

–Nietzsche

ACKNOWLEDGMENTS

I had help, support, and advice from various quarters while working on this project. I thank various family members, friends, many students I have neglected to name, librarians, booksellers, colleagues and correspondents–some for their work, some for generous advice, some for keeping me in good humor, and others simply for helping me learn the virtue of patience. I thank in particular John Bidwell, Page duBois, Kathleen Forni, Ralph Hanna, Sandra Prior, Frank Spellman, Stephen Tabor, Daniel Terkla, William Watterson, and various staff members of the Huntington and the Clark Libraries. Chapter 1 and much of Chapter 6 appeared in *Huntington Library Quarterly* 57 (1994): 98-123 and *TEXT* 4 (1989): 59-79; I thank the editors for permission to print the slightly revised versions here. A brief form of the Conclusion appeared in *The Center and Clark Newsletter* 29 (1997): 1-3. I owe other debts as well, to commentators on and teachers of things nautical, and I could not have completed this particular work without having incurred them: to Charles and Nancy Woolley, to the owner of the Silver Dollar from Beals Island, Maine, whose singular civilities will be repaid with what I owe many others, and to the very banality of Jeffrey's curses as he probed the intricacies of a line impossibly snarled, a fix entirely of his own making (a true scholar for you!). First among these is David, now one more decade silenced; his influence continues. My greatest thanks go to Lawrence, Susan, and now Sarah Green. And for his opposeless intellect and will, I thank Seth Lerer, to whom I dedicate all of interest in what follows.

INTRODUCTION

The following study concerns the history of Chaucer reception and the unstable nature of the material on which that history is based. This material has been described, defined, and organized by constantly changing institutions and traditions of Chaucerianism. And all has often been the subject of brief critical histories—histories conventionally narrated in the opening pages or notes of articles and monographs under such real and implied headings as Survey of Previous Scholarship, Previous Editions, Manuscript Evidence. Yet the coherence implied by these brief histories is a function of their genre rather than their materials. The materials themselves and the individuals who have studied them (individuals that collectively form the institution of Chaucerianism) often resist such orderly and coherent histories. We can speak generally of resistance, recalcitrance, incoherence; but the obstinacy of the material is more accurately seen as a persistent recurrence of specific exceptions, anomalies, and simple errors.

My main interest is in what I will call the Chaucer book and its complex relation to identifiable Chaucer editions. These entities are to be distinguished from Chaucer's text. Chaucer's text is reproducible exactly; it can be quoted, edited, even modified in support of critical readings. The Chaucer book, by contrast, is never reproducible exactly, whether it is considered a manuscript, a printed book, or a group of book-copies of either kind. Chaucer manuscripts are unique and (except under the extreme pressures of textual criticism) they are generally treated as such. The printed book is similar: it is theoretically reproducible or, in some of its senses, the product of

1

the myth of reproducibility; but no two books are ever found to be the same and the singularity characteristic of manuscripts continues long after the supposed rise of print culture.

The multiple understandings of the word *book* mean that the Chaucer book both embodies the edition and is itself a member of an edition. And even the word *singularity* will not in this context refer always to a particular object at hand, since there are singular book-copies with their own histories (Sloane's copy of Caxton's *Canterbury Tales*) as well as singular editions, which vary in their individual copies and in the institutional responses they generate (the edition of 1721 by John Urry). To the modern Chaucerian, this conflict between the singular book and the text-based edition can be repeated on higher levels, as the edited and suddenly coherent text becomes transformed into the psychologically coherent master of that text, the author—an author who is not a historical Chaucer at all, but rather what those now known as early moderns might refer to as *Chaucerus noster*. The book, then, becomes a basis for a series of transformations—to an imagined author, to a sane and coherent psychology, to what may well be a nostalgic image of ourselves.[1]

In the chapters below, I have laid great emphasis on two editions: the 1532 edition edited by William Thynne, and what appears to be the first corporate edition, the edition of 1721 by Urry. It is against the background of these two editions that a transformation of Chaucer studies and Chaucer books takes place in the eighteenth century, first with a series of translations and imitations and finally in the production of small-format edition of Thomas Tyrwhitt.[2] Because these eighteenth-century editions were more readily available than previous editions, Chaucer scholars suddenly had choices and needed to face the question of alternative editions and further questions such as what purpose editions serve and what constitutes a legitimate edition. These editions defined issues that have since dominated Chaucer studies: questions of canon and the relation of these questions to the edition; the very notion of a modern edition; the function such editions serve both for the amateur (the general reader) and for self-styled professionals (eighteenth-century antiquarians and twentieth-century professors).

Several excellent surveys of these editions have been written by William L. Alderson, W. W. Greg, Eleanor Prescott Hammond, John Hetherington, and Charles Muscatine.[3] Of equal interest to me are what many bibliographers would now consider erroneous histories or erroneous assumptions within book histories: the persistent assumption that inclusion of a text within a book constitutes evidence of its canonicity; the modern notion that textual criticism proceeds incrementally toward perfection; the various descriptive bibliographies of the Chaucerian book that flatly contradict material evidence, and the vitality of such descriptions among Chaucerians.

As one primary example, we can consider what late nineteenth-century Chaucerian bibliographers referred to as "the First Folio"— the 1532 edition edited by Thynne. However strained the allusion to Shakespeare, this relation seems promoted with no irony by W. W. Skeat in his introduction to the 1905 facsimile of this edition:

> The credit of being the first to print a collected edition of the Works of Chaucer (and others) belongs to William Thynne . . . who published the First Folio edition (here reproduced) in 1532, just a century before the appearance, in 1632, of the Second Folio edition of Shakespeare's Plays.[4]

To modern Chaucerians, the bibliographical facts concerning the 1532 Chaucer are so obvious that confusions by earlier scholars seem barely worth consideration. Its colophon is unambiguous: "Thus endeth the workes of Geffray Chaucer. Printed at London by Thomas Godfray. The yere of our lorde. M.D.xxxii. Cum privilegio a rege indulto." Copies are readily available and two of them have been reproduced in facsimile.[5] Those who did not have this colophon and formed opinions that contradict it were simply wrong.

But eighteenth-century scholars without ready access to this colophon had a different definition of evidence: they relied on a statement by the first scholar of that book and its production, John Leland, whose 1540 commentaries on British writers, always available to Chaucerians, were edited and published in 1709: the 1532 Chaucer was printed, not by Godfray, but by Berthelet, indeed "our Berthelet": "Vicit tamen *Caxodunicam* editionem *Bertholetus* noster opera *Gulielmi Thynni.*"[6]

And why not? Which of the two statements is more authoritative— Godfray's or Leland's? Even with a copy of the book in hand, one could not use the colophon to refute an authority of Leland's stature. The book, after all, is only one witness and arguably a witness only of its own existence. And Leland did not deny that such physical books as one might happen to have in hand existed. So there must be another book. Leland's comments, erroneous as they were, defined evidence that could not be produced, and thus could not be refuted.

The difference between the consensus of twentieth-century and early eighteenth-century scholars reflects the difference in their respective foundations. What has happened is not a correction of an earlier consensus, but a redefinition of what constitutes evidence: new descriptions of physical books, modern facsimiles, and modern editions.

The facts on which such fluid consensus are based do not stay firmly in place. The inscription on Chaucer's tomb in Westminster Abbey, the subject of the lead essay here, provides an example. The facts are elusive, and advances in photography have done nothing to change this. Anyone can go to Westminster Abbey and transcribe these lines; and anyone can buy a post-card with a picture. But in my experience, neither the transcriptions taken of the inscription by reliable witnesses, nor the official photos by Westminster Abbey represent what must be on that tomb or must *have been* on that tomb. What the lines might say doesn't seem any clearer to us than it appears to be to the mythical Victorians walking reverently past the illegible inscription on the tomb in the frontispiece of the Moxon edition (see frontispiece). The largely inferential history of the deterioration of these lines, their creation, their reinscription, is itself the history of Chaucerianism.

Chaucer's book presents an even more problematic multiplicity, for it is composed of thousands of book-copies (each with its own unique history) and conflicting descriptions of each of its various units. Chaucer's book remains Chaucer's book, even when absurdly edited, badly produced, or unread. It is no less Chaucer's book when damaged, annotated, rebound. That there is some stable entity behind all this is surely an illusion, but it is one that Chaucerians can hardly do without.

A century ago, the Westminster coroner gave measurements for what he claimed to be Chaucer's "principal long bones." I have yet to discover any official doubt cast on those laughable measurements, which—remarkably enough!—accord perfectly with Chaucer's own description of himself in the *Canterbury Tales*. I certainly cannot provide Chaucer's bones myself; so why should I question the integrity of the one person who has so graciously taken the trouble to root them up?

States, Issues, and the Edition of 1561

Scholars customarily organize Chaucer's book through the classificatory units of editions, issues, variants, and copies. I will take a moment here to discuss a particular example (for the bibliographically inclined an unnecessary reminder) of the insecurity of some of our most basic notions regarding such matters. As soon as books are considered in terms of editions and issues, the notion of the book itself is dematerialized, since in the strictest sense, the only material books that exist are individual copies. At this point, many Chaucerians might begin to feel some unease. We might well appeal to an authority for the determination of these definitions (STC or the ESTC for pre-1800 books, and less usefully, the NCSTC for nineteenth-century books), but not many Chaucerians I know can tell me off-hand the difference between a Chaucer edition and an issue, or explain why these definitions do not apply well to books produced after new printing processes were introduced in the early nineteenth century; and I hope I am not alone in the difficulties I have in trying to cite accurately the various editions, issues, and reprints of even such basic material as Skeat's Chaucer publications.

A Chaucer history generally distinguishes sixteenth-century editions as follows: 1532 (edited by Thynne), 1542 (re-edition, adding the Plowman's Tale), 1550(?) (Plowman's Tale moved and inserted prior to the Parson's Tale); 1561 (edited by John Stow; numerous additions; one issue with woodcuts); 1598 (first Speght edition); 1602 (second Speght edition, with arguments included prior to each tale and glossary). But the dates of these are still unsettled, there being no external evidence for the date 1550. And definitions of various issues are purely bibliographical. The revised STC defines these in a hierarchy: variant—"a major change in title, imprint or colophon"; issue—"the addition, deletion and/or substitution of leaves or sheets constituting up to half of a book's original sheets"; edition—"an item having a majority of sheets (usually all) from reset type."[7] The four versions of the 1550 edition are distinguished only by differences in the printers named in the colophon: STC thus defines these as variants (the first edition of STC in 1926 considered them "issues").

Other cases are less clear. Prior to the revised STC, most bibliographies of Chaucer speak of two "issues" of 1561 (so the 1926 STC), distinguishing them by their most prominent feature—the presence or absence of woodcuts in the General Prologue.[8] The revised STC, however, identifies three items here: (1) STC 5075 (with woodcuts, and colophon *J. Kyngston f. J. Wight, 1561*); (2) STC 5076, "another issue" (with general title page reset and without woodcuts; colophon identical to STC 5075); (3) STC 5076.3, a "variant" (title page identical to STC 5076, with woodcuts, colophon *H. Bradsha, 1561*). I think the reason this last is a variant rather than an issue is that it presumably has the same title page as the issue of STC 5076. Thus, STC means this book is a variant of the particular issue STC 5076, not a variant of the edition represented by the two issues STC 5075-76.[9]

Chaucerians, of course, are more concerned with the most prominent features of these books—the woodcuts. A copy that has woodcuts is a copy of STC 5075, one without woodcuts is a copy of STC 5076; and thus the Variorum Chaucer sigla distinguish STw from ST. Nonetheless, Chaucerians who rely on such features are, bibliographically speaking, simply in error. Even the three STC entries to some extent misrepresent the nature of variant copies. Since the variant sections are two title pages, two prologues, and two colophons, why should there be three bibliographical units? Why not two, with variants? Or why not eight, corresponding to the eight possible combinations of these three pairs? Note that the particular copies listed under each of the three variants in STC do not conform to the ideal descriptions. The Texas copy of STC 5076 has woodcuts (a feature of STC 5075). And the support for the STC category 5076.3 is very tenuous: the defining copy has the STC 5076 title page (or its "general" title page, whatever that might mean) and prologue with woodcuts,but the second copy is described thus: "The Aldenham copy w. this colophon [as in STC 5076], sold at Sotheby's, 22 March 1937, lot 106 (bought by Sawyer, untraced), app. had gn. tp as in 5076 and prologue without woodcuts." Why the revised STC claims the title page is a general variant of STC 5076, I don't know, since the transcription of that title page in the Auction Catalog itself doesn't match either issue of 1561—in fact, it isn't even close.[10]

In the context of the book trade, such differences can be crucial and costly, even though to many Chaucerians they are mere curiosities at best. If the Texas copy of STC 5076 were accorded the status of an issue, collectors could justify buying it even if they could match each of its sheets with their other copies of STC 5075 and STC 5076. If it is a made-up copy (a product of fraud, if from the hands of Thomas J. Wise, or a legitimate copy, if it comes from what one London dealer described to me somewhat ominously as their "Hospital"), its value plummets. All early Chaucer editions and most of the individual copies that define those editions—both central to the history of Chaucer reception—are mediated by the book trade. They are subject to the conventions of value associated with that trade—conventions that are far from stable. For the bibliographer and for a contemporary book-dealer, a book-copy made up after, say, 1800 has a different status from one made up before, say, 1600. But a turn-of-the-century book-dealer would have had no qualms about completing STC 5076 with a section of STC 5075 containing wood-cuts (this may be what STC thinks of the Texas copy, although I am not certain).[11] Nonetheless, such late made-up copies of the 1561 Chaucer are no less "books" because of their history, and no less influential on Chaucer scholars because of their failure to conform to the units defined in STC.

Pollard and Redgrave were primarily concerned with cataloguing books as a function of their production, and their classifications attempt to circumvent the notion of such made-up copies—that is, the real physical copies that exist. As such bibliographical descriptions become more precise, their objects are dematerialized. No one, for example, has ever actually held STC 5076 or consulted it. What one has done is to consult a copy of a Chaucer that resembles other Chaucers supposedly edited by Stow; quite likely, that copy contains the briefest of bibliographical notes, typed or handwritten at an inde-terminate period—notes that can be very misleading. No one has yet compared the individual book-copies of these various issues and vari-ants of the Stow Chaucer to determine their relations beyond what is readily apparent from their title-pages, woodcuts, and colophons. Textually, no two copies are likely to be the same. And even on such basic matters as paper, no two copies I have examined show the same use and distribution of various paper stocks—a situation that is typical of books of this and earlier periods. Their natures are determined by accidents at press, corrections at press, and the chance of collation. When one has two copies in hand, one can speak of the material exis-tence of each during the present, but to project that material presence into the past and to write a history of that presence very quickly devolves into pure speculation. For despite what some bibliographies may claim, there is no secure way to speak of early and late copies in a press run or, in many cases, even corrected and uncorrected sheets of a press run.[12]

According to most histories of the Chaucer book, the modern tradition of editing began in the eighteenth century. If there is any truth to this, it is important to add that what could be described as modern bibliography began at the same time. As we shall see, the bibliographical history of Chaucer was not easy to construct, and a number of factors were involved: ideological notions of what should be Chaucer, traditions of what had been Chaucer, and most important, the simple recalcitrance of the material evidence—evidence that for better or worse would not take on a decisive character. The Caxton editions that were necessary to form the beginning of a coherent history of Chaucer editing were imperfect, and the description "imperfect at the beginning and end" occurs many times in Thomas Hearne's descriptions of books he is handling. These gaps, both material and textual, were then filled by tradition and conjecture. And sometimes not filled at all. An imperfect Caxton missing the Retraction might be compared with the 1532 edition, or one of the later folio editions to 1687—in all of these, the Retraction was omitted. The material absence (a damaged Caxton) along with the textual absence (in the folio editions) provided the basis for a conspiracy theory that could explain a manuscript presence—manuscript versions of the Retraction were suddenly evidence of "monkish forgery" (see below, chap. 5).

The following series of studies focuses on this problem of the Chaucer book and the tradition of Chaucerianism within which that book and its attendant mythology is transmitted. The arrangement of chapters is roughly chronological in subject. Those in Part One deal with various topics of concern identified in the production and reception of the Chaucer book from the sixteenth to the early eighteenth centuries—a period dominated by the single-volume folio Complete Works: the surprising unreadability of the inscription on Chaucer's tomb; the authorship of Thynne's preface and the typography of the early Thynne edition; the notion of Chaucer as a Wycliffite (by Foxe), and the erroneous bibliographical history that supported that error. The chapters of Part Two consider what has been defined as the modern period of Chaucerianism. This period is marked by an increasing ambivalence of modern editors and critics in relation to the book of Chaucer, and various attempts to provide alternative sources of authority. Among the topics I raise here are: the reception of the 1721 edition and its relation to modern editions; codicological theories of the booklet and the implications of those theories on matters of canonical units of text; changing notions of evidence in modern Chaucer studies; and what I call the tradition of the "unbooking" of Chaucer—a tradition with its roots in Dryden. Together, these sections show a tradition of Chaucerianism wrestling with the problems posed by the physical books that very tradition produces, and an attempt by modern Chaucerians to transcend the authority those books embody.

The chronology, of course, is not absolute. Although history suggests a movement from manuscripts to printed books, scholarly history often proceeds in reverse: codicological concerns are historically later than bibliographical ones. And only in the past decade or so has this field begun to exert a strong influence on American and English bibliography—itself moving away from its roots in what was once the New Bibliography of R. B. McKerrow, W. W. Greg, and Fredson Bowers.[13] The Chaucer book is itself a physical object that exists, changeable and poorly described, over time. And the history of Chaucerianism is one of backing and filling, forgetting, and repeated misdirection.

My concern with the history of the Chaucer book is in part a rejection of critical theories of coherence—theories that several years ago I characterized as conspiratorial in nature.[14] While I don't doubt that Chaucer at one time had a plan (of some sort), that he worked for people who had other plans, that Chaucerians later disputed about Chaucer in devious self-serving ways, I have been struck repeatedly by how seldom any of these plots and counterplots form any coherent pattern and further by how much effort I must expend to be persuaded by arguments that Chaucer's plan or the plans of earlier generations of Chaucerians are similar to our own. Neither Chaucer nor Chaucerians seem remarkably conspiratorial—and there is little convincing evidence that the plots and counterplots occasionally hatched achieved much success. This in spite of, or perhaps because of, the obvious eccentricity and sheer belligerence of a number of key figures in this history: Leland, Francis Thynne, Hearne, Urry, F. J.

Furnivall, and Skeat. What good or evil they may have intended seemed balanced by the social irrelevance of their scholarly concerns; the books they produced (and did not produce) are at best (or at worst) benign.

My study is addressed primarily to Chaucerians, and my initial assumptions are conservative; my own skepticism and the skepticism I hope to provoke depend on these assumptions. Chaucerianism has, like antiquarianism, survived on the textuality of its tradition, and although I have attempted to counter this textuality, I am aware that in many respects this study constitutes an extension of it. By defining a tradition of Chaucerianism, I have discussed one aspect of this book history, and have necessarily omitted the aspects that are not specific to this history, aspects that involve many who have contributed to Chaucerianism while deriving none of its intellectual benefits—those engaged in the industries of type-founding, papermaking, ink manufacture, and transportation, as well as those students unwittingly engaged in supporting the modern institution of Chaucerianism. If they have any voice whatsoever here, it is in what I have deliberately characterized as the sheer intractability of the material itself. It is this intractability and its resistance to coherent explanation that is my subject here.

Chapter 1

WHO IS BURIED IN CHAUCER'S TOMB?

T he following chapter is a preliminary statement of the problems in Chaucer studies and their traditions; it attempts to expose the difficulties attendant on the transmission of and even the expression of seemingly simple textual information. The tradition I investigate here is full of secondary works claiming to be primary works, simple errors, and in one case the invention of a non-existent witness. The chapter itself is paradigmatic of my approach, but those readers who find their patience tried are invited to skip to its concluding paragraphs and then to move to some of the more "storial matter" in later chapters. To pose as a preliminary question a seeming tautology is irritating, as is the tangle of detail that surrounds it; for both the question and the detail get in the way of the felicitous speculation one can indulge in if one assumes that Chaucer, after all, might just as well be in Chaucer's tomb as anyone else. As long as we don't get embroiled in such questions as who is in that tomb or, as here, what is on that tomb, we can speculate on the relation of Chaucer to the Church, to London politics, then follow that with the same series of heady questions focused on his texts (assuming of course, as no self-respecting twentieth-century or nineteenth-century Chaucerian would, that Chaucer wrote Chaucer's Workes). And if anyone were to raise questions about that much-restored tomb, and if scholars cared much about it (they don't), it would be time simply to "roll up one's sleeves" (or someone else's sleeves), go to the source, read it, perhaps move a few stones around to unearth whatever might be needed, and get back to the basic activities of literary scholarship.

I don't know whether Chaucer is in Chaucer's Tomb, nor am I conversant with the techniques that could be used to find out. What interests me are questions that stand in the way. And I begin with a literary question: what does the tomb say? Prior to posing such ambitious questions as "Who is Buried in Chaucer's Tomb?" or the more speculative "Why is Chaucer Buried in Chaucer's Tomb?"[1] we ought at least to be able to read the inscriptions that claim he is there. And if we can't, then what business do we have going to the tomb with our bone-measuring instruments?

The Inscription(s)

There are three texts inscribed on or directly related to the tomb. A version of all three texts was incorporated into the "Life of Chaucer" included in Speght's 1602 edition (c1v; see fig. 1)[2]:

(1) a four-line inscription (a version is now in Westminster Abbey) ("Qui fuit Anglorum vates . . .");

(2) the last two lines of a poem by Surigone, often found printed in early Chaucer editions ("Galfridus Chaucer vates . . .");

(3) references to verses "about the ledge" of the tomb ("Si rogites . . ."); interestingly enough, all sources that quote these last verses claim they are either illegible or completely worn out.

The first printed reference to any of these texts is to the "old verses" by Stephano Surigone. It occurs in Caxton's epilogue to Chaucer's translation of Boethius in 1478. Caxton claims that the English language "shal endure perpetuelly," as will the memory of Chaucer:

> of whom the body and corps lieth buried in thabbay of Westmestre beside london to fore the chapele of seynte benet. by whos sepulture is wreton on a table hongyng on a pylere his Epitaphye maad by a poete laureat wherof the copye foloweth.

Caxton then prints a thirty-line poem by this "poete laureat" Surigone, and ends with the following often-quoted distich:

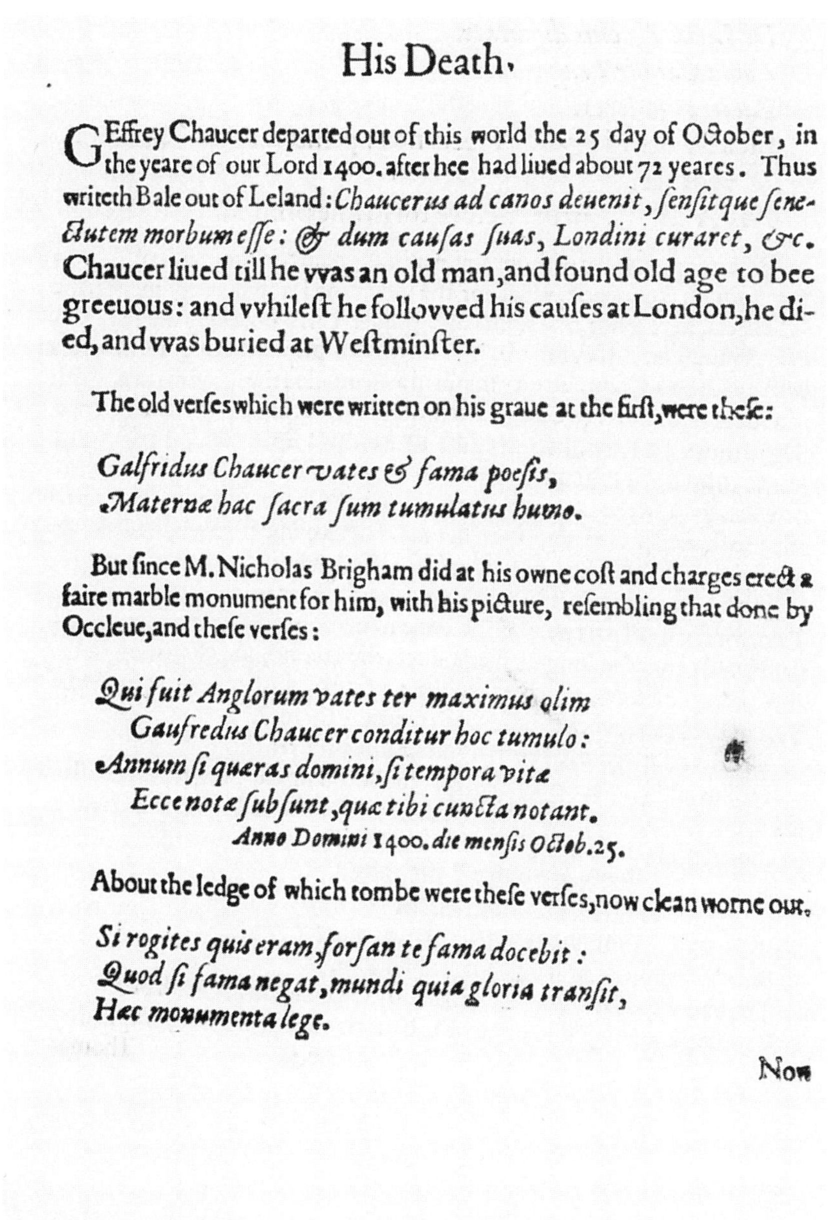

His Death,

G Effrey Chaucer departed out of this world the 25 day of October, in the yeare of our Lord 1400. after hee had liued about 72 yeares. Thus writeth Bale out of Leland: *Chaucerus ad canos deuenit, fenfitque fene-Elutem morbum effe: & dum caufas fuas, Londini curaret, &c.* Chaucer liued till he vvas an old man, and found old age to bee greeuous: and vvhileſt he follovved his caufes at London, he died, and vvas buried at Weſtminſter.

The old verfes which were written on his graue at the firſt, were theſe:

Galfridus Chaucer vates & fama poefis,
Materne hac facra fum tumulatus humo.

But fince M. Nicholas Brigham did at his owne coſt and charges erect a faire marble monument for him, with his picture, refembling that done by Occleue, and thefe verfes :

Qui fuit Anglorum vates ter maximus olim
    Gaufredus Chaucer conditur hoc tumulo :
Annum fi quæras domini, fi tempora vitæ
    Ecce notæ fubfunt, quæ tibi cunEla notant.
        Anno Domini 1400. die menfis OElob.25.

About the ledge of which tombe were thefe verfes, now clean worne out.

Si rogites quis eram, forfan te fama docebit :
Quod fi fama negat, mundi quia gloria tranfit,
Hæc monumenta lege.

Now

Figure 1. Thomas Speght, "Life of Chaucer," in *The Workes of our Antient and Learned English Poet*, Geffrey Chaucer (1602), sig. clv.

Galfridus Chaucer vates . et fama poesis
    Materne . hac sacra sum tum(u)latus humo.[3]

As for the pillar or tablet, no physical traces of it remain. The four-line inscription—the text most often meant in references to the inscription on the tomb—was written ca. 1556, when Nicholas Brigham erected the present monument (conventionally called a "tomb") on the east wall of the south transept. The two lines "about the ledge" exist only in verbal accounts of the tomb's history.[4]

Simple as this story is, most of the specific details are subject to dispute. An earlier floor-slab (no one has ever described what may have been on it) was sawn up to make room for Dryden and a new floor-slab with a modern inscription (not at issue here) placed there after 1714. And some of the more self-assured witnesses have not been disinterested. Caxton's account is an advertising blurb; no one has explained why he and an obscure Italian poet should have known more about Chaucer's burial place than an early eulogist such as Hoccleve, who says nothing about Chaucer's resting place although much lamenting his death. Later authenticating claims are combined with overt pleas for funds: one scheme to restore Brigham's monument bases its appeal in 1850 on researches by unspecified "competent authorities" proving that the monument is indeed *"the original tomb* of the Poet."[5] Other claims combine minute detail with striking vagueness: Chaucer's bones were presumably "exposed" in 1889 to make room for Browning, and the Westminster coroner's account of the measurement of Chaucer's "principall long bones" is given in a one-paragraph letter of 1897 (the actual examination having occurred "some years back"). But how he knew the bones were Chaucer's rather than those of some other pious poet piled on top of him is unexplained.[6]

The "Old Verses": Caxton's "Table Honging On a Pyler" and Leland's "Nivea Tabella"

One of the first problems to be encountered in dealing with these traditions concerns the "ii old verses." Although the text itself is relatively stable, the words of Caxton documenting their existence have undergone some odd transformations. And it is here that we will first confront John Leland's *Commentarii de scriptoribus Britannicis* (ca. 1540)—a work that, although buried quietly in bibliographical discussion of Chaucer, is one of the most deviously influential works in the entire history of Chaucer studies.[7] My chapters below will be referring often to it. The interpretation of a passage from Leland controls recent discussion of the epitaph and of the relations between Caxton and Surigone. Leland has been credited by Chaucerians with a number of misleading statements; his remarks concerning Surigone's epitaph in Westminster Abbey and his own "nivea tabella" should now be included among these.

In a very level-headed article of 1967, N. F. Blake gives the following version of events:

> While in England, [Surigone] either spontaneously or more probably by request composed an epitaph on Chaucer. This was then placed by some admirer or by Surigone himself on a pillar by Chaucer's tomb. . . . When Caxton came to Westminster, he saw and copied the inscription. This he subsequently printed in his edition of Boethius together with four of his own verses. ("Caxton and Chaucer," 160)

Blake was reacting against a speculative version of the story, based on Leland, first offered by R. Weiss in 1937, according to which Caxton met Surigone in 1471 in Cologne and may later have collaborated with him on the edition of Chaucer's *Boece* (1484).[8] According to Blake's rejoinder, Surigone need not have been in England in the 1470s; Caxton need not have even met Surigone.[9] But Leland's account has a way of reasserting its airy-thin authority. Blake's critique of Weiss continues:

> Leland says that Surigone composed the Latin epitaph on Chaucer at Caxton's request and that the last two lines from that epitaph were engraved on the tomb also at Caxton's request. . . . But Weiss neglected the fact that Leland goes on to say that all the verses were inscribed on a tablet (*tabella*) which Surigone had caused to be fixed to a pillar near Chaucer's tomb: ". . . elegos in nivea tabella depictos, quos Surigonus Visimonasterii columnae, Chauceri sepulchro vicinae, adfixit." Leland's account of the epitaph is therefore as follows. Caxton asked Surigone to make an epitaph for Chaucer. This epitaph Surigone had inscribed on a tablet which he affixed to a pillar by Chaucer's tomb. (160)

Is Blake right about what Leland claims was affixed to the column? Here are Leland's closing lines in full, from the 1709 edition used by all modern scholars:

> Habes nunc, humanissime lector, elegos in nivea tabella depictos, quos Surigonus Visimonasterii columnae, Chauceri sepulchro vicinae, adfixit. Tu saepe eosdem in nostri vatis gratiam legas. Sic tibi, quisquis eris, faveat suadela, leposque.

Lounsbury's translation of these lines, well-known to Chaucerians, is as follows (note the ambiguity, not in the Latin, in the antecedent of "which"):

> You have now, O most courteous reader, the elegiac lines inscribed on a snow-white tablet *which* Surigon affixed to the Westminster column adjoining the tomb of Chaucer. May my persuasion and their attractiveness dispose you, whoever you are, to read them often for the sake of our poet. (italics added) [10]

According to Blake's interpretation of these lines (Leland's or Lounsbury's), Leland says that a tablet, apparently a "nivea tabella," was caused by Surigone to be fixed to a pillar—apparently the very table mentioned by Caxton. But what Leland says is that Surigone had the elegiacs, not a snowy tablet, affixed to a column near Chaucer's tomb ("elegos . . . quos" and not *"tabella . . . quam"). You, reader, now have these same elegiacs "painted in a snowy tablet." The word *tabella* is a common classical word for a writing tablet; in the plural, the word is a metaphor for writing itself. And the snowy-white nature of paper was a cliche used even in Chaucer: "Upon a thikke palfrey, paper white" (*Legend of Good Women*, line 1198).[11] Leland has transformed what Caxton calls the *table* in Westminster Abbey into the *nivea tabella* which the reader is now reading—the page of his own book; and future readers will be able to enjoy Surigone's verses over and over. Although Lounsbury a hundred years ago complained about Leland's propensity to soar into verse, no one to my knowledge as pointed out that he does so here. Leland's last line is a hexameter and a clear warning that something in this account is afoot.

The Inscription: Recent Witnesses

The texts of the main inscription and the attendant "verses about the ledge" are transmitted in several overlapping traditions: in Chaucer editions and biographies, in written surveys of physical antiquities, and in engravings found in these and other works.[12] Before examining these early witnesses, let us consider the information about Chaucer's burial and tomb in the most recent biography of Chaucer: Pearsall's excellent *Life of Geoffrey Chaucer*. The tomb is not central to Pearsall's project, and in his discussion, various traditions surrounding it collide. On the matter of Chaucer's burial, Pearsall relies on the main Chaucerian tradition represented by Crow and Olson's *Life Records* of 1966:

> [Chaucer's] remains were moved in 1556 to a new tomb set against the east wall of the south transept, a part of the abbey which has since become known as "Poets' Corner" (plate 1). It is the inscription on this tomb, reported in 1606 but now illegible, that provides the date of his death (plate 14).[13]

Plate 1 in Pearsall's *Life* should show the tomb with an illegible inscription; plate 14 should show a 1606 report of the date of Chaucer's death. But this is not what the plates show. In plate 1 illustrating Chaucer's tomb (on the page facing the quotation above), labelled "by courtesy of the Dean and Chapter of Westminster," the inscription is clearly readable (although Pearsall's text claims it is not) (the text is in small capitals; I transcribe u and v according to modern conventions):

M. S.

Qui fuit Anglorum vates ter maximus olim
   Galfridus Chaucer conditur hoc tumulo
Annum si quaeras Domini si tempora mortis
   Ecce notae subsunt quae tibi cuncta notant
      25 Octobris 1400
      Ærumnarum requies mors
N. Brighham hos fecit musarum nomine sumptus
      1556

The photograph in Pearsall's plate 1 must have been retouched. Pearsall is right that the tomb is not this legible (at least, not according to absolutely reliable reports from 1993); nor is the text as legible in any of the black-and-white or color photos I have seen from the Abbey. The word *sumptus* is not readable, nor are the first two digits of Chaucer's death date. In other words, the tomb itself and photos that accurately portray what is *now* on the tomb are consistent with what Pearsall says in his text about its illegibility.[14] Furthermore, and more important, Pearsall's statements are also consistent with a venerable Chaucerian tradition: that the tomb is *now* illegible (whenever that may be). Chaucerians have made this claim at least since the early nineteenth century, despite the efforts of various restorers to prove them wrong. The engraving by Todd, dated 1809, follows a convention whereby inscriptions are represented by a wavy line. Nonetheless, a break in the line clearly indicates that part of the inscription is illegible. The engraving also shows one of the shields as no longer visible (see fig. 5 below).[15]

Plate 14 in Pearsall's biography should depict something "reported in 1606." Instead, it depicts a 1652 engraving from Ashmole's *Theatrum Chemicum Britannicum* (see fig. 2), in fact the first pictorial representation of the tomb. The date 1606 is one often assigned in Chaucer studies to Camden's report of the inscription, although the report was first published in 1600.[16] Camden is the first to quote the inscription roughly as we find it in the Westminster Abbey photo, quoted above (compare the variant *tempora vitae* in the Ashmole plate, fig. 2). My point here is not to criticize Pearsall, whose discussion is excellent, nor his plates, which are helpful and very traditional. I only wish to point out the confusion and conflation of sources here— something perfectly in accord with the tradition in which they are transmitted.

The Editorial Tradition

The first Chaucer editions to contain substantial prefatory material are the 1598 and 1602 editions of Thomas Speght. Each contains a "Life of Chaucer" in which the tomb inscription is quoted. The Life is generally attributed to Speght, although Stow claimed to have collected the material and passed it on to Speght. This is of some importance, for if the text of the inscription is part of that material, it is

Figure 2. Elias Ashmole, *Theatrum Chemicum Britannicum* (1652), p. 226. Photo courtesy of the Henry E. Huntington Library, San Marino, Calif.

secondhand at best.[17] The 1598 edition contains a text of the "old verses" and one of the earliest published version of Brigham's inscription. Speght's English text is in Roman type, his vernacular quotations in blackletter, and the Latin quotation in italics (sig.c1v). In the 1602 edition, Speght adds a citation to the verses "about the ledge," thus becoming the first published source to contain all three of the texts (see fig. 1 above).

In the text of the old verses, the 1602 edition changes *Maternae haec* (1598) to *Maternae hac*—readings that alternate in later works.[18] The text of the verses "about the ledge" is subject to more variation (see Table of Variants below). The statement that these verses are "clean worne out" is curious.[19] The only earlier published witness to these lines I know of is Camden (1600), who says nothing about their legibility or his source.

The most significant features of what Speght gives as the inscription itself are the absence of the heading *M.S.* (i.e., *Manibus sacrum*), the absence of the attribution to Brigham, the reading *tempora vitae,* and the form in which the date is given: *Anno Domini 1400. die mensis Octob. 25.* No other texts I have seen follow Speght in providing the date in this form. But Speght's variant *tempora vitae* survives into modern discussions through the 1652 plate in Ashmole, the biographies included in the edition by Urry (1721) and the various Aldine editions (1845 et seq.), the introduction in Skeat's edition, and even in the text printed in small capitals as Brigham's very own in Spurgeon's *Chaucer Criticism,* 1:94. In other particulars (Ashmole's *nota* is unique), these texts are identical to the restored text shown in the Westminster Abbey photo in Pearsall's biography. Skeat's discussion, for Chaucerians one of the more obvious sources for such information, is taken verbatim from the biography of Chaucer by Nicolas Harris Nicolas included in the many issues of the 1845 Aldine edition of Chaucer. Nicolas derived the inscription he gives there from the versions in Urry's edition—following the editorial tradition even when citing the antiquarian one.[20]

If there is for Chaucerians a "vulgate text" of the epitaph, this is it: either the text of Speght with the heading *M.S.* and the form of the date altered to read *25 Octobris 1400,* or, if one prefers, the Westminster Abbey restored text (as depicted in Pearsall's biography), with the variant *tempora vitae.* None of these editors claims to give a first-hand account of the tomb. They do not note variant readings and contradictions in their own sources; they do not clearly and accurately give the source of their own readings; and, with the exception of the repeated phrase concerning the verses "clean worne out," they do not refer to the deteriorating state of the tomb itself. What I might regard as unsporting—"examination . . . of the tomb itself" (the words of the 1850 "Weekly Gossip" quoted in n. 5 above)—these editors might quite rightly have considered unnecessary and useless.[21]

Even in the reports of my colleagues, reports which I have characterized as absolutely reliable, I corrected (silently) a transcription
error.

Antiquarians and Monument Surveys: Camden (1600)
through Crull (1722)

The most important witness to the inscription not in an edition of
Chaucer is in William Camden's *Reges, Reginae, Nobiles . . .* of 1600—
the work cited by Chaucerians following Hammond and Crow-Olsen
in its third edition. Chaucer's monument is one of those listed "In
Australi plaga Ecclesiae." Camden omits the heading *M.S.* and the
date after the final line, "N. Brigham hos fecit Musarum nomine
sumptus." With these exceptions, it is Camden's text that finds its way
into the various "restorations" (for example, Poole's in 1881 and the
Westminster Abbey photo published in Pearsall's biography), probably through John Dart's *Westmonasterium* of 1723. In his notes on the
inscription, Camden is the first to report a 1555 date for Brigham's
monument: ("Anno vero 1555. Nicholaus Brigham Musarum nomine
huius ossa transtulit"), although all other early witnesses claim that
1556 is the date inscribed on the monument itself. Camden is thus
the apparent source for John Pits (*De Rebus Anglicis*, 1619), who, like
Camden, gives the date for Brigham's monument as 1555 while omit-
ting the date from the inscription itself.[22] Camden adds the verses
that Speght, in 1602, will describe as "about the ledge" and "now
clean worne out." He says nothing about position or legibility:

> Si rogitas quis fueram, forsan te fama docebit;
> Quod si fama neget mundi quia gloria transit,
>   Haec monumenta lege.[23]

Another early witness is John Weever, *Ancient Funerall Monuments*
(1631). Weever is often cited, for example, by Crull in the monument
survey of Westminster Abbey and in Dart's Life in the 1721 edition of
Chaucer. Weever refers in his text to Speght's Life, "written at large,"
and follows his citation of the three sets of verses with passages from
Hoccleve, Lydgate, Douglas (all in Speght; the Douglas citation
appears only in the 1602 edition), as well as from Spenser and Sidney.
His text of the "old verses" contains the variant *Materna* (for

Maternae), giving a readable text, but one shared only by Ashmole (1652). For the inscription itself, Weever relies on Camden, including in his description Camden's reported date of 1555 and the reference to Brigham's burial of his daughter Rachael. Like Camden, he omits the *M.S.* and gives no date after the line identifying Brigham. He also uses Speght's phrase "about the ledge of the Tomb" for the verses "Si rogitas . . .". The variants in Weever (*rogitas, eram, negat*) are not precisely those of Camden (*rogitas, fueram, neget*) or of Speght (*rogites, eram, negat*), although any set of these could be derived from the other (see Table of Variants below). Weever introduces his texts with the statement: "The Inscriptions upon his Tombe at this day are after this manner." Weever had at least two texts before him—Speght and Camden. Does the phrase "at this day" mean that Weever is claiming to give an eye-witness account as well?

Camden's text of the four-line inscription is used also in the surveys of Westminster Abbey by Henry Keepe (1683) and Jodocus Crull (1711; 1722).[24] Keepe's text of the inscription is identical to that in Camden; it is in italics and lacks the *M.S.* Unlike Camden, Keepe adds the date 1556 after a comma following *sumptus*. Crull, in his 1711 edition, quotes the inscription in the form given by Camden and Weever, citing Weever directly. Crull includes the introductory *M.S.* and, like Keepe, adds the date 1556 after a comma following the word *sumptus*. For the remaining verses, Crull cites Weever. In the "old verses," Crull prints the ungrammatical although metrically acceptable variant *Materni*, probably a simple error. The verses about the ledge have another unique variant: *Hoc monumentum Lege*—this one grammatical, but unmetrical.

In the 1722 edition, Crull introduces some changes: the date is now given as 1555. This was the date reported by Camden, seconded by Weever, but not included in either of their transcriptions of the inscription itself. Crull is the first to claim that that date is actually on the tomb. The "old verses" are quoted not from "Mr. *Wever*" (as Crull claimed in 1711), but from Caxton's edition of Chaucer's *Boethius*, and the 1711 error *Materni* is corrected. The verses "about the ledge" are also corrected: *Hoc Monumentum* (1711) becomes *Haec Monumenta*; and Crull uses the Camden variant *neget* for 1711 *negat*. I assume Camden is the source for both inscription and verses.

Engraved Inscriptions (Ashmole to Todd)

The textual tradition is obviously unstable; but the pictorial tradition is no better, both in its visual details and in the engraved texts. The details below should be considered not in terms of their accuracy ("are they right or wrong?") but rather with reference to the question: "what in the days before photography constitutes a first-hand account or even a primary source?"

The earliest pictorial representation of Chaucer's tomb is the engraving contained in Ashmole's *Theatrum Chemicum Britannicum* (1652), a collection of English alchemical texts with extensive Prolegomena and Annotations.[25] The engraving of Chaucer's tomb is on the page 226 facing the beginning of the Chaucer Canon's Yeoman's Tale (see fig. 2).

Significant features of the text in this engraving include the clear error in line 4 (*nota*), the short form of the death date (*25 Octobris 1400;* so Camden), and the variant *tempora vitae* (so Speght). In addition, it contains all the surrounding material (*M.S., Ærumnarum . . . 1556*), material that could not have been derived directly from any of the earlier written versions of Speght, Camden, or Weever.

Ashmole states in his diary that Vaughan "wrought and finished" all the cuts for this collection at Ashmole's own house. Presumably, Vaughan worked from drawings of the actual tomb (even the placement of the arms is in accord with what can be seen in all photos, from the Royal Commissions photo of 1926 to the more recent Abbey photos). But sources apart from these hypothetical drawings are involved as well. The portrait of Chaucer probably comes from Speght's Chaucer: "The *Picture* of *Chaucer* is now somewhat decay'd, but the *Graver* has recovered it after a *Principall* left to *posterity* by his worthy Schollar *Tho. Occleve,* who hath also these *Verses* upon it" (*Theatrum Chemicum Britannicum,* 472).[26] Even the italics in this engraving function as do italics in a printed source: they are nonrepresentational, that is, they do not reproduce the form of anything that was on the tomb.[27] Thus the italics over the figure on the left are a simple identification: "Imago Chauceri." And thus the variant *vitae* appears, from Speght, engraved on the tomb itself. Ashmole presented to his engraver as the text on the tomb both the words and in part the form (italics) of the text *as reported by Speght and the surveys.*[28]

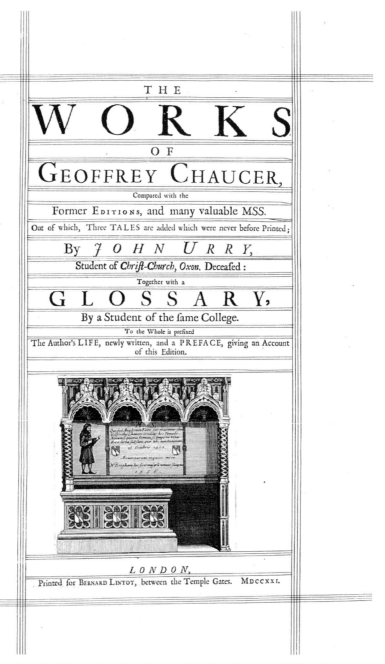

Figure 3. John Urry, ed., *The Works of Geoffrey Chaucer* **(1721), title page. Photo courtesy of the Henry E. Huntington Library.**

The unsigned engraving that appears on the title page of Urry's 1721 edition (see fig. 3) is clearly traced directly from the Vaughan engraving in Ashmole, with differences only in shading and in details of Chaucer's image. The dimensions of the two engravings are identical, and in both, the figure of Chaucer holds a book rather than rosary beads he holds in the Hoccleve portrait. The inscriptions are in script, although the Urry engraving sets its verses flush left. The texts are identical with the exception of the correction of the obvious error *nota* to *notae* in the Urry plate. The same words are capitalized and in the surrounding text, the same abbreviation occurs: *musarũ*. No other account of the inscription contains these features.

But the text of the inscription on the title page differs from that given in the prefatory Life of Chaucer (written in part by John Dart). All three inscriptions are printed in this Life (sig. e2).[29] The date for Brigham's addition is given as "about the 1555" [sic] with reference to Weever, *Funerall Monuments*, but the text (italicized) is not identical to that in Speght, Weever, or the plate on the title page; it is, rather, what I have called the "vulgate" text, with the *M.S.*, the variant *tempora vitae*, and a variant of the short form of the date *25. Octobris. 1400.*

For the verses "about the Ledge," ("Verses now quite worn out"), Dart cites Speght and Weever in his notes. The phrase "now quite worn out" is apparently taken from Speght's edition, as are the variants *rogites* and *negat*. Dart's text, thus, is largely what it claims to be—a conflation of Weever and Speght—the edition Dart later claims he uses in preference to the Urry Chaucer in which this very biography appears. The *M.S.*, however, is not included in any of these texts. Did Dart, even before he took the survey of Westminster in 1723, transcribe this from the tomb itself? Or did he simply look at the 1652 Ashmole plate, a plate he knew and to which he refers in this same survey (see below, n. 32)?

The most important and most elaborate early engraving appears in Dart's *Westmonasterium* (1723), a full-page engraving signed J. Cole (see fig. 4).[30] The text has the variants *mortis* (cf. Speght's *vitae*) and the short form of the date, *25 Octobris, 1400.* This engraving differs in various details from all other representations of the monument: the capitals, the placement of the arms, and, most notably, the inclusion of a figure "in Tudor costume" to the right of the inscription, symmetrically placed against Chaucer's image on the right. This figure has been tentatively identified as Brigham himself.[31] The text is low-

Figure 4. From John Dart, *Westmonasterium* (1723), 1: 85. Photo courtesy of the Henry E. Huntington Library.

ered, such that the arms flank not the date but the text itself. This does not accord with what seems to be visible in the early photos, nor is it consistent with the Ashmole engraving. Furthermore, this placement of text and arms causes a visible problem in line three, cramping the letters of the final word, *mortis*.

The Cole engraving probably results from examination of the tomb itself. The conventional italics found in all previous sources (written and engraved) here are changed to roman capitals; and none of the significant Speght-Ashmole variants finds a place here, even though Dart refers to the Ashmole engraving.[32] The cramping of the word *mortis* may mean that Dart began with Speght's text of the inscription (containing the word *vitae*) and changed it to *mortis* after the engraving had been blocked out.

For Cole, the Roman capitals were an integral part of the text, just as they seem to be in the printed versions of the epitaph in Nicolas and in Spurgeon (see n. 20 above). Cole is not concerned with its precise appearance (thus its eccentric relation to the arms). The roman capitals are a statement of what kind of text is or should be on a tomb, not necessarily what text is there, just as the blank right panel calls out for what may be an *Imago Discipuli* to balance the *Imago Chauceri*, still with Ashmole's book, in the left panel.

Cole's is the last engraving of the tomb to contain a text. Other early engravings include those in Crull (1722), Todd (1809; fig. 5), and a color engraving in Ackermann's history of Westminster Abbey (1832); but none of these contains a legible text. The text of Ackermann's description of the tomb and his version of the inscription itself are taken directly from Dart's *Westmonasterium*.[33]

John Foxe and "One M. Brickam"

There are two other early witnesses cited by Chaucerians: Foxe, in *Actes and Monuments*, whose text of the inscription is very distinctive, and Robert Commaunder (before 1613). Commaunder has achieved some notice among Chaucerians for claiming that the author of the inscription is not Brigham but "Hickeman." In Crow and Olson's *Life-Records* (1966), this Hickeman is still given credit for "part of the work" (549 n.2). It is time to dispose of this mysterious Hickeman, who is no authority on anything whatsoever; he is nothing more than a ghost, resulting from a mistranscription of Foxe.

Figure 5. Henry J. Todd, *Illustrations of the Lives and Writings of Gower and Chaucer* **(1810). Photo courtesy of the Henry E. Huntington Library.**

Foxe's *Actes and Monuments* appeared in six editions before 1613, and the section on Chaucer's monument appears first in the second edition (1570).[34] Foxe cites "these ii old verses" in familiar form and identifies the author of the mid-sixteenth century monument as "one M. Brickam." The inscription itself reads as follows:

> Qui fuit Anglorum vates ter maximus olim,
> Galfridus Chaucer conditur hoc tumulo.
> Annum si quaeras Domini, si tempora mortis,
> Ecce nota subsunt, quae tibi cuncta notent.
> Octob. An. 1400

The significant variants here are *mortis, nota, notent,* the form of the date, and the absence of all surrounding text (*M.S.,* the line concerning Brigham). In later editions of Foxe, *Brickam* is spelled *Brickham; nota* is corrected to *notae,* and the abbreviation *An.* expanded to *Anno.*

The testimony of Robert Commaunder (d. 1613) was discovered by F. J. Furnivall in 1904; Commaunder's notes are from a commonplace book (now Egerton 2642).[36] Commaunder quotes the epitaph and seems to attribute it to an otherwise unknown "Hickeman": "Carmina Epitaphica magistri Hickeman Auditoris composita Anno domini 1556." Furnivall asked in a 1904 *Notes and Queries* article whether such a person was known: "Who *is* Hickeman?" To my knowledge, he received no reply. But the correct answer is "No one."

Commaunder's version of the epitaph contains the variants *mortis, note, notent,* and the date in the form *25 Octobris, Anno 1400;* it also omits the surrounding text (*M.S.* and the line concerning Brigham).[37] Furnivall, noting the variant *mortis,* states: "In one point Commaunder's text of the epitaph is better than Brigham's as given by Skeat, . . . for 1400 is clearly the date *mortis* of the poet, and not his *vitae.*" But every text that has the variant *vitae* is, as we have seen, indebted to Speght's edition. Commaunder's variants are easy to identify; his text is from Foxe—a book he would be as likely to know as any other, and a much more accessible source for the inscription than the tomb itself. No other witness gives the date in a similar form; and only one other (Pits, in 1619) has the variant *notent.* Foxe's earlier reading *nota* is corrected to *notae* in the 1583 edition. Commaunder either got it from there or corrected it himself, just as he expanded an abbreviation for *Octobris* while retaining the distinctive form in which Foxe gives the date.

Spurgeon, in 1908, suggested that Commaunder had simply misread the name *Brigham* on the tomb: "As Nicholas Brigham's name is carved on the tomb of Chaucer in the Abbey as its restorer, we can only suppose that Commaunder mistook the name" (*Chaucer Criticism,* note at 1:186). I think Spurgeon is right; Commaunder misread the name. But he did not misread the roman capitals on the tomb. What Commaunder misread were the references to "one M. Brickam" or "Brickham" printed in blackletter in a copy of Foxe: the same source for the distinctive variants that appear in his text of the epitaph itself.[38]

Conclusions

For most Chaucerians, the original readings of these verses are of no great consequence: they are not by Chaucer, but about Chaucer (or so it is said). As long as the date on the tomb is more or less accurate (to precede by a whisker the earliest *Canterbury Tales* manuscripts), as long as Chaucer's bones are somewhere in the vicinity (and who can prove they aren't?), then textual criticism, literary criticism, and social criticism of Chaucer can proceed as before.

The variants of these texts show clearly that editors follow editors (Skeat is dependent on Speght), and monument surveys are based on previous monument surveys (Weever is in debt to Camden). But the actual text of any of the three inscriptions is difficult to determine. The verses about the ledge, if they existed at all, were probably on the ledge before the physical monument became "Chaucer's Tomb" in 1556, and were removed. Stated succinctly: the verses about the ledge of Chaucer's tomb were never about the ledge of Chaucer's Tomb. Surigone's verses have as many variants as printings. And the four-line inscription itself shows substantive variants (some involving "life" and "death") which textual criticism can hardly resolve.

So why not just look at the tomb?

Since Dart's survey of 1723, eyewitnesses consistently report the inscription as "defaced" or "obliterated." Neale and Brayley reported in 1818-23 that the inscription was "now almost obliterated" and printed a text derived from Camden and Dart.[39] But Henry Poole in 1881 determined to put an end to such obscurity:

> Fifty years' more disintegration [since the survey of Neale and Brayley] followed with still further obscuration, when the writer closely scrutinized and cleansed the slab, discovering traces of all the letters but four. Without any attempt to strengthen the engraving, the lettering was developed by painting all the remaining traces with gold-coloured paint, and with the same pigment reproducing the four absent letters;

and now the inscription of 1558 [*sic!*] is quite distinct and perfectly durable.[40]

Surely, those who in the past century have chosen to restore the tomb according to the text of Camden, Weever, and Dart have acted rationally. And most of the recalcitrant variants in, say, Speght can be reasonably explained away on textual-critical grounds.[41] But what is rational is not necessarily what is correct. Whether Poole or any of his successors (those responsible for the perfectly legible text reproduced in Pearsall's photo) could see an original inscription through and past this tradition, and whether, if they did see such an inscription, they could have detected anything in its traces that contradicted their chosen authorities—there is no way of knowing such things.

Questions such as who is in (or near) that tomb, whether it is (or was) a tomb, and the precise political import of this possible tomb—these are matters on which many authorities in the Chaucer tradition have for centuries pronounced with no small fervor. If it is permitted to compare great things with small, we might include in these discussions the uncertainties surrounding the words many of these same authorities claim are carved in stone.

TABLE OF VARIANTS

Substantive variants and selected spelling and formal variants appear below. Cited in order of date; 1598, 1602 denote Speght's editions.

Inscription:

M.S.: Ashmole (plate); Urry (plate and text); Crull, Dart (plate), Nicolas-Skeat
[*M.S.* absent]: Foxe, 1598, 1602, Camden, Commaunder, Pits, Weever, Keepe

mortis: Foxe, Commaunder, Camden, Pits, Weever, Keepe, Crull, Dart (plate)
vitae: 1598/1602, Ashmole (plate), Urry (text and plate), Nicolas-Skeat

nota: Foxe (1576), Ashmole (plate), Urry (plate)
notae: Foxe (1583), 1598/1602, Camden, Commaunder (spelled *note*), Pits, Urry (text), Crull, Keepe, Dart (plate), Nicolas-Skeat

notant: 1598/1602, Camden, Ashmole (plate), Urry (text, plate), Dart (plate), Crull, Keepe, Nicolas-Skeat
notent: Foxe, Commaunder, Pits

25 Octobris 1400: Camden, Pits, Weever, Ashmole (plate), Urry (text and plate), Dart (plate), Keepe, Crull, Nicolas-Skeat
Anno domini 1400, die mensis Octob. 25: 1598/1602
25 Octob. An. 1400: Foxe, Commaunder (*Octobris, Anno*)

N. Brigham . . . 1556: Ashmole (plate), Urry (text and plate), Dart, Crull (1722), Keepe, Nicolas-Skeat
N. Brigham . . . 1555: Crull (1711)
N. Brigham . . . [no date]: Camden, Weever (date 1555 in text)
[lines absent]: Foxe, 1598/1602, Commaunder, Pits

Verses about the ledge:

rogites: 1602, Ashmole, Urry, Nicolas-Skeat
rogitas: Camden, Weever, Crull, Dart,

eram: 1602, Weever, Ashmole, Urry, Crull, Dart, Nicolas-Skeat
fueram: Camden

negat: 1602, Weever, Ashmole, Crull (1711), Urry, Dart, Nicolas-Skeat
neget: Camden, Crull (1722), Dart

Chapter 2

WHO WROTE CHAUCER'S WORKES?—
THE AUTHORITY OF [WILLIAM THYNNE?]

For though it had ben in Demosthenes or Homerus tymes / whan all lernyng
and excellency of sciences florisshed amonges the Grekes / or in the season that Cicero
prince of eloquence amonges latynes lyued /
yet had it ben a thyng right rare & straunge
and worthy perpetuall laude / that any clerke
by lernyng or wytte coulde than haue framed a tonge before so rude and imperfite /
to such a swete ornature and composycion/
lykely if he had lyved in these dayes /being
good letters so restored & reuyued as they
be/ if he were nat empeched by the envy of
suche as may tollerate nothyng /whiche to
understonde their capacite doth nat extende /
to haue brought it unto a full and fynall perfection.

(*Workes of Chaucer*, 1532, sig. A2v)

This chapter focuses on the 1532 edition attributed to William
Thynne (STC 5068).[1] Thynne's edition was the first printed edition
whose physical form shows that as a project it was begun and completed as a complete works. The book itself is not without precedent:
Caxton editions were published as small units, but clearly sold to be
bound by individual owners as larger collections; and most incunabu-
lists describe such distribution practice as if not a norm at least rou-
tine.[2] Pynson's 1526 edition is a unit composed of three parts

33

independently published; and an even more striking precedent is Cambridge University Library MS Gg.4.27—a manuscript which better illustrates the notion of a complete works than any of the printed precedents for Thynne. Nonetheless, for 200 years, the Thynne edition defined both the form and content of Chaucer's book: the large, double-column folio, with works arranged in a sequence roughly according to magnitude and importance: *Canterbury Tales, Romaunt of the Rose, Troilus and Creseyde, Legende of Good Women, Boece, Book of the Duchesse,* "Envoy to Bukton," *Parlement of Fowls,* etc. Its goal was in part to preserve and in part to expand "Chauceriana"—the most striking example being Henryson's "Testament of Creseyde," inserted at press after the edition had been foliated.[3] Each subsequent edition to 1602 continued that trend, with a number of works added, and none dropped.

Modern bibliographers have little difficulty with this edition: it is printed by Godfray, and the preface, containing the passage quoted above, is actually by Brian Tuke, not Thynne. In this chapter, I focus on several problems, all regarding the recalcitrance of the evidence on which Chaucerians base their views of this edition and the way that evidence is received in modern scholarship. The chapter is in three parts: (1) What does Thynne say in the simple statement quoted above? The answer involves the notion of editorial truth—the notion of a Chaucerian book that exists over time rather than at a point in time. (2) Why is there a consensus that the statement is not made by Thynne? This involves the history of authentication; here the weight of evidence is presumably inversely proportionate to its extent. (3) What did Thynne, as editor, mean by a "works" of Chaucer?

I. A LIKELY STORY

The simple statement quoted at the head of this chapter occurs in the preface signed by Thynne, and appears to be a tissue of prefatory cliches many scholars have noted.[4] I seem to be one of very few Chaucerians who have difficulty with this statement. It is quoted without comment by Brewer (*Critical Heritage,* 1:88, with full context), reprinted in roman type by Skeat in the introduction to his 1905 facsimile, paraphrased by James E. Blodgett, and included as well among the introductory Testimonies in Urry's 1721 edition.[5] Furthermore, despite the clear statement "I William Thynne, Chief Clerk of the

Kitchen," it is routinely credited to Brian Tuke, based on a statement in Leland (again Leland!) and on some hand-written comments in the Clare College copy—the copy of the book used in the recent Brewer facsimile.

Consider the version of this text as quoted in the Testimonies to the Urry edition of 1721:

> For though it had been in *Demosthenes* or *Homerus* times, when all learn-
> ing and excellencie of sciences flourished amonges the *Greeks*, or in the
> season that *Cicero* prince of eloquence amonges *Latines* lived, yet had it
> ben a thinge right rare and straunge and worthie perpetuall laude, that
> any clerke by learninge or witte coulde then have framed a tonge, before
> so rude and imperfite, to such a swete ornature and composition; likely,
> if he had lived in these dayes, beinge good letters so restored and revived
> as they be (if he were not empeched by the envie of such as may tolerate
> nothing, whyche to understande their capacite doth not extend) to have
> brought it unto a full and finall perfection. (sig. g2v)

"Likely": Similarly? By the same token? If he had lived in *these* enlightened days . . . ?

Among the changes Urry makes here is a rationalization of Thynne's ambiguous punctuation. Strictly applying the implied con-
ventions of Urry's punctuation (or that of his own editors), Thynne's *lykely* must be construed as an adjective: the grammatical phrase is "any clerke . . . likely . . . to have brought it unto a full and finall per-
fection."[6] But isn't Thynne attempting to draw parallels? Had Chaucer lived in classical times, the result would have been X; and similarly, had he lived in modern times, the result would be Y. Isn't that supported by the typographical accident involving the setting of the word *lykely* at the left margin? And doesn't the material accident support what we know Thynne must be trying to say?

The only recent Chaucerian to comment directly on the passage is Blodgett. Blodgett's construction of the passage, which omits the misleading *likely*, is as follows:

> Especially striking is Thynne's readiness to measure Chaucer most favor-
> ably against classical standards: [above passage quoted to the phrase
> "swete ornature and composycion"]. Had Chaucer been fortunate
> enough to live in the present, "being good letters so restored & reuyued

as they be," he might have been able to bring the English language to "a
full and fynall perfection." (Blodgett, "William Thynne [d. 1546]," 36)

This is an admirable paraphrase and I believe that is what Thynne
means (or may mean) here. But Blodgett changes the meaning of the
final sentence, and his paraphrase leaves no room for the word *likely*
at all, which is the first word following his quotation above.[7]
Blodgett's Chaucer is not someone likely to have transformed the
English language, had he been so fortunate to have lived in these
times, but less grandly someone who might have so transformed the
language. That is perhaps what Thynne means, and it is certainly
much more in accordance with what a modern scholar might be willing to concede; but it is not what Thynne says.

Something is left out. There is an apparent elision (a rhetorical
one by the writer or an accidental one by the compositor): either "he
were" ("even in Demosthenes' time, Chaucer's feat would have been
remarkable; [*he were*] likely, had he lived in these times, . . .") or "he
were like" ("likely, had he lived in these times, *he were like* to have
framed the tongue . . .").

The best solution is to conclude that both readings are correct, the
strictly grammatical reading (*likely* as adjective) and what might be
called the rhetorical one (*likely* as a conjunction)—that what Thynne
means is that there are three possible "times"—ancient, modern, and
medieval—and that Chaucer simply picked the least congenial time
for a learned cleric like himself. Thus Thynne is saying: "even in
Demosthenes' times, Chaucer's accomplishments would have been
remarkable" and "imagine what Chaucer could have done in these
enlightened times, why, he would have absolutely perfected the language." The entire last series of clauses in Thynne's statement is parenthetical, describing as an afterthought what Chaucer would do in
these troubled times. But this solution involves an uncomfortable
paradox that has many variants in the history of Chaucer studies: we
can solve most of the difficulties evidence presents by assuming that
we know what the evidence must mean before we consult it.

The "Trew Copie"

There are many common but conflicting ideas competing for
Thynne's attention here: (1) praise for Chaucer who would have

succeeded in any time; (2) praise for the sovereign; (3) praise for the present, which is under the enlightened control of the dedicatee King; (4) the similarity of the present age to the imagined classical age; (5) the similarity of the present age to the rude medieval times of Chaucer in the struggles of clerics relying on their native wit and learning. For all ages have (6) obstructive enemies—ignorant, rude, unenlightened—opposing these struggles. Thynne uses these cliches to draw an analogy between his own preservative editorial work and the progressive illuminating work of Chaucer. And all is placed within the framework of a general history of writing, ending in the invention and development of printing (sig. A2r).

Holding this history together is the notion of a "trew copie" of Chaucer. The notion of a true copy is fundamental to early Chaucer editing, and fundamental as well to modern editing—appearing in phrases of such stupendous ambivalence as "original reading." But the nature of the true copy is no less elusive than a "true reading" of Thynne:

> Wherfore, gracious souerayne lorde / takynge suche delyte and plea-sure in the workes of this noble clerke . . . I haue of a longe season moche vsed to rede and visyte the same: and as bokes of dyuers imprintes came vnto my handes / I easely and without grete study / might and haue deprehended in them many errours / falsyties / and deprauacions / whiche euydently appered by the contrarietees and alteracions founde by collacion of the one with the other / wherby i was moued and styred to make dilygent sertch where I might fynde or recouer any trewe copies or exemplaries of the sayd bokes / whervnto in process of tyme / nat without coste and payne I attayned / and nat onely vnto such as seme to be very trewe copies of those workes of Geffray Chaucer / whiche before had ben put in printe / but also to dyuers other neuer tyll nowe imprinted. (sig. A2v)

Just as Chaucer is a polisher of language, Thynne's task is to polish a text: to restore and publish Chaucer's works, clearing up various "errours / falsyties / and deprauacions" by diligently following "trew copies or exemplaries."

But what is Thynne's idea of this true copy? the basis for the elu-sive perfect edition of Chaucer?

This "trew" copy is, of course, mythical, and like other myths, has a history. Caxton's preface to his second edition of the *Canterbury Tales* contains the much repeated story of having received a book "that was very trewe," owned by the father of a gentleman who wanted a newly printed volume. Caxton's second edition is an updating of the first: Caxton uses the manuscript only to make changes in the original edition ("by whiche I have corrected my book").[8] De Worde reprints the entire preface; and Pynson, in his revision of this preface in 1526, speaks of his edition as "dyligently and trewly corrected / by a copy of Willyam Caxtons imprinting / acording to the true makinge of the sayd Geffray Chaucer."

The notion of a true copy is behind all these statements, although no definition of *true* will accommodate these various uses. In Thynne's case, the true copy has multiplied, and if I am not mistaken, in the above passage, he rejects these early printings entirely (prints which for Pynson are the very embodiment of "truth"): they are not true copies, and it would be an easy matter, had he cared to expend the energy, to discover their defects. Wherefore, he searched for *other true copies* of works not yet in print.

It has become part of the mythology of print that printing results in a stable text, and this has recently been argued specifically in relation to English texts by Tim Machan.[9] But note here that what reveals the problem of variation to Thynne are printed copies, not manuscripts. The destabilization of the text is the direct result of print, not the result of manuscripts: the correct print will thus recover the true text (the stable text) represented (somewhere) in the manuscript tradition. It is noteworthy that in the history of Chaucer's text, these "most trew" copies have remained conveniently hidden. In the case of the *Canterbury Tales,* "most true" copies, "hitherto undiscovered" were still being unearthed in the nineteenth century. The two most important manuscripts in contemporary editing, the Ellesmere and the Hengwrt, formed no part of editorial history until the Chaucer Society imprints.[10]

What Thynne means by a "trew" copy is an authenticated copy. And since no eminent Chaucerian as yet exists, only the King can provide such authentication: "none coulde to my thynkyng occurre / that syns / or in the tyme of Chaucer / was or is suffycient / but onely your maieste royall / whiche [could] adde or gyue any authorite hervnto." Henry, then, assumes the role of the ideally perfect Chaucerian, whose authority is equal to Chaucer's own.[11]

II. THE AUTHORSHIP OF THE PREFACE: BRIAN TUKE, JOHN LELAND, AND THE AUTHORITY OF AUTHORITY

But the Thynne preface, to modern Chaucerians, is not Thynne's preface. It is, rather, assigned to Brian Tuke without any serious objection. Although I do not dispute this attribution, it seems a tenuous one, particularly in view of the repeated identification of the author in the Preface itself as Thynne, and the fact that Thynne's son Francis Thynne, in his *Animadversions* of 1598, says only that his father "vsed the helpe of that lerned and eloquent knighte and antiquarye Sir Briane Tuke" (*Animadversions*, 6).

The principal reasons for the attribution are two: (1) handwritten comments in the Clare College copy, presumably by Tuke, and (2) the confused, but oddly authoritative, comments by "that painful antiquary" John Leland. The Clare College copy, complete with this handwritten note, was used for the recent facsimile edition by Brewer; so the note has become part of what amounts to a Standard Edition of the Thynne book itself. Tuke's handwritten note claims he wrote the dedication at Greenwich while (Thynne was?) waiting for the tide. ("This preface I sir Bryan Tuke knight wrot at the request of Mr Clarke of the Kechyn then being / tarying for the tyde at Grenewich"). Brewer claims this is "his [Tuke's] own copy of Thynne's Chaucer," although I am not certain there is any evidence to that effect, beyond the handwritten note itself.

The first to argue for Tuke's authorship was Henry Bradshaw, whose statements were reproduced by Furnivall in his edition of Thynne's *Animadversions* (p. xxvi) and reprinted by Skeat in the 1905 facsimile (p. xxi). Bradshaw:

> When Leland tells us that Sir Brian Tuke wrote a limatissima praefatio to the edition of Chaucer published by Berthelet, we are all puzzled; and when Leland tells us that Thynne edited the edition, we are still more puzzled, because no such edition is known. . . Curiously enough, there is a copy of Godfray's edition in one of the College Libraries here . . . in which, at the top of Thynne's dedication, Sir Brian Tuke has written with his own hand: "This preface I sir Bryan Tuke knight wrot at the request of Mr Clarke of the Kechn then being / tarying for the tyde at Grenewich." It would be difficult to find a prettier coincidence in all points—the tarrying for the tide at Greenwich, when we learn from

quite other sources (1) that Thynne's office was at Greenwich, and (2) that he lived down the Thames at Erith. You will allow that it is not often one has the pleasure of hitting off things so prettily. Observe the words "then being. . . ."

There is no question that this is "prettily hit off." But there is serious reason to doubt Bradshaw's conclusion. The major source is Leland, the same Leland whose accuracy has been continually disputed in Chaucer studies.[12]

Leland states that the first printer of Chaucer was Caxton, whose "one volume edition" (inexistent today) was superseded by that of Berthelet's (also inexistent today). Despite these errors, the rest of his statement is apparently to be believed:

> Vicit tamen *Caxodunicam* editionem *Bertholetus* noster opera *Gulielmi Thynni*; qui, multo labore, sedulitate, ac cura usus in perquirendis vetustis exemplaribus, multa primae adjecit editioni. Sed nec in hac parte caruit *Brianus Tucca*, mihi familiaritate conjunctissimus, et *Anglicae* linguae eloquentia mirificus, sua gloria, edita in postremam impressionem praefatione elimata, luculenta, eleganti.
>
> [Our Berthelet superseded the Caxton edition through the efforts of William Thynne. Who, after great labor, assiduousness, and care in seeking old exemplars, added much to the first edition. Nor did Brian Tuke lack his share in this—a great friend of mine, and marvelous in the eloquence of the English tongue,—his glory being an ornate, lucid and elegant preface in the last impression.]

Leland then says he gets his table of contents from a later edition (the edition of 1542, differing from the 1532 edition in its inclusion of the Plowman's Tale).[13]

As Bradshaw notes, we are puzzled by certain statements in this account, particularly those we know to be false: first and foremost, there is no Berthelet Chaucer, or if there is, it is identical to the 1532 Godfray edition. Even the editors of the 1721 edition remained confused about this, and Timothy Thomas in the Preface cited two 1532 editions (Urry, *Works* 1721, sig. l2r).

To Lounsbury in 1892, Leland represented everything wrong with Chaucer scholarship. According to Lounsbury, Leland's influence was a direct result of the extent of his errors:

Leland is, in fact, a shining example of a man who has been saved by the multitude of his blunders. Had merely one or two mistakes marred the general accuracy of his account, these would never have been forgotten by any, and would occasionally have been magnified by some. But they were so numerous that they led in time to the quiet ignoring of the whole narrative in which they were contained. His account of Chaucer came in consequence to be generally forgotten. With it disappeared the memory of its errors and the knowledge of its utter worthlessness. But it left Leland as a name still to conjure by. (*Studies in Chaucer*, 1:143)

Leland may well have no independent authority on any of the details of this story. This story of the epitaph comes from Caxton's Preface. His story of Thynne's efforts comes directly from Thynne's Preface. His table of contents is calqued out of a later book. His reference to Berthelet could be an intrusion of a note on Gower. Why would his reference to Tuke be any more than a repetition of hand-written notes in the copy now at Clare College?[14] Nonetheless, despite the denunciation of Leland by Lounsbury, the modern account of early Chaucer printing and Leland's place within this history is virtually the same as that found in a long note in Tyrwhitt's 1775 edition (Appendix to the Preface, 1: ix-xvii, note e). Tyrwhitt's account of early editions, from Ames's *Typographical Antiquities* of 1749, is roughly what we find in modern bibliographies, that is, he corrects the apparent confusion of Berthelet and Godfray. Although criticizing several of Leland's inaccuracies, he seems to accept Leland on Tuke:

the Preface of *Brianus Tucca* (Sir Brian Tuke) which he commends so much, was nothing else but the Prefatory address, or Dedication, to the King, which is prefixed to Godfray's and other later editions in the name of Mr. William Thynne. The mistake may not have been so extravagant, as it appears to be at first. It is possible, that Berthelette might be concerned in putting forth the edition of 1532, though it was printed by Godfray; and it is very probable, that the dedication, (which is in such a style as I think very likely to be commended by Leland,) though standing in the name of Mr. William Thynne, was composed for him by Sir Brian Tuke. Mr. Thynne himself, I apprehend, was rather a lover, than a master, of these studies. (xi-xii, note e)

But Tyrwhitt's logic is faulty here. Leland does not praise the preface in a dispassionate judgment of its elegant style, but rather because it is by his friend Tuke ("mihi familiaritate conjunctissimus"). Furthermore, if Thynne were a "lover" rather than a "master," where he needed help was in editing. Not in the writing of the preface. Tyrwhitt has advanced a reasonable argument against the very case he seems to be arguing.

The problem with Leland's authority ought to be more clearly faced by modern Chaucerians.[15] If his independent authority on *res Chaucerianae* is inexistent (as many Chaucerians imply), then his account is no more than the *fons et origo* of a number of Chaucerian myths that have been centuries in the undoing. The reference to Tuke should occupy no privileged place here. Perhaps Brian Tuke did write the preface, and perhaps the man in the moon wrote it. But the confirmation from Leland should in no way decide the case. There is no evidence that the physical and material evidence we have today is not exactly what Leland had in the 1540s.[16]

A further issue bears on the matter of attribution for the preface, and that is the source of the language borrowed in this preface. Thynne (or Tuke) claimed to have consulted earlier printed books in his edition; he has seen books of those works "whiche before had ben put in printe." And Blodgett has shown that the copytext used by Thynne for *Boece* is Caxton's edition of 1478 (STC 3199), a copy of which contains Thynne's pressmarks. Caxton included a preface for his Boece edition, and this contains comments that are close to what we find in the preface for the 1532 Chaucer:

> Therfore the worshipful fader & first foundeur & embelissher of ornate eloquence in our englissh. I mene / Maister Geffrey Chaucer hath translated this sayd werke oute of latyn in to oure vsual and moder tonge. Folowyng the latyn as neygh as is possible to be vnderstande. wherein in myne oppynyon he hath deseruid a perpetuell lawde and thanke of al this noble Royame of England. (Caxton, Preface to Boece, ed. Crotch, 37)

Later in this preface, similar language appears:

> the sayd worshipful mann Geffrey Chaucer / first translatour of this sayde boke & embelissher in making the sayd langage ornate & fayr.

whiche shal endure perpetuelly. and therfore he ought eternelly to be
remembrid. (ibid)

Caxton's words seem to reappear in Thynne's own reference (quoted
in full above) "thyng right rare & straunge and worthy perpetuall
laude."

That Thynne used Caxton's *Boece* is not surprising and has drawn no
comment. But what the language of the Chaucer preface indicates is
that *the writer of the preface* had access to Caxton's book and paid direct
attention to it. Obviously, if this preface-writer is also the editor of the
edition, that makes perfect sense: the writer of the preface has seen earlier printed books of Chaucer, and the editor has used those books as
copytext. And that, of course, accords exactly what the preface says,
identifying its author as "I your most humble vassal / subiecte and seru-
aunt Wylliam Thynne / chefe clerke of your kechyn" (sig. A2v). But it
does not accord with the notion (or myth) of Tuke's or anyone else's
separate authorship of this preface. Tuke, after all, claims and is only
credited with some form of elegant preface. Taking the written notes in
the Clare College copy at face value, this is something done while "waiting for the tide" (apparently it is Thynne, not Tuke, who is doing the
waiting). I do not know the tides of the Thames, which are undoubtedly complicated by river currents; but surely less than half a day is
involved here. A few hours might be sufficient time to write a preface;
but that is not sufficient time to have performed any editorial work,
and probably not sufficient time to have studied a Caxton *Boece* carefully enough to reproduce the very language of its preface.

De Worde, Pynson, and [Caxton's] Preface to the Canterbury Tales

As noted above, Thynne's preface is enmeshed in a tradition of
what might be called "prefatorial authorship"—a tradition that for
Chaucer began with prefaces by Caxton. In this tradition, an authorial signature does not necessarily mean authorial composition.
Thynne's borrowing of Caxton's language from the *Boece* preface had
precedent in the history of Caxton's preface to the *Canterbury Tales* of
1483. This was reprinted by de Worde in 1498 and a version of it
appeared in both Pynson editions (of 1492 and 1526).

De Worde's 1498 edition has a strong material relation to
Caxton's edition and in the preface de Worde retained Caxton's

own signature: "AMEN By William Caxton His soule in heuen won."[18] But the Pynson editions of 1492 and 1526 printed heavily-revised versions of this preface, and in 1492, Pynson signed it as his own: "AMEN By Richard Pynson."[19] Pynson omits Caxton's detailed account of the discovery of the manuscript but recasts some Caxton's sentiments and some of his editorial history as his own (less successfully in 1492 than in 1526):

> of whom emonge all other of hys bokes / I purpose temprynte by the grace of god the book of the tales of caunterburye in which I fynde many a noble hystorye . . . (Caxton, 1484)

> Of whom I among alle other of his bokes the boke of the tales of Canterburie in whiche ben many a noble historie . . . (Pynson, [1492])

> of whome amonge all other of his bokes / I purpose to emprinte by the grace of Iesu / the boke of the tales of Caunterburie / in whiche I fynde many a noble hystorie . . . (Pynson, 1526)

Pynson pays tribute to Caxton, but in 1526 takes credit for some of Caxton's editing. Caxton's phrase "by which I haue corrected my boke" refers to his use of the gentleman's manuscript by which he has corrected his first edition. In Pynson's 1492 version, this statement is ambiguous:

> to whiche boke diligently ovirsen and duely examined by the pollitike reason and ouirsight. of my worshipfull master william Caxton (Pynson, [1492])

In 1526, Pynson is more certain about this editorial history, which he rewrites as follows:

> Whiche boke is diligently and trewly corrected / by a copy of Willyam Caxtons imprintyng . . . (Pynson, 1526)

Pynson thus retells Caxton's story in his own voice, and eliminates in his second edition the more obvious incongruities or incompetencies of his first,[20] and takes credit (in a revision of Caxton's own words) for some of Caxton's editorial endeavors.

Chaucerian prefaces had thus been misattributed well before Thynne signed his own preface in 1526. And perhaps it is perfectly consistent with this tradition to assume that Thynne (or a mythical Thynne) revised and re-signed the prefatory remarks he had before him (perhaps one written by a personal friend?), just as his predecessor Pynson had done with the Caxton preface. And that consistency may be just enough for Leland (or his enthusiasts) once again to assert his murky authority.

III. THE CANON AND THYNNUS NOSTER

The most important issue on which Thynne's authority is still felt in modern Chaucer criticism is the Chaucer canon, and that will be the focus of this final section. As we have seen, the editorial matter in the early Chaucer editions is shot through with misattribution and deceit. If these editors did not provide clear and unambiguous information on who was writing their own introductions, why should they be expected to offer a coherent statement on what Chaucer himself wrote? Yet the question of canon seems to require some sort of answer; and modern scholars, by assuming rightly that canon is determined by physical books, assume much more problematically that the statement provided by or embodied in those physical books is necessarily a coherent one.

Each edition in the series of editions based on Thynne added material to its predecessor, material for which no claims of Chaucer's authorship were necessarily implied. The most extensive addition (to Tyrwhitt, a "heap of rubbish" 5:xxii) was that made in Stow's edition of 1561, a number of items taken from Cambridge, Trinity College, MS R.3.19.[21] The way such "Chauceriana" might become "the Chaucerian" was suggested in an ingenious reading of the title page of Stow by Skeat—an interpretation that in its strained virtuosity has all the marks of the overly nuanced and clever bellettrism Skeat claimed to avoid. The question at issue is that of the canon. The title-pages of the editions in question read as follows:

1532: The workes of Geffray Chaucer newly printed/ with dyuers workes whiche were neuer in printe before: As in the table more playnly dothe appere.

1561: The Woorkes of Geffrey Chaucer, newly printed with diuers
Additions which were never in printe before: With the siege and
destruccion of the worthy Citee of Thebes, compiled by Jhon Lidgate,
Monke of Berie. As in the table more plainly doeth appere.[22]

According to the argument of Skeat, Thynne's 1532 title meant
only that he had printed works by Chaucer "and diverse others" hitherto unprinted by other authors. The change in Stow's title (for
"divers others," Stow prints "divers additions") indicates that Stow
claimed for Chaucer all the works previously included as related to
Chaucer; what were "divers workes" in Thynne become "divers workes
by Chaucer" in Stow.[23]

> Here [in Stow] the authorship of Chaucer was, *for the first time*, practi-
> cally claimed for the whole of Thynne's volume. At the same time,
> Stowe did not really mean what he seems to say, for it was he who first
> added the words—'made by Ihon lidgate'—to the title of "The Flower
> of Curtesie." . . . It is clear that Thynne's intention was to print a collec-
> tion of poems, including all he could find of Chaucer and anything
> else of a similar character that he could lay his hands on. In other
> words, the collection was, from the beginning, a collection of the
> Works of Chaucer and other writers. (Skeat, *Works of Chaucer*, 7:ix-x)

According to Skeat, Stow and Speght used "misleading titles that
actually assigned to Chaucer all the poems in the volume."
On the face of it, Skeat's reading, albeit ingenious, is preposterous:
all Stow's title means is "this is the book called 'The Works of
Chaucer' (a book that contains diverse other texts) to which this edition makes diverse additions"—and that simple interpretation is completely supported by the contents themselves. Skeat himself seems to
have come up with the argument only after most of his editorial work
had been completed; there is not one word about Stow's title or its
implications in the many discussions of the edition in the first six volumes of Skeat's edition (see *Works of Chaucer*, 5:x and the lengthy discussion on 1:31-43). And Skeat does not seem to be committed to the
argument in his later work.
Skeat's argument has been revived, however, as the target of an
often-cited 1984 article by Robert Yeager. Yeager objects to the argument on canon-formation that Skeat's reading of the title page

implies. At issue for Yeager is not Skeat's logic but his assumption that Thynne simply printed "what he could lay his hands on."[25] The basis of the argument thus shifts from the title page to the table of contents, although Yeager seems to imply a connection—that a dubious reading of the title page somehow entails an erroneous interpretation of the canon. According to Yeager, the contents of Thynne's volume are not the result of economic and material factors; rather they constitute choices of a literary-critical nature. That is, Thynne in 1532 was somehow engaged in the same canonical debates (even if only in his own head) that embroiled the Chaucer Society and Skeat in the late nineteenth century, and which have been renewed this century.

Yeager's article, although flawed in detail, is interesting in its unstated assumption of universality—that what is contained in early books is a product of the same literary choices that might be made by modern critics, and that this earlier editorial work is thus to be judged by standards applicable to modern editorial work. Yeager argues that because Caxton and Thynne read more than they could publish, they were forced to make choices, "necessary" choices (139). These were both economic and literary. Thynne's decision to include all he found in Caxton and early editions, including non-canonical works, was purely economic (and thus non-literary): Thynne presumably wanted to produce the "large volume" that Caxton himself had not produced, and in order for such a volume to have maximum value, it must operate on a principle of inclusion, not exclusion. Subsequent to these "necessary" choices were a second set of literary decisions, and these decisions involved works selected to include in addition to those already in the printed canon. Only these decisions reveal Thynne's idea of a Chaucer(ian) poem. Yeager assumes crucially that these literary decisions must be, if not rational, at least principled: that is, they must be intelligible as an early form of literary criticism. We have reason thus "to inquire after the theory underlying those judgments" (140).

By this logic, Yeager excludes from consideration the "25 or so apocryphal pieces contained in 1532" as a legacy of Caxton (148). Thynne's choice to include these is neither "deliberate" nor "critical." What remains are 18 or so pieces of apocrypha, and it is on the basis of these that Yeager will characterize Thynne's own vision, or version, of Chaucer: "Thynne must have found something about these poems which corresponded to his idea of Chaucer's style" (155).[26] The implication of this reasoning is that reputable Chaucer editors do not go about wantonly adding to the canon; each addition they make to an edition is an index of an opinion (perhaps erroneous) concerning an author's canon.

But the reasons editors make decisions are various and in some cases simply economic, as we can see by comparing the series of editions that led to Urry's of 1721 with those that led to Skeat's edition. Until 1721, each successive edition is larger than its predecessor; after 1721, the canon shrinks precipitously. When the canon becomes so large as to require overly-large or expensive volumes, scholars gain their reputations by defining a new leaner canon (as Tyrwhitt did in 1775). Yeager's dispute with Skeat on the canon makes editorial history more coherent than it is, and threatens to turn both Thynne and Caxton into members of the old Chaucer Society.

In order to recuperate Thynne, Yeager initially defines criticism in broad terms as "the act of making deliberate choices" (136). But as Yeager's argument proceeds, it is clear that his understanding of the function of a critic is quite different from this. He bases his argument less on the strict criteria he had used to determine evidence (in the tradition of Skeat) than on his ability to "read" certain pieces of evidence. Yeager reads Thynne not as a late nineteenth-century critic on the model of Skeat (an editor struggling with the choices of canon), but finally as a critic of the 1980s in the tradition of George Lyman Kittredge.[27] What is legitimized is not Thynne's status as a critic, but the modern critic's status as an existential "maker of choices." Thynne claimed to be a diligent editor. By late nineteenth-century standards, he was certainly not that; but I can't see how redefining him as a mediocre critic is any vindication.

Skeat and Yeager share one assumption and goal: that Thynne is to be judged on the basis of what they themselves do. Skeat had defined himself as an editor and as a scholar of the Chaucer canon. It was Skeat also who defined the two stages of the editorial history of Chaucer: the first, the series of folio editions that culminated in the supposed "worst" edition of Urry; the second, the modern edition, beginning with Tyrwhitt and culminating with his own multi-volume edition. To Skeat, the changes between Thynne and Stow must be interpreted in this context; the differences constituted a step in the progress of the old-fashioned edition that Tyrwhitt's and his own would discredit. For Yeager, the relation to Thynne is a different one; he bypasses the obvious profession of Thynne (a publisher) and links him to modern criticism by redefining him as a critic.

Under this analysis Caxton and Thynne, thus, enact a double history of Chaucer criticism. First, their own. But more important, that of the twentieth century and the transformation of Chaucer studies from Skeat to contemporary criticism, and the revival of literary studies within the context of bibliographical ones.

Chapter 3

TOWARD A TYPOGRAPHICAL HISTORY OF CHAUCER: THE BLACKLETTER CHAUCER

T he reception of Chaucer is a process that involves not only the author Chaucer and his text, but also the Chaucer book and the various aspects of that book. Just as Chaucer is involved in all periods of English reception, so too is the book that embodies him—representatives of the Chaucer book can be found for nearly every period of English book production and typography. I focus here on typography because it is an aspect of the book that most readers recognize quickly: for most readers, it constitutes what might be called the "character" of the book (a word used by fifteenth-century printers to describe a typeface). In its own evolution and in the often naive classifications that are applied to type, we can see Chaucer first defined as a canonical author, and later transformed into a medieval author and finally a classical one. What I am concerned with in this chapter is the deceptively simple representation of Chaucer in the early varieties of blackletter—reserving for later chapters the history of the transformation of Chaucer into a classic writer with all the dignity of roman type. The history of Chaucerian typography is one marked by persistent anomalies, much like the more familiar literary history of Chaucer.

Typography and the Book

Typography and the typographical aspects of a book are unlike most other aspects of the material book. Despite claims in recent scholarship to the contrary, most of the material aspects of a book are individual: the paper used for a particular book is not of uniform stock, and various book-copies of the same issue do not combine paper stocks in the same way; the binding and trimming are also individual—the products of individual booksellers and owners. Typography, by contrast, like the text itself, is both abstract and reproducible. Those singularities of typography of concern to bibliographers—turned letters, broken type, etc.—are incidental; they are part of a text only to the extent that the resultant words formed by such accidents are textual. In discussing typography I refer to an aesthetic abstraction, like a text, composed of typeface and page format—one that is strictly reproducible, even if the details of individual copies may vary within the same issue; anything worth saying about this subject should be to some extent contestable with facsimile evidence and bibliographical description. I will be distinguishing the "production genre" (the classification pertaining to events at press) from "consumer genre" (how a book was classified when read). What I call the "production genre" has two parts: first, the mechanical (actual history of particular physical type fonts), and second, the aesthetic (the projected consumer genre—how the printers imagined a production would be received). In the case of Chaucer, the extant evidence is largely confined to matters of production. Although valid inferences concerning the consumer genre might well be drawn, direct evidence as to how specific typefaces and page formats were read and interpreted in the period of early printing does not exist; for later periods, such evidence as exists is chaotic, with typefaces misidentified, misclassified, and, especially before the age of mechanical reproduction by facsimile, misremembered.

Typographical History of Chaucer: A Skeletal Narrative

Most histories of Chaucer books have been constructed around a simple chronological narrative. This narrative is useful for indicating general aspects of the history of Chaucer's book as well as for opposing some persistent banalities one hears about that book. This narrative can be summarized verbally or pictorially. Caxton's one-column, small-folio editions (folios from half-sheets, see fig. 6) give way to double-column, full folio editions: Pynson's *Canterbury Tales* of 1492, where only the prose is in two columns; de Worde's *Canterbury Tales* of 1498, entirely in two columns (fig. 7). Since the early Pynson edition was dated much later by eighteenth-century bibliographers, the priority of

Me haue J not pij d? With in my hol x
Ye knowe wel that J am poure and? of x
Rithe pour almes ou me poure wrecche
May than quod he the foule fend? me fecche
If J the excuse though thou holdist he spilt
Allas qd? he god? woot J am not in the gilt
Pay me quod he or he shete saint anne
J wol anone here awey thyn nelle panne
For ætte whiche thou owest me of of x
When that thou madist thyn husbond? cokeolde
J paye at hoom for thy correction
Thow lixt quod she he my sauacion
Me was J neuer or now widow or wyf
Sompned? vnto pour court in al my lyf
Me neuer y was but of my body trewe
Vnto the deuyl blak and? rowgh of helle
Yeue J thy body and? eke my panne to
And? when the deuyl herde hir curse so
Vp on her knees he sayde in this manere
Now mabylle myn owen moder dere
Js this pour wyl in ernest as ye saye
The deuyl quod she fette hym or he dey
And? panne and? al but he wol hym repent
May ol x stot that is not myn entent
Quod the sompnour forto repent me
For ony thing? that J haue had? of the
J wolde J had x thy smook and? euery cloth
Now brothir quod the deuyl he not wroth
Thy body and? this panne is myn he right

Figure 6. *Canterbury Tales,* **first Caxton edition (Westminster: Caxton, 1478) (20 lines = 135 mm.). Photo courtesy of the William Andrews Clark Memorial Library, University of California, Los Angeles.**

The second nonnys tale

full wrongfully began thou quod he
And in wrong is yet all thy perseueraunce
Wolt thou not how our pryncis myghty & fre
Haue thus comaunded & made ordenaunce
That euery cryften wyght fhall haue penaũce
But yf that he his cryftendom wythfey
And gon all qwyt yf that he woll it reney

℣Your pryncis crien as your nobley doth
Quod tho cecyly in a wood fentence
Ye make vs gylty and it is not foth
for ye that knowen well our Innocence
for as moche as we do ay reuerence
To cryft and for we bere a cryften name
Ye put on vs a cryme and eke a blame

But we that knowen that name fo
for vertuous we may it not wythfeye
℣Almache anfwerde chefe one of thyfe two
Do facrifyce or cryftendom reney
That thou mowe afcape by that weye
At whyche worde this holy blyffull mayde
Gan for to laugh and to the Juge fayde

℣O Juge confufid in thy nycete
Wolt thou that I renye Innocence
To make me a wycked wyght quod fhe
Lo he diffymuleth here in audyence
he ftaryth and woodyth in his aduertence
To whom almache fayd o fely wretche
Ne wolt þ not how fer my myght may ftretche

Haue not our myghty pryncis yeuen
To me both power and auctorpte
To make folke bothe deyen and lyuen
Why fpekeft thou they fo proudly to me
I fpeke not but ftedfaftly quod fhe
Not proudly for I fay as for my fyde
We haten dedly that vyce of pryde

And yf thou drede not a foth for to here
They woll I fhewe all openly by ryght
Thou that haft made a full grete lefynge here
Thou fayft thy pryncis haue yeue the myght
Bothe for to fle & for to quycken a wyght

That thou mayft but only lyf bereue
Thou haft noy other power ne none leue

℣But þ mayft fay thy pryncis hath þ makid
Mynyftre of deth for yf thou fpeke of mo
Thou lyeft for thy power is full nakyd
Do way thy boldnes fayd almache tho
And do facrifyce to our goddis or thou go
I retche not what wrong thou me profre
for I can fuffre as can a phylofophre

But that wronges may I not endure
Thatlthou fpekyft of our goddis here quod he
Cecyly anfwer o nyce creature
Thou fayde̍ſt no word fith thou fpakeſt to me
That I ne knewe therwyth thy nycete
And that thou were in euery maner wyfe
A lewde offycer and a veyne Juftice

There lackyth no thyng of thyn vtter eyen
But thou art blynde for thynge that we fe all
That is a ftoon that mowe men well afpyen
That ylke ftoon a god thou wolt it call
I rede the lete̍ thyn honde vpon it falle
And tafte it well & ftoon thou fhalt it fynde
Syn that thou feeſt not wyth thyn eyen blynde

It is a fhame that the peple fhall
So fcorne the and laughe at thy folye
for comynly men wote it well ouer all
That myghty god is in heuens hye
And thyfe ymages well thou mayft afpye
To the ne to hemfelf may do no profyte
for in effect they be not worth a myte

℣This and fuche other wordes fayd fhe
And he war wrothe & bad men fholde her lede
Home vntyll her hous & in her hous quod he
Brenne her in a bath of flames rede
And as he bad ryght fo it was do in dede
for in a bath they gonne her faft fhytten
And nyght & daye fyre they vnder betten

℣The longe nyght and eke the day alfo
for all the fyre and eke the grete hete

o iij

The knyghtes tale.

Let euery felowe tell his tale about
And let se nowe/who shall the supper wyn
And there I leste/ I wyll agayne begyn.

This duke/of whom I make mencyoune
Whan he was come/ almost to the towne
In all his wele and his most pryde
He was ware/ as he cast his eye asyde
Where that there kneled in the highe wey
A company of ladys/ twey and twey
Eche after other/ cladde in clothes blake
But suche a crye/ a suche a wo they make
That in this worlde/ nys creature lyuynge
That euer herde suche a waymentynge
And of this crye/ they nolde neuer stynten
I pray they the reynes of his brydell henten
What folke be ye/ þ at myn home comyng
Perturben so my feest with cryeng
Quod Theseus: haue ye so great enuy
Of myn honour/that thus complayne a cry?
Or who hath you myspode/ or offended?
Lowe telleth me/ if it may be amended.
And why that ye be clothed thus in blake?
The oldest lady of them all spake
Whan she had swowned with a deedly chere
That it was ruthe for to se and here
She said lorde/to whom fortune hath yeue
Uyctory/ a as a conquerour to lyue
Nought greueth vs your glory a honour
But we beseke you of mercy a socour.
And haue mercy on our wo and distresse
Some drope of pyte/through thy gentylnesse
Upon vs wretched wymmen/ let thou fall
For certes lorde/there nys none of vs all
That she ne hath be a duchesse or a quene
Nowe be we captyfes/as it is well sene
Thanked be fortune/and her false whele
That non estate assureth for to be wele.
Nowe certes lorde/ to abyde your presece
Here in this temple of the goddesse Clemece
We haue be waytyng all this fourtenyght
Helpe vs lorde/sythe it lyeth in thy myght.

I Wretche/ that wepe and wayle thus
Whylom wyfe to kyng Campaneus
That starfe at Thebes/cursed be þ day
And all we that ben in this aray

And maken all this lamentacyon
We losten all our husbondes at that towne
Whyle that the siege there aboute laye
And yet the olde Creon (Wel awaye)
That lorde is nowe of Thebes cyte
Fulfylled of yre and of iniquite
He for dispyte/and for his tyranny
To done the deed bodyes vyllanye
Of all our lordes/Whiche that ben slawe
Hath all the bodyes on an heape ydrawe
And wyll nat suffre hem/ by none assent
Neyther to be buryed/ne to be brent
But maketh houndes to eate hem in dispyte
And we at that worlde/Without more respite
They fallen grosly/and cryen pytously
Haue on vs wretched wymmen some mercy
And let our sorowe synke in thyn hert.
This gentle duke down fro his hors stert
With hert pytous/Whan he herde hem speke
Hym thought that his herte wolde breke
Whan he sawe hem so pytous a so mate
That whylom were of so great astate
And in his armes/he hem all vp hent
And hem comforted in full good entent
And swore his othe/as he was true knyght
He wolde don so ferforthly his myght
Upon the tyrante Creon hem to wreake
That all the people of Grece shulde speke
Howe Creon was of Theseus yserued
As he that had his dethe full well deserued
And ryght anon withouten more abode
His baner he displayed/and forthe rode
To Thebes warde/ and all his hoost besyde
No more Athenes nolde he go ne ryde
Ne take his ease fully halfe a day
But onward on his way that nyght he lay
And sent anone Ipolita the quene
And Emely her yonge syster shene
Unto the towne of Athenes to dwell
And forth he rydeth/ther nys no more to tel.

He red statue of Mars with spere a targe
I So shyneth in his whyte baner large
That all the feldes glytteren vp a doun
And by his baner / borne is his penon
Of golde ful ryche/ i Which there was ybete
The mynotaure/that he slan in Crete
Thus

Figure 8.   William Thynne, ed., *The Works of Geoffrey Chaucer* (London: Godfray, 1532). (20 lines = 94 mm.). Reproduced by permission of William Andrews Clark Memorial Library.

The second Nonnes tale. Fol.lv.

And whiles that the organs made melodie
To God alone thus in herte song she
O lorde, my soule and eke my body gie
Unwemmed, lest I confounded be
And for his loue that died vpon a tre
Euery second or thirde day she faste
Aye bidding in her orisons full faste.

The night cam, and to bed must she gone
With her husbonde, as often is the manere
And priuely she said vnto him anon
O swete and wel byloued spouse dere
There is a counsaile, and ye wol it here
Which that right faine I wold to you saine
So that ye me ensure, it not to bewraine.

Valerian gan fast vnto her swere
That for no case, ne thing that might be
He should neuer to none bewraien here
And than at erste, thus to him said she
I haue an angel, whiche that loueth me
That w gret loue, where so I wake or slepe
Is redy aye, my body for to kepe

And if that he may selen out of drede
That ye my touche or loue in bilony
He right anon will slee you with the dede
And in your youth thus shall ye dye
And if that ye in clene loue me gye
He wol you loue as me, for your clennesse
And shewe you of his ioye and brightnesse.

This Valerian, corrected as God wolde
Answerd ayen, if I shal trust the
Let me that aungel se, and him beholde
And if that it a very aungel be
Than wol I done as thou hast prayed me
And if thou loue another man forsothe
Right w this sword tha wol I sle you bothe

Cecile answerd anon in this wise
If that ye lust that Angel shul ye se
So that ye trowe on Christ, and you baptise
Goth forth to via apia (q she)
That fro this toun ne stante but miles thre
And to the pore folke that there dwell
Say hem right thus, as I shal you tell.

Tel hem that I Cecile, you to hem sende
To shewen you the good vrban the olde
For secret nedes, and for good entent
And whan that ye saint vrban han beholde
Tel him the wordes, that I to you tolde
And whan that he hath purged you fro sinne
Than shal ye se that Angel er ye twinne.

Valerian is to that place igon
And right as him was taught by his lernin
He founde this holy vrban anon
Among these saintes burials louting
And he anon, without tarieng
Did his message, and whan he had it tolde
Vrban for ioy, gan his hondes vp holde.

The teres from his eyen let he fall
Almighty God, O Jesu Christ (q he)
Sower of chaste counsaile, hierde of vs all
The frute of thilke sede of chastite
That thou hast sowe in Cecile, take to the
Lo like a besy bee, withouten gile
The serueth aye thine owne thral Cecile

For thilke spouse, that she toke but newe
Ful like a fierse Lion, she sendeth here
As meke as any lambe was to ewe
And with that word, anon there gan apere
In olde man, clad in white clothes clere
That had a boke with letters of gold in hon
And gan biforne Valerian for to stond.

Valerian as deed fel doun for drede
Whan he this olde man saw standing so
Whiche forthwith anon he herde him rede
O lord, O faith, O God withouten mo
Of Christendome, and father of al also
Abouen al, and ouer al euery where
These wordes al with Gold written were.

Whan this was rad, than said this olde man
Leuest thou this thing or none, say ye or na
I leue al this thing (q Valerian)
Under the heuen no wight ne thinke may
Sother thing than this, I dare well say
Tho banished the olde man, he nist where
And pope vrban him christened right there.

Valerian goth home, and findeth Cecile
Within his chambre, with an aungel stonde
This aungel had of rose and of lillye
Crounes two, the whiche he bare in honde
And first to Cecile, as I vnderstonde
He yaue that one, and after gan he take
That other to Valerian and her make,

With body clene, & w vnwemmed thought
Kepeth aye wel these crounes (q he)
From paradise to you I haue hem brought
Ne neuer more shullen they rotten be
Ne lese her swete sauour, trusteth me
Ne neuer wight shal sene him with eye
But he be chast, and hate bilonie
         L.i.   And

Figure 9. John Stow, ed., *The Workes of Geoffrey Chaucer* (London, 1561).

The firſt booke of Fame.   Fol.261.

But ye ſhall ſee the day ý ye ſhal curſe ý while,
That ye ſo buſily did your entent
Hem to beguile,that failhed neuer ment.

For this ye know wel,though I would lie,
In women is all trouth and ſtedfaſtneſſe,
For in good faith I neuer of hem lie,
But much worſhip,bountie,and gentilneſſe,
Right conning,ſarte,and full of mekeneſſe,
Good and glad,and lowly I you enſure,
Is this goodly angeliike creature.

And if it hap a man be in diſeaſe,
She doeth her buſineſſe,and her full paine,
With al her might,him to comfort and pleaſe,
If fro his diſeaſe ſhe might him reſtraine,
In weyb us deed twis ſhe well not faine,
But with all her might ſhe doth her buſineſſe,
To bring him out of his heauineſſe.

Lo what gentilleſſe theſe women haue,
If we could know it for our rudeneſſe,
How buſie they be vs to keepe and ſaue,
Both in heale,and alſo in ſickneſſe,
And alway right ſorie for our buſtreſſe,
In euery manner,thus ſhew they routh,
That in hem is all goodneſſe and trouth.

And ſith we find in hem gentilneſſe & trouth,
Worſhip,bountie,and kindneſſe euermore,
Let neuer this gentilleſſe,through your ſlouth,
In her kind trouth be aught to loſe,
That in women is,and hath ben full yore,
For in reuerence of heauens queene,
We ought to worſhip all women that beene.

For of all creatures that euer wer get & borne,
This wote ye wil a woman was the beſt,
By her was recouered ý bliſſe ý we had loſt,
And though ý woman ſhall we come to reſt,
And ben ſaued,it that our ſelfe leſt,
Wherefore me thinketh,if that we had grace,
We oughten honour women in euery place.

Therefore I rede,that to our liues end,
For this time for it,while that we haue ſpace,
That we haue trepaſſed,purſue to amend,
Praying our Ladie,wel of all grace,
To bring vs vnto that bliſſfull place,
There as ſhe ý all good women ſhal be in ſere
In heauen aboue,among the angels clere.

Explicit.

The Houſe of Fame.

In this booke is ſhewed how the deedes of all men and women,be they good or bad,are carried by report to poſteritis.

Od courſe by euery ý came to
good,
For it is wonder thing by the
Rood
To my wit,what cauſeth ſwe-
uens
On the morrow,or on euens,
And why the effect followeth of ſome,
And of ſome it ſhall neuer come.
Why that it is an auiſion,
And why this is a reuelacion,
Why this a dreame,why that a ſweuen,
And not to euery man liche euen,
Why this a fantome,why that Oracles,
I not:but who ſo of theſe miracles
The cauſes know bet than I,
Define he,for I certainly
Ne can hem not,ne neuer thinke,
To buſie my wit for to ſwinke,
To know of her ſigniſications
The gendres,ne diſtinctions
Of the times of hem,ne the cauſes,
Or why this is more than that is,
Or yeue folkes complexions,
Make hem dreame of reflexions,
Or els thus,as other ſaine,
For the great feeblenſſe of her braine,
By abſtinence,or by ſickneſſe,
Priſon,ſtrife,or great diſtreſſe,
Or els by diſordinaunce,
Or naturall accuſtomaunce,
That ſome men be too curious
In ſtudie,or Melancolius,
Or thus,ſo inly ful of dred,
That no man may him bote red,
Or els that deuotion
Of ſome,and contemplation,
Cauſen ſuch dreames oft,
Or that the cruell life vnſoft
Of hem that loues leden,
Oft hopen much or dreden,
That purely her impreſſions
Cauſen hem to haue viſions,
Or if ſpirits han the might
To make folke to dreame on night,
Or if the ſoule of proper kind,
Be ſo perſite as men find,

Chat

Figure 10. Thomas Speght, ed., *The Workes of our Antient and Learned English Poet,* **Geffrey Chaucer (London: Islip, 1602)**

356   The firſt Book of Boecius.

Cautels who ſo vſeth gladly, gloſeth,
To eſchewe ſoch it is right high prudence,
What ye ſayd ones, mine hart oppoſeth,
That my writing payes in your abſence,
Pleaſed you moch better than my preſence:
Yet can I moze, ye be not exeuſable,
A faithfull harte ever is acceptable.

Quaketh my penne, my ſpirit ſuppoſeth,
That in my writing ye find woll ſome offence,
Min hert welkneth thus ſone, anon it riſeth,
How hotte, now colde, and eſt in feruence:
That miſſe is, is cauſed of negligence,

And not of malice, therefoze beth merciable,
A faithfull harte ever is acceptable.

¶ **Lenuoye.**

Forth complaint, forth lacking eloquence,
Forth little letter of enditing lame,
I haue beſought my ladies Sapience,
Of thy behalfe, to accept in game,
Thine inabilitie, doe thou the ſame:
Now forth, I cloſe thee in holy Clenus name,
Thee ſhall vncloſe my harts gouernereſſe.

Boecius de Conſolatione Philoſophiæ.

In this Book are handled high and hard obſcure Points, *viz.* The purveyance of God; The force of Deſtiny; The freedom of our Wills; and the infallible Preſcience of the Almighty; and that the Contemplation of God himſelf is our *Summum bonum.*

Carmina qui quondam ſtudio florenti peregi
Flebilis heu mæſtos cogor inire modos.

Alas, I weeping am conſtrained to begin verſe of ſozowful matter, whilom in floziſhing ſtudie made deliſtable dities. For lo, rending Muſes of Poets, enditen to me things to be written, and dzerie teares. At laſſe no dzede ne might overcome tho mules, that they ne werten fellowes, and folowden my way, that is to ſay: when I was exiled, they that weren of my youth, whilom weelful and grene, comfozten now ſozowful wierdes of me old man: for elde is commen vnwarely vpon me, haſted by the harmes that I haue, and ſozow hath commaunded his age to be in me. Heeres hoze aren ſhad ouertimeliche vpon my head: and the ſlacke ſkinne trembleth of mine empted body. Chilke death of menne is weleful, y ne commeth not in yeres that be ſwet, but commeth to wzetches which yeleped: Alas, alas, with how deafe an eare death cruell turneth away from wzetches, and naieth foz to cloſe weepying iyen. While Foztune vnfaithfull, fauoured me with light goodes, the ſozowful houre, that is to ſay, y death, had almoſt dzeint mine hedde: but now foz Foztune cloudie, hath chaunged her deceiueable chere to meward, mine impitous life dzaweth along vngreable dwellings. O ye my frends, what, oz whereto auaunted ye me to been wilfull? Foz he that hath fallen, ſtode in no ſtedfaſt degree.

Hæc dum mecum tacitus ipſe reputarem, queri-
moniamque lacrimabilem ſtili Officio deſigna-
rem; aſtitiſſe mihi ſupra verticem viſa eſt mu-
lier reuerendi admodum vultus, oculis arden-
tibus, & ultra communem, &c.

In the mean while, that I ſtil recozded theſe thynges with my ſelf, and marked my wepely complatnte, with office of pointell: I ſaugh ſtondyng abouen the hight of

mine hed a woman of full great reuerence, by ſemblant. Her iyen bzennyng e clere, ſeyng outer y common might of men, with a liuely colour, e with ſoch vigour e ſtrength y it ne might not been nempned, all were it ſoy ſhe were full of ſo great age, that menne woulden not trowen in no manere that ſhe were of our elde.

The ſtature of her was of doutous iudgement foz ſometime the conſtrained e ſhonke her ſeluen, like to y common meaſure of men: And ſometime it ſeemed, that ſhe touched y heauen, with y hight of her hedde. And when ſhe houe her hedde higher, ſhe perced y ſelf heauen ſo that the ſight of men looking was in vell: her clothes were maked of right delie thzedes, e ſubtell craft of perdurable matter. The which clothes ſhe had wouen with her owne honds, as I knew well after, by her ſelf declaring, e ſhewing to me the beauty: The which clothes a darkeneſſe of a fozleten and diſpiſed elde had duſked and darked, as it is wonte to darke by ſmoked Images.

In the netheteſt hemme oz bozder of theſe clothes, men redde iwouen therein, a Grekiſh A. that ſignifieth the life Actiue: e aboue that letter, in y hieſt bozdure, a Grekiſh T. y ſignifieth the lyfe Contemplatiſe. And betwene theſe two letters, there were ſeen degrees nobly wzought in manner of ladders, by which degrees men might climben from the nether reſt letter to y vppereſt: natheleſſe, handes of ſome men hadden kerue that cloth by violence oz by ſtrength, e eueriche man of hem had bozne away ſuch peces as he might getten. And fozſothe this fozeſaid woman bare ſmall bookes in her right hand, e in her left hand ſhe bare a Scepter. And when ſhe ſawe theſe Poeticall Muſes approchjng about my bed, and endityng wozdes to my wepinges, ſhe was a little amoued, e glowed with cruell iyen. Who(qd.ſhe) hath ſuffred approchen to this ſicke man, theſe commen ſtrompets, of which is the place that men callen Theatre, the which onely ne aſſwagen not his ſozowes

---

Figure 11. *Works of Geoffrey Chaucer* (London: W.H., 1687). Photo courtesy of the William Andrews Clark Memorial Library.

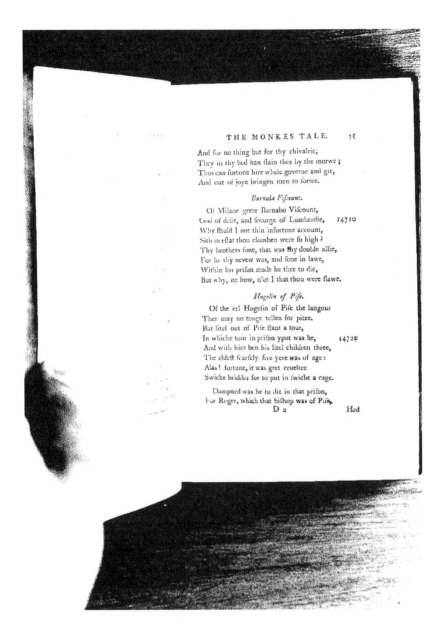

THE MONKES TALE.   35

And for no thing but for thy chivalrie,
They in thy bed han flain thee by the morwe ;
Thus can fortune hire whele governe and gie,
And out of joye bringen men to forwe.

Barnabo Vifcount.

Of Milane grete Barnabo Vifcount,
God of delit, and fcourge of Lumbardie,   14710
Why fhuld I not thin infortune account,
Sith in eftat thou clomben were fo high ?
Thy brothers fone, that was thy double allie,
For he thy nevew was, and fone in lawe,
Within his prifon made he thee to die,
But why, ne how, n'ot I that thou were flawe.

Hugelin of Pife.

Of the erl Hugelin of Pife the langour
Ther may no tonge tellen for pitee.
But litel out of Pife ftant a tour,
In whiche tour in prifon yput was he,   14720
And with him ben his litel children three,
The eldeft fcarfely five yere was of age :
Alas ! fortune, it was gret crueltee
Swiche briddes for to put in fwiche a cage.

Dampned was he to die in that prifon,
For Roger, which that bifhop was of Pife,
D 2   Had

Figure 12. Thomas Tyrwhitt, ed., *The Canterbury Tales of Chaucer* (London: T. Payne, 1774). Reproduced by permission of the William Andrews Clark Memorial Library.

these editions has varied in the history of Chaucer studies. The first complete works is by Pynson of 1526—a complete works formed by combining three independent sections (*Canterbury Tales, Troilus and Criseyde,* and *House of Fame,* now STC 5086, 5088, and 5096).[1]

The second stage is represented by the series of double-column folio editions from 1532-1687, beginning with William Thynne's edition of 1532. These effectively eliminated the editions of single works for Chaucer until translations began to appear in the eighteenth century (see figs. 8-11).

The third stage begins in the eighteenth century with two developments: the (apparent) rejection of blackletter with Urry's 1721 folio edition and the creation of small format, multi-volume editions, the most important by Tyrwhitt in 1775-78 (fig. 12). Tyrwhitt's edition was followed by a number of piracies as Chaucer was included in such large popular series as Bell's *Poets of Great Britain* (1782).[2] For Chaucerians, the legacy of this tradition is the multi-volume edition by Skeat and the various single-volume scholarly editions that follow from it.

Let us first consider the utility of the brief history sketched above. What this history shows immediately is a bifurcation in the manufacturing elements of the book and in its very conception. This can be exemplified by a number of aspects of the book: type (blackletter vs. roman); layout (double vs. single column); size (folio vs. octavo and smaller); press-run (the development of large press runs). These changes could be paralleled by textual and linguistic changes, for example, the development of a tradition of vernacular translations and imitations.

But a further bifurcation is also implied—one of audience. The typographical history I have sketched above has been twice written this century, once by John Hetherington in a typescript and again by Charles Muscatine in *The Book of Geoffrey Chaucer.* These studies are directed not to professional Chaucerians, but rather to book buyers and book dealers. Hetherington's manual, eminently readable, modest in its stated goals, and amateurish in its production, is intended to help dealers and owners identify the particular Chaucer they are trying to buy or sell; Muscatine's book was produced for the Book Club of California.[3] These works do not define Chaucerians as, say, readers of academic journals. Hetherington performed his research by simply taking the books off his personal library shelf and comparing them

(Hetherington, *Chaucer*, 1). The history of typefaces is directly related to such opposing audiences: one considers the book an aesthetic object; another considers the book a repository of a text (see the twentieth-century variant of this history sketched in my conclusion on the Fine Press Chaucer).

The series of figures also exposes some persistent mythology among Chaucerians. A glance through any bibliography of Chaucer will show that the interest of most Chaucerians writing on early printing is Caxton, not his more directly influential successors. Yet the centrality of de Worde's typeface to English typography and the obsolescence of Caxton's early Burgundian type is immediately apparent (see fig. 6). As early as 1598, Caxton's type was characterized as "a ragged letter" (Thynne, *Animadversions*, 71); the term is descriptive, not judgmental, and indicates that Caxton's type was very early seen as eccentric. In terms of English book production, Caxton's editions are singular; they resemble neither the English manuscripts against which they competed nor the later editions that replaced them. That singularity has little to do with Caxton or his intentions: the typographical appearance of Caxton's books was dependent on the tastes of his continental typecutter, Johan Veldener. When Veldener changed from Flemish to what Hellinga calls an "international" style, Caxton had no choice but to follow suit, as did Caxton's own successor de Worde.[4] What might be called the zero-degree of blackletter in English culture is the typeface of de Worde (fig. 7); and it would be difficult to distinguish in ordinary language a de Worde typeface from any number of late sixteenth-century English blackletter fonts.[5] De Worde, thus, presents what might be called a typographically unmediated Chaucer. Caxton's Chaucer, by contrast, is much earlier a commodity—a rare book, whose value is enhanced by its visual singularity.

At the other extreme of this series is the 1687 edition (fig. 11). This edition has become the object of some Chaucerian bibliolatry, even though it is probably the edition least seen (either physically or in facsimile) by Chaucerians. To a collector, it is the least valuable of Chaucer folios, and to most scholars the least interesting. But it still stands as the culmination of a series of what are often called the "tall handsome folios" of Chaucer. Brewer, in his *Critical Heritage* volume has called the type a "handsome rather mannered blackletter" (35): "An edition, with the conscious antiquarian appeal of blackletter (i.e.

Gothic) type (very mannered and beautiful), was published in 1687"
(1:13-14).

The 1687 folio is neither particularly tall nor handsome; it has
never had much antiquarian appeal, and even today, copies are quite
cheap. Whether the type is beautiful is a matter that cannot be argued,
but I have never heard it so described by anyone other than Brewer
(and a bookseller who once tried to sell me a copy); it has no place in
any history of English typography I have read. I am not sure whether
"mannered" means that the typeface is eccentric in relation to other
blackletters of the period or to blackletter in general. But even the
limited selection of figures included in this chapter suggests a steady
progression (by most accounts a decline) in English typography from
the sixteenth to the late seventeenth century, and the 1687 Chaucer
seems no exception. That aesthetic judgment accords with most type-
founding histories.[6] It also accords with Alderson's suggestion that the
book is a stopgap edition designed only to secure copyright (*Chaucer
and Augustan Scholarship*, 48). The renewal of English typography in
the late seventeenth century did not affect the books under consideration here.[7] The attention of printers and founders was largely confined to roman type; blackletter was becoming a specialty type, and the
larger market that seemed to exist for Chaucer in the eighteenth century received Chaucer in large part through translations and modernizations—all in roman type. The Chaucer editions noted above lapsed
into the peculiar history accorded them by the book-trade—a history
largely determined by economic considerations.

The Presumed Opposition between the Blackletter and Roman Chaucer

The apparent coherence of the above typographical history, however, can be as misleading as it is useful. Some of the more important
editions are anomalies—their very monumentality highlighted by
their resistance to the coherence of any smooth narrative. In the sections below, I will outline some general problems with the notion of
the blackletter Chaucer and discuss in particular the anomalous
nature of the 1532 edition that presumably initiates the series of
blackletter folios. In a later chapter, I will return to this problem with
reference to the Urry edition of 1721.

To begin with, the history defines Chaucer from a distinctly modern point of view: Chaucer is an author of a large body of works

represented in an edition, and a coherent history of these editions is thus a coherent history of Chaucer—a Chaucer monumentalized in folio, transformed into roman type, and finally marketed in popular affordable format. So stated, the difficulties of this history become apparent. The Chaucer book itself is not a creation of printing. Cambridge University Library, MS Gg 4.27 is the first extant complete-works edition of Chaucer, and was produced in the early fourteenth century—a hundred years prior to the edition of Pynson. Most important, the very terms central to this history are misleading; they are the products of modern classifications and have variable relations to classifications available at the time the books were produced. The very notion of a blackletter Chaucer is a product of developments in the history of typography (English and continental) and the efforts of early antiquarians and modern bibliographers to impose on this history a coherent system of classification.

The term *blackletter* and its meanings develop as a way of describing the resources available to late seventeenth-century English type-founders and printers and the manner in which eighteenth-century bibliographers and amateurs looked at earlier books. Eighteenth-century bibliographers routinely spoke of "the old black letter," and Joseph Moxon in *Mechanick Exercises* (1683) classified typeface according to this scheme: Roman, Italic, and English, with a further set of imprecisely defined terms designating body and face size (producing such categories as "English English").[8] The classification is asymmetrical and insecure, since roman comes to oppose italic in a way for which there is no blackletter counterpart.[9] Furthermore, what Moxon describes as "English" (a family of blackletter now known as textura) is closest to what was originally a script used for Latin, and still functioned that way in Caxton's use of type fonts. In the history of English typography, this typeface appears to reverse its initial meaning and function.

Library catalogs have more or less followed Moxon, adding brief typographical information when space permits. In many of the British Museum catalogs, this is B.L., G.L., meaning "blackletter" or "Gothic letter"—descriptive categories that add inadvertent support for the traditional myth concerning the transformation of blackletter into roman.

These classifications can suggest something about the consumer genre of a text at a particular period in history—a period that spans both the low point of Chaucer reception and book production (late seventeenth century) as well as a period of vitality and revival (early to mid-eighteenth century). Obviously Moxon—as well as the early eighteenth-century English editors of Chaucer, modern literature, and medieval chronicles—felt that the difference between blackletter and roman was fundamental. Kynaston's translation of *Troilus and Criseyde* (1635) prints the Chaucer text in blackletter, with a facing Latin translation in roman type. And this was the convention followed by the one extensive textual commentary on Chaucer printed in the seventeenth century (by Brathwait).[10] But such classifications obscure the production genre in all its aspects.

To describe earlier periods, a different language of typography is required and a different system of classification. The system of F. S. Isaac involves simple measurement and classification of types within large families: for blackletter or Gothic, these are textura, rotunda, bâtard.[11] The type used in the 1532 Chaucer is thus a 94B. The numbers indicate 20-line type measure (in millimeters); the letters suggest broad families of type. Together, the classification provides information about the actual book production and history (what type case was used in production), as well as some minimal information on how the printer intended the book to be categorized by a reader. For sixteenth-century English books, his system works fairly efficiently.[12]

The transformation of one type into another, specifically blackletter into roman, is to some extent a product of late-seventeenth-century type mythology, since there are various families and even sizes of blackletter, and these are not used interchangeably during the early period of printing.[13] Even in 1700, that mythology of binary opposition is weak. As a means of describing the typographical features of Chaucer's book and, consequently, the classicization of his text, the myth is seriously inaccurate and misleading. There are first of all several non-blackletter Chaucers prior to Urry's of 1721: first, the Canon Yeoman's Tale included in Ashmole's *Theatrum Chemicum Britannicum* (1652), where the Prologue is in italic and the text in roman; second, the texts included in Dryden's translation of 1700 (both are noted by Alderson). When Dryden speaks of putting Chaucer "in English habit," he clearly refers only to the language of the text, not its appearance, since the Middle English texts appear, like the translations, in roman type.[14] There is a third non-blackletter Chaucer, rarely mentioned by Chaucerians. This is the 1606 print of the

Plowman's Tale, in roman type, complete with marginal gloss (STC 5101). The fact that this book is no longer a "non-blackletter Chaucer" today means only that it has been banished from the twentieth-century Chaucer canon. To us, this book seems to be an anomaly, but in the history of Chaucer typography, it has precedent: it is based on the earlier independent Plowman's Tale (1535, STC 5099.5) printed in single column by Godfray (the printer of the 1532 Chaucer)—and the text in that independent print also contains marginalia.[15]

Thus, in speaking of a Chaucer transformed from blackletter to roman, we are actually describing the development of a particular genre of the Chaucer book as it was conceived at a particular time in Chaucer history. The transformation of Chaucer into roman type describes Chaucer being confined to and eventually defined by the bounds of a complete-works edition. Such an edition sets standards and rules that may well be inapplicable to a more popular Chaucer— one where Chaucer is represented in single-text editions and anthologies. And this tradition, paradoxically, has more venerable roots in the earliest printed editions of Chaucer.

The Edition of 1532 and the Early Canon of English Authors

I have indicated above how the simple opposition between blackletter and roman glosses over one quite radical change in English typography—that from Caxton's early bâtard types to de Worde's more familiar texturas. The 1532 edition is a somewhat less obvious example of similar historical forces; like the earlier Caxton editions, it initiates a series of editions, and also like these editions, its own typographical appearance, due to continental factors, was never duplicated.

The 1532 edition of Chaucer edited by William Thynne is a landmark edition in many ways, and twice within the last century, it has been reproduced in facsimile. It is also the last edition that generally retains the status of a manuscript in modern editions, that is, it is the last edition that modern editors suspect may have been printed, in part, from manuscripts no longer available.[16] It is also the first printed edition that is designed from the beginning of its production as a complete edition, and thus all arguments concerning the Chaucer canon, up to and including those by Skeat, take as their

foundation the inclusion of a work in Thynne. In nearly every complete works since, the *Canterbury Tales* is printed first. The Retraction
stays firmly out of the canon until the eighteenth century. Minor
works are added, but always at the end of the edition, and none of
those included in Thynne's edition are omitted until the nineteenth
century. Since all Chaucer editions follow the physical format of
Thynne (the double-column folio) until the mid-eighteenth century,
any reader picking up a Thynne edition would recognize it as a basic
Chaucer edition. As late as 1905, Skeat refers to it as the "First Folio"
edition—a description that functions intelligibly even though it is historically inaccurate and from a bardolatric point of view preposterous
and overreaching (*Chaucer 1532*, Introduction, xvi-xvii).

Yet despite its status as the basic Chaucer edition, it is also typographically one of the most eccentric—as eccentric as the Kelmscott
and Fine Press editions would be centuries later. It is printed not in
the textura characteristic of de Worde, but in a continental bâtard—a
typeface similar to Pynson's type 2 (the bâtard 101mm used in the
prose sections of the 1492 edition). This font was not entirely familiar
to the printer of the Chaucer edition, and once worn out it apparently could not be replaced or recast. Chaucer was never again
printed in any type resembling this. The 1532 edition thus firmly
established the large folio format for the Chaucer editions and the
text for them, but its visual appearance was not reproduced.

English printers since Caxton were entirely dependent on continental type-cutters, and because of this, they had only a limited
choice of type. They could not continue working with a type that had
proved successful to them unless there was a demand for the same
type on the continent. Whether Thynne's edition could establish a
typographical tradition would thus depend not on the intentions of
the English printers, but rather on those of continental printing communities. The "well of English undefiled" would be defined visually by
French and Dutch artisans.

The 1532 Chaucer has often been associated with the 1532 Gower
(printed by Berthelet). Even though the typefaces are classified as different families (bâtard vs. rotunda), the typographical context of
each shows that from the standpoint of the consumer genre, the two
are very similar. As noted in a previous chapter, the first piece of
external evidence concerning the 1532 Chaucer is by Leland, who in
defiance of the colophon, attributes it to Berthelet:

Vicit tamen Caxodunicam editionem *Bertholetus* noster opera *Gulielmi Thynni,* qui . . . multa primae adjecit editioni. (Leland, *Commentarii,* 423)

Judged according to modern bibliography, Leland is simply in error: the printer of the 1532 edition was Godfray, not Berthelet, as the colophon found in all surviving copies states. Modern bibliographers assume that Leland is simply confusing or conflating Godfray's Chaucer and Berthelet's Gower. But Leland's authority is not easy to refute, and his (inadvertent) association of Godfray and Berthelet has been confirmed through a number of details in the printed books: it has long been known that Berthelet and Godfray shared an ornamental border, and more recently, Andrew Wawn pointed out that works by both printers show a peculiar "4", set apparently at 90 degrees. This discovery by Wawn is an important one. It was relatively easy to pass around a single woodcut border, but the sharing of a numerical type font is clearly a more serious matter.[17]

There are further associations as well, regarding not so much the material production genre (sharing of type) but the implied consumer genre: how these works were intended to be received. Both are produced in a format that is extremely rare for this period, a folio in 6s (quires of six leaves, consisting of three sheets folded once).[18] And each is in a typeface that for literary works was an exotic. The monumentality of these editions is borne out by other factors. First, the type used by Godfray for the Chaucer was either new or its use with English texts unfamiliar to him, the proof being in the use of the *w.* Continental type fonts did not supply sufficient *w*'s for the needs of English-language printing and various solutions were adopted. In the seventeenth century, *w*'s for roman type are generally imported from other fonts and thus ill-matched. Isaac long ago pointed out the problems in use of the bâtard *w* by Godfray in the 1532 Chaucer. But as I have shown elsewhere, the conventions for the use of that *w* changed as Godfray progressed in his printing. In the early portions, the bâtard *w* alternates with a textura *w* (see fig. 8) for lower case; upper case is supplied by a double *V* or the bâtard *w.* In later sections, the bâtard *w* (proper to the font), becomes the upper case *w,* with all lower case *w*'s from a textura.[19] I have seen no other example of this in contemporary uses of similar type. The final typographical product (large folio in 6s, bâtard type) associates Chaucer with what are generally considered "humanist" productions, for example, the plays of

Thomas Heywood. The rotunda of Berthelet had similar uses, used most noticeably in the works of Thomas Elyot.[20]

Berthelet and Godfray, whatever their economic association, were engaged in the same publishing venture: the promotion of a vernacular author in an expensive, monumental edition—an edition that would appear in an exotic typeface—one that in the case of the Godfray Chaucer, may have been inspired by the earlier Pynson edition. The source of the texts was Caxton in both cases, but the appearance of each constituted a radical break with previous printing traditions in England.

Again, considering these editions only in their contemporary English context, we can draw a number of ancillary conclusions. Any charting of the development of traditional "major writers in English" or the "fathers of English poetry" must begin with the affected and deliberate monumentality of these two editions and their authors, Chaucer and Gower. This physical monumentality overshadows other attempts to produce a triumvirate of English authors, parallel to those in Italy or France, that is, a triumvirate that generally includes Lydgate.[21]

The absence of several English writers included in the nineteenth- and twentieth-century versions of the medieval canon is not surprising. Langland was not printed until the small editions of Crowley in 1550 (STC 19906, 19907).[22] But Lydgate's absence is more surprising, since his publication record is on the whole far more impressive than that of any medieval English writer, including Chaucer and Gower. A list of Lydgate's books fills two columns in STC. Yet only one of those productions fits the monumental format developed by Godfray and Berthelet in the 1530s, and that is one only partially attributed to Lydgate: *Fall of Princes,* printed by Pynson in 1527 as a work by Boccaccio. In my opinion, this has nothing to do with what Lydgate says: his prolixity, his ragged rime—characteristics that can be easily matched in much of Chaucer and Gower. Materially, Lydgate's work does not conveniently fit this format. Conceptually, Lydgate texts had been long associated with the small folio editions of Caxton and de Worde (a size equivalent to the quarto printed from full sheets in which most of Lydgate's works appear). Lydgate was typographically and visually old-fashioned.

All of these writers had been printed by at least one of the three major printers, Caxton, de Worde, Pynson. And the formats chosen persisted (the quarto for Lydgate, the double-column large folio for Chaucer and Gower).[23] As literary scholars we have been trained to be sensitive to strictly textual evidence. In this case that consists of evidence both internal and external—the texts themselves and what fifteenth-century poets say about them. Such evidence points in a number of these instances to one set of conclusions: the threesome of Gower, Chaucer, Lydgate; the direct relation of Chaucerian apocrypha to religious pamphlets. But the evidence from specific books leads us in an entirely different direction: the monumentality of Gower and Chaucer, the irrelevance of such bibliographical red-herrings as the Pilgrim's Tale, the marginality of Langland, the old-fashionedness of Lydgate, the inexistence of the Gawain poet. The history of what I would call the "materialization" of these texts has yet to be written.

Continental Factors

The above narrative history isolates English type and gives it a degree of autonomy: there is the historical development of canonical English writers, and there are book formats that parallel this history. But just as the choice of an English canon is affected by continental forces (English authors are sought to match French or Italian ones), so is the typographical appearance of those authors.

The invocation of continental analogies with English poets is common: Chaucer is the English Petrarch, Dante in English, the English Alain.[24] This clearly responds to and affects readings of Chaucer. The case of typography is similar, but the material basis of the relation is more precise. Here that material (a type font) may have cultural meanings and implications that are directly opposed. The typographical mark of monumentality in one culture may be vulgar and old-fashioned in another. The attempt to legitimize England as a nation with its national authors, thus, cannot be represented with an appropriate type that would be recognized internationally.[25]

Seen within the context of English typography, the following narrative might be constructed: that both Chaucer and Gower were distinguished or marketed in 1532 with exotic type fonts, that within two decades, both had been domesticated and appear in the same typographical dress (de Worde's textura) as other English writers—Lydgate, Langland, Malory. Major English writers were specifically English insofar as they resembled minor English writers.

Yet that apparent domestication was determined not by forces in England but by forces on the continent. Printers' intentions are like all other intentions—authorial, critical, and institutional. They are not always coherent, often frustrated, and difficult to recover. English printers did not have the luxury of controlling the physical appearance of their books: they used what type was available to them—the type supplied and priced by continental typefounders—not what typeface might continue the tradition of monumentality initiated by Godfray and Berthelet. The available supply of type determined such apparent domestication: typographically, Chaucer could not be distinguished from Lydgate even if a printer had thought this desirable.

Type wore out. And although some type might be recast (Caxton's Type 2* is an example), the type used by English printers in the sixteenth century was for the most part uncorrectable.[26] Because of this dependence on continental materials, we cannot speak of the particular meaning of a particular type in English typography, and we have little way of determining how the actual product reflects the intended product.

Consider the bâtard of the 1532 Chaucer. Within the context of English printing, this seems reserved for such humanist productions as Heywood. But within the context of European printing, this bâtard has a completely different meaning: in French printing, it was used for vernacular works; in the general change during 1530s and 1540s to roman and italic fonts, the older bâtard became associated with popular vulgar texts.[27]

This French bâtard was retained in later type fonts only as a way of representing medieval vernacular, in the same way that blackletter continued to be used by English printers for medieval works long after roman type had become the normal type. A glance at French sixteenth-century books shows the fate of this letter. Rabelais scholars often note that the first two books, *Pantagruel* (1532) and *Gargantua* (1534), were printed in pamphlet form in bâtard; the first book to appear in roman type is the third, *Tiers Livre* (1546). Rabelais, so the myth goes, was transformed from a popular into a classical or humanist writer—a myth that in turn can be supported by the contents of these books.[28]

The myth has some foundation, yet Rabelais simply underwent the same changes affecting the entire spectrum of French typography. The bâtard that had characterized French manuscript and printed literature simply disappeared. And far from being marked, the succession of individual Rabelais editions simply partake of differing "zero-degrees of typography." We don't know what a reader might have thought who in 1555 picked up an early bâtard Rabelais (Book 2) instead of the more modern roman version. Was Rabelais dated? That is a matter of the history of the consumer genre. But we can speculate on what the printer may have thought.

In mid-century, continental books and their implied typographical conventions are already circulating in England. When the implications of this typeface changed in mid-century, there would be no possibility of an English printer designing a book as a typographical successor to Godfray's 1532 edition. For English printers, there were fewer alternatives to roman or italic. English authors were forced, by the exigencies of French typography and transformations taking place on the continent, to *become* medieval in the blackletter fonts provided by foreign typefounders.

Scholars of these editions have also done their part to domesticate the exotic typefaces of the 1532 Chaucer and the 1532 Gower. Again, the traditional language of typography is in part responsible. In the early eighteenth century, Thomas Hearne recognized Godfray's odd type, but did not have the means to describe it in any detail, and characterized it only as "other" than what he had seen in the rest of the editions.[29] In the twentieth century, this typeface has fared little better, as we can see in the case with the early printings of Heywood and their modern reproduction. As I have noted, the plays of Heywood were originally printed by Rastell in a monumental format similar to that used for Gower and Chaucer: large folios, although single- rather than double-column. Several of these were printed in bâtard type.[30] Yet when the Malone society issued its type-facsimile reprints—reprints that give at least the illusion of reproducing the appearance of the books on which they are based—all of these, whether their originals were printed in textura or bâtard, were issued in ordinary textura; that is, the apparent efforts of Rastell to promote his authors in exotic typeface are obliterated. The Malone society reproduces, inadvertently, a situation that Rastell himself may have faced due to the realities of type-founding and type-reception. The bâtard type either could not be cheaply replaced, or, equally plausibly, it had assumed on the continent a meaning contrary to that Rastell had tried to give it. The result was a domestication in two historical periods: the sixteenth-century domestication of Heywood, and the twentieth-century domestication of Rastell by the Malone Society. In the history of typography, exotic types lose autonomy and develop into a refined version of ordinary type.

The blackletter that in 1532 would have made Chaucer appear like all other writers (the textura type font used two years later to produce the Plowman's Tale) was readily available to Godfray and used for the Preface of the Thynne Chaucer. This blackletter is so standard that some Chaucerians have mistaken it for the blackletter used in the 1542 Chaucer.[31] But that typeface category—the very one under which most modern Chaucerians classify the typography of this edition through their reference to a generic blackletter—was rejected by its printer.

The history of Gower's *Confessio Amantis* provides a useful comparison.[32] There are only two editions of Gower in the sixteenth century, one in 1532, the other in 1554 (a column-for-column reprint). And as was the case with Chaucer, the distinctive typeface of the 1532 edition (for the Gower, a rotunda) was not available in mid-century. Nonetheless, for the 1555 edition, something of the character of the 1532 edition is maintained: a large elegant typeface, double-column folio (see figs. 13 and 14). There is no mistaking this Gower for any of the Chaucers produced between 1542 and 1561; it retains the elegance of the earlier 1532 prints. In terms of popularity, however, it may well suffer from the very monumentality it exhibits—a monumentality that is at the same time a singularity. Unlike Chaucer (who in the 1550s appears in a standard blackletter) Gower appears in exotic dress, and is not reprinted until Chalmer's English poets edition of 1810.

Chaucer was thus caught in two transformations: (1) the standardization of English typography—whereby all medieval works would be printed in a blackletter in the genre of the textura used by de Worde, and (2) the transformation of French typography, from bâtard to roman. These in turn led to a third: the narrative of Chaucer reception, whereby the individual editions become part of a series. The discrete series of Chaucer editions with their separate type fonts become transformed into a coherent continuum—a narrative that conveniently supports the narrative of all Chaucer scholarship: the transformation of ancient criticism (however defined) into modern criticism, always curiously contemporary.

PROLOGVS. Fol.4.

(Ut dicitur) rerum euentus necessario contingit/
sed potius dicendum est/quod ea que nos prospe
ra et aduersa in hoc mundo vocamus/ secundum
merita et demerita hominum/ digno dei iudicio
proueniunt.

And netheles yet somme men wryte
And sayn fortune is to wyte/
And some men holde opinion
That it is constellacion/
whiche causeth all that a man dothe
God wote of bothe whiche is sothe/
The worlde/as of his propre kynde
was euer vntrew/and as the blynde
Improperly he demeth fame
He blameth/that is nought to blame
And preyseth/that is nought to preyse
Thus whan he shall the thynges peyse
Ther is deceyt in his balaunce
And all is that the varyaunce
Of vs/that shulde vs beter auyse
For after that we fall and ryse
The worlde ariste/and falleth with all
So that the man is ouer all
His owne cause of wele and wo
That we fortune clepe so
Out of the man hym selfe it groweth
And who that other wyse troweth/
Beholde the people of Israel
For euer/whyle they dydden welle
Fortune was them debonayre
And when they dydden the contrayre
Fortune was contraryende
So that it proueth wele at ende
why that the worlde is wonderful
And may no whyle stande full/
Though that it seme wele besyn/
For euery worldes thynge is vayne
And euer goth the whele about/
And euer stant a man in doute/
Fortune stant no whyle stylle
So hath ther no man his wylle
Als far as any man may knowe
There lasteth no thynge but a throwe

Boetius.
O quam dulcedo humane vite multa amaritu-
dine asperfa est.

The worlde stante euer vpon debate
So may be syker none astate/
Now

Now here/now there/now to/nowe fro
Now vp/now doun/the world goth so
And euer hath done/and euer shall
wherof I fynde in specyal
A tale wryten in the byble
whiche must nedes be credible
And that as in conclusyon/
Seyth/that vpon diuisyon
Stant/why no worldes thing may laste
Tyl it be dryue to the laste
And fro the fyrst reygne of all
Vnto this daye howe so befall
Of that the reygnes be meuable
The man hym selfe hath be culpable
whiche of his gouernaunce
Fortuneth all the worldes chaunce

Prosper et aduersus obliquo tramite uersus
Immundus mundus decipit omne genus
Mundus in euentu uersatur, ut alea casu,
Quam celer in ludis iactat auara manus.
Sicut imago uiri uariantur tempora mundi,
Statq; nihil firmum preter amare deum.

Hic in prologo tractat de statua illa/qua rex
Nabugodonosor viderat in somnis/ cuius caput
aureum/pectus argenteum/venter eneus/ tibie
ferree/pedum vero quedam pars ferrea/queda
fictilis videbatur:sub qua membrorum diuersitate
secundum Danielis exposicionem huius mundi
variacio figurabatur.

The bigh almygbty purueyaunce
In whose eterne remembraunce
From fyrst was euery thynge present
He hath his prophecye sent
In suche a wyse/as thou shalt bere
To Daniel of this matere
How that this world shal torne & wede
Tyll it be falle vnto his ende
wherof the tale tell I shall
In whiche is betokened all
As Nabugodonosor slepte
A sweuen him toke/the whiche be kept
Til on the morowe be was aryse
For therof he was sore agryse
Tyl Daniell his dreme be tolde
And prayed hym fayre/that be wolde
A rede what it token may
And sayde/a bedde where I lay
Me thought I seygbe vpon a stage
wher

Figure 13. Gower, *Confessio Amantis* (London: Berthelet, 1532) (20 lines = 87 mm.). Photo courtesy of the Henry E. Huntington Library.

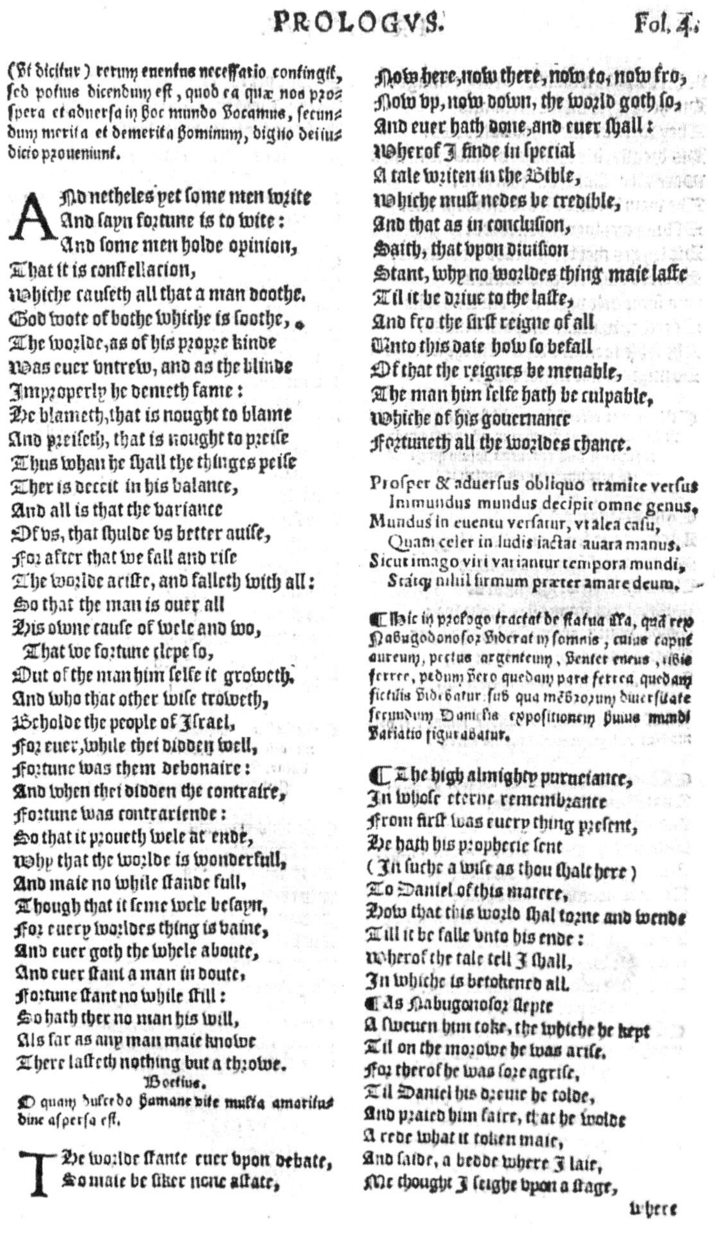

Figure 14. Gower, *Confessio Amantis* (London: Berthelet, 1555) (20 lines = 73mm.). Reproduced by permission of the William Andrews Clark Memorial Library.

Chapter 4

THE BOOK AND THE TEXT: TWO STUDIES ON THE TESTAMENT OF LOVE

If the determination of the Chaucer canon were to proceed entirely on the basis of what is contained in early manuscripts and what internal evidence those texts provide, it would not be difficult to settle questions of attribution for such texts as the *Testament of Love*, the Plowman's Tale, *Jack Upland*, and the Retraction. The *Testament of Love* cites Chaucer directly, as does Henryson's *Testament of Criseyde*, also contained in the sixteenth-century folios. Neither the *Testament of Love* nor the Plowman's Tale exists in early manuscript form, and the copy text for the version of *Jack Upland* contained in the Speght Chaucer folio is Foxe's *Actes and Monuments*. The Retraction, on the other hand, is Chaucerian in language and appears in every manuscript that contains a complete version of the Parson's Tale. The decisions of modern editors concerning the authorship of these texts ought to be easy ones to make.

The historical debate concerning these texts has proceeded on different grounds, however—grounds both ideological and material. On the one hand, the suitability of such works for inclusion in the Chaucer canon has been judged according to their politics. A reformist text has a good claim to have been written by a reformist Chaucer—that is, by that particular Chaucer who emerged in the mid-sixteenth century. On the other hand, such ideological arguments (and interpretations of Chaucerian history) sometimes mask more banal material matters: the inclusion of a work within the Chaucer canon and the subsequent canonical debate concerning that work are products of its material inclusion within an early

Chaucer book. Debate continues over the Retraction, and debate over these other texts continued far longer than now seems reasonable.

The subject of the present chapter is the *Testament of Love*. This text has interested Chaucerians for several reasons: it provides convenient biographical information (for whoever might be assigned its authorship),[1] and helps define what is or is not Chaucerian (again, regardless of its authorship). But the value it has for Chaucerians is due to a simple fact of editorial history: it happens to have been included in the Chaucer book—Thynne's 1532 folio.

In what follows, I consider the *Testament of Love* from two perspectives: (1) the ideological, and (2) what might be called the codicological and bibliographical. The first focuses on Foxe's ideological interpretation of the *Testament of Love* and the response by John Dart—a contributor to the 1721 Chaucer; the second on the now accepted rearrangement of the text of book 3 by Henry Bradley and Skeat in the late nineteenth century. The reconstruction by Bradley and Skeat provided an apparent solution to an anagram confirming the hypothesis of Usk's authorship; this in turn effectively ended further discussion of Chaucer's authorship and nearly eliminated the particular text (or text version) that had gone under his name.

Both types of argument develop because of a persistent myth concerning the printed book, another example (or variant) of what I have called the mythology of coherence so prevalent in Chaucer reception and scholarship. This myth assumes on the basis of the material object (the book) that some sort of textual coherence in contents, in some cases alluded to on the title page, must exist: this textual coherence is then labeled "Chaucer," the "Chaucerian," or the "Chaucerian context." Even the modern debate over the Chaucerian canon must begin with the physical placement of the works in the multi-volume edition of Skeat—the first to relegate works declared spurious to a separate volume.[2] But the material coherence of the book itself is in part illusory—one that masks the intractable incoherence of the texts represented. It is this illusion that canon debates in the eighteenth and nineteenth century began to combat.

I. CHAUCER THE RIGHT WYCLIFFIAN: JOHN DART AND "OLD MR. FOX"

Chaucer's identity as a reformer was a prerequisite to his appearance in Foxe's *Actes and Monuments*. Chaucer was first cited in the 1570 edition, and the sections on Chaucer expanded in subsequent editions.[3] Chaucer had been assigned a number of reformist works in the 1530s and 1540s, and claims to Chaucer's authorship were made on the title-pages themselves: *Jack vp Lande compyled by the famous G. Chaucer* (1536?; STC 5099); *The plouumans tale compylled by syr G. Chaucher knyght* (1548?; STC 5100). The 1548 Plowmans Tale was itself printed from the 1542 Chaucer.[4] But *Jack Upland* was included in a Chaucer folio only in 1602, printed directly from the second edition of Foxe (1570) and deriving its Chaucerian authorship from Foxe's discussion and authority.[5] If Chaucer's identity as a reformer were assumed, there would be no reason to contest these attributions; thus Foxe simply accepted what the title page of *Jack Upland* claimed. By modern standards, Foxe's Chaucer is a fiction, since the works Foxe cites and the works that seem to define his Chaucer are works modern Chaucerians claim Chaucer never wrote.

The *Testament of Love* has a longer Chaucerian history than any of these texts. It appeared in all Chaucer editions from 1532-1721, kept there unquestioned in part due to its very obscurity. There are no manuscripts; all printed versions are derived from the 1532 Chaucer, and all early references to it are to the text printed in this folio edition. Unlike the Plowman's Tale, whose ideology is clear, the obscurity of the *Testament of Love* renders it relatively safe from ideological objection. It could serve Foxe in several ways: first and foremost, it tells a tale of martyrdom; in addition, it includes within that tale reference to "highest matters." Foxe's championing of the *Testament* as reformist propaganda was not challenged until Dart's objections to "old Mr. Fox" in the Urry's 1721 edition.

The obscurity of the *Testament of Love* seems deliberate; at its conclusion, the author (now conventionally known as Usk, earlier known as Chaucer) states the following:

In this boke be many priuy thinges wimpled & folde / vnneth shul
leude men the plites vnwinde / wherfore I pray to the holy gost he lene
of his oyntmentes mens wittes to clere / & for goddes loue no man

wonder why or how this question come to my mynde / for my great
lusty desyre was of this lady to ben enfourmed / my leudenesse to
amende. . . . I desyre not onely a good reder / but also I coueyte and
pray a good booke amender / in correction of wordes and of sentence.
(*Workes*, 1532, sigs. 3R1vb-3R2ra)[6]

Usk has had no lack of emenders and correctors. The most important
have been Bradley and Skeat, who, in arguments rarely challenged,
unwound some of the pleats in book 3 by radically rearranging its sections. What is now called Usk's *Testament* is a text resulting from the
rearrangement of the final chapters, such that the initial letters in
these sections occur in a sequence "T.INVSK" ("thine Usk") rather
than "TSKNVI" (Skeat first solved this as an anagram for an unidentified "Kitsun"). If Bradley and Skeat are right (and Chaucerians
assume they are), the text received as Chaucer's from 1532-1900 was
disordered and thus had far more wimpled pleats than the text cited
by twentieth-century readers in Skeat's edition. In other words,
Chaucer's *Testament of Love* (or "Kitsun's")—the only one available
until the late nineteenth century—is a lot more obscure than Usk's
Testament of Love with the concluding anagram identifying its new
author. In the pre-Skeat edition, readers were left to their own
devices to construe such sentences and transitions as the following:
"What wonder syth god is the greatest loue / and the ne ought to
loke thynges with resonnyng to proue / and so is instrumet of wyl /
wyl: and yet varyeth he from effect & vsing bothe" (sig. 3Q3va), and
"This instrument may ben had /although affect a usage be left out of
doyng / right as ye have sight and reson / and yet alway use ye
grettest wisdom in hem shal he be/ and they in god" (sig. 3R1vb).
Compare Skeat: "This instrument may ben had, although affect and
usage be left out of doing; right as ye have sight and reson, and yet
alway use ye * l- nat to loke, [ne] thinges with resonning to prove; and
so is instrument of wil, wil"; (*Works*, 7: 130-31)[7]; "What wonder, sith
god is the gretest love and the * gretest wisdom? In hem shal he be,
and they in god" (7: 143). Usk (the author of Skeat's *Testament of
Love*) writes more clearly than his master Chaucer (the author of pre-
Skeat *Testament*) was assumed to do.[8] Yet despite the apparent corrup-
tion of the text, the *Testament* has proved a useful source for
biographical detail—oddly enough, once for Chaucer and now for
Usk.

The Reading by Foxe

The pre-Skeat *Testament* (what could be called Chaucer's *Testament*) is the object of one of the stranger readings in Chaucer reception—a reading by John Foxe, of a passage he does not bother to identify. Foxe's reading is extremely rich, containing as it does an interpretation of printing (that the production of a massive and expensive folio edition is tantamount to vulgarization); an embracing of Chaucer (whose religious views seem to foreshadow Foxe's own and those of his readers); and a claim of hermeneutical ingenuity, whereby Chaucer, Foxe, and Foxe's readers share a critical vision not granted to their enemies. Foxe's reading was included (in part) in the Testimonies of Urry's 1721 Chaucer, and became an apparent classic of Chaucerian reception. I quote it in full (from Foxe's 1570 edition) with a brief following summary:

Chaucers woorkes bee all printed in one volume, and therfore knowen to all men.

This I meruell, to see the idle life of the priestes and clergye men of that tyme, seyng these lay persons shewed themselues in these kynde of liberall studies so industrious & fruitfully occupied: but muche more I meruell to consider this, how that the Bishoppes condemnyng and abolishyng al maner of Englishe bookes and treatises, which might bryng the people to any light of knowledge, did yet authorise the woorkes of Chaucer to remayne still & to be occupyed: Who (no doubt) saw in Religion as much almost, as euen we do now, and vttereth in hys workes no lesse, and semeth to bee a right Wicleuian, or els was neuer any, and that all his workes almost, if they be throughly aduised will testifie (albeit it bee done in myrth & couertly) & especially the latter ende of his thyrd booke of the Testament of loue: for there purely he toucheth the highest matter, that is the Communion. Wherin, excepte a man be altogether blynd, he may espye him at the full. Althoughe in the same booke (as in all other he vseth to do) vnder shadowes couertly, as vnder a visoure, he suborneth truth, in such sorte, as both priuely she may profite the godlyminded, and yet not be espyed of the craftye aduersarie: And therefore the Byshops, belike, takyng hys workes but for iestes and toyes, in condemnyng other bookes, yet permitted his bookes to be read.

So it pleased God to blinde then the eyes of them, for the more commoditie of his people, to the entent that through the readyng of

his treatises, some fruite might redounde therof to his Church, as no
doubt, it did to many: As also I am partlye informed of certeine, whiche
knewe the parties, which to them reported, that by readyng of Chausers
workes, they were brought to the true knowledge of Religion. And not
vnlike to be true. For to omitte other partes of his volume, whereof
some are more fabulous then other, what tale can bee more playnely
tolde, then the talke of the ploughman? or what finger can pointe out
more directly the Pope with his Prelates to be Antichrist, then doth the
poore Pellycan reasonyng agaynst the gredy Griffon? Under whiche
Hypotyposis or Poesie, who is so blind that seeth not by the Pellicane,
the doctrine of Christ, and of the Lollardes to bee defended agaynst
the Churche of Rome?[9]

In sum: since Chaucer's works are now in one volume, they are
"known to all men." Once the truth is out, the authorities can no
longer hoodwink the public with obviously false interpretations of
readily-available texts. Thus it is a marvel that the authorities allowed
these works to pass uncensored, since Chaucer saw almost as much as
we do, and the interpretation of his works is straightforward. That
marvel (the laxness of the authorities) is due to God's intervention,
who blinded them. In fact Chaucer caused many to be converted.

Several things need to be remarked here. First, Foxe's interpretation of Chaucer is based almost exclusively on works Chaucer did not
write (or rather, works that Skeat, in the late nineteenth century,
claimed he did not write)—the *Testament of Love, Jack Upland,* and the
Plowman's Tale. Moreover, Foxe's reading seems opposed to the one
piece of external evidence about Chaucer's works and readers that he
cites: the exclusion of the works of Gower and Chaucer from the
Prohibitions of 1542. This text, with its reference to Chaucer, itself
became a canonical part of Chaucer's reception history through
Foxe; it is cited in Dart's Life of Chaucer in the 1721 Chaucer (sig. f1r
with reference to Foxe), and quoted later by Spurgeon (of course)
and by Brewer in the more selective *Critical Heritage* series.[10]

The tactics of Foxe's reading and the elements that make it up are
familiar ones in the history of literary criticism: (1) a new radical
reading utterly at odds with the past evidence of readings; (2) the
claim that it is self-evident; (3) a myth offered to explain away the
incontestable evidence of past contrary readings (that Chaucer and
Gower were specifically exempted from the prohibition). Foxe's is

one of the earliest examples of the conspiracy-theory reading, based as it is on an implied conspiracy of Chaucerians suppressing the truth of his (Foxe's) own eccentric reading.[11] This reading by Foxe, however peculiar, gained entry into the mainstream Chaucer industry as well-indexed editions of Foxe continued to be produced through the seventeenth century.[12]

The edition of Urry in 1721 included a Life of Chaucer written in part by John Dart. This Life was revised by William Thomas, against Dart's wishes, before being printed,[13] but for the moment, I will identify the following as Dart's own. The subject here is the association of Chaucer with Wyclif, an association Dart insists on elsewhere (sig. d2v): "There can be no doubt of *Chaucer's* intimacy with *Wickliffe*, being probably of the same College with him, a Follower of his Opinions, and both Retainers to the Duke of *Lancaster.*"

Chaucer how much soever he had espoused those Opinions, thought it prudence to conceal them more than he had done, seeing the inconveniences and danger they had occasioned; so that after the Prosecution by *Rich.* II and the Duke of *Lancaster's* changing his mind, he thought it proper to be more circumspect. Nor doth it appear that at any time time [sic] he ran all the lengths of that Opinion. His resentments were chiefly against the personal Vices of the Clergy, not their Doctrines; for the Pilgrimage to *Canterbury* is spoken of with reverence; and he calls *Becket* the *holy blissful Martyr.* And the Parson, tho' he would not *ren to St. Powles* to procure Livings, makes one in the Expedition to *Canterbury.* This I say, not as if that Journey was real; but *Chaucer* would never have been guilty of so great an impropriety as to make Persons act contrary to their Opinions. Nor did even the Leaders of that Party scruple the Ceremonies then used: They opposed them in opinion, but seldom differed from them in practice. Even *Wickliffe* himself always conformed, and held his Living of *Lutterworth* without interruption, and died in it of a Fit of the Palsy; which seized him while he was saying Mass. But *Chaucer* differed much from them even in Opinion, for in his *Testament of Love,* he confesses the Real Presence [Mr. *Fox* seems to be of a contrary opinion. Acts and Mon. 1684. Vol. II. p. 42.] which passage, because it exposes the neglect of Religion in his time, and shews his regard for Divine Worship, shall be here set down at large. *Lo! it accordeth for soche there ben that voluntarie lustes haunten in courte with ribaudrie, that til midnight and more wol playe and wake, but in the church at matins he is behinde, for evil disposicion of his stomake.—His aulter is broke, and lowe lithe in pointe to gone to the yerthe, but his horse must ben esy and hie, to bere him over grete waters. His chalice pore, but he hath riche cuppes. No towaile but a shete, there* God shall ben handelid. *And on his mete bord there shall been bordeclothes and towelles many paire. At masse serveth but a clergion: five Squiers in hall. Pore chauncell, open holes in every side: Beddes of silk, with tapites going al about his chambre. Pore masse boke and leude chapelaine, and broken surplice with many an hole: gode houndes, and manye, to hunte after harte and hare, to fede in ther festes.* In the *House of Fame* [In the Beginning of the First Book] we find him again going on Pilgrimage. We may gather his opinion of the Invocation of Saints, from his *Priere de nôtre Dame,* his Ballad in commendation of our Lady, and several other Pieces. But however *Chaucer* might despise some extravagancies of the Church of *Rome,* yet that he died a Member of it, seems plain by his Retractation. (*Works,* 1721, sig. c2r)

As in the case of Foxe, some of the works cited here are now considered spurious (for example, the "Ballad in Commendation of our Lady"). The interpretation of others is eccentric: the *House of Fame* is here interpreted as a religious pilgrimage. Moreover, Dart is not reacting to the passage apparently cited by Foxe. The passage cited by Dart is not from the end of book 3, but rather from the beginning of book 2 (*Workes,* 1532, sig. 3N2v), and it is in the mouth of the allegorical lady (Boethius's Philosophia?).

The passage from the *Testament* cited by Dart is part of a satire on the deterioration of Religion.

These thinges me greven to thinke, and namely on passed gladnesse, that in this worlde was wonte me disporte of highe and lowe, and nowe it is failed. . . . I made grete festes in my time, and noble songes, and maried damoselles of gentill feture, withouten golde or other rychesse. Pore clerkes, for witte of schole, I sette in churches, and made soche persones to prech . . . But nowe the leude for simonie is avanced, and shendeth al holye churche. (*Works,* 1721, 492; compare *Workes,* 1532, sig. 3N2r; Skeat, *Works of Chaucer,* 7: 50-51)

The passage Foxe has in mind, or at least a passage that might be relevant for his opinions, is the conclusion to the entire work at the end of book 3:

How was it the sightfull Manna in desert to children of Israel was spirituell mete? bodily also it was, for mennes bodies it norisheth. And yet never the later, Christe it signified. Right so a jewell betokeneth a gemme, and that is a stone vertuous, or els a perle. Margarite a woman betokeneth race, lernyng, or wisdome of GOD, or els holie churche. If bred through vertue is made holie fleshe, what is that our God saith? It is the spirit that yeveth life, the fleshe nothyng it profiteth. Fleshe is fleshly understanding: Fleshe without grace and love naught is worthe. The letter sleeth, the spirite yeveth lifelich understandyng. Charitie is love, and love is Charitie, God graunte us all therin to be frended. And thus the Testament of love is ended. (*Works*, 1721, 517; compare *Workes*, 1532, sig. 3R2r; Skeat, *Works of Chaucer*, 7: 145)

This passage concludes the *Testament* in the versions printed in the 1532 and 1721 editions as well as in the text reconstructed by Skeat. It is possible, I suppose, to construe it as a satire against Communion, although, despite Dart, I am not at all certain Foxe does that.

The conflict between Foxe and Dart over the proper interpretation of Chaucer is based first on a work Chaucer did not write, and second on two different passages from that work. Furthermore, both passages from the *Testament* are figurative. In the first, cited by Dart, the reference to Mass is illustrative of a general decline of religion. But it is part of a venerable tradition of metaphors whereby deterioration is expressed as raggedness (the most obvious example in medieval literature is Alanus, *De Planctu Naturae*, where man's lapse into homosexuality is portrayed as a shredding of Nature's garments). Theologically, the metaphor (but not the passage itself) could be read quite differently: the validity of the Mass has nothing to do with the material elegance of the accoutrements.

The final passage, although indeed touching "the highest matter," makes a claim only concerning the symbolic and literal functions of certain objects. Biblical images (Manna) are given both a literal and spiritual interpretation; secular images (Margarite) are given flexible spiritual interpretations. And there is nothing in and of itself to give offense to either Foxe or his opponents. If this is the passage cited by Foxe (Dart thinks it is not), then it "toucheth the highest matter, that is Communion" only in a very oblique fashion.

The concluding section of Dart's Life concerned the canon, and part of his frustration with the Urry Chaucer of 1721 resulted from his discovery that his own views on the canon were not properly represented either in the book itself or in the final version of the very biography he had written for the edition. In *Westmonasterium* (1723), Dart objected to the editing of his Life of Chaucer by the editors of the edition (William and Timothy Thomas) and objected as well to their inclusion of the Plowman's Tale in the final edition:

> But after the verse, *By this the Manciple had his Tale I ended*, &c. comes on
> *The Parson's Prologue* and *Tale;* whereas they have in the printed Copies
> thrust this in between, and, to favour the Deceit, chang'd the very
> Verse, and made it, *By this the Ploughman had his Tale y ended*, &c. (Dart,
> *Westmonasterium*, 86)

Dart is speaking of the placement of the Plowman's Tale prior to the Parson's Tale in editions subsequent to the 1542 edition, when it first appeared. Here Dart's arguments are based on the ideal of decorum and fitness. In the earlier Life of Chaucer from the 1721 edition, his argument seems more strictly ideological:

> tho' I cannot go so far as to suppose he scurrilously reviled the
> Established Religion of those times, and therefore cannot think that
> either the Plowman's Tale or Jack Upland were written by him . . . But
> that he was a Favourer of the Lollards . . . is evident from several places
> in his Writings, where he bitterly inveighs against the Priests and Fryers.
> (Life of Chaucer, *Works*, 1721, sig. c1r)

Particularly irritating to Dart was the authority granted "Old Mr. Fox" in the apparently revised version of his Life:

> After which, when the Book had been some time out, I found upon
> perusing it, that all these Arguments were entirely omitted, and I am
> barely made to assert, by my own Authority, that *Chaucer* never wrote
> this Piece: Yet the Alterer has made me so modest (without my knowl-
> edge, I am sure) to refer to the Preface. Upon which, at least, I
> expected the ingenious Gentleman who wrote it, (and, I believe, knew
> nothing of what was said in the Life,) had some better Arguments for
> what I had said. But suddenly, to my Surprize, old Mr. *Fox* was set there
> to stare me in the Face, and give the Lye. (*Westmonasterium*, 87)

The "Alterer" Dart refers to was William Thomas; the other editor, Timothy Thomas, refers only obliquely to Dart's Life in the Preface to this edition:

> [Urry] left some Extracts out of Records, which were intended for *Chaucer's* Life; but as they were very few, and those for the most part relating to *Thomas Chaucer*, who is supposed to be his Son, it was judged necessary to employ a Gentleman who had made some Collections that way, to draw up the account of our Author's Life, which is prefixed to this Edition. (Preface, *Works*, 1721, sig. i2v)

But there is no further reference in this Preface to Dart or to old Mr. *Fox*.

What Dart sees and what irritates him, then, is not the note quoted above—a note to his own Life of Chaucer ("Mr. *Fox* seems to be of a contrary opinion, Acts and Mon. 1684. Volume 2 p. 42")—but rather the heavily-edited section concluding his Life of Chaucer; this is part of the list of works (a section that would be further revised in the hand-written notes in the British Library copy of the edition). The published version reads as follows:

> Leland says, that by the consent of the Learned in his time, the Plowman's Tale was attributed to Chaucer, but was suppressed in the Editions then extant, because the Vices of the Clergy were therein exposed. Fox is of the same Opinion,[note] who also ascribes the little Piece called Jack Upland to him; as some have that Poem called Piers Plowman's Visions, confounding it with the Plowman's Tale. (*Works*, 1721, sig. f2r)

The note here reads "Acts and Mon. Vol. II. p." The page reference surely should have been filled in, since the passage is the same one included in the Testimonies, and the language itself is taken from the earlier note by Dart ("Mr. *Fox* seems to be of a contrary opinion"). But Mr. Fox's Opinions are on two different subjects: the argument in the earlier passage is only over what the *Testament of Love* refers to. "He confesses the Real Presence" (Foxe denies this!). Here Foxe only claims that the Plowman's Tale is Chaucer's. Is it possible that Dart's (or Thomas's) irritation at the "contrary opinion" of Foxe concerning the authorship of the Plowman's Tale became the "contrary opinion" over the reference in *Testament of Love*—the opinion that the Plowman's Tale does *not* confess the True Presence?[14]

Like Foxe's *Actes and Monuments*, Urry's Chaucer is a committee production. The elements are determined ideologically, but unlike Foxe's *Actes and Monuments*, there is no overriding ideology to make that edition coherent.[15] The *Testament of Love*, however, found its coherence on somewhat different grounds late in the nineteenth century, and it is this coherence that eventually would become the basis of new ideological readings of it.

II. THE BRADLEY-SKEAT SOLUTION TO THE ANAGRAM, AND THE RECONSTRUCTION OF THE LOST MANUSCRIPT OF THE TESTAMENT OF LOVE

The most important question about the *Testament* concerns its authorship, and the way that question was answered is the subject of the section below. Thynne's 1532 Chaucer edition is the sole authority for this work, and the attribution to Usk was the result of the discovery and solution of an anagram found in the apparently disordered text Thynne prints at the end of book 3. The now-accepted solution came in stages. Tyrwhitt accepted the *Testament* as genuine without question (*Canterbury Tales*, 1:xxiv, 5:xvii) and William Godwin used it as the basis for his biography of Chaucer in 1803. But that the text refers to Chaucer and contains praise of Chaucer made the text suspect.[16] Skeat's discovery of an anagram in the concluding pages confirmed these suspicions, and the work was omitted from his edition of 1894:

> I have lately made a curious discovery as to the Testament of Love. The first paragraph begins with a large capital M; the second with a large capital A; and so on. By putting together all the letters thus pointed out, we at once have an acrostic, forming a complete sentence. The sentence is—MARGARET OF VIRTW, HAVE MERCI ON TSKNVI. Of course the last word is expressed as an anagram, which I decipher as KITSVN, i.e. Kitsun, the author's name. The whole piece is clearly addressed to a lady named Margaret, and contains frequent reference to the virtues of pearls, which were supposed to possess healing powers. Even if 'Kitsun' is not the right reading, we learn something; for it is quite clear that TSKNVI cannot possibly represent the name of Chaucer.[17]

After Skeat's Chaucer edition appeared, and prior to the appearance of the edition of the *Testament* Skeat included in his *Supplement* of spurious works (1897), Henry Bradley rearranged the sections of book 3 and discovered (or formed) the acrostic "THINVSK"—one that in turn provided a new author for the work—Thomas Usk. The hypothesized disorder was the result of an apparent shuffling of sheets within one of the final quires of the manuscript that served as Thynne's copytext, a disorder Skeat would later attempt to explain in detail.[18]

The arguments of Bradley and Skeat are not easy to follow in their details: Bradley apologizes for his own explanation and "the repellent form of a series of numerical references to page, column, and line of Chalmer's edition" (231). Yet Bradley's explanation is a model of clarity compared to what one finds in Skeat's *Supplement*, where Skeat attempts to reconstruct the actual quire of the hypothetical manuscript behind Bradley's rearranging of the text:

> It is not difficult to account for this somewhat confusing dislocation. It is clear the original MS. was written on quires of the usual size, containing 8 folios apiece. The first 10 quires, which we may call [*a-k*] were in the right order. The rest of the MS. occupied quire *l* (of 8 folios), and quire *m* (of only 2); the last page being blank. The seventh folio of *l* was torn up the back, so that the two leaves parted company; and the same happened to both the folios in quire *m*, leaving six leaves loose. What then happened was this: —first of all, folios *l*1-*l*4 were reversed and turned inside out; then came the former halves of *m*1, and *m*2, and the latter half of *l*7; next *l*5 and *l*6 (undetached), with the former half of *l*7 thrust in the middle; so that the order in this extraordinary quire was as follows: *l*4 *l*3 *l*2 *l*1 all inside out, half of *m*1, half of *m*2, the latter half of *l*7, *l*5, *l*6, and the former half of *l*7, followed by the six undetached leaves. The last quire simply consisted of *l*8 (entire), followed by the latter halves of *m*2 and *m*1, which were kept in the right order by the fact that the last page was blank. (*Works of Chaucer*, 7: xx-xxi)

Any professional Chaucerian with some bibliographical experience, a few numbered slips of paper, a high tolerance for the vagueness and inconsistency of nineteenth-century codicological language, and about three or four hours of uninterrupted concentration should be able to make some sense of this. For those without such assets, I provide the diagrams below. I am guided in part by Skeat's somewhat more lucid discussion in his introduction to the 1905 Thynne facsimile.[19]

The language of Skeat's explanation is if not inaccurate at least misleading. By "folio," he means what we would call a "bifolium" (a single folded sheet). The hypothesized manuscript is a manuscript in 16s, not one in 8s. Skeat's signing of quires is also misleading, since such signatures need not have existed, and the quire structure (contrary to Skeat's conjecture) need not have been consistent through the manuscript. All that matters for Skeat's argument, however, is the quire structure of the two hypothetical quires in question (those labeled by Skeat *l* and *m*). And for purposes of clarity (if such can exist), I have represented those quires pictorially and assigned leaf numbers 1-20. The first figure below represents the hypothesized lost manuscript; the second shows the disordered leaves of that manuscript as Skeat assumes it existed in Thynne's shop.

What Bradley and Skeat propose is the following: somewhere between the writing of the manuscript and its printing, a particular manuscript of Usk underwent the following dislocation:

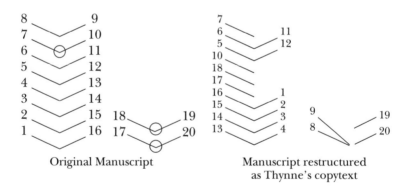

Original Manuscript   Manuscript restructured
                             as Thynne's copytext

The textual implications of this argument may be presented in tabular form as follows. The first column represents what Bradley and Skeat think was the lost manuscript used as a copytext by Thynne; the numbers are those of the leaves of the manuscript before its dislocation. The second column gives the corresponding page numbers in Skeat's edition, along with the relevant initials contained in the section and a note when the hypothesized physical break corresponds to a textual break (note that Skeat and Bradley change the particular *N* that will make up the anagram). The third and fourth columns, which I shall refer to later, give the relative amount of text in the sections, expressed as lines in the Skeat edition.

Lost Manuscript	Skeat text	Total lines	Lines per leaf
13-18	Skeat 135-43; *S* and *K*	301	50
10	Skeat 131-32; ends with break	65	65
5-7	Skeat 124-28; begins with *N* in Thynne; ends with break	149	50
11-12	Skeat 132-35; begins with *V*	9	47
1-4	Skeat 118-24; *I*	221	55
8-9	Skeat 128-31; begins with *N* in Skeat	97	48
19-20	Skeat 143-45	64	32+

The solutions offered by Bradley and Skeat are impressive, despite Skeat's modest disclaimer. Let us look first of all at Bradley's argument. Bradley's reconstruction may be correct, but the question I wish to raise is how did Bradley arrive at this solution and how does his argument supporting that solution proceed? (Note that the logic behind each will be different, and further that the argument itself may be no less valid for all that.)

According to Bradley's summary, his attempts at rearrangement began due to the "bewildering obscurity of the third book":

> the bewildering obscurity of [the author's] third book is for the most part not his own fault, but is due to extensive dislocations of the text, produced by a disarrangement of the leaves in a manuscript (229).

On the first two pages of this brief article, Bradley identifies breaks in logic and syntax in the book and defines various thematic units that can in turn be reorganized as larger coherent units of text. By the third page, all problems are solved: "All these difficulties disappear, and a consecutive and intelligible text is obtained, when the disjointed fragments are rearranged in what I conceive to be their original order" (231).

I by no means intend to disparage Bradley's scholarship here, for these two pages are the record of what must have been an extraordinary amount of work. I am concerned rather with what follows, as Bradley proceeds to what seems an afterthought: his reordering of book 3 into the form it would soon assume in Skeat's 1897 edition has the additional benefit of solving questions of authorship:

> Students of the 'Testament of Love' . . . will remember that some years ago Prof. Skeat discovered that the initial letters of the sections formed an acrostic, reading Margaret of virtu, have merci on T.S.K.N.V.I. Prof. Skeat thought that the concluding letters were an anagram on the author's name, which he supposed to be *Kitsun*. I always felt that the assumption of an anagram was extremely improbable, but was unable to make any better suggestion. When I had completed my rearrangement of the text I was naturally curious to see whether my transpositions had rendered it possible to read the acrostic straightforward; and on examination I discovered the correct order of the mysterious initials to be T.H.I.N.V.S.K. (The H is the first letter of the sentence 'here of this matere,' &c., which in Chalmers is printed without break, but in the editio princeps is clearly marked as the beginning of a section, though Thynne's printer has omitted the ornamental initial.) (229)

There is nothing wrong with Bradley's conclusion nor his logic. But his narrative of discovery seems suspect, as does the emphasis he places on the *H*, a letter which plays a great part in the solution Bradley proposes.

Bradley presents his solution as what Henry Bradshaw or F. J. Furnivall might earlier have called a "happy hit"; suddenly a "vigorous arrangement of facts" has yielded a solution.[20] Yet Bradley's actual procedure may have differed from what he describes. Bradley did not seek a solution; he began with one. And the facts he was presumably arranging to support that conclusion were in some cases of his own making:

> I have for a long time felt all but sure, on historical grounds, that the 'Testament of Love' was the work of Thomas Usk, the 'clericus familiaris' who betrayed his master, John of Northampton, and was beheaded in March, 1388. The agreement between the author's career as he describes it, and the known career of Usk, is itself almost decisive.

I have hitherto abstained from publishing my view for various reasons, one of them being my inability to make anything of the acrostic. Now that the sentence is clear—'Margaret of virtue, have mercy on *thine Usk*'—I venture to say definitely that the 'Testament of Love' was written by Thomas Usk in the year 1387. (232)

This paragraph should give pause. By Bradley's own admission, the only thing standing in his way toward identifying the author was the acrostic, not the obscurity of the text. Indeed, Bradley had apparently found a coherent authorial career in the text despite its incoherence.

What Bradley did was the reverse of what he claims. He began with an anagrammatic solution *VSK* and used that to make sense of the thematic sections he claims to have first identified. The initial letters in Thynne's text read as follows: T H (neither set as woodblock initials but both clearly beginning new sections and so represented typographically on sigs. 3P5v and 3P6v) S K N V I. Skeat had not acknowledged the H, and had tried to solve the anagram TSKNVI. Bradley, by contrast, knew the answer to the anagram—Thomas Usk. He was not distracted by an anagrammatic puzzle—how to arrange letters—but could proceed directly to a different puzzle—how to arrange the text.

Now we can see why Bradley accepted *H* as part of the anagram as Skeat originally had not. It was correct not because it would provide the happy reading "thine" but rather because it already was part of the solution Bradley had in his mind from the beginning—*Thomas.* Bradley says nothing of this, but Skeat in 1905 makes Bradley's actual thinking clear: "Mr. Bradley has since kindly pointed out to me that Usk's first design seems to have been to make his sentence end with THOMAS VSK instead of THIN VSK" (*Chaucer 1532,* xl). The "first design" in question here is more accurately Bradley's, not Usk's.

To support the solution he had already determined, Bradley needed to move the section containing the initial *V* (Skeat, 132-35) to precede the section with the initials *S* and *K* (Skeat, 135-43; see diagram above). He thus read backwards from the *S* until he found a break—one of the more prominent, reading in Thynne: "in whiche heuen is euerlastynge presence / withouten any mouable tyme there / fole haue I not said . . ." (sig. 3Q1r). He would insert there the section with *V,* and to find the end limit of such a section, he merely read forward from *V* to discover a suitable break, which the phrase "frute that is nothyng preterit ne passed" easily provided (sig. 3Q5v). "Frute" could be joined with "fole" with a minimal addition and the section *VSK* came into being.

After Bradley had formed the name Usk, he had an anagram reading TH.VSK NI—almost what he wanted. Somewhere in the manipulations of the final sections, he eventually transformed "Thomas" into "Thine." There are a number of ways that blocks of text could be moved to provide this solution. But Bradley must have arrived at this solution after much trial and error, and he does not mention (nor does Skeat) that he has changed one of the elements that make up the anagram. I doubt this is accidental and it may be discussed in the correspondence between them to which Skeat refers. But the capital chosen as the *N* in the Skeat edition ("'Now, lady,' quod I . . .''; Skeat, 128) is not the ornamented *N* in Thynne's edition ("Nowe trewly lady I haue my ground wel vnderstonde . . ."; sig. 3Q3v)—a sentence introducing the block of text in Skeat, 124-28. The Thynne *N* won't do because in the reconstruction, it is only a paragraph away from the *I*. Bradley's innocent manipulations involved adding elements to the anagram and re-identifying the accepted elements of that anagram, in addition to rearranging the text itself.

Skeat's hypothesized manuscript is the "codicization" of Bradley's argument, and for all its ingenuity, no less problematic. The table above reveals several anomalies in Skeat's hypothetical manuscript. Leaf 10 contains one-third more text than any other proposed leaf and, crucially, the end of a chapter. The nature of the text in this leaf is important in that the leaves that follow (11-12) contain the *V* that is required to form the name Usk. The proposed conjunct leaf (leaf 7) also ends a chapter. Leaves 19-20 contain the same number of lines as the single leaf 10, and to explain this, Bradley and Skeat hypothesize an entire blank page. The manuscript Skeat proposes thus is much less neat than his solution. What we are dealing with is not a manuscript suddenly disordered in Thynne's shop but rather a disorderly one to begin with.

Skeat makes an important but misleading statement in his argument: that the hypothesized manuscript is one of "the usual size" of 8 folios. This sounds like a manuscript in 8s, but in fact, because of Skeat's loose terminology, what he is actually conjecturing is a manuscript in 16s—a much rarer entity, and one that would have to contain a substantial amount of writing on each leaf: the equivalent of some 55 printed lines per leaf, or roughly 2/3 of Skeat's printed page for each page of the manuscript.

Skeat does not note the rarity of such manuscripts. Most manuscripts in 16s are double-column Bibles. In a short survey of American manuscript catalogues with easily accessible information, I could find only two examples of the type of secular manuscript Skeat conjectures: both from the Huntington. Interestingly, these are both the exact kind of manuscript Skeat would want the text to appear in—collections of Chauceriana: HM 114 and HM 140. Skeat's argument and his deattribution of the text implies that the disordering of the manuscript occurred in Thynne's press-room: what I have called Chaucer's *Testament of Love* (the disorderly text printed in Thynne) is a product of the sixteenth century; Usk's *Testament* (printed in Skeat's *Supplement*) was more orderly. But the type of manuscript hypothesized in Skeat's argument suggests something else: it implies that the canonization of this text as Chaucer's or as Chaucerian, in the same form modern editions define it as Usk's, must have occurred earlier, in the fifteenth century.[21]

I have no reason to doubt Bradley and Skeat's attribution. The hypothesis of Usk's authorship has already led to some interesting political and ideological studies by Paul Strohm. But I suspect also that the relegation of that book to the pages of Skeat's *Supplement* is a product of the same type of thinking that produced the Wycliffian Chaucer canon imagined by Foxe on the basis of the same text.[22]

Chapter 5

[CHAUCER'S] RETRACTION AND THE EIGHTEENTH-CENTURY HISTORY OF PRINTING

The following chapter concerns the ways in which the critical fortunes of Chaucer's Retraction in the early eighteenth century were both expressed and conditioned by the bibliographical history of the Chaucer book. I consider two aspects below: first, the changing typographical conventions in which the dubious canonicity of the Retraction had to be represented, and second, the fluid nature of the definition of a book—how the defects of individual book-copies led to misconceptions of the book-edition those copies represent.

The texts associated with the Retraction in the early eighteenth century—the Plowman's Tale and the *Testament of Love*—are almost universally considered non-Chaucerian today. The Retraction denounces those tales central to Chaucer studies, and its canonicity is still felt to need defense today.[1] The legitimizing basis for this controversy (or its material analog) is found in printing history and in misconceptions of that history: the question of whether the Retraction is by Chaucer is a question of whether the Retraction has appeared, does appear, and should appear in Chaucer editions.

According to standard histories of Chaucer editions, Urry's edition of 1721 is the first edition in roman letter. Yet on the page containing the Retraction, the Urry edition seems to be the *last* of the blackletter Chaucers; text is printed in blackletter, commentary in roman (see fig. 15). This page constitutes the tentative reestablishment of the Retraction in the Chaucer canon after an absence of nearly two centuries. The typographical conventions reflect the conflicting and often self-contradictory forces and voices that characterize the edition

95

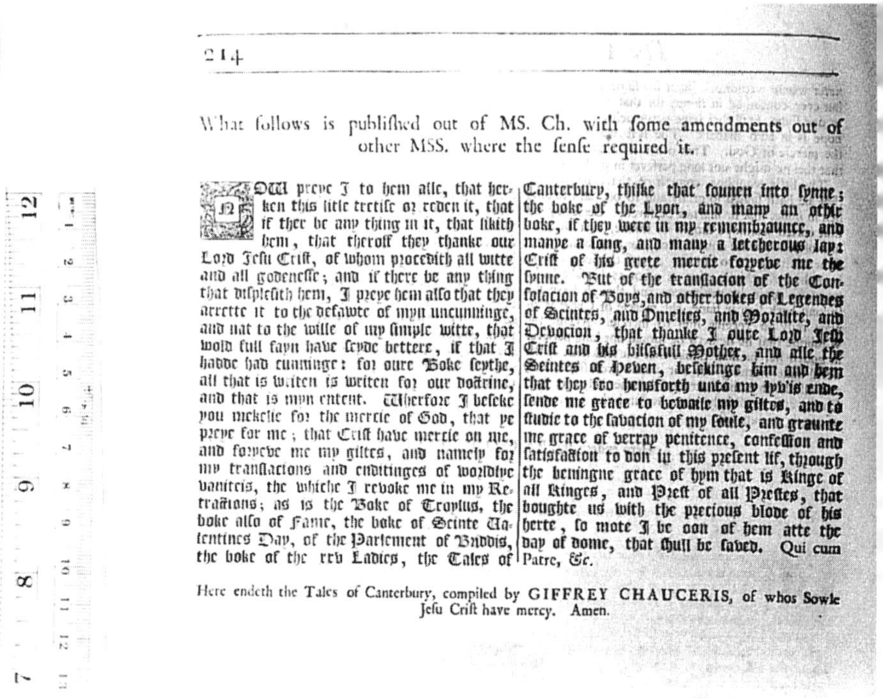

214

What follows is publiſhed out of MS. Ch. with ſome amendments out of other MSS. where the ſenſe required it.

NOW preye I to hem alle, that herken this litle tretiſe or reden it, that if ther be any thing in it, that likith hem, that theroff they thanke our Lord Jeſu Criſt, of whom procedith all witte and all godeneſſe; and if there be any thing that diſpleſith hem, I preye hem alſo that they arrette it to the defawte of myn uncunninge, and nat to the wille of my ſimple witte, that wold full fayn have ſeyde bettere, if that I hadde had cunninge: for oure Boke ſeythe, all that is writen is writen for our doctrine, and that is myn entent. Wherfore I beſeke you mekelie for the mercie of God, that ye preye for me; that Criſt have mercie on me, and foryeve me my giltes, and namely for my tranſlacions and enditinges of worldlye vaniteis, the whiche I revoke me in my Retractions; as is the Boke of Troylus, the boke alſo of Fame, the boke of Seinte Valentines Day, of the Parlement of Briddis, the boke of the xxv Ladies, the Tales of Canterbury, thilke that sounen into ſynne; the boke of the Lyon, and many an other boke, if they were in my remembraunce, and manye a ſong, and many a letcherous lay: Criſt of his grete mercie foryeve me the ſynne. But of the tranſlacion of the Conſolacion of Boys, and other bokes of Legendes of Seintes, and Omelies, and Moralite, and Devocion, that thanke I oure Lord Jeſu Criſt and his bliſsfull Mother, and alle the Seintes of Heven, beſekinge him and hem that they fro hensforth unto my lyv'is ende, ſende me grace to bewaile my giltes, and to ſtudie to the ſavacion of my ſoule, and graunte me grace of verray penitence, confeſſion and ſatisfaction to don in this preſent lif, through the beningne grace of hym that is Kinge of all Kinges, and Preſt of all Preſtes, that boughte us with the precious blode of his herte, ſo mote I be oon of hem atte the day of dome, that ſhull be ſaved. Qui cum Patre, &c.

Here endeth the Tales of Canterbury, compiled by GIFFREY CHAUCERIS, of whos Sowle Jeſu Criſt have mercy. Amen.

Figure 15. John Urry, ed., *Works of Geoffrey Chaucer* (London: Lintot, 1721), Retraction, p. 214.

as a whole. These conventions cannot be analyzed as the product of a coherent intention nor are they even the result of a single recoverable decision.

The Retraction had been omitted from the series of folio editions from 1532-1687, despite an ever-increasing growth in the number of texts defined either as authored by Chaucer or as sufficiently Chaucerian to warrant inclusion in an edition. Urry himself, the named editor of this edition, could have had nothing directly to do with the appearance of this page (he died before the type for this particular page was chosen); but the blackletter of the Retraction is in part a tribute to Urry's belief that it was spurious. These are not the words of the great English author Urry thought he was editing, but rather the words of what Urry considered a "monkish" forger. Blackletter, in this context, signals editorial suspicion.

Urry's London Journey and his Blackletter Chaucer

John Urry died in 1715, six years before his edition appeared. Urry was a close friend of Thomas Hearne, and during the early years of the Chaucer project, the two were in close communication. It is from Hearne's diaries that much of the information surrounding the Chaucer edition is derived. Urry's death on 19 March 1715 is recounted in detail by Hearne; Urry had gone to London to argue his case for the blackletter. Such a new blackletter had been promised to subscribers by the printer, Lintot, earlier in the year. The original Proposals of Subscriptions for Urry's Chaucer end with: "N.B. A new black letter, Accented, has been cast on purpose for this Work, for the Ease of the Reader" (*Daily Courant*, 27 Jan. 1715, reprinted two days later).[2] But Lintot apparently changed his mind, due either to the expense of the new type or to concerns that a book of this nature would not sell. And in the printed proposals of the following year (30 June 1716) there is nothing about a new type font: "Three entire New Tales of this Author in *Manuscript* (never yet printed) have been recovered, and will be added to this Edition; by which *Alterations, Amendments*, and *Additions*, this work is in a manner become new." The proposals included a sample sheet of prologues, printed in roman.[3]

As early as 1717, Hearne claimed that Timothy Thomas, who completed the edition after Urry's death, was dissatisfied with the decision to print the edition in roman. Thomas Rawlinson predicted that the edition would be "a very bad one" and Francis Atterbury, one of the initiators of the edition, had also been in favor of a blackletter edition.[4] In 1735, Hearne looks back at the financial problems of the 1721 edition and blames them on its typography:

> The more I look upon such old black-lettered editions, the more I wish that the late edition had been printed in the black letter, which was what my friend Mr. Urry intirely designed, as I have often heard him say, tho' the managers afterwards, for frivolous reasons, acted contrary to it. Curious men begin to esteem the old editions more than the new one, partly upon account of the letter, and partly upon account of the change that hath been made in the new edition, without giving the various lections, which would have been of great satisfaction to critical men.[5]

By this date, Hearne was successfully publishing small octavo editions of medieval historical works at Oxford; and since his expulsion from the Bodleian in 1715, he had relied on these editorial ventures for a living. These editions were printed for the most part in small blackletter. Yet even in these volumes, there are visible problems in the type. Some of the letters used in Hearne's blackletter are not appropriate to the font, but are imported from exotic fonts designed for lexicons. An example is the most famous of these volumes, Robert of Gloucester's *Chronicle* of 1724.[6] The text of the chronicle itself is printed in small blackletter, but does not have an appropriate thorn or yogh—both of which are cut considerably thinner than rest of the font (see fig. 16 below). The font does not have an italic thorn although the conventions seem to require one (the problem still exists in some modern fonts), and it lacks a blackletter dotted *y*. In other words, even for these elegant volumes, what seems to be a fairly easy adjustment (recasting or recutting of two letters) does not seem to have been possible.

The problem Hearne faced in 1724 would have been far worse in 1715. Caslon began casting type in London only in 1728, and the successful London foundries of the earlier eighteenth century were entirely dependent on imported punches and matrices.[7] Advances for cutting and design of blackletter proceeded at an even slower pace than for roman. It was becoming a specialty type. The single blackletter cast by John Fell in the late seventeenth century was created only to provide a proper type size for printing quotations and words in glossaries.[8]

The promise of new "black letter, Accented" in the initial Proposals for the Urry edition of 1715 (the Proposals claim that the letter has already been cast) does not seem realistic. Such a font would need not only casting, but cutting and even designing, and I know of no examples of a blackletter accented in the way the roman of Urry's edition is. The double-column folio that Urry foresaw would require, among other expenses, a complete font of type, not the limited fonts available for quotations and display. Given what seems to be Lintot's careful cap on costs,[9] it is unlikely that he would have been willing to invest in the huge, untested font required for such a production—particularly in a typographical climate where the low standards that marked seventeenth-century English printing were no longer tolerated by customers.[10] What was planned as Urry's Chaucer was to be monumental in every possible respect. From the standpoint of distribution and sale, there proved to be insufficient subscribers to support the print run of 1500 copies. And from the standpoint of design and execution, there were no type-cutters or foundries in London that could have produced the new blackletter Urry wanted and Lintot even once promised. Urry's Chaucer was unrealistic from the start: the material conditions of English typefounding would not have permitted its production, even if the market for it had existed.

To Urry, blackletter was authenticating, not, as it would prove to be in the edition that bears his name, the mark of something spurious (see fig. 15). Urry, in conceiving of his edition as blackletter, was in part a victim of a bibliographical myth—that there are two type styles, blackletter and white (both roman and italic), that these have their special meanings, and that the material world of English typography somehow was organized in support of these abstractions. Urry held to that myth (as his publisher Lintot did not) despite the economics of typefounding.

The Typography of Authentication and the Voices of the 1721 Edition

The authenticating nature of typographical script has a long tradition in medieval English studies. Roman capitals are classical (or classicizing!); blackletter constitutes a claim of antiquity. And what I call the typographical mythology that Urry fell prey to has been held by many Chaucerians before and after him. The implied conventions of blackletter, roman, and italic are easily visible in the introduction to the 1602 Speght edition (see above, chap. 1, fig. 1). Three centuries later, Spurgeon, inadvertently authenticates Speght's italicized version of the tomb inscription by reproducing this same text in roman capitals facing a photo of the tomb itself.[11]

In his editions, Hearne himself had had occasion to print Chaucer's Retraction. It occurs in a "Letter to Bagford" (1709) included as an appendix in his 1724 edition of Robert of Gloucester's *Chronicle*. This letter is one of the major published sources for Hearne's influential opinions on the Retraction. The typographical conventions are clear: medieval quotations are printed in blackletter. Hearne quotes the Retraction in blackletter, and pronounces (in roman) his famous dictum on its inauthenticity.

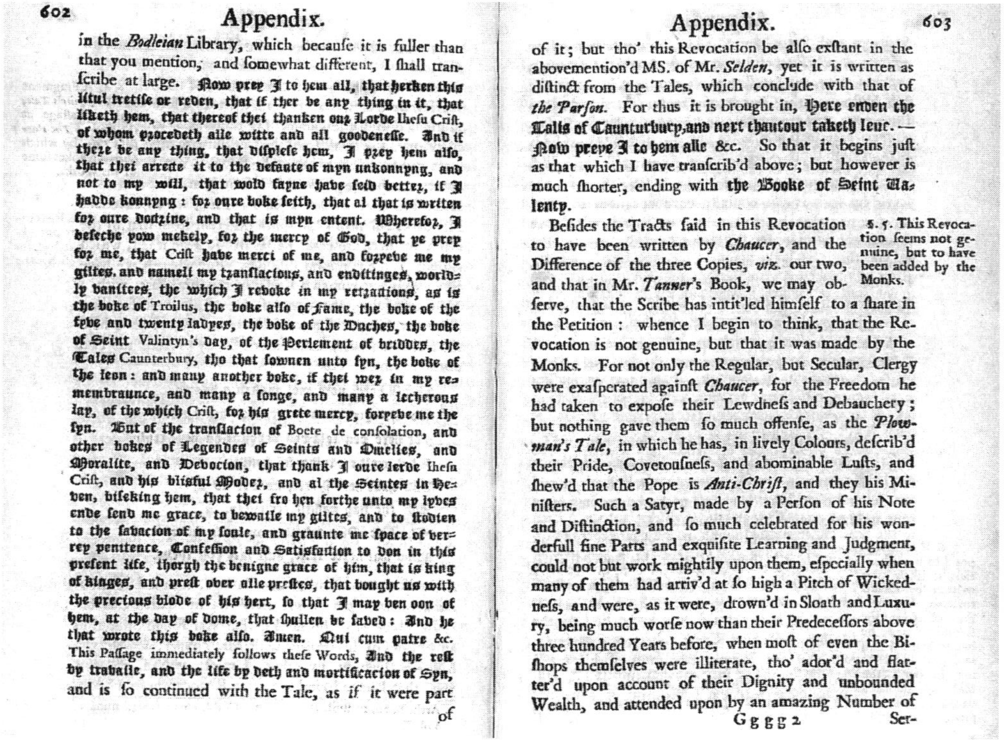

602 Appendix.

in the *Bodleian* Library, which becauſe it is fuller than that you mention, and ſomewhat different, I ſhall tranſcribe at large. **Now prey I to hem all, that herken this litul tretiſe or reden, that if ther be any thing in it, that liketh hem, that thereof thei thanken our Lorde** Iheſu Criſt, **of whom procedeth alle witte and all goodeneſſe. And if there be any thing, that diſpleſe hem, I prey hem alſo, that thei arrecte it to the defaute of myn unkonnyng, and not to my will, that wold fayne have ſeid better, if I hadde konnyng: for oure boke ſeith, that al that is writen for oure doctrine, and that is myn entent. Wherefor, I beſeche yow mekely, for the mercy of God, that ye prey for me, that** Criſt **have merci of me, and foryeve me my giltes. and nameli my tranſlacions, and endittinges, worldly vanitees, the which I revoke in my retractions, as is the boke of** Troilus, **the boke alſo of Fame, the boke of the fyve and twenty ladyes, the boke of the Duches, the boke of Seint** Valintyn's **day, of the Perlement of briddes, the Tales** Caunterbury, **tho that sownen unto syn, the boke of the leon: and many another boke, if thei wer in my remembraunce, and many a ſonge, and many a lecherous lay, of the which** Criſt, **for his grete mercy, foryeve me the syn. But of the tranſlacion of** Boece de conſolation, **and other bokes of Legendes of Seints and Omelies, and Moralite, and Devocion, that thank I oure lorde** Iheſu Criſt, **and his bliſful Moder, and al the Seintes in Heven, biſeking hem, that thei fro hen forthe unto my lyves ende ſend me grace, to bewaile my giltes, and to ſtodien to the ſavacion of my ſoule, and graunte me ſpace of verrey penitence, Confeſſion and Satiſfaction to don in this preſent life, thorgh the benigne grace of him, that is king of kinges, and preſt over alle preſtes, that bought us with the precious blode of his hert, ſo that I may ben oon of hem, at the day of dome, that ſhullen be ſaved: And he that wrote this boke alſo. Amen. Qui** cum patre &c. This Paſſage immediately follows theſe Words, **And the reſt by travaile, and the life by deth and mortificacion of Syn,** and is ſo continued with the Tale, as if it were part of

Appendix. 603

of it; but tho' this Revocation be alſo extant in the abovemention'd MS. of Mr. *Selden*, yet it is written as diſtinct from the Tales, which conclude with that of *the Parſon*. For thus it is brought in, **Here enden the Talis of Caunturbury, and next thautour taketh leue.— Now preye I to hem alle** &c. So that it begins juſt as that which I have tranſcrib'd above; but however is much ſhorter, ending with **the Booke of Seint Valenty.**

Beſides the Tracts ſaid in this Revocation to have been written by *Chaucer*, and the Difference of the three Copies, *viz.* our two, and that in Mr. *Tanner*'s Book, we may obſerve, that the Scribe has intit'led himſelf to a ſhare in the Petition: whence I begin to think, that the Revocation is not genuine, but that it was made by the Monks. For not only the Regular, but Secular, Clergy were exaſperated againſt *Chaucer*, for the Freedom he had taken to expoſe their Lewdneſs and Debauchery; but nothing gave them ſo much offenſe, as the *Plowman's Tale*, in which he has, in lively Colours, deſcrib'd their Pride, Covetouſneſs, and abominable Luſts, and ſhew'd that the Pope is *Anti-Chriſt*, and they his Miniſters. Such a Satyr, made by a Perſon of his Note and Diſtinction, and ſo much celebrated for his wonderfull fine Parts and exquiſite Learning and Judgment, could not but work mightily upon them, eſpecially when many of them had arriv'd at ſo high a Pitch of Wickedneſs, and were, as it were, drown'd in Sloath and Luxury, being much worſe now than their Predeceſſors above three hundred Years before, when moſt of even the Biſhops themſelves were illiterate, tho' ador'd and flatter'd upon account of their Dignity and unbounded Wealth, and attended upon by an amazing Number of Ser-

§. 5. This Revocation ſeems not genuine, but to have been added by the Monks.

Gggg 2

Figure 16. Hearne, Letter to Bagford, in *The Chronicle of Robert of Gloucester* (Oxford: Sheldon Theatre, 1724), 2: 602. Photo courtesy of the Henry E. Huntington Library.

To Hearne, the Retraction was "authentic" in the sense that it was medieval, thus worthy of being printed in blackletter. But it was not Chaucer's; rather, it was "made by the Monks."[12]

The controversy over the authenticity of the Retraction finds full expression in the 1721 edition. The conflicting voices we hear are those of Urry, his editorial executors Timothy and William Thomas, Dart, and behind these we can hear Hearne and Bagford. Even the most diligent investigators of this edition have not thought it possible to distinguish these voices, nor, indeed, have they felt it worth the effort. But as in the conflicting statements on Chaucerian metrics, individual voices occasionally become clear. Urry himself apparently intended to omit the Retraction. In this, he was following the opinions of Hearne. Moreover, he was following what he considered the mainstream editorial tradition (the Retraction is included in none of the folio editions from 1532 to 1687).[13] The only reference to the Retraction in this edition that could be from Urry (possibly through Thomas Ainsworth)[14] is in an introductory note to the Plowman's Tale:

> This and the Tale is in none of the MSS that I have seen, nor in any of the first Printed Books; Caxton and Pynsent, I presume, durst not publish it: The former printed this Poet's Works in Westminster-Abbey, and both before the Abolition of Popery; and the MSS being before that, I fancy the Scriveners were prohibited transcribing it, and injoyn'd to subscribe an Instrument at the end of the Canterbury Tales, call'd his Retraction. So that if this Tale had not been carefully collected and preserv'd in Master Stowe's Library, as the Editor of Islip's 1602 Book says he has seen it, in a hand near to Chaucer's time for Antiquity, in all likelyhood it had been lost.[15]

The attitude of this writer (I am assuming it is Urry himself) toward the Plowman's Tale and the Retraction is related to a number of ideological convictions and simple errors: the Tale was saved from destruction through the efforts of Stow, who had it in an early manuscript; it is anti-institutional, and thus deserves an uncontested place in the canon. The Retraction, by contrast, is a mere "Scrivener's Instrument"—a late addition to Chaucer's text. The logic and the manipulation of material evidence from physical books are noteworthy. Because the Plowman's Tale is absent from the 1532 edition but is printed in all subsequent editions, it must have been earlier "suppressed"—thus the manuscript presumably reported by Speght. The absence of a material fact is thus evidence of its importance—and in this case, all proves the canonicity of the Plowman's Tale. This is logic similar to that used by Francis Thynne in his *Animadversions*.[16]

The case of the Retraction is quite different. Urry knew full well that manuscripts contained the Retraction; those Thomas characterizes as containing the Retraction include MSS I (Ha2), V (En1), VII (Ry), and XII (Mm):

> Mr. Urry gives an account of a manuscript. of the late Bishop of Ely which he had collated, containing all the Tales with *Gamelyn*, and the *Retractation* thus introduced at the end of the *Parson's Tale*, *Here takith the maker of this book his leave*; and after it this Rubrick, *Here endith the Canterbury tales compiled by geffrey Chaucer, of whose soule Jhu Crist have mercy. Amen.* (*Works*, 1721, Preface, sig. k2r)

Thomas knows these only from Urry's notes and states directly two pages later that MS Ch is the first one he has seen containing the Retraction.

But this history of the Retraction and the Chaucer canon has little to do with the existence of the Retraction in the manuscript. Its place in the canon has to do with its ideology and even more important with an erroneous history of its place within printed books—a history written in large part after Urry's death although included in the edition that bears his name.

Thomas Hearne and the Early History of Caxton

For at least a century, scholars have been interested in the manuscripts used in early editions of Chaucer, and those involved in the Urry edition and in Tyrwhitt's later edition have for the most part been identified.[17] Less attention has been paid to the early printed books involved in these editions and the nature of individual copies of those books. Nonetheless, in discussing questions of canon, these are extremely important. The Chaucer canon is a question of what belongs in a printed edition of Chaucer. And what belongs in a printed edition of Chaucer has always been considered in the context of what was included, rightly or wrongly, in other printed editions of Chaucer.

The early editions of the *Canterbury Tales* are these: Cx1, (STC 5082); Cx2 (with Preface) (STC 5083), Pynson (1492) (STC 5084), de Worde (1498) (STC 5085), Pynson 1526 (STC 5086), Thynne 1532 (STC 5068). In modern bibliographies, both Caxton editions contain the Retraction as do those of de Worde and Pynson 1526. Only the 1492 Pynson omits it. The folio editions beginning with Thynne's of 1532 all omit it. These are the facts that correspond to copies of these books in the twentieth century. But modern bibliographies do not reflect the fluid nature and contents of these (same) early printed books as known, handled, and described in the eighteenth century. An eighteenth-century Caxton is unique, and not an exemplar of the "ideal copy" of twentieth-century bibliography and producers of facsimiles. And the best collection of Caxtons, by Harley, was not formed until after the Urry edition was produced.[18]

The letters surrounding the Urry edition refer to three Caxton editions for the *Canterbury Tales* (one owned by Bagford, another owned by Sloane, and a third "with Mr. Tanner"). Other copies existed and may have been available, but references are often vague, and even of these three, I have some question about what the copy "with Mr. Tanner" actually is. The contemporary conception of what these books contained was also vague.[19]

In 1709, John Bagford writes Hearne for information on manuscripts and early printings of Chaucer: "My desier is onley to haue the printed Copeyes loked ouer with the dates & printers Names" (Spurgeon, *Chaucer Criticism*, 1: 297).[20] An entry in Hearne's diary of 1709 listing Chaucer's works and early documents about him in the Bodleian lists a number of manuscripts, but only two editions: "His Workes printed by Richard Pynson" (1526) and the edition by Speght ("Pedigree of Geff. Chaucer. See at ye Beginning of his Works. Edit. opt.").[21]

Hearne, however, is convinced at this time that Caxton did not print Chaucer's complete works, and may not have printed the *Canterbury Tales*.

For soon after Printing was established in this Island, *William Caxton,* besides divers other good Books, set himself carefully about searching out and publishing the several Pieces of *Geffry Chaucer;* but I much

question whether he printed divers of them together. For tho' *Stow* and
some others inform us, that he was the first that publish'd his Works,
yet I believe they are to be understood of some Pieces printed by him
in distinct and small Volumes, and not after the Method that was follow'd by his Successors. For *Richard Pynson*, in his Preface to his Edition
of the *Canterbury Tales* (which we have amongst Mr. *Selden's* manuscripts, and contains nothing else) acquaints us, that he printed them
from a Copy, that was prepar'd for the Press by his Master *William
Caxton*, but gives not the least Hint that they had been before
printed.[22]

Hearne is reacting against the notion promulgated by Leland that
Caxton had collected Chaucer's works in a single volume.[23] Because
he has not physically examined this Caxton, he is able to deny its existence: Leland is wrong, and Stow is wrong as well. So convinced is he
by this idea that he even misreads the testimony of Pynson, who states
about as clearly as he can that an earlier edition of Caxton does in
fact exist.

Hearne's language shows that he is inadvertently projecting what
we might consider later printing practices onto Caxton: the word
divers was a cliche of later printings, which included such newly-discovered works in a series of bigger and presumably more complete
editions. In addition, a good many of the books Hearne himself
would have handled were just such compilations; the combination of
different books in one volume is an ordinary practice of eighteenth-
century printers and binders—a fact that bibliographies, library catalogs, and literary histories themselves tend (for very good reasons) to
conceal. Why should Caxton have proceeded any differently from
modern booksellers?

The idea that the *Canterbury Tales* was a collection of "diverse" works
of the same status (to Caxton) as were the "diverse" other works by
Chaucer is completely consistent with Hearne's other conjecture that
the Retraction was a "monkish forgery." The notion of an authoritative
Chaucer Book yields to the notion of a collection of Chaucerian booklets. And through such a notion, the canonicity of any unit within that
book (a particular poem), or any unit within a larger poem (individual
Canterbury tales), becomes much more flexible.[24] The argument is
both appealing and reasonable, but Hearne's apparent stake in its
validity is quite remarkable, since an extraordinary reading of Pynson's

Preface is required to maintain it. Pynson's 1492 Preface includes the following unambiguous statement:

> Of whom I, among alle other of his bokes the boke of the tales of Canterburie in whiche ben manye a noble historie of wisdome, policie, mirth and gentilnes. And also of vertue and holynes which boke diligently ovirsen & duely examined by the pollitike reason and ovirsight. of my worshipful master william Caxton accordinge to the entent and effecte of the seid Geffrey Chaucer, and by a copy of the seid master Caxton purpos to imprent. by ye grace, ayde and supporte of almighty god.

In his 1709 Letter to Bagford, Hearne addresses this passage:

> The Title Page of our Pynson's Edition of Chaucer's Tales, amongst Mr. Selden's MSS. is wanting, as is also the date. But there is the Preface of Mr. Pynson. From that Preface it appears that he printed these Tales according to a Copy prepared in due Method by Mr. Wm. Caxton, but I much doubt whether Caxton ever printed all the Tales, & am of opinion that he printed only some Pieces of his works, notwithstanding what Stow and others say.[25]

Pynson clearly considers the "boke of the tales of Canterburie" a single unit, comparable to other books by Chaucer. That book has been diligently overseen by Caxton, according to the "entent and effecte" of Chaucer and by a copy Caxton owns. But Hearne simply denies this. Pynson, whose complete text is right before him, must have compiled his text from other sources, despite what Pynson himself says and despite "what Stow and others say." Thus, Caxton never prints a complete works (true enough), but by the same token, he never prints a complete *Canterbury Tales*. The phrase "some Pieces of his works" allows these two arguments to be conflated.

Obviously, a close comparison of the Pynson and Caxton editions would have forced Hearne to revise these statements. But that was not practical. Hearne is here chained to Leland's statement: Leland had claimed that Caxton published Chaucer "in one volume." And perhaps Hearne felt that the book he could not find simply could not exist. Therefore Leland was wrong and Caxton had printed individual works only. If Leland could be wrong concerning the whole of

Chaucer's works, there was no reason any other bibliographer should be right concerning an individual compilation (the *Canterbury Tales*) included within that whole.[26]

But Hearne was not consistent, and in these same extracts, presumably of the same date, Hearne faces the evidence of the Caxton itself. This Caxton seems to be complete, and contains the Retraction, which Hearne's earlier logic had denounced as spurious. Again, in his letter to Bagford of 1709:

> And whereas you mention a Passage, intit'led *Penitentia ut dicitur pro fabula Rectoris*, by which *Chaucer* revok'd several of his Books, that you found printed in an Edition of his Poems with Mr. *Tanner*, which you have not seen in any other, I must, withall, acquaint you, that I have found the same Revocation in a MS. in the *Bodleian Library*, which because it is fuller than that you mention, and somewhat different, I shal l transcribe at large. *Now prey I to hem all.* . . .

This book may be one of the two early Caxton editions, or possibly a copy of de Worde's 1498 edition. The Pynson edition of 1492 omits the Retraction, and the de Worde edition of 1498 omits what Hearne calls its title.[27]

Two years later, Hearne claims to have access to a second early printed edition, this, the imperfect Caxton copy owned by Sloane:

> Dr. Sloane hath an imperfect Copy of William Caxton's Ed. of Chaucer's Canterbury Tales. It is now in Mr. Urry's hands. Caxton's Name does not appear. But, I think, there is no doubt of his being the Printer, the Letter agreeing with the other Pieces I have seen printed by Caxton.[28]

The particular book Hearne is describing here is now in the British Library (IB 55095). The edition here is the second edition, and the reason Caxton's name does not appear is that this particular copy lacks all prefatory matter before sig. m2. It also lacks all after sig. K, including, of course, the Retraction.[29] Sloane's copy must not long have stayed with Urry, since it was not among the books and MSS demanded and returned to Sloane following Urry's death; these include a 1598 Chaucer marked P. 150 and returned with two Sloane MSS at Urry's death.[30] With Urry's death (1715), a concerted effort was made by owners to get their manuscripts and books returned, and one of these was a Caxton *Canterbury Tales* owned by Bagford (Bagford does not own such a book in 1709).[31]

The relative inaccessibility of these Caxtons and the inaccuracies in descriptions of individual copies in the history of the Retraction are extremely important, since Pynson's 1492 edition and all the six-teenth-century folio editions omit it. A Chaucerian of the eighteenth century would be used to a text without the Retraction. And although all manuscripts containing full texts of the Parson's Tale also contain the Retraction, many manuscripts, due to the loss of end-leaves, do not. A serious bibliographer of Chaucer would have every cause to suspect this text.

Hearne had very early regarded the Retraction as a forgery, as he states in his 1709 letter to Bagford:

> Besides the Tracts said in this Revocation to have been written by *Chaucer*, and the Difference of the three Copies, *viz.* our two, and that in Mr. *Tanner's* Book, we may observe, that the Scribe has intit'led him-self to a share in the Petition: whence I begin to think, that the Revocation is not genuine, but that it was made by the Monks. For not only the Regular, but Secular Clergy were exasperated against *Chaucer*, for the Freedom he had taken to expose their Lewdness and Debauchery; but nothing gave them so much offense, as the *Plowman's Tale.*[32]

The three copies here include two manuscripts and the printed copy "with Mr. Tanner." Hearne showed some hesitation on these matters, but his opinions were more fixed than is sometimes implied and, con-trary to what appears in some standard Chaucer histories, he never seems to have changed his mind entirely.[33]

To Hearne, the tradition of the book was powerful. The first and most accessible Chaucer book he had encountered was in the tradi-tion of the Thynne folios—books that did not contain the Retraction, but did contain the Plowman's Tale. For some time, Hearne's opin-ions on the canon and on early book history were an extrapolation of the contents of this particular book. And only later did the impact of other books (the incunable Chaucers) convince him that these opin-ions were inaccurate. Even when the only authority was a late book, Hearne could imagine some "early authority" at its origin.[34]

The History of Chaucer Editions: The Version of 1721

One printed book that would provide evidence contradicting Hearne's view of the Retraction is "Mr. Tanner's book"—a fifteenth-century Chaucer that Hearne knew contained the Retraction. Unless this is the same copy referred to as "Mr. Bagford's," somewhere in the production of the Urry edition, its existence was forgotten or information about what it contained inaccurately transmitted. Hearne's well-known view that the Retraction was a monkish forgery could well have led to a misunderstanding of any early Chaucer discovered that was "imperfect at the end."

William and Timothy Thomas, who completed the Urry edition, had to base their history of editions on many such imperfect copies, and they were working from what were obviously unsystematic notes. Many of the books and manuscripts Urry had gathered were returned to their owners, and when it came time to make the final revisions on the book list, the Thomases no longer had access to them. The Thomases later made use of the Caxton in Harley's library, although Humphrey Wanley in his notebooks implies that their chief interest was in the manuscripts.[35] The summary they give, although sound in its general outlines, contains two serious errors: the first concerning the contents of Caxton's editions and the early history of the Retraction, the second concerning the nature of the 1532 edition, which (because of Leland) they believe is two editions—one by Berthelet, another by Thynne.

Copies of Caxton were extremely rare. Under Wanley, the Harley collection obtained many of these: in a letter to Hearne of 1731, he speaks of owning a "great number of books printed by Caxton."[36] Yet this interest was recent, and Wanley's early catalogs do not mention Caxton at all.[37] The early publication history of Chaucer begins to resemble what we now have in STC with Ames, *Typographical Antiquities*, published in 1749 but referred to earlier in hand-written corrections in the British Library copy of Urry—notes Tyrwhitt identified as by W. Thomas.[38] Timothy Thomas knows of these editions in part through Thynne's reference to "divers Imprints" of earlier Chaucer works:

> But when his Edition came out, which was much more compleat as well as more correct than the former ones, they were totally neglected, and

therefore it is very rare to meet with any Copies of them but what are imperfect, especially at the beginning and end; so that the Reader is not to expect here an exact account of the Dates of the first Impressions. (*Works*, 1721, Preface, sig. 11v)

But what is striking to us about Thomas's history of these editions is not the dates, but the contents. Thomas corrects Stow's date of 1466 for the first Caxton, and claims to have seen single copies of each of the two editions of Caxton's *Canterbury Tales*. The first is "imperfect both at the beginning and end." On the second edition, with woodcuts: "But the Copy which I saw of this Edition being likewise imperfect, there appears no date." He does not know of de Worde's edition.[39]

His remarks on Pynson's edition are also, in their published form, garbled, and many of these are corrected in the hand-written notes in the British Library copy:

Pynson published Two Editions. But the Copy of it which I perused wanting the Title Page, I cannot determine the year wherin it was published, but Mr. Bagford says it was in 1520, or 1522.

Thomas then claims inaccurately that both the Pynson edition and the "large two-column folio with Caxton cuts" (the edition of 1532) contain the Retraction:

Pynson's Second Edition came out in 1526, and is printed in two Columns, and contains, besides the Canterbury Tales, and the Retractation at the end of the Parson's Tale (which was the first, and I believe the only time it was printed before the present Edition of it) the Poems following:[41]

Pynson is given credit for being the first to print the Retraction—a tradition the Urry edition revives. In fact, Pynson's first edition is the first to *omit* the Retraction, a tradition that Urry himself intended to continue. Since the two copies of Caxton to which the Thomases claim to have had access were imperfect, they simply interpreted them in a way that gave credit to their own endeavors.

The second error in the Thomas Preface concerns the 1532 edition:

Besides the Tales and other Works of Chaucer mentioned in the fore-
going Article, it contains the Retractation, (which is in none of the subsequent Editions that I know of) . . . *The Testament of Love* is imperfect
in the Copy I perused, both the beginning and end of the Book being
lost; so that I cannot determine whether this be the first Edition put
out by William Thynne, printed (as Leland says) by Berthelet, to which
Brian Tucca added an elaborate and elegant Preface; or the second,
increased by Mr. Stow; and printed by Thomas Godfray in 1532.[42]

Leland's clear (but misleading?) statement that Thynne edited an
edition printed by Berthelet now becomes corrupted to imply that
there were two editions. The Godfray edition became the basis for
later editions (such as Stow's). Thomas had not seen the supposed
Berthelet edition, but neither had he seen the colophon to the
Godfray edition, and he simply accepted Leland.

By the end of this editorial project, there was apparently no possibility of collating copies of these editions. Anyone with easy access to a
series of physical editions would soon suspect that the 1532 Berthelet
edition was a ghost. But the problem is "easy access." In the early eighteenth century, the 1532 edition was not easy to find, and even those
who encountered a copy, despite its distinctive bâtard typeface, might
have dismissed it as yet another blackletter double-column folio.

The following is from Hearne, 1712, and recounts his first acquain-
tance with it. Hearne claims that Urry has brought him an old
Chaucer edition in folio, like so many other early editions these scholars had access to, "mutilated at the beginning and end." It is probably
the same copy to which Thomas refers above.

Hesterna die D. Urry ex Aede Xti mihi ostendit vetustam Editionem
Chauceri, sed mutilam cum ad initium tum ad finem. Est in folio, mul-
tis adjectis quae non comparent in Edd. Caxtoni & Pynsoni. Quisnam
Editor fuit mihi non constat. Edisci tamen, ni fallor, potest e schedula
quadam mecum a Bagfordo communicata. Typi sunt alij ab ijs qui in
ceteris, quas vidi, Edd. habentur. In una parte libra haec verba *constat*
W. *Thynne* leguntur.[43]

For these early editors, the 1532 edition, the basis of all folios until
1687 was as rare as "Edd. Caxtoni & Pynsoni," and an ideal copy
equally elusive.[44]

The very rarity of this edition might explain Thomas's further errors. Thomas also claims (perhaps unwittingly) that the mythical 1532 Berthelet includes the Retraction, but this statement is corrected (as others are not) in handwritten corrections of the British Library Urry. As printed, Thomas claims the following:

> Besides the Tales and other Works mentioned in the foregoing Article, it contains the Retractation, (which is in none of the subsequent Editions that I know of), *The Romaunt of the Rose . . . .*

The correction makes this sentence read:

> Besides the Tales and other Works mentioned in the foregoing Article, (except the Retractation, which is in none of the subsequent Editions that I know of) it contains *The Romaunt of the Rose. . . .* (*Works*, 1721, British Library copy, sig. 12r)

The error conflicts with the (equally inaccurate) statement made a half-page earlier and may be accidental. But it does reflect the conflicting notes and sources from which the Thomases were working. Since the 1532 copy was imperfect, as were the early Caxton copies of Sloane and Bagford, bibliographers were able to imagine their contents however they wished.[45]

The Retraction: Urry's Place in the Urry Edition

Those involved in the Urry edition did not have a clear idea of the early publication history of the Retraction, nor did they have an easy method for sorting out the early manuscript tradition. Dart, who denied that Chaucer had written the Plowman's Tale, in all likelihood believed the Retraction was genuine; and in the List of Books (perhaps with Thomas's revision) we read: "The Book of *the Lion* is mentioned in his Retractation, and by *Lidg.* in the Prologue to the *Fall of Princes*; but it is now lost . . ." (*Works*, 1721, sig. f1v). On the authenticity of the Retraction, the Thomases seem to agree. But Urry, perhaps under the influence of Hearne, had very early on decided that the Retraction was not genuine, and this eventually led Thomas into a self-laudatory reinvention of the wheel in his supposed discovery of manuscript copies of it.

In the 1721 Preface, Timothy Thomas seems to take the blackletter of the Retraction as an authenticating mark of its antiquity:

> When the greatest part of the Tales were printed off, there came to my hands another MS. of the *Canterbury Tales*, which Mr. *Urry* had not seen. It belongs to *Charles Cholmondley* Esq; of the *Vale-Royal* in *Cheshire*, whose Name should be mentioned with particular respect for his readiness in communicating this MS. without any previous application, as soon as he understood where a new Edition of *Chaucer's* Works was preparing. It is imperfect at the beginning and in most of the Tales; but those of the *Frere* and *Sompnour* are entirely lost. This MS. hath the *Retractation* at the end of the *Parson's Tale*. Though this was the first Copy of it which I had seen, yet I had an opportunity of collating it with other Copies before it went to the Press; and thererefore the Reader may expect to find it more compleat and correct than any single MS. represents it. (*Works*, 1721, Preface, sig. llr)

That Thomas had not seen a copy of the Retraction before finding MS Ch. confirms his statement at the beginning of the Preface that he was "a stranger to Mr. *Urry* and his Undertaking, till some time after his Death" (*Works*, 1721, sig. i2r). What this means also is that at the time of producing the edition, he was a complete stranger to the contents of the early editions of Chaucer:

> but as I did not expect to have this Task enjoined me, I took no Notes of what I heard from him from time to time relating to this matter: I shall therefore acquaint the Reader with every thing just as it occurs to my memory upon a Recollection; adding such particulars as I find noted in those Papers of Mr. *Urry* which have come to my hands. (ibid)[46]

One of the many ironies of this edition is that the blackletter type Urry himself foresaw as appropriate for the edition became the type used to print what he considered a monkish forgery.

Although Alderson was skeptical about recovering Urry's opinions, he implied that Urry's contemporaries would simply read this page as following clear and unambiguous conventions: "The headnote to the Plowman's Tale, whether it be the work of Urry or of Thomas, echoes Hearne's view that this revocation is a monkish forgery and would undoubtedly have led an Augustan reader to conclude that it was not authentically Chaucerian" (Alderson, *Chaucer and Augustan Scholarship*, 118). Alderson studied this edition more carefully than anyone. But I cannot agree that an Augustan reader would have known what to make of this. Clearly, Urry intended that the Retraction be considered a forgery. But the inclusion of the actual Retraction in this edition would surely leave even the most studious of Augustan readers in the dark.

The Urry edition, then, conflates the views of several editors. First, Urry was following Hearne, for whom the Retraction was simply a "monkish forgery." This view would be consistent with that of Foxe, who sees Chaucer as a proto-reformer. Dart, however, denied Foxe's premises, and specifically denied that the Plowman's Tale was by Chaucer—a disagreement then projected onto a vague reference by Foxe to an allusion to the Eucharist in the *Testament of Love*. William and Timothy Thomas, in turn, came to the project with different views. From the appearance of the edition, it would seem that they worked within the editorial tradition of inclusion: none of Urry's attributions were questioned, and the only text included in earlier folios omitted from this edition was Lydgate's *Siege of Thebes*. The Preface claims that tales are included "lest it should be thought that any thing is omitted in this Edition, which was intended by Mr. *Urry*. As to the Tale of *Gamelyn*, Mr. *Urry's* Sentiments concerning it may be seen in the Note before it" (*Works*, 1721, sig. k2r). The Retraction itself was also included, contrary to what must have been Urry's intentions. According to Dart's own testy retraction, much of his Life of Chaucer was rewritten by the Thomases, and it must have been rewritten to reflect one overriding concern—to make the Urry Chaucer as large and inclusive as possible.

> There is very little to be added to what has been said before concerning the other Two Pieces added in this Edition . . . . It may (perhaps with some shew of reason) be suspected that *Chaucer* was not the Author of them, but a later Writer, who may have taken the hint from what is suggested in v. 796 of the *Prologues*, that the Pilgrims were to tell Tales in their Return homewards; but as to that the Reader must be left to his own Judgment. But supposing they were not writ by our Author, we are however obliged to Mr. *Urry's* diligence for finding out and publishing Two ancient Poems, not unworthy our perusal: And they have as good a right to appear at the end of this Edition, as *Lidgates* Story of *Thebes* had to be printed in former ones. (sigs. k2v-l1r)

With the Tale of Beryn, the Urry edition becomes another in the series of earlier folio editions—concluding with a spurious continuation of the *Canterbury Tales.*

Rather than the monumental edition Urry envisioned, the consortium seems to have attempted to produce a mainstream one—"more complete and correct" than any preceding. As we shall see in a subsequent chapter, the only serious innovations (the respelling and representation of text) are those most Chaucerians have summarily dismissed.

Chapter 6

THE RECEPTION OF CHAUCER'S
EIGHTEENTH-CENTURY EDITORS

One of the stated purposes of the ongoing Variorum Edition of Chaucer is to "afford a starting point for future scholarship."[1] In the new Riverside edition, an edition designed, as its predecessors, for students as well as professional Chaucerians, the same language appears: "Our notes . . . are intended . . . to supply the reader with the information needed to begin the study of the work and to provide references for further investigation."[2] According to this formula, an edition merely puts before the reader the text (or what is called a text) as well as the ancillary information from which an interpretation might arise.[3] An edition is a first step, a beginning. Electronic editions, with far more opportunities for text manipulation, extend this theory.

That such a notion is more a myth about editions than a principle regarding their production has been tacitly acknowledged in much textual criticism. The most noteworthy example in medieval English studies of the last twenty years is the Kane-Donaldson edition of *Piers Plowman*—an edition where the text is less a premise for future scholarship than a distillation of Kane's past scholarship and thinking about *Piers Plowman*—to many, a subject hardly less interesting.[4] The relation of such a text to future texts and scholarship is less in the groundwork it lays than in the challenge it issues. The present chapter examines this myth from an historical perspective, based on the production and reception of eighteenth-century editions of Chaucer. What does our evaluation of past editions tell us about the principles guiding our own editorial projects?

The eighteenth century is of particular interest in the history of Chaucer scholarship, both for the development of the text (and the idea of the text) and for the development of the language in which the text will be discussed. The eighteenth century produced what in modern scholars' eyes is the first modern edition of Chaucer (Tyrwhitt's *Canterbury Tales* of 1775) as well as what many scholars regard as the worst edition (Urry's 1721 edition). I will be dealing here with these two editions and also with the relatively neglected partial edition by Thomas Morell of 1737.[5]

A Consensus on the "Worst Edition": Urry's 1721 Edition

For many editors, a new edition is justified if it is better than its predecessors. "The Variorum Edition . . . offers the best text possible" or "the text which is as near as it is possible to get to what Chaucer must have written."[6] The Variorum claim is based on evident slippage between the terms "base-text," "best-text" (referring to textual-critical methods) and the notion of a "best edition" (the intended result of textual-critical methods). Such language is no more persuasive than earlier claims based on the consultation and collation of "very trewe copies" and "dyvers others never tyll nowe imprinted."[7] What might be judged a "best edition" is an historical matter. And it is a delusion to imagine that the best edition of one culture will be the best for any other, or, less obviously, that the history of editions is progressive, with its *telos* constituted by the most recent edition or editorial project.

While there is no consensus on the best edition among Chaucerians, there is a consensus on the worst one: nearly all scholars agree that this is the Urry edition of 1721. The strength of this consensus, which seems to have little to do with evidence or the definition of evidence, is worth investigation; it can serve to highlight our evaluative principles, or at very least demystify some modern statements of editorial principle. Presumably, if we can agree on what is bad we should have similar principles for determining what is good.

Credit for establishing this consensus is generally given to Thomas Morell, whose edition of 1737 I will discuss below. To Morell, Urry's edition is the worst only by default. That honor would have gone to John Entick, whose competing edition of Chaucer never got beyond his proposals of 1736. In a letter to Entick, Morell criticizes Entick's reliance upon Urry: Urry's text and authority "is actually the worst that is extant, except the little I have seen of yours."[8] In 1775, Tyrwhitt states flatly that Urry's is "the worst that was ever published," and in his "Advertisement to the Glossary" (1778) adds "Mr. Urry's edition should never be opened by any one for the purpose of reading Chaucer."[9] Nichols, in *Literary Anecdotes*, repeats Tyrwhitt's statement:

> The strange licence in which Mr. Urry appears to have indulged himself, of lengthening and shortening Chaucer's words according to his own fancy, and even adding words of his own without giving his readers the least notice, has made the text of his edition by far the worst ever published.[10]

And with the exception of Alderson, most modern scholars have been content to repeat these sentiments. Skeat: "This edition is the worst that has appeared" (*Works of Chaucer*, 1:30). Spurgeon: "This edition is, from the point of view of the text, the worst ever issued" (*Chaucer Criticism*, 1:353). The Variorum editors agree. Pearsall: "the most ravaged of all the printed texts" (*Nun's Priest's Tale*, 116); Ross: "a travesty, condemned out of hand by Urry's contemporaries" (*Miller's Tale*, 106).[11] Baker is more restrained: "The obvious fact is that [Urry's] is the most eccentric edition of all" (*Manciple's Tale*, 69); as is Pace: "So many harsh things have been said of the text of this edition that I shall not add to them." Pace notes further: "any collection of isolated examples from [Urry], however, will exaggerate the badness of the text."[12] Pace's last point is worth emphasis. Modern readers of Chaucer are in no position to judge the quality of Urry's text (to Pace, its degree of "badness") simply because it is so unlike anything we have come to regard as Chaucer, that is, so unlike modern editions.

Urry believed that Chaucer's verse was regular (contrary to the recent statements of Dryden). So he added syllables, used apostrophes to indicate an unpronounced syllable (or what he thought was an elided one), respelled plurals and preterits as "-is" and "-id" when they were to be pronounced—all in an attempt, as his editor Thomas claims, "to restore him, (to use his own Expression) *to his feet again.*"[13] To a reader used to the appearance of Skeat, Robinson, or any text based on Ellesmere or Hengwrt, the result is odd:

> Our Host saw that he dronkin was of Ale,
> And seide, abide, Robin, myn levè brother,
> Some better man shall tell us first another,
> Abide, and let us werkin thriftily.
> By Godd'is Soule, qd he, that woll not I,
> For I will speke, or ellis go my way.
>
> Miller's Prologue, 3128-33 (*Works*, 1721, 24)

But the passage is hardly unintelligible, and not much stranger than what appears in many Chaucer manuscripts or, for that matter, in previous editions.[14] Despite the criticism brought against Urry for such practices, he has much precedent here, and his methods find support in modern textual-critical theory as well as in editorial practice. Classical editors normalize spellings and routinely emend for metrical reasons. Chaucer editors such as Skeat and Robinson also reject eccentric spellings and emend for metrical reasons. Greg's influential notion of copy-text is not simply a call for an authoritative text; it is rooted rather in the very practical need for standardized spellings. How will the editor spell those variants that are chosen or conjectured?[15]

Urry had planned to defend his editorial practices in a preface, but had written nothing when he died in 1715. Timothy Thomas, in the published Preface, explains what he can of Urry's system but admits that he was a "stranger to Mr. Urry and his Undertaking; till some time after his Death" and claims that the whole task of a preface might have been "better performed by others, of themselves inclined to this sort of Study who . . . were thought to have been made acquainted with his whole Scheme" (sig. i2r).[16] Thomas is presumably thinking of Thomas Ainsworth. Ainsworth, once employed by Urry, completed Urry's text, promised to explain all in a preface, and like Urry, died before he could do so.

The result, then, is not Urry's edition at all, but an edition by a committee, with all the consequent inconsistencies. In his Life of Chaucer included within the edition, Dart disagrees strongly with Urry's metrical theories. In the Preface, Thomas disguises his criticism of Urry's spelling system under a veil of scholarly objectivity: "Whether the assistance of this Final *è* be not here too frequently, and sometimes unnecessarily called in, is not my business to enquire into" (sig. i2v). Thomas also takes Urry to task for philological errors: to print the genitive singular as *'s* (as if a contraction of "his") is, according to Thomas, a simple mistake. He is at a loss to explain why the original idea to use brackets to indicate emendations was dropped (sig. k1r).

In the Proposals for the edition, subscribers had been promised a Glossary: "A more Useful and Copious *Glossary*, for the better Understanding of this *Poet*, than has yet been printed, will be added at the End by Anthony Hall, A.M. Fellow of Queen's College, Oxford." Hall is not mentioned by name in the edition itself, and the task of a Glossary fell to Thomas. Thomas concludes his preface with a sternly ironic reference to a certain "worthy Gentleman" who backed out of doing the glossary at the last minute. Thomas then ironically takes credit for all its failings, for "I would not have his Reputation suffer by the imperfection of this Performance" (sig. m2r).[17]

The committee assigned to the completion of the edition included the printer Lintot, and this too led to problems. Thomas claims he has discovered a new manuscript, and wished to include some of its readings at the foot of the page, but "my direction being misunderstood at the Press, some of them were inserted in the text" (sig. l1r). The half-page following the Table of Contents is filled by an engraving of a knight: over it is printed in large type "N.B. The FOLLOWNIG [*sic*] cut should have been placed before the Rhime of Sir THOPAZ" (sig. n1r).[18]

As a committee production, Urry's edition is not unique, nor is consistency and editorial unanimity necessarily a virtue for such editions. In the edition of Manly and Rickert, similar disclaimers and contradictions appear, due in part to Rickert's death. Manly prints part of Rickert's essay on authorial variants, even though he notes that the essay was unfinished, was written when Rickert's powers were failing, and promulgates a thesis that he finds unconvincing.[19] Such contradictions appear as well in Robinson's second edition (1957). Here, Robinson is discussing Manly-Rickert's classification of manuscripts, which appeared in 1940 (well after Robinson's first edition of 1933): "Since it was based upon all known manuscripts, over eighty in number, the classification of authorities there given [in Manly-Rickert] completely supersedes the tentative one in this work" (xxxvi). Yet Robinson's "completely superseded classification" of 1933 is again printed in 1957 on pages 886-89, after a three-page list of readings that he has changed based on Manly-Rickert, readings which are then ignored in the textual notes that follow.[20]

The innovations of Urry's edition were confined to the text itself. Materially, and on matters of canon, it was simply a dressing up in roman type of the earlier folio editions. It was a "Complete Works" in folio—that is, a large volume containing all the works by, and many works relevant to, a particular poet. Pearsall's claim that the edition "was in every gentleman's library in the eighteenth century" (*Nun's Priest's Tale*, 119) is dubious. The edition did not sell well, and even those who contributed to it did not feel compelled to buy one; Dart, who wrote the Life of Chaucer, claims he is content with his blackletter edition.[21] For those who could read Chaucer already—that is, for Chaucer scholars—Urry offered nothing new, beyond a text of two obviously spurious tales.

So what did Urry do to earn his reputation? We are told that he altered, disfigured, and travestied the text. But what text? Caxton's? Ours? The words in Ellesmere or Hengwrt which he had never seen? The very language criticizing Urry surreptitiously introduces the notion of a norm, or worse, a definitive text from which Urry's text supposedly deviates.

Urry invented a new form of normalized writing for Chaucer, one not respecting the vagaries of scribal caprice, but rather one intended to be read metrically (perhaps aloud), by his eighteenth-century audience—all according to an ingenious but perfectly intelligible system of diacritical marks and spelling changes. These marks, strange as they appear to modern Chaucerians, have a function, and they can be understood in far less time than any of the metrical theories that took their place in later editions (for example, the discussions by Tyrwhitt or Skeat). Urry thus made the text accessible (to a restricted audience, to be sure) and claimed further that this easily accessible text, a text to which any amateur Chaucerian would have access, was the best text. This, according to modern Chaucerians, is dangerous. What is most striking (and to some scholars, most pernicious) about Urry's edition is the breakdown in authority: Urry fails to delegate responsibility (so Alderson); printers misread their instructions and renege on promises; lexicographers refuse to do their job; biographers disagree with metricians; and worst of all, the text is completely given over to its readers. Urry thus paid no court to those who could be considered serious Chaucer scholars—scholars who do not need diacritical marks to know when final syllables are to be dropped, and who certainly do not need a text that can be picked up and read according to a prevailing theory of metrics by any literate amateur. Serious Chaucerians know such things; non-Chaucerians and students do not know about such things. And true textual criticism, apparently—that is, textual criticism in the so-called "Great Tradition" of Ruggiers—is one way to ensure that that structure of power remains intact.

Tyrwhitt and the Modern Edition

Tyrwhitt's *Canterbury Tales* appeared in four volumes in 1775; a fifth volume containing the glossary was printed in 1778. Tyrwhitt states his purpose as follows: "The first object of this publication was to give the text of *The Canterbury Tales* as correct as the Mss. within the reach of the Editor would enable him to make it. . . . The Editor therefore has proceeded as if his author had never been published before" (*Canterbury Tales*, 1:2). Tyrwhitt claims to proceed as if there were no past; printing, according to Tyrwhitt, has not promulgated truth but obscured it. Tyrwhitt's edition of Chaucer will overcome the past of publishing just as the edition of a classical text overcomes the medieval past of errant scribes.

Windeatt, the most recent student of this edition, claims that the edition marks "a new departure in Chaucer editing." As for Tyrwhitt himself: "Such scholarly responsibility, and relative deference to the medieval documents themselves, makes Tyrwhitt the founder of modern traditions of Chaucer editing."[22] The implications of this new departure and the scholarly acceptance of its importance, are the subjects of the pages below.

Windeatt is in a long line of eulogists for Tyrwhitt. And the consensus began early. In 1789, Philip Neve in *Cursory Remarks on some of the Ancient English Poets* says:

> Chaucer is not now what he was, before the year 1775. In that year, Mr. *Tyrwhitt*, a gentleman who can never be named, without respect and gratitude, by any scholar, or reader, of *Chaucer*, published the *Canterbury Tales* with a glossary, Notes, and Illustrations, executed with method, acumen and perspicuity, no where exceeded, among all the commentators on books. In this edition, the text is published in its

original purity; and a reader, to go through with it, has only to consult
his faithful guide the editor; who will equally amuse and instruct him
on the pilgrimage. (Spurgeon, *Chaucer Criticism*, 1: 488)

The reader of Tyrwhitt becomes a pilgrim—virtually one of the characters on the Canterbury journey itself. This metaphor is a commonplace of Chaucer criticism, but the judgment on the edition and the
notion of a text "in its original purity" seem to be taken from Tyrwhitt
himself. Dibdin also is extravagant in his praise, calling his edition a
"model of editorship."[23]

Tyrwhitt had detractors, most notably Thomas Wright. Wright,
whose edition of the *Canterbury Tales* appeared in 1847, attacked
Tyrwhitt both in the introduction to this edition and in his earlier
Anecdota Literaria (1844): "there is perhaps not a single line in
Tyrwhitt's edition of the Canterbury Tales which Chaucer could possibly have written."[24] But by the end of the century, praise for Tyrwhitt is
again high. "No more thorough and conscientious editing had ever
been applied to the elucidation of a great English classic" (Lounsbury,
Studies in Chaucer, 1:301). Skeat echoes this praise, speaking of "the
honoured name of Thomas Tyrwhit, whose diligence, sagacity, and
discrimination have never been surpassed by any critic . . . I would add
my humble testimony [to that of Lounsbury] to Tyrwhit's unfailing
greatness" (*Works of Chaucer*, 6: xx).[25] The consensus on Tyrwhitt has
grown stronger, and today no praise is too unstudied as to deserve
neglect, as the volumes of the Variorum Chaucer attest. In a one-page
article in 1950, Hench quotes the opinions of Pace concerning the
"pains-taking devotion of a great scholar to his task." This quotation
(with variants) has found its way into several volumes of the Variorum
edition, but with little acknowledgement that it is a second-hand opinion, appearing in a one-page article—an article itself based only on a
single page of Speght's Chaucer that *may* contain Tyrwhitt's notes.[26]

Although praise for Tyrwhitt has become traditional, the precise
object of that praise varies. Hammond praises Tyrwhitt for his contribution to the canon (*Manual*, 210-11); Lounsbury for his glossary
(*Studies in Chaucer*, 1:297). Ross claims Tyrwhitt is the "first scholar to
explain in detail how one should read the lines of the *CT* as heroic
meter, correcting Dryden's error" (*Miller's Tale*, 45)—praise that
seems factually in error. Pearsall praises Tyrwhitt's "systematic and
intelligent use of good manuscripts" (*Nun's Priest's Tale*, 119).

The notion of Tyrwhitt's greatness has assumed the status of a myth among Chaucerians, but this myth rigorously excludes a good deal of information: Tyrwhitt as a Chaucer editor is judged in the context of Chaucer editors only.[27] Important contemporaries such as Thomas Warton and Thomas Percy (who were not Chaucer editors) thus rarely figure into such discussions, even though Tyrwhitt himself claims that his discussion of English poetry could have been omitted "if he had foreseen that Mr. Warton's *History of English Poetry* would have appeared so soon" (one year before Tyrwhitt's edition).[28] Furthermore, the focus on Tyrwhitt as a great Chaucer editor necessarily excludes his work on the classics; the rhetoric of his posthumous edition of Aristotle's *Poetics* provides a useful corrective to the quiet and gentle Tyrwhitt in Chaucerian mythology.[29]

The myth of Tyrwhitt's greatness also ignores a material fact. Tyrwhitt's popularity was due less to his excellence as an editor than to the physical convenience of the book itself: the octavo volumes of his edition made the *Canterbury Tales* available for the first time in a size smaller than folio; all earlier small-format Chaucers had been translations. The text of the edition became readily available in several authorized and pirated reprints in poetry collections of the late eighteenth and early nineteenth centuries.[30] Furthermore, Tyrwhitt's text was not challenged until the edition of Wright for the Percy Society in 1847. For these reasons, Tyrwhitt *ought* to have dominated Chaucer studies in the nineteenth century. Yet the evidence of his influence is inconsistent, particularly from the early period, and the main scholarly lines of Chaucer criticism often developed without the direct consideration of Tyrwhitt's text. Readers of Chaucer had a number of choices, including, of course, translations, and Tyrwhitt was only one of many editions.[31]

William Blake's opinions on Chaucer had lasting influence. But Blake scholars disagree as to what editions Blake used. Karl Kiralis, the most thorough scholar of his quotations, saw Tyrwhitt's text behind them, but a better case has been made by G. E. Bentley and Alexander S. Gourlay for Speght's blackletter edition.[32] Keats refers directly to a blackletter edition, but wrote "Flower and the Leaf" in a volume of the Bell edition (not his own), which contained Tyrwhitt's edition of the *Canterbury Tales* and Urry's of the rest.[33] In 1806, Lamb writes Wordsworth to say he has found a copy of Urry for him, and Wordsworth earlier quotes Urry (I assume from Anderson's reprint).[34]

Coleridge uses Tyrwhitt when available, but quotes Urry for *Troilus and Criseyde.* Leigh Hunt quotes Tyrwhitt in 1816 as does William Hazlitt in 1818. But George Nott (1816) objects to the metrical theories of all three eighteenth-century editors (Urry, Morell, and Tyrwhitt), then argues for his own metrical theory from manuscript evidence. Walter Scott often quotes Tyrwhitt, but just as often uses an idiosyncratic combination of archaisms and modernizations that I assume is his own.[35] So while Tyrwhitt was the preferred text for scholars (Hazlitt), he was used indifferently by those with an arguably greater effect on future scholarship (Blake and Scott).

The scholarly reputation of Tyrwhitt can be traced also through the various editions of a single work, Warton's *History of English Poetry,* often reprinted in the nineteenth century and the subject of two major revisions—in 1824 by Richard Price (itself revised in 1840) and in 1871 by W. Carew Hazlitt.[36] What Warton says in all these revisions is much the same; but what Chaucer says, that is, the edition in which Chaucer is cited, changes. Warton's first volume, containing sections on Chaucer, was published in 1774 (one year before Tyrwhitt's edition appeared) and quotes Chaucer exclusively in Urry's version. The 1824 edition substitutes Tyrwhitt's edition for that of Urry. An acknowledgement of greatness? Perhaps. But perhaps not. In the revision of 1871, Tyrwhitt is himself displaced by the 1866 Aldine edition by Richard Morris (printing Wright's 1847 text for the *Canterbury Tales*).[37] Is this the "best" Chaucer? or simply the latest Chaucer?—a Chaucer who after 1824 happens to be Tyrwhitt, and after 1871 happens to be Wright, or Wright in the *persona* of Morris.

The apparatus of these later editions of Warton becomes quite complex. Even in 1871, most of Warton's original notes of 1774 are retained. But the authorities vary. So in the second volume, we find on page 310 quotations from "Morris" for the Knight's Tale; note 3 on page 311 quotes the Reeve's Tale in "Wright" (the text used by Morris), followed by a note from Tyrwhitt; note 5 then quotes the Knight's Tale in Urry's edition. But on page 298, the "ingenious editor of the *Canterbury Tales*" (Warton's own note of 1778) means Tyrwhitt.[38]

The eighteenth century saw a radical shift in material aspects of the text from a large, unmanageable folio to the smaller octavo volumes of Tyrwhitt, and the even smaller volumes of the later reprints of Tyrwhitt. But these volumes pose problems of their own: to read any line of Tyrwhitt in his original edition, three volumes are necessary: (1) text, (2) notes, (3) glossary. The confused reception of Tyrwhitt is thus a reflection of the basic paradox of his edition: it was an erudite work in the material form of a popular one.[39] Three years passed between the appearance of Tyrwhitt's text and his glossary, and in some later editions, the text appeared stripped of both glossary and notes.[40] Tyrwhitt's *Canterbury Tales* was in many ways a popular book that very few could read with ease. Even Chalmers, who in 1810 reprinted Tyrwhitt for his English Poets series, concedes this: "Mr. Tyrwhitt, since this advice was given [ref. to Warton] has undoubtedly introduced Chaucer to a nearer intimacy with the learned public, but it is not probable that he can ever be restored to popularity" (1:xv).

Thomas Morell and the Open Edition

Thomas Morell's edition of 1737 is a partial edition, containing only the General Prologue and the Knight's Tale. With the exception of the chapter by Arnold C. Henderson in Alderson's *Chaucer and Augustan Scholarship*, Morell's edition has been neglected by Chaucerians. Tyrwhitt makes little use of it, and the references by Nott (noted above) are exceptional.[41]

Morell was a school-teacher, and certainly the only Chaucer editor who wrote opera libretti (for Handel's oratorios *Judas Maccabaeus*, *Theodora*, and *Jephtha*). He was also an editor of Greek texts for use in schools; and it is here that his innovations in Chaucer appear. A Greek text for Morell had several components—the Greek text, a facing-page Latin translation, and finally notes (which might appear both at the bottom of the page and in an appendix; see fig. 17).[42] His Chaucer (fig. 18) takes the same general form. The edition is an octavo, the same size as his school editions, smaller than any previously printed Chaucer.[43] Chaucer's text appears with notes at the bottom of the page; and the page is divided roughly in half. Following the text is a modernization by Dryden and others (the equivalent of the Latin translation of the Greek school text). And following that is an Appendix consisting of "Annotations" (349ff.) and "Various Readings" (425-43). A glossary follows. Morell turned Chaucer into the genre he knew best—the school text. And the Chaucer we have here is a startling one. It is well-printed, eminently accessible, with an

EURIPIDIS HECUBA.   5

POLYDORI Umbra.

I A M B I.

VENIO, defunctorum latebra & caliginis portis
Relictis, ubi Pluto seorsum habitat à Diis,
Polydorus, Hecubæ filius Cisseidos
Priamique patris, qui me, cum Trojanæ civitati
Periculum effet, hasta ne caderet Græca,   5
Metuens, clam emisit ex Trojana terra,
Polymestoris ad domum Thracii hospitis,
Qui feracissimos Cherronesi campos
Seminat, bellicosum populum regens hasta.
Multum vero mecum auri emittit occulte   10
Pater, ut si quando Ilii mœnia caderent,
                                                  Viven-

ΣΧΟΛΙΑ.

EΥΡΙΠΙΔΟΥ ΕΚΑΒΗ.   4

ΠΟΛΥΔΩΡΟΥ Εἴδωλον.

I A M B O I.

Ποл. ΗΚΩ, νεκρῶν κευθμῶνα ϗ σκότε πύλας
Λιπών, ἳν' Ἄδης χωρὶς ᾤκισαι θεῶν,
Πολύδωρος, Ἑκάβης παῖς γεγὼς ϗ̔ Κισσέιας
Πριάμε τε πατρὸς, ὅς μ', ἐπεὶ Φρυγῶν πόλιν
Κίνδυν⊙· ἔχε δορὶ πεσεῖν Ἑλληνικῷ,   5
Δείσας, ὑπεξέπεμψε Τρωϊκῆς χθονός,
Πολυμήστορ⊙· πρὸς δῶμα Θρηϊκῆ ξένε,
Ὅς τὴν ἀρίςην Χερρονησίαν πλάκα
Σπείρει, φίλιππον λαὸν εὐθύνων δορί.
Πολὺν ϑ̔ ἅμ' ἐμοὶ χρυσὸν ἐκπέμπει λάθρα   10
Πατήρ, ἳν' εἴπστ' Ἰλίε τείχη πέσοι,
                                            Τοῖς

ΠΑΡΑΦΡΑΣΙΣ.

ΣΧΟΛΙΑ.

Figure 17. Thomas Morell, *Euripides Hecuba* (London, 1748). Photo courtesy of the Department of Special Collections, Van Pelt Library, University of Pennsylvania.

2

The PROLOG.

5 Eke whanné Zephyrus with his fote Breth
Enſpirede hath, in every Holt and Heth,
The tendir Croppys, and the yongé Sonne
Hath in the Ramme half his Courſe yronne,
And ſmalé Foulis maken Melodye,
10 That ſlepen allé Night with open Eye,
(So prykyth hem Nature in her Corages)
Than longen Folk to go on Pilgrimages,
                        And

v. 6 Holt, A.S. holt, a Wood or Grove. *Linc.*

v. 7 Croppys. *Crop* in old Engliſh ſignified the Top of any thing. Fr. *Crop, Croupe.*

  The Lilly Croppis one and one
  He ſmote off——   *Gower,* p. 169.

Overblydand lichtly the Croppis of the Wallis.
——*Summas periabitur undas.*   Dougl. Virg. i. 150.

So here it ſignifies the Twigs or Tops of Trees.

  And for to kepe out well the Sonne
  The Croppis were ſo thick yronne
  And every Braunch in other knit, &c.   R.R. 1396.

v. 11 Hem and her, *i.e.* them and their, *vid.* Pref.

v. ib. Corages, *i.e.* Minds. So *Boeth. de Conf.*
   Si veſtros Animos, Amor,
   Quo cælum regitur regis.

Oweful were Mankynde, if thilke Love that governeth the Heerth governed your Corages. *Summum laſſerum ſolamen animarum,* Thou art Soverain Comfort of Corages anguiſhous. *Ib. Chaucer.*

The PROLOG.   3

And Palmers for to ſeken ſtraungé Stronds,
To ſerven Halowys, couth in ſondrie Londs,
15 And ſpecially from every Schieres End
Of Englond, thei to Canterbury wend,
That Holy bliſtul Martyr for to ſeke,
That hem hath holpen, whanné thei were ſik.
It ſo befel that Seſon on a Daye
20 In Southarke at the Taberre as I laye,
Redy to wendin on my Pilgrimage,
To Canterbury with devout Corage ;
                        That

v. 13 Palmers. Pilgrims, who after having viſited Jeruſalem or other holy Places, at their Return carried in their Hands a Staff or Bough of Palm-tree, in token of their having perform'd their Vow of Pilgrimage. Lat. *Palmarii, ſeu Palmati.* vid. Append.

v. 14 Halowys. Saints. A.S. Halig, holy. *Thei Schewden out the Blas of Halowys and Prophets.* Apocai. 16. Wickl. Teſt.

v. ib. Couth. A.S cuð, known, famous.
  In Story as is *Cowth.* Lidg. Theb.
  His Name for ever ſchall be *Couth.*   Gower 135.

v. 16 Wend, *i.e.* go. A.S. Wendan, to go; *wade,* Went.

v. 18 That bliſful Martyr. *Thomas Becket,* Archbiſhop of Canterbury, who was aſſaſſinated *An. Dom.* 1171, and canonized for a Saint by Pope *Alexander* the 3d. *Vid.* Append.

v. 20 Taberre. The Sign of a Taberre, or Taberde. Fr. *Tabarre,* It. *Tabarro.* A Jacket or Sleeveleſs Coat, worn in time paſt by Noblemen in the Wars, but now only by Heralds, and is call'd their Coat of Arms in Service. Sp. This Sign is ſince changed into the Sign of a Talbot with this Inſcription, *This is the Inn where*

                            v. 13

B 2

Figure 18. Morell, *The Canterbury Tales of Chaucer* (London, 1737). Photo courtesy of the Department of Special Collections, Van Pelt Library, University of Pennsylvania.

ingenious system of glosses on the page, and with cross-references to discussions of particular words in the glossary (the same page format chosen for the Riverside edition and the earlier edition by A. C. Baugh).

Tyrwhitt mentioned Morell's edition with respect:

> He appears to have set out upon the only rational plan of publishing Chaucer, by collating the best Mss. and selecting from them the gen-uine readings; and accordingly his edition, as far as it goes, is infinitely preferable to any of those which preceded it. (Tyrwhitt, *Canterbury Tales*, Appendix to the Preface, 1:xx-xxi)

But Tyrwhitt's notes do not suggest any further links with this edition. Tyrwhitt has a note about every forty lines; Morell's notes are far more numerous. But Tyrwhitt and Morell rarely note the same line, and when they do, their notes are quite different. On *palmeres* (Gen. Prol. line 13), Morell offers copious Latin quotations. Tyrwhitt counters with only Italian quotations. I do not think this is accidental. On *not heed* (line 109), Morell suggests an Anglo-Saxon root and cites Shakespeare; Tyrwhitt says only "nut, round-head." Then there is "as Austyn bit" (line 187). A note? Of course. We need to know who "Austin" is, and Morell tells us: "St. Augustin, that famous Doctor, and Bishop, wrote more Books than ever did any in the Church of the Latins." Tyrwhitt doesn't tell us a thing about Augustine, but rather uncharacteristically, and unnecessarily, gives us a paragraph on the grammatical form "bit." On *vavasour* (line 360), Morell gives us an entire page of Latin quotations, all extremely useful, and right on point. Tyrwhitt ignores them: "The precise import of this word is often as obscure as its original. See Du Cange in v. In this place it should perhaps be understood to mean the whole class of middling Landholders" (4:205).[44]

Even when Tyrwhitt had available to him a helpful note by Morell, he suppressed it, either intentionally or by neglect. And with that he suppressed any sense of a continuing tradition. To Tyrwhitt, an edi-tion is not the foundation for future scholarship, since he did not avail himself of the one earlier edition that drew his praise. The future acts rather to suppress its own origins in that past. And occa-sionally Tyrwhitt proceeds not, as he claims, as if Chaucer had never been edited before, but rather as if Chaucer had never been the sub-ject of commentary before.

Tyrwhitt knew what he was about—the production of the best edition. But Morell's intentions are wonderfully uncertain, as is clear from his preface:

> Such Variety of Prefatory Matter here presents itself, that, in this *dubiâ coenâ* I know not where to begin, or what Dish to fix upon in the Bill of Fare.—Shall I entertain you, courteous Reader, with a Dissertation on the Study of Antiquity in general?—But a Study so pleasant in the Theory, and so useful in the Application, needs no further Recommendation than what itself carries along with it.—There may be, indeed, some light and flattering Wits so averse to the more severe and recondite Studies of the learned, as to censure even the elaborate Works of Dr. *Hickes*, or *Thomas Hearne*, and to look upon all Antiquaries as a Set of dull and stupid Animals. But for Men to find fault with what they do not understand, shews more of ill Manners than sound Judgment; which is generally the Case here.[45]—Or shall I enlarge upon the Beauties and Excellencies of our Author in particular?—but this has been already executed by the masterly Hand of Mr. Dryden; and I would not pretend to attempt a *Venus* after *Appelles*.—Or shall I defend him from the Charge of *Verstegan* and *Skinner*, of having spoiled and corrupted that Language, which he is generally and justly allowed by others to have polished and refined, nay, almost perfected?—. . . But herein likewise have I been happily prevented by many abler Hands, especially the learned Dr. *Hickes*. (xxi-xxii)

What then is the purpose of the edition? Morell has no answer:

> However, as I shall have an Opportunity of prefacing each Volume, I shall speak to these and many the like Particulars in their turns.

The subsequent volumes, although supposedly completed, were never published.

No previous editor of Chaucer had addressed his readers in quite the same way as Morell. Speght's reference to "all friendly Readers" in his 1598 preface is only a traditional appeal that they point out his errors; Tyrwhitt's coldly objective tone has no room for a reader at all. But what role are we to assume as we read Morell? His "courteous Reader" is no antiquarian, no professional scholar. As we read his preface, we are transformed into novel readers, about to read what appears to be a school edition of a medieval work. Morell's edition is thus the first of the largest and almost certainly the most influential genre of Chaucer editions—the school edition. But in 1737, such readers, and such supporting institutions, did not exist.

There are, of course, many reasons to prefer, as the Chaucer tradition has done, the edition of Tyrwhitt. But why should we read the history of eighteenth-century Chaucer editions the way Tyrwhitt himself asks us to read it? Tyrwhitt's text today is hardly of more authority than Urry's. And his notes have survived simply because they are easy to incorporate into multi-volume editions.[46] The tradition of an accessible Chaucer, represented by the editions of Urry and Morell, was never directly supported by professional Chaucerians. The tradition was kept alive only indirectly—through modernizations, and most important, through the school edition. Skeat edited a student Chaucer in conjunction with his own six-volume edition. And one of the primary virtues of the Robinson edition in America has been its attempt to combine two increasingly well-defined groups of Chaucerians—students and professionals. An open tradition of editing is not necessarily one that points to new directions in scholarship, but rather one that offers the text to a new set of readers. And if Tyrwhitt is to be considered within such a tradition, credit is due primarily to those who pirated his edition, such as Bell in 1782.

Morell's edition is by no means a monumental one, nor, as its reception proves, an influential one. I call it an "open" edition not in spite of these facts, but in part because of them. It is ragged and unfinished, and consequently neglected. It stands thus (to its credit) as a monument to no one—neither to its author, nor to the scholarly tradition that inadvertently gave birth to it.

Excursus: The Urry Frontispiece and the Notion of an "English Classic"

Brewer's *Critical Heritage* volume characterizes both the 1687 folio and the 1721 edition in similar terms: the 1687 edition is a "tall handsome folio"; the Urry edition is a "large handsome volume" (1:35-36). This language reinforces the basic contrast that Brewer and others have attempted to make: it isolates typographical differences between the two editions that show the transformation of Chaucer from a gothic author into a modern, or from an author with only antiquarian appeal into a classic author. I have already noted that the change in typography from blackletter to roman is itself accidental. Other details of these editions have also been interpreted according to the basic paradigm implied by the typographical myth. Here, I am concerned with one of the eccentricities of the Urry edition—its two full-page engraved frontispieces—one of Urry himself by N. Pigné ("Iohannes Urry Armiger Aedis Christi Alumnus"), the other of Chaucer by Vertue ("Geffrey Chaucer: Our Antient & Learned English Poet").

The myth that these frontispieces constitute a classicization of Chaucer begins with a casual description by Alderson, concerning the format of the Urry edition:

> [Lintot] did not stint himself in providing it [Urry] with a format appropriate to a major edition of an English classic, and he had confidently assured one of the collaborating editors that the planned printing of 1250 copies would "go off." (Alderson, *Chaucer and Augustan Scholarship*, 81)

I believe this is in part the source for Brewer's statements concerning the actual details of this format. Brewer is here reading the Urry edition (the classic) against the 1687 edition (with what Brewer calls its "conscious antiquarian appeal"):

> This large handsome volume continues the process of presenting Chaucer as an 'ancient'. As in editions of the Latin Classics, pride of place is given to a large engraving of the editor, Urry . . ., and an engraving of Chaucer follows on the next leaf. . . . Chaucer's 'Retracciouns' to CT are printed for the first time. (1:36)

The statement concerning the Retraction is simply false: such a claim occurs only in the Preface by Thomas of this very edition, a statement later hand-corrected by William Thomas. Brewer has probably been misled by Alderson, who describes it (accurately) as "Missing in all printed texts of Chaucer from Thynne (1532) through Speght" (*Chaucer and Augustan Scholarship*, 117).

Brewer's statement concerning the frontispiece, however, has been repeated by Machan, who elaborates: the 1721 edition is "complete with a frontispiece of Chaucer and a critical apparatus on the model initiated by Speght." This "renders Chaucer's texts in appearance very much the equal of contemporary presentations of the texts of Homer or Vergil" (*Middle English Textual Criticism*, 44). I believe Machan's detail is simply an elegant variation on the word *classic*, since no contemporary editions of Homer or Vergil are specified.

Alderson's comment on format has taken on a life of its own. Brewer was speaking of the frontispiece portrait of the editor Urry—a frontispiece which he (rightly or wrongly) felt was in the tradition of classical editions. Thus, the book is to be classified in this genre. Machan seems to be repeating the same argument (I assume inspired by Alderson): the 1721 edition presents Chaucer as a classic as proved by its frontispiece. Yet Machan is now talking about the other frontispiece—not of the editor Urry, but of the author Chaucer.

What classics, if any, did its editors and printers have in mind? And which frontispiece (or frontispieces) enforce this association?

The edition originated with a plan by Atterbury in 1711 as Dean of Christ Church College to produce a series of editions: Hearne says, without further identification, that these were to be "well-known writers" ("bonae notae scriptores").[47] Hearne's notes on this enthusiasm of Atterbury mention *only* the Chaucer edition, giving us no idea of who these other "bonae notae scriptores" might be.

The purchases and publishing record of Lintot should inspire further skepticism. Lintot's major investments were in Pope and contemporary authors, such as Gay (the records include 25 pounds for his "Wife of Bath" and 75 for its revival in 1717). What classics he is printing are translations: Pope's Homer, and one by Theobald. The accounts quoted by Nichols show several thousand pounds paid to Pope between 1714 and 1721, and on 1714, an agreement to pay Theobald for all the *Odyssey*, four tragedies of Sophocles (2 pounds for every 450 Greek verses), along with the Satires and Epistles of Horace (1 pound for every 120 Latin lines). As mentioned earlier, the agreement with Urry requires no outlay of money at all. If then there were a concerted effort to produce classics (of any sort), Lintot was simply not involved. And the context of his investments show that he was interested in modern writers or at least ancients in modern dress (a translated Homer; a roman type Chaucer).

The statement concerning the two frontispieces is one I have considered for some time and I still see no basis for it. I am certain that Brewer has some specific edition in mind, but I do not know what it is. My own examination of title-pages and frontispieces from the period suggests that the Chaucer example is almost unique and that the appearance of the editor with the author would have meant nothing to the eighteenth-century reader. A book's frontispiece was certainly of import, but the typical frontispiece portrayed the author. One of the major contemporary editions is the four-volume, large-quarto edition of the works of Joseph Addison printed by Tonson in 1721, which includes a frontispiece of the author; Iola Williams describes this as: "the almost common form for the frontispiece of really imposing editions published about this time" (8). Williams mentions another book by Tonson, the 1718 large folio edition of Matthew Prior's works ("the most imposing book of the time") (12). But the frontispiece engraving here is allegorical, as is the series of small engravings throughout the book. The Addison engraving is by George Vertue, as is the Chaucer portrait in the Urry Chaucer. But the engraving of Urry is by a N. Pigné. French work predominates in English books of the early part of the century, and Pigné is one of the lesser-known of these artists.[48] The appearance of the Urry portrait here is like much else in the volume; it is not a matter of editorial calculation or design, but rather an accident, in this case, due to Urry's death. And it is not consistent with other nearly contemporary editions of classic authors with presumptuous editors. Richard Bentley's edition of *Paradise Lost* surely is an example of an editor with the reputation of the highest notion of self-aggrandizement (London: Tonson, 1732). It contains a Vertue engraving of Milton, but Bentley's image does not appear. Nor do I find anything comparable in any of the other more obvious candidates, such as Pope's Shakespeare and the early editions of classics edited for Cambridge by Bentley.[49]

I picked up the following books in a casual search of a small Special Collections department.[50] These books are not exceptional, and many eighteenth-century readers might have had access to them; but not one duplicates the frontispiece conventions that we are told guide the eighteenth-century reader in placing the Urry Chaucer squarely within the genre of "classic."

Homer (London: Th. Wood, 1736), 8o; no engraving.

Iliad, tr. Pope (4th ed., London: Lintot, 1736), 12mo; no engraving.

Horace, *Odes, Satyrs, and Epistles*, tr. Creech (5th ed., London: Tonson, 1720); engraving of Creech.

Horace, *Odes and Satyrs,* tr. eminent hands (London: Tonson, 1721); allegorical frontispiece.

Juvenal and Persius (London: Sales, 1707); no frontispiece.

Juvenal and Persius (London: Tonson, 1726); allegorical frontispiece.

Lucan, tr. N. Rowe (London: Tonson, 1718), folio; allegorical frontispiece.

Pindar, *Odes,* tr. Gilbert West, 3 vols. (London: Dodsley, 1706); medallion bust of Pindar.

Plutarch, *Lives,* 5 vols. (London: Tonson, 1711?); allegorical frontispiece.

With the exception of the engraving of Creech, no editors or translators appear.

English classics show the same trend:

Cowley (London, 1710); engraving of Cowley.

Shakespeare, "A collection of Poems," 2 vols. (London, 1710); engraving of W.S.

Shakespeare, ed. Rowe (London: Tonson, 1709); medallion of Shakespeare surrounded by allegorical personages.

Shakepeare, ed. Pope (London: Tonson, 1725); engraving of Shakespeare (by Vertue)

Shakespeare, ed. Theobald (London: Tonson, 1733); engraving of Shakespeare.

Shakespeare, ed. Johnson (London: Tonson, 1765); frontispiece of W.S.

Again, there are no engraved portraits of editors. The only example I can find in my unsystematic search is the 1751 Pope edition edited by William Warburton (9 volumes), where, in a rather modest frontispiece (octavo), unidentified medallion portraits of both Pope and Warburton appear, following a convention of seventeenth-century title pages whereby author and translator would appear in two medallion portraits, top and bottom.[51] The case is not quite parallel to the Urry edition, since Warburton is both Pope's editor and one of his correspondents (letters to Warburton are included in the final volume). And neither A. F. Johnson nor Margery Corbett list in their studies a single example of a book with two frontispieces showing either author and editor or author and translator. Even the double medallion title pages seem overrepresented in Corbett's sample and discussion.[52]

The Urry frontispiece, then, is not the sign of a "classic" in any sense, because contemporary editions of classics simply did not print large, folio-sized portraits of their editors. It is, rather, a belated tribute to an editor who had died in the production of the volume—just what the engraving itself claims: "Iohannes Urry Armiger Aedis christi Alumnus Obijt Anno dom. 1714. Aetat. 51."

Chapter 7

THE BOOK AND THE BOOKLET

I. THE PECIA SYSTEM

One of the most significant recent contributions to the study of Chaucer's text has been the theory of the booklet—a theory heavily promoted in the important 1989 anthology *Book Production and Publishing in Britain, 1375-1475*, edited by Jeremy Griffiths and Derek Pearsall. This chapter will examine both the origins of the theory outside Chaucer studies (specifically in the work of Jean Destrez) as well as the development of the theory within Chaucer studies, beginning with the work of Hammond and Brusendorff. To what extent should this appealing theory be applied to Chaucer and what are its implications regarding fundamental units of study?

The theory is primarily codicological, focusing on the manuscript as a material entity; but in Chaucer studies, and in literary studies generally, these interests (like bibliographical ones) are in the service of textual ones. In its simplest form, the theory posits that the production and distribution of texts in the late medieval period and the period of early printing operated with a textual and physical unit of a "booklet" rather than a "book." The theory was applied to Chaucer's minor works by Hammond and Brusendorff; and in Norton-Smith's recent facsimile of MS Fairfax 16, the term is used without definition, describing what appears to be the organization of the manuscript itself into five units—units that vary in size from a few leaves to over 300. Ralph Hanna has described the Hengwrt MS of the *Canterbury Tales* as composed in booklets.[1] Such a term potentially breaks down the modern view of what constitutes a book—a large, stable object containing a text, marketed as a single unit, which can be given a single entry in a catalog. If the primary unit of production and reception is the booklet, then such catalog descriptions are misleading, and our entire notion of what constitutes a book may be overturned. Because of the potentially revisionary nature of this concept, it requires serious examination.

The notion of the transmission of books by booklets has been lurking in Chaucer studies for quite some time. Henryson's *Testament of Criseyde* was included within Chaucer *Works* for two centuries, after being added as a single unnumbered quire following *Troilus and Criseyde* in the 1532 edition. Henryson associates his own writing with just such a unit in his single reference to Chaucer within this text. Henryson speaks of reading Chaucer quire by quire, and wondering, at the same time, whether Chaucer is responsible for the text that results.

> I toke a queare / and lefte al othere sporte
> Written by worth Chaucer glorious
> Of fayre Creseyde / and lusty Troylus
> (*Testament of Creseyde*, from Chaucer, *Workes*, 1532, sig.2Q3r)[2]

As we have seen in an earlier chapter, Thomas Hearne also made use of, or fell prey to, a version of the theory. His knowledge that Caxton printed "diverse works" by Chaucer, but never a complete works, led to his notion that the *Canterbury Tales* itself was such an example of a collection of "diverse works," thus possibly one that Caxton never printed (!), and also one whose individual sections could be treated as autonomous units (see above, chap. 5). Either of these views of Caxton could support his idea that the Retraction was a forgery.

For modern medievalists, the notion of a text consumed and transmitted as small units (booklets) has been part of a fundamental shift in the conception of basic units of study: from the book and the individual works it contains to the transmitted group. Both the book and the individual work are represented by, and to a certain degree products of, the tradition of editions. The fluctuating allegiances of texts within transmitted groups, however, oppose editorial endeavors, since the basic textual units—called booklets—are unrepresentable in traditional editions.

The booklet theory with its attendant emphasis on the physical transmitters of the text following the author's death appeals also to modern Chaucerians in the diminishing role it assigns to the author. By further removing the author from the production and transmission of the fundamental units of book and text, the booklet theory extends on the bibliographical plane what has already taken place in criticism on the biographical one, where the notion of an "author" has increasingly given way to that of a "compiler"—the very word used by Henryson to describe Chaucer. Since the now-classic formulation of the concept by M. B. Parkes and later by his student A. J. Minnis, the term has become a staple of discussion of late medieval texts.[3] The theory changes the very definition of what constitutes Chaucer's book—under the booklet theory, the physical book is necessarily more editorial than authorial.

Among the questions for which the theory seems to offer solutions are the following:

(1) Canon and the minor poems. According to the booklet theory, the major Chaucer manuscripts are formed (or customized) from units intermediate between the single poem and the complete book. The physical unit might be described as a fascicle; the textual unit is a group of poems. These poems could be combined in different ways, and the various units expanded or contracted.[4]

(2) Tale order in the *Canterbury Tales*. The theory finesses the entire question, since each Canterbury tale is itself arguably of booklet length, and thus these booklets (authorial) could be combined or compiled in various ways, whether by author (genuine links) or editor (spurious links). Tale order is perhaps no more (and no less) Chaucerian than the order of poems in, say, Fairfax 16.

(3) The status of incomplete manuscripts. Obviously, the problem simply disappears.

(4) The ambivalent attitude of modern scholars to the printing revolution. The revival of interest in the history of printing seems related to the threat (or promise) of an analogous technological change. The appeal of the pecia system theory to Chaucerians may be a function of this concern.[5]

There are many unproblematic examples of booklet construction, for example, certain late-medieval sermon collections.[6] The stronger and more interesting forms of the theory, however, involve its application to individual works or coherent groups of works, for example, a unit such as "Chaucer's poems." The first part of this chapter deals with the constraints involved in such extensions of the theory. The focus is on the pecia system—a well-documented method of production of certain university manuscripts. Before the implications of the booklet theory for Chaucer can be considered, the specific restrictions implied by the studies of this system need emphasis.

Modern Theories of the Booklet: Destrez and the Pecia

The most influential study of booklet production of manuscripts has been the classic study by Jean Destrez on the pecia system—a means of book production used in university publishing in the thirteenth and fourteenth centuries. That the system studied by Destrez is analogous to various systems of reproducing Chaucer texts has been implied by several Chaucerians, most notably, by Pearsall in the 1989 anthology on late medieval book production—an anthology containing as well the influential articles by Julia Boffey and John J. Thompson, A. S. G. Edwards, and Ralph Hanna—all of whom make reference to book production by the booklet unit.[7] In Destrez's definition of the pecia, the unit of production and sale was one sheet, folded in quarto. A "book text" consisted of a number of peciae used as exemplars individually rented out for copying. The book produced was copied from individual peciae. Destrez's notion of a "booklet" thus has little flexibility: the value and persuasiveness of his findings are dependent on the specificity of this definition.[8]

The indications of such a system are material: (1) marks in particular manuscripts indicating that they were copied from exemplars, and (2) the exemplars themselves. In Destrez's published study, he claims to have found about 30 exemplaria and almost 1,000 manuscripts containing these indications: 340 in Paris; 300 in provincial libraries, and 350 in foreign libraries (19).[9]

The strong basis of Destrez's work in material evidence must be stressed. The books he includes in his study are not those that merely seem to be composed in units, but rather those with material features that can be explained no other way. Destrez claimed that all of these manuscripts contain texts taught in universities. Non-university texts simply did not contain the specific marks Destrez was looking for: "Par contre, ne sont pas manuscrits universitaires, donc ne portent pas d'indications de pièces et, par suite, échappent à nos observations" (20). According to Destrez, the pecia system had been in existence by the ninth century, but left almost no traces except in the thirteenth and fourteenth centuries. Destrez claims that he could find no twelfth-century manuscripts and few fifteenth-century manuscripts that contained pecia marks (19).

There are a number of particulars in Destrez's argument that deserve note:

(1) His researches were confined to "professional" manuscripts, since personal manuscripts leave no trace of marks.[10]

(2) Destrez repeatedly claims that the institution fell into disuse due to printing, which rendered it obsolete as a means of professionally reproducing texts.

(3) The purpose of the institution is the production of stable texts, and the existence of these texts in turn makes it possible to deduce the existence of such an institution. Because the university approved the texts being lent, texts tended to be relatively stable (the texts are produced by radiation rather than in a linear series).

(4) Mixed texts are produced when more than one exemplar is copied, or when a professional copyist uses a different exemplar for a particular pecia. Destrez is insistent that this was not an official use of system, and that when different pecia are used, they come from different universities (68). Universities approved different texts successively, so that when a particular text is found marked with different peciae, the one with the most peciae is latest (scribes lengthened text).[11]

The significance of Destrez's findings for textual critics is obvious. Pecia marks provide convincing external, non-textual evidence for the grouping of manuscripts into textual families. This generally onerous task, inevitably circular when based on textual evidence alone, becomes simple and mechanical. But equally important are its obvious restrictions: the theory and its evidentiary support apply only to cases involving professional copying, a controlled stable text, and a clear opposition of manuscript production and printed book production.

Chaucerians can easily see why I emphasize the points above. Each involves evidence or defines a historical situation that has no clear analogue in early Chaucerian text and book production. Destrez's work cannot be extended to cover the situation of fifteenth-century Chaucer manuscripts without ignoring his assumptions. Pecia marks, the external evidence on which Destrez's rests, are not found in any Chaucer manuscript. Furthermore, for Chaucer, we have individual manuscripts, not institutional ones, and these are sometimes produced by amateurs (whose manuscripts Destrez claimed could not be studied scientifically); no Chaucer manuscript is the institutional product of a university. In Chaucer studies, the texts to be explained by a theory of fascicular production are unstable, not stable. And finally, the received text for Chaucerians is one formed in the fifteenth and sixteenth centuries, and the opposition central to Destrez between manuscript production and print thus is not generally maintained.

The Booklet Theory in English Studies

The one application of Destrez's work to England was by Graham Pollard in 1978. The strength of Pollard's work is due, as Destrez's, to its restrictions.[12] Pollard studied manuscripts from English universities and found evidence that could extend Destrez's theories to England: the pecia system was developed in university towns to promote the rapid production of multiple, identical copies of texts for students. And the same demise of the system occurs well before the advent of printing. Nonetheless, the evidence itself was less extensive, and, like Destrez, Pollard could find none of what he called the "stationer's exemplars" (what Leonard Boyle calls epipeciae)—those institutionally owned and rented quires from which individual copies were made:

> We must now consider the original source—the stationer's exemplar from which he had the *peciae* made. So far as I know, no such manuscript has yet been identified, so I cannot supply any physical features by which it could be recognized. (Pollard, "The Peciae System," 158)

The system defined and studied by Pollard should have little bearing on printing history or on the production and dissemination of secular manuscripts in the fifteenth century.

Destrez's work sits uneasily with Chaucer studies. It has often been cited, but warily. It should be contrasted with the work of P. R. Robinson and Ralph Hanna, who are very familiar with Destrez, but work with different fields and different levels of evidence. Robinson's evidence derives from Anglo-Saxon manuscripts; the restrictions defined by Destrez and Pollard—manuscripts produced within a university environment—are inapplicable. Robinson's findings, although less precise, are consequently more easily generalized.[13] What Robinson calls booklets are codicologically defined units, that is, they are neither textual units nor paleographical units, and Robinson distinguishes the booklet from the "scribal stint."

The criteria used to define a booklet in the case of Anglo-Saxon manuscripts are various; a booklet is indicated when a physical unit (for example a quire) coincides with the beginning and end of a text or group of texts, or when the outer pages of such units are "soiled or rubbed." Like Destrez, Robinson defined the booklet narrowly, with reference to external and internal evidence: "It must be emphasized that the existence of a booklet is established only if its content forms a self-sufficient unit" ("Self-Contained Units," 232). In this 1978 article, there is no reference to Destrez, and (by implication) no evidence of a codicological "back-formation."

In 1986, Ralph Hanna critiqued Robinson's notions, objecting in particular to her conflation of two units (or perspectives): the booklet as an "object found" or as an "object intended," that is, the difference between a manuscript that is put together by buyers and owners (what would be now indicated by an entry in a library catalogue and the object of provenance studies) and a manuscript that is put together deliberately by its producers (the object of study for descriptive bibliography).[14]

Although Hanna begins with an objection to Robinson's blurring of a necessary distinction, he seems to be arguing overall with an eye to extending rather than refining Robinson's definition, which he paraphrases as follows: "a group of leaves forming at least one quire, but more likely several and presenting a self-contained group of texts."[15] Hanna questions in particular the emphasis on the notion of "self-sufficiency," on which Robinson based her own definition. Once the booklet is "codicized" (!) that self-sufficiency is lost: and this is the case with Huntington Library manuscripts HM 114 and HM 144, both consisting of multiple booklets stitched together.[16]

Hanna admits the "common debilities" of the criteria both he and
Robinson define for booklet production: "none of them necessarily
appears in any given booklet; [and none] is the exclusive property of
the booklet as a codicological unit" (109). Hanna's redefinition and
reranking of these criteria move in two directions. On the one hand,
his notions of "contextualization" and "codicization" undermine the
autonomy of the booklet implied by Robinson. On the other hand,
Hanna's privileging of material and codicological features as defining
elements of a booklet (rather than codicological and textual "self-sufficiency") somewhat paradoxically moves the entire notion of the
booklet further toward the abstract: in Thornton MS, Lincoln
Cathedral 91, Hanna notes "hidden booklets."[17] And as the critical
notion of booklet becomes abstract, the codicological and textual-critical foundations for the booklet theory seem to crumble. What
Hanna calls a "hidden booklet" is no longer a material entity, but an
imagined one, or perhaps the act of imagination itself.

The difference between Robinson and Hanna reflects their various
interests. Robinson's work is almost exclusively codicological;
Hanna's work has always tended toward textual criticism. His conclusions show precisely this interest: to Hanna, Robinson "leans too
much on the notion of textual self-sufficiency, and not enough on the
notion of separately conceived production" (107). For Hanna, the
distinguishing mark of a booklet is "postponement of any overall plan
for a finished book." "The literary manuscript is a commonplace
book, a gathering of materials which meet, for whatever reason, the
interests of a compiler . . . an eclectic miscellany" (108). For Hanna,
the material acts as evidence for an ideal: the critical object is not the
historical event of manuscript provenance but the historical ideas and
ideals that drive or are imperfectly realized by these historical
events.[18] It is obviously a short step from here to basic problems in
Chaucerian texts, a step Hanna himself makes in his 1989 "The
Hengwrt Manuscript and the Canon of *The Canterbury Tales*" (*Pursuing
History*, 142). But the closer we get to Chaucer, the further we get
from the type of material evidence on which the work Destrez and
Pollard was based.

The various essays in the important Pearsall and Griffiths anthology of 1989 continue this redefinition of basic textual and manuscript
units. The studies attempt to define new modes of production for late
medieval manuscripts and early printed books, and with that, new

units of production as well. The dispersal of authorship among other producers means a breaking up of the monolithic book:

> The characteristic form of author-initiated production is the copy made at the author's instigation among friends or for presentation to a patron; the characteristic form of consumer-initiated production is the copy made by the consumer himself, or to the order or commission of a customer, whether acting as an individual or as an institution (such as a monastery). The third form of production, that initiated by the producer or entrepreneur is crucially important to the history of book-production and most obviously coincides with our notion of 'publishing'. . . This book deals with extent to which entrepreneur production as distinct from commissioned or bespoke was characteristic. (Pearsall, "Introduction," 1-2)

According to Pearsall, the institution of printing "brought in a dominantly producer-initiated form of book-production" (3).[19] As these modes of production are considered, the specter of Destrez arises. In their description of the production of *Canterbury Tales* manuscripts, Pearsall and Edwards use the now classic study of Doyle and Parkes to deny Manly-Rickert's notion of bookshops: "What we have, in fact, is a group of professional scribes, used to working independently, perhaps in adjacent premises, brought together to execute a specific commission" (262).[20] Edwards and Pearsall continue:

> The exemplar was split up and circulated in quires for simultaneous copying. The practice was well known in monastic scriptoria, and has some resemblance to the university pecia system, but it was evidently a ticklish operation in the hand-to-mouth world of the London booktrade, which is perhaps why it was so rare. (262)[21]

That the confident "in fact" yields so quickly to the qualifiers "perhaps," "rare," and "ticklish" is noteworthy (in such an environment, the word "evidently" means its opposite!). Again, the evidence is circumstantial and textual. The imagined system may be analogous to that of Destrez, but the nature of the evidence is quite different.

Destrez was not interested in texts. He was interested in the institution of manuscript production and the material evidence for such production. The application of his work to textual studies would be simple: *less work on textual studies.* But Chaucer studies never have and

never can move in this direction. Whatever the differing interests of
Chaucerians, they share one concern—the text—even if they pretend
to deride a fellow Chaucerian's concern for the same thing.

II. EVOLVING DEFINITIONS OF TEXTUAL UNITS IN MODERN CHAUCER BIBLIOGRAPHY

Until recently, the primary means of determining canon in
Chaucer studies was not the manuscript (despite numerous protests
to the contrary) but the tradition of the printed book. The basis for
canon is "what appears in the book," that is, an edition. Before the
late eighteenth century, the process was generally additive. Tyrwhitt,
in an essay accompanying his edition of the *Canterbury Tales* (1775-
78), suggested a new definition of canon—one that proceeded by
exclusion rather than inclusion; Tyrwhitt's conclusions were embodied in several nineteenth-century re-editions of Chaucer (for example, the Moxon edition of 1843) and finally in Skeat's edition of
1894.[22] In 1897, Skeat effectively established a "canonical apocrypha"
with the publication of his *Supplement*—volume 7 of his once six-volume edition.[23] The Chaucer canon, thus, was editorially defined as
Tyrwhitt's text of the *Canterbury Tales* plus the works listed in his
Appendix; this was done initially through the numerous editions of
reprinted texts, selections, and piracies that attempted to cash in on
the popular market for British authors, and finally through the
embodiment of this canon in Skeat's edition.

In the early part of this century, two important Chaucerians registered an unspoken objection to this book-centered and edition-cen-
tered canon: Eleanor Prescott Hammond and Aage Brusendorff.[24]
Many of their findings have been challenged, and some of their interests are no longer central to Chaucer studies.[25] Yet their recognition
of units of "the Chaucerian" other than those of the individual work
or the large book that contains those works has found a receptive
audience among recent Chaucerians, even though such a notion goes
against the main editorial tradition within which it was developed.

The Collection and the Booklet

Most of the questions Brusendorff would take up were first raised
by Hammond in a series of articles leading to and supplementing her

1908 *Chaucer: A Bibliographical Manual.* Skeat was aware of the relations of many of the manuscripts of the minor poems, but in Hammond's opinion, he had not placed much emphasis on these relations, and his discussion of manuscripts themselves was cursory:

> Skeat, I:48-58 and Minor Poems xlff., is very unsatisfactory in his hasty and summary remarks, which called forth from Flügel, Anglia 22:510ff. (1899), a censure accompanied by a collection of facts from the pages of the Chaucer Society prints, etc. A list of MSS, but without annotation, had previously been made by Koch, Anglia 4: Anz. 112-117 (1881). (Hammond, *Manual*, 326)[26]

The manuscripts for the minor poems are then discussed in toto by Hammond, based on locations: British Museum, London, Oxford Bodleian, other Oxford, Cambridge Univ. Library, Cambridge colleges, private hands.[27]

According to Hammond, individual poems had to be discussed in relation to manuscript context. In the conclusion to an early article (1905), Hammond states directly:

> For if the text of some Chaucer-poem, imbedded in a codex largely Lydgatian, . . . can be better estimated by evaluation of the rest of the volume, something is gained for the Chaucer canon. Such Chaucerian texts have been thus far too regularly regarded as entities in themselves. In my paper on the text of the *Parlement of Foules* [1902] I put forward a conjecture suggested to me by that study,—that a comparison of the codices of the Oxford Group (Fairfax, Bodley, Tanner, and Digby), would introduce another and important element in to the erection of a critical text. I hope that the results of that comparison for the Oxford Group, and of a similar study of the Shirley MSS . . . will substantiate that conjecture in the opinion of Early English specialists, and direct attention, so long concentrated upon the problem of the text, to the problem of the volume ("Two British Museum Manuscripts," 28)

This manuscript context directed scholarly focus away from classical nineteenth-century issues of textual criticism and attribution. Hammond, particularly in her articles on John Shirley and later manuscript groups, made repeated statements that her findings had little direct bearing on classical textual-critical questions; the manuscripts

she studied were often those furthest from Chaucer and thus from a
textual-critical point of view least authoritative:

> When we have made this investigation, and compared the three copies of
> Lydgate's *Secrees* in this man's hand, and clarified the relations of his
> *Canterbury Tales* transcripts, we shall have won nothing for literature, and
> very little for text-history. We shall have identified perhaps a few minor
> copyists, perhaps only one, of the latter fifteenth century; and we shall
> have had occasion to censure this man's irresponsibility. But even while
> we recognize that those future gains can be solely negative, that no
> ground firm enough for textual argument exists, we have at least a clearer
> knowledge of the general situation. ("A Scribe of Chaucer" 1929, 33)

This summarizes many statements Hammond had made earlier, for
example, on "Ashmole 59 and other Shirley Manuscripts":

> The interest which we feel in the group above mentioned is, however,
> entirely antiquarian. Textually these codices have no value for us. The
> process of elimination may seem destructive, but it is necessary. (348)
> Since Shirley wrote from memory, "Neither Harley nor Ashmole can
> deserve or can be permitted recognition in a critical text" ("Ashmole
> 59," 345).[28]

For Hammond, the only manuscripts of great textual importance
were those in her "Oxford group" (Tanner 346, Bodley 638, and
Fairfax 16):

> The great value of the Oxford Group lies, then, in the clearness with
> which each step of its descent can be traced, and the certainty with
> which we can work back to a MS. two degrees nearer Chaucer than the
> existing volumes.[29]

Brusendorff's *Chaucer Tradition* appeared in 1925, and is closely
linked with Hammond's work. Brusendorff was primarily interested
in what he calls "traditions" and distinguishing between the genuine
and the spurious:

> If . . . we cannot establish the continuity in time and space of some tra-
> ditional account we are pretty certain to have to do not with any true

tradition, but with late legends representing mere fancies or speculations, and originating as often—or oftener—among the learned as
among the vulgar. (27)

In this sense, Brusendorff was no different from Lounsbury in 1892,
who distinguished the Life of Chaucer from the Legend. But
Brusendorff, following Hammond, went further. Like Hammond, he
directed a good part of his attention to Chaucer's minor poems. And
this choice of subject led to a new version of Chaucer.

At the heart of this enterprise is the question of authorship and
authenticity. Skeat, following Bradshaw and F. J. Childs, had already
attempted to develop quantitative tests of authenticity, for example,
philological tests regarding final *y/ye* rimes. Skeat's quantitative tests,
however, served to confirm previous assumptions rather than to revo-
lutionize the definition of what constituted evidence. Skeat simply followed Tyrwhitt, attacking the additive nature of edition production
(particularly the additions made by Stow) and eliminating from the
canon most of the works that were so added. Like Tyrwhitt, he
assumed a fundamentally author-centered poem, denying Chaucer's
writing of the "Assembly of Ladies" and the "Flower and the Leaf," in
part because their female personae implied a female author.[30]

Brusendorff's discussion of the minor poems shows that his notion
of authorship and its relation to the history of the Chaucerian book is
a less traditional one. Brusendorff's chapter on the minor poems does
not begin as other chapters do with "The Principles of Textual
Criticism" but rather with "The MS. Collections" themselves (chap. IV,
178ff.). That is, the starting point, like Hammond's, is a different unit:
the manuscript collection. For the minor poems, Brusendorff defined
three major collections, naming them after the scholars who had
relied on them: the Hammond group, the Tyrwhitt group, and the
Bradshaw group. To these groups, Brusendorff added another group,
the Shirley group, defined as those six (or seven) manuscripts in
Shirley's own hand, as well as those previously identified by Hammond
as using a Shirley manuscript as copytext or as having a Shirley text as
ancestor.[31] Not only do these groups circumscribe the authorship
question, they also deny the manuscript unit. The important MS
Fairfax 16 becomes Fairfax I and II, defining two units; the Bradshaw
group, with Gg at its center, is made up largely of "fugitive" copies,
appearing on the flyleafs of Cotton Cleopatra D.vii and Ellesmere.[32]

And interestingly, not one of the three scholars who gave their names to these groups had actually edited the minor poems contained in these groups.

Like Hammond, Brusendorff denies the textual value of much of this; Shirley's attributions are more reliable than the details of his texts:

> But in other respects Shirley's information is so remarkably accurate that in spite of this single, though rather serious, offence his notes about the Chaucerian authorship of certain poems form a highly important body of evidence towards the final settlement of the Chaucer Canon. (236)[33]

Hammond and Brusendorff posed a challenge to traditional Chaucer editing and studies in the canon. Traditional editorial enterprises of necessity took as their primary units of investigation the individual poem, the individual copies of that poem, and the relation of these to an individual author—a goal never renounced by Hammond or Brusendorff. Hammond even concludes her later work with what appears to be a Retraction of sorts. But the fundamental units of investigation were now redefined as two: the collection and the booklets that make up that collection.

Brusendorff's "the manuscript collection" is a fluid concept—a "manuscript containing a collection of poems." Such a definition at first glance seems to refer to actual material entities, such as Fairfax 16. Yet Fairfax 16, under this definition, is two collections, with what Brusendorff calls a separate manuscript beginning at fol. 187: "Part II of the Fairfax volume forms an interesting little MS. (ff. 187-201)" (192). These material entities are not Brusendorff's main concern; they are defined not materially (in modern terms, codicologically), but textually. And what Brusendorff is interested in are these textual relations and the history that brought them into existence:

> While it sometimes happened that several scribes were at work copying one long work, this was much more frequently done when making collections of such brief items, since it was naturally much easier in this case to get several copies for transcription. (178-79)

The precise definition of a "collection" and even a "manuscript" is elusive. Hammond addresses directly the problem of defining a manuscript in *Manual*, 52-53: "The term 'manuscript' is applied roughly to various sorts of Chaucer volumes written by hand." A Borgesian list of four such sorts then follows: volumes of single works, works written by commission, private works, and volumes increased as they pass from owner to owner. What constitutes a "collection" or a "manuscript" can become further blurred in the notion of a "group," which again, is less a material entity than a history of affiliations (relating parts of manuscripts to parts of others). As in all textual-critical schemata, such groups consist both of real manuscripts, the texts of those manuscripts, and the conjectured texts and manuscripts that are behind such groups.[34]

The second most important unit defined by Brusendorff and Hammond is the smaller unit of the booklet: once again, not a unit consisting of a single text or work, and not one that must always appear in material form.[35] The word "booklet," so frequent in modern Chaucer studies, is used often by both Hammond and Brusendorff:

> Cambridge MS. [Trin. College R.3.21] is composed, like Trin. Col. Cambr. R. 3, 19, of several fascicules or booklets, used separately and bound together afterwards. (Hammond, "Two British Museum Manuscripts," 10)

Manuscripts themselves have no autonomy. Ashmole 59, one physical manuscript, is historically two. And Hammond's study of Pepys 2006 showed a title page hidden between 377 and 378—two pages gummed together; Hammond thus speaks of each unit as a "separate fascicule or book" ("Pepys 2006," 197). Even a manuscript produced as a single unit need not be a single unit:

> Manuscripts of the *Canterbury Tales* are not necessarily entities, are often of double, even of multiple, source; and the variants of scribes are in part, sometimes in large part, negligible for purposes of classification. (Hammond, "A Scribe of Chaucer," 31)

Brusendorff agrees:

Another and earlier group of texts is formed by four Bodleian MSS: Fairfax 16, Bodl. 638, Tanner 346, Digby 181 [ref. to Hammond] . . . . Evidently the four sections [of Tanner 346] were worked on by the two scribes at the same time, but the care taken to make the various parts self-contained through adding single sheets shows that they were kept separate and probably sold separately, the buyer making his own selection. (182-3)

And on Fairfax 16:

The correctness of this theory is emphasized by the view adopted here, that all the five parts of the MS. were originally separate booklets, offered for sale among many others by a copying and publishing firm, and together with some blank quires at beginning and end made up the present volume for a noble customer, who had the frontispiece executed for him, with his coat of arms inserted . . . it may be argued that the original sources [of Tanner] and the ancestor of Bodley-Fairfax I were a number of independent booklets, each containing one longish poem, like the *Legend*, or several shortish ones, like *Pity &c*, and copied in different order by different scribes. (186-7)[36]

The Editorial Legacy of Brusendorff and Hammond

Like Hammond, Brusendorff was ambivalent about the textual-critical value of these collections. He also felt, as some modern textual critics do not, that there was a fundamental difference between such collections and manuscripts of single works:

It might be added that yet another test, based on external evidence, has been set up, it being argued that when a poem occurs in a MS. together with other poems, admittedly Chaucer's, it must be his too.[37] This test fails, however, resting as it does upon a complete misconception of the MS. collections in which Chaucer's Minor Poems have been handed down to us. These collections are really anything but authoritative, and there is in fact a pronounced difference between MSS. chiefly containing one long work, and MSS. offering a batch of comparatively brief pieces, a difference so decisive as to make a separate study of the latter necessary. (51-52)

Nonetheless, Brusendorff ended each discussion with a suggestion as to how individual poems were to be edited. Hammond seemed to claim in her last articles that from a textual-critical point of view, the principal advantage of her findings would be in a Lachmannian *eliminatio* of the textual evidence these manuscript groups implied.

In Robinson's edition of 1933, Hammond's studies play little part. Robinson's editing proceeded on independent pieces of a canon determined in large part by studies of Skeat.[38] The second edition of 1957 did nothing to change this. The recent third Riverside edition (counting the early edition by Gilman as the first Riverside edition) announces on its title page that it is "based on F. N. Robinson"; this statement functions (for some texts) as an editorial disclaimer justifying an uncritical promulgation of Robinson's editorial assumptions.[39] In the notes to the Minor Poems by R. T. Leneghan (1185ff.), the authorities cited in the opening paragraph include Skeat and Robinson, H. Frank Heath (an editor of the Globe Chaucer), George Pace and Alfred David (editors of the Variorum Chaucer), but not Brusendorff or Hammond. In later notes, I find only one reference to Brusendorff (1188, on "Womanly Noblesse") and none to Hammond.

In 1982, the Variorum Chaucer put out as one of its first volumes *The Minor Poems: Part One,* edited by Geoge B. Pace and Alfred David. Like Urry's edition, this is a group production, and the main editor (Pace) died before its completion. The single most important assumption of the Pace and David edition is that the fundamental units are the individual poem and its author. In addition, the way this edition groups poems is by modern notions of literary genre:

> The fourteen poems here presented as Part One comprise a much more heterogeneous assortment [than those in Part Two]. . . . No attempt has been made to arrange these poems chronologically, but as far as possible each poem is placed alongside those with which it has affinities in form or subject. (David, "Introduction: The Poems of Part One," 3)

There is not one word in this introduction by David of the manuscript collections or the means of circulating the texts in the fifteenth century.

The second part of the Introduction, by Pace, defines the particular problems of the Variorum:

> If I thought that I could unfailingly provide a text approximating one
> "from the poet's own hand" [quoting Lounsbury], I would use that text
> here.
>
> The Text for this Variorum Edition must serve a function different
> from that of most texts: it must be an instrument of collation. Against
> the Text will be read a large number of manuscripts and editions and
> the results of the collation recorded. For editions, the common source
> behind them all, when such a source exists, would be the best instru-
> ment. That would be the manuscript from which the editors have, all
> and sundry, departed in seeking a text near one "from the poet's own
> hand." (Pace, "Introduction: The Text for This Edition," 10)

This seemingly measured statement conflates entities that are from a
textual-critical point of view distinct: a critical text and a basis for collation (something that precedes the critical text).[40] It reveals as well
that the object of Pace's research is still "Chaucer's text"—a text Pace
states directly is irrecoverable. Manuscripts and editions (products of
editorial intervention) are then "read" against this suddenly extant
text (or a near version of it), almost as an afterthought. They are considered degradations of that original text, not as active participants in
its transmission or creation.

Pace, apparently more than David, was concerned about the studies of Hammond and Brusendorff (see the section "Special Topics,"
17-19). Nonetheless, there the discussion remains; the implications
of Hammond's arguments and her critique of Skeat's casual handling of manuscripts are ignored. So too are her textual-critical comments (the main thrust of this edition): "The Minor Poems
manuscripts are a mixed lot. One manuscript, Fairfax 16, is outstanding" (Pace, 22). An outstanding manuscript from some points
of view perhaps, but not, according to Hammond, from a purely textual-critical point of view. In the major section on "The Manuscripts"
(Pace, 22-27), the manuscripts are simply listed, with brief, unsystematic notes: Ashmole 59—"Miscellany, with much Lydgate; fols. 1-
134 by John Shirley"; Bodley 638—"Miscellany Chaucer, Lydgate,
etc."; Cambridge Gonville and Caius College MS 176—"Miscellany
(much medical)"; Cotton Otho A.Xviii—"Original, possibly ultimately from a Shirley MS, burned (charred fragments remain)"
(22). Pace claims: "To give full descriptions for the fifty-five manuscripts appearing below would obviously be far beyond the scope of

this work" (ibid). But in a work of this length, that is not at all obvious.[41] For each poem in the edition, Pace provides a "Textual Essay" with full bibliography of previous work. What results is a fragmentation of the manuscript sources for these poems, something dealt with in brief cross-references:

> Fairfax 16 (F) is the proper copy-text for this edition of "Envoy to Bukton". F has been described briefly in the Textual Essay for *Purse* (143)
>
> The excellence of many of F's texts is well known (127)

But this is no description of Fairfax 16, for which one must turn to Hammond or to the facsimile by Norton-Smith. And the manuscript context of each copy of a poem, while not completely ignored by Pace, is effectively unrecoverable by a reader of his edition:

> To avoid needless repetition, foliation [of manuscripts] is not included; the lists of authorities for the various poem at the beginning of the Textual Essays supply foliation, where it is most needed. (22)

Pace and David's work is squarely within the main editorial tradition for Chaucer's texts, or what might even be called the "received-text tradition" of Thynne, Urry, Skeat, Robinson. It ignores the codicological tradition initiated by Hammond and Brusendorff and culminating now in the publication of manuscript facsimiles. The striking brevity of manuscript description is countered by Pace's detailed and extremely accurate descriptions of printed editions (28-36); the last representative of this series is (for the moment) the Variorum edition itself.[42]

Alternative Editions: The Facsimile

The alternative edition is that of the facsimile. The facsimile embodies (or seems to embody) the new emphasis on codicology and the elevation of material codicology over abstract principles of textual criticism. For Chaucer's minor poems, a series of facsimiles has become available, including those of Hammond's Oxford group: Fairfax 16, Tanner 346, and Bodley 638.[43] The status of these is paradoxical. They originate in the claim of the importance of material evidence, but have the effect of de-materializing that evidence. The facsimile, as many have noted, is *not* a reproduction of a material entity, but is, rather, an edition—editorial from first to last.[44] While facsimiles seem to promote the material entity (the manuscript), they are themselves only a material reproduction of a history of a manuscript production. The introduction for a facsimile-edition recounts that history and precedes a photograph; the key piece of information (the manuscript itself) is missing.[45] A facsimile remains a reproduction and, like the edition, is only as good as the principles of its own production. Even the $15,000 Ellesmere facsimile has been trimmed.[46]

Nonetheless, if cheap, black-and-white facsimiles (or more accurately "facsimile-editions") provide something to be read by various Chaucerians, that is probably not a bad thing, although it is surely less ambitious than the Canterbury Tales Project, which provides not only the visual facsimile, but might in its textual sections provide scholars the chance to create the texts they choose to read.[47] But the question of the Hammond-Brusendorff "text" remains. The object of the Hammond-Brusendorff enterprise is, for all practical purposes, unrepresentable, since the preposterous nature of an edition of a "lost manuscript" or "group of booklets" would be only too apparent.

The problem is exactly that of classical textual criticism—a field that neither Hammond nor Brusendorff claimed to transcend. Under the claims of recension, the hypothesized archetype can only be reconstructed after all the intermediate manuscripts in the textual-critical stemma are constructed. The edited and printed archetypal text can presumably only be produced after all hypothesized sub-archetypes have been completely constructed. If we have four manuscript readings, ABCD, and these are in two groups AB CD, which in turn suggest a reading in O', then prior to constructing O' the textual critic must be able to construct $\sqrt{AB}$ and $\sqrt{CD}$ in toto. In the case of the Manly-Rickert edition, individual editions of the groups *a*, *b*, *c*, and *d* should be theoretically possible. For individual variants, of course, this has been done. But for extended readings, I have never seen this very basic principle put into practice.

No one wants an edition of Manly-Rickert's *b* group of the *Canterbury Tales*. And similarly, no one wants an edition of Hammond-Brusendorff's lost Shirley manuscript, or the booklets behind the

Oxford group of manuscripts. Nonetheless, two primary fictions of modern Chaucerians depend absolutely on this hypothetical and unrepresentable entity: (1) that there is an author responsible, in some way, for these texts; and (2) that there is an equally interesting and recoverable tradition in which that author is received.

The Individual as Object of Study: Private Manuscripts, Private Owners, and Private Readings

Destrez defines his subject matter (page 43) by eliminating from consideration any manuscript written by a master or student simply for their own use. According to Destrez, these do not resemble at all manuscripts written by professionals. I am not certain what particular manuscripts Destrez has in mind, but certainly the comparable manuscripts I have seen confirm this: often unruled, difficult to read, poorly constructed. According to Destrez, these were the work of private individuals, and more important, scientific study of them is impossible (43). The literary extension of Destrez's theories, however, immediately involves such elements of individuality and singularity that Destrez wished to avoid: singular authors, private compilations, unique manuscripts.

For Chaucer studies, the shift in focus from Chaucer to an historical Chaucerian (the scribe, compiler, or owner) retains the focus on individuals. See for example Shirley's comments, quoted by Hammond:

> This litell booke / myth min hande
> wryten I haue /. . .
> And doon hit bynde / In þis volume
> Þat boþe þe gret / and þe comune /
> May þer on looke / and eke hit reede
>   (Hammond, quoting MS Add. 16165, *English Verse*, 195)

The study of specific manuscripts through production of facsimiles is justified on these grounds: their producers are individual readers of literary texts. The St. John's College manuscript of *Troilus and Criseyde* provides "information about how the work was received and understood by some of its earliest readers."[48] The difference between Bodley 638 (an amateur production) and the similar Fairfax 16 (a commissioned, professional one) is evidence of the difference between the tastes of two individual readers.[49] But as we move from the authorial presence (that which links the Bodley, Fairfax, Tanner and Digby manuscripts) to the readers' presence, we move away from the collective and institutional toward the individual manuscript—that entity for which Destrez speculated "no scientific study was possible."

Destrez's statement is not an article of faith, but it does indicate the dilemma for Chaucerians, and a further dilemma for modern enthusiasts of manuscript study. The object of what Destrez called scientific study can only be the socialized object, that is, one that leaves a trace of its own collective or rule-bound production. This is the material correlative to the abstract object of the studies of Hammond and Brusendorff, and would also constitute what Jerome McGann characterizes as a socialized text, resulting from the dispersal of authorship—the proper concern of editorial endeavors.[50] In Chaucer studies, one of the more interesting attempts to analyze such a socialized object is the reading of the Ellesmere manuscript by Edwards and Hanna—a reading that takes as its primary objects the non-Chaucer flyleaf poem and the historical provenance of the manuscript.[51] But many other studies simply reproduce the mechanics of author-centered critical readings on the manuscript level.[52] The revitalization of the editorial tradition in late twentieth-century Chaucer studies has thus far functioned to promote both the codicological materials as well as the institution of authorship these materials seem to undermine.

Chapter 8

UNBOOKING CHAUCER: THE DRAMA OF CHAUCER THE *PERSONA*

T hrough the eighteenth century, Chaucer studies are dominated by self-styled antiquarians, for whom modern literary values seem secondary. In the late eighteenth century, Thomas Warton's *History of English Poetry* changes this; his specific attacks on a generation of earlier antiquarians (with whom his own work might well be associated) serves to legitimize the competing belletristic line of Chaucer studies—that is, a line beginning with Dryden's *Fables* of 1700 and its influential introduction characterizing Chaucer as "one of us"—the genial poet who would be revived as the Chaucer central to Chaucer studies of the twentieth century.

> The antiquaries of former times overlooked or rejected these valuable remains, which they despised as false and frivolous; and employed their industry in reviving obscure fragments of uninstructive morality or uninteresting history. But in the present age we are beginning to make ample amends: in which the curiosity of the antiquarian is connected with taste and genius, and his researches tend to display the progress of human manners, and to illustrate the history of society.[1]

The following chapter discusses what I call the "unbooking" of Chaucer—one of several movements in Chaucer criticism that wrest the authority for Chaucer away from the physical books in which that authority was embodied. The particular line of criticism I consider here originates with Dryden and culminates in the major tradition of twentieth-century American criticism. It is at times quite radically at odds with the work discussed previously. Instead of antiquarians, we

159

have modernizers. Instead of editors, we have Kittredge; and instead of Donaldson the editor, we have Donaldson the genial essayist. Central to this line is the notion of decorum—a specifically dramatic decorum—defined classically as fitness of voice to speaker. That such fitness was somehow "natural" led in Warton's own discussion of drama, to the equation of decorum and naturalness itself.[2] What this notion of decorum does is to remove Chaucer from his embodiment in the Chaucerian book, and transform him into the voice and, by implication, the *persona* of the reader.

My subject below is the history of two common words in twentieth-century Chaucer criticism—the words *persona* and *drama*—and the origins of these words and attendant concepts in Dryden. I leave these undefined, since it is that very lack of definition that has permitted them to assume such importance in this century. It is because of such language that twentieth-century Chaucerianism has been able to develop its own apparently coherent history—a history that maintains its coherence in spite of, or perhaps because of, its steady polemic and the constant claim of revisionism.

The American institution of Chaucerianism is now nearly a century old; it has been dominated by questions articulated by Kittredge in 1915—questions reasserted strongly in the work of E. Talbot Donaldson and later by Donald R. Howard reacting against what are now known as the historicist theories of D. W. Robertson, Jr. Lee Patterson has outlined some of the major elements in this history (stressing the centrality of Robertson). Although excellent on the issue of historicism, Patterson's history understates I think the importance of Kittredge; it also ignores the reassertion of Kittredge's principles and techniques in the work of Howard and the series of *PMLA* articles Howard himself refereed—articles whose strengths lay in the individual interpretive reading (and not in the outlining of what Robertson claimed was a collective understanding).[3]

The easiest way to extract a congenial political message from the Chaucer text is to attribute it to Chaucer himself (for example, Gavin Douglas's notion of Chaucer as "wommenis friend").[4] Yet the studies of the past two decades considered here have tried to avoid this move. They privilege the notion of voice over speaker, a disembodied voice that in cultural terms would exist physically as a sound rather than as authorized markings on parchment, and take as a polemical target the notion of the Chaucerian *persona* popularized by Donaldson.

The theories of voice are the critical counterpart of the textual-critical studies that privilege the variant (oral, written, and performed) over the authorized, definitive text.[5] The political implications of both arguments seem egalitarian; despite the limited settings in which a Chaucerian voice might have been heard in the fourteenth century, that voice would clearly have been more accessible than the physical objects (manuscripts) that either represented that voice or were its actual origins.

My skepticism over the critical notion of a Chaucerian voice or Chaucerian voices is due to the indifference of the modern Chaucerian community to the practical realization of such political implications. Chaucerian readings are rarely presented as simple alternatives: they are produced under the assumption that some are better or, as a recent variant, more powerful than others. Furthermore, the basis of these readings and consequently of their critical evaluation is in part a stable text, the very existence of which undermines all theoretical pronouncements and polemics privileging voice.

Dryden, Kittredge, and Chaucer's Human Comedy

The *fons et origo* for American Chaucer criticism is in Dryden's well-known Preface to his 1700 folio edition of *Fables*.[6] The book itself is of some note: it contains in an appendix some of the first Chaucer texts to be printed in roman type. As texts or as editorial productions, they are negligible, taken from Speght's 1598 edition. Alderson states that these were never considered by Dryden and his publisher Tonson as editions or in any way as autonomous productions; they were rather appendices to this particular book.[7] Yet Dryden established a lasting canon of taste, and the tales he translated (the Knight's Tale, the Wife of Bath's Tale, the Nun's Priest's Tale) are still those that dominate modern anthologies.

Dryden repeats many of the familiar cliches of Chaucer criticism: "*Chaucer* (as you have formerly been tolde by our learn'd Mr. *Rhymer*) first adorn'd and amplified our barren Tongue fro the *Provencall*, which was then the most polish'd of all the Modern Languages" (*Fables*, sig. *A1v).[8] "From *Chaucer*, the Purity of the *English* Tongue began" (sig. *B1r); he is the "Father of English Poetry" (sig. *B2r); "*Chaucer* follow'd Nature every where; but was never so bold to go beyond her" (sig. *B2r); "For Mankind is ever the same, and nothing lost out of Nature . . ." (sig. *C1v). Chaucer's rudeness finds a place here as well, although unlike earlier Chaucerians, Dryden attributes this to Chaucer himself, rather than to his times. As for his verse, "There is the rude Sweetness of a *Scotch* Tune in it, which is natural and pleasing, though not perfect" (sig. *B2v); "*Chaucer*, I confess, is a rough Diamond, and must first be polish'd, e'er he shines. I deny not likewise, that, living in our early Days of Poetry, he writes not always of a piece" (sig. *C2r).

Chaucer's own texts are fragmented, as are those of Ovid. The Wife of Bath's prologue was considered by Dryden "too licentious" to be translated (sig. *D1v), and her tale appears as an autonomous narrative. But the fragmentation of the individual author implied here is an illusion; for the very basis of that fragmentation is the authorial personality, in this case, Dryden's own: "I found I had a Soul congenial to his Own" (sig. *C2v).

That "soul" is a unifying force; for it is around the coherent, unifying soul that diverse dress and habits can appear. So words themselves adorn the thoughts which are their essences (sig. *C2v); and so Chaucer, essentially "a perpetual Fountain of good Sense," can be excused for material faults, since he only "indulg'd himself in the Luxury of Writing" (sig. *B2r). The concept of a unifying character is central to Dryden's essay. And behind this, due in part to Dryden's seemingly casual reliance on Aristotle, is the notion of a dramatic or theatrical character.

Characters themselves are analyzed in terms of a theory of decorum: "The Matter and Manner of their Tales, and of their Telling are so suited to their different Educations, Humours, and Callings, that each of them would be improper in any other mouth" (sig. *C1v).[9] The notion of a specifically dramatic decorum is never far away, even when Dryden claims to be writing in purely essayistic fashion: "Besides, the Nature of a Preface is rambling; never wholly out of the Way, nor in it. This I have learn'd from the Practice of honest *Montaign*, and return at my pleasure to Ovid and Chaucer" (sig. *B1v). As Dryden makes this remark, he is in the midst of a discussion organized around the first four of the six parts of tragedy as defined by Aristotle: he has been discussing their fables and inventions (sig. *B1r-v). And thus a discussion of *ethos* must follow:

Both of them [Ovid and Chaucer] understood the Manners; under which Name I comprehend the Passions, and, in a larger Sense, the Descriptions of Persons, and their very Habits: For an Example, I see *Baucis* and *Philemon* as perfectly before me, as if some ancient painter had drawn them. (sig. *B1v)

The next categories are again Aristotelian: "The Thoughts and Words remain to be consider'd, in the Comparison of the two Poets" (sig. *B1v).

Dryden thus considers the *Canterbury Tales* from first to last as a drama, one cut off from the large, unreadable, gothic book in which (for Dryden) those tales had appeared. The central organizing principle becomes one of character: first the fictional characters and finally the character of the author himself.[10] Just as a character's words and actions are reflections of the fictional character itself, so is the fictional character in turn a reflection of the author who creates that character:

The very *Heroes* shew their Authors: *Achilles* is hot, impatient, revengeful, *Impiger, iracundus, inexorabilis, acer, &c.* Aeneas patient, considerate, careful of his People, and merciful to his Enemies; ever submissive to the Will of Heaven, *quo fata trahunt retrahuntque, sequamur.* (sig. B1r)[11]

Kittredge

It was for Kittredge to turn Dryden's remarks into a theory of the *Canterbury Tales* text itself. In all of *Chaucer and his Poetry*, Dryden is the only Chaucerian (unless Lydgate counts as one) to be quoted.[12] There is, as far as I can see, only one other reference to a Chaucerian by name (Lounsbury at p. 22). Certainly the lecture format of this book was largely responsible for this. But Chaucerian scholars are (somewhat paradoxically) far more influenced by the chatty Kittredge of this often reprinted book than by the more scholarly Kittredge of his articles. Every university library I have been in has one or more copies; and these are often extensively marked up, either by once-future Chaucerians, or by students of past ones.

Kittredge cites, from Dryden, the cliches of past Chaucerians—that Chaucer lived in rude times, that he was a polisher of language. Kittredge modifies these familiar cliches in such a way that they refer, not to Chaucer, but to Dryden himself: in imagining that Chaucer's obsolete language was rude, Dryden "knew better; but he was arguing Chaucer's case before a prejudiced jury" (18); in his translations, Dryden understood Chaucer's concision, but in his own expansiveness "could not free himself from the prejudices of his age" (19). The "rude times in which he lived" seem here to be Dryden's.

Having introduced Dryden in the introduction, Kittredge quotes him extensively in the first section of the *Canterbury Tales* chapters. The reason Dryden compares Ovid and Chaucer is not because of the stories themselves, but because of the characters contained both in the tales and in their telling:

> This, no doubt, is what Dryden had in mind when he wrote, comparing Chaucer with Ovid: "Both of them understood the manners, under which name I comprehend the passions. . . . I see Baucis and Philemon as perfectly before me, as if some ancient painter had drawn them; and all the pilgrims in the Canterbury Tales . . . as distinctly as if I had supped with them at the Tabard in Southwark; yet even there too the figures in Chaucer are much more lively, and set in a better light." (153-54)

It is here that Kittredge introduces the notion of the *Canterbury Tales* as a Human Comedy; and the notion is attributed specifically to Dryden:

> I am much deceived if Dryden is not here treading on the verge of the proposition that the *Canterbury Tales* is, to all intents and purposes, a Human Comedy. . . . The Canterbury Pilgrimage is, whether Dryden meant it or not, a Human Comedy, and the Knight and the Miller and the Pardoner and the Wife of Bath and the rest are the *dramatis personae*. (154-55)

The tales themselves Kittredge characterizes as "merely long speeches expressing, directly or indirectly, the characters of the several persons" (155). Dryden does not use the word *comedy* to refer to the *Canterbury Tales*; but the Dryden that most Chaucerians know—a Dryden delivered by Kittredge—means what Kittredge claims he means. And before proceeding to the most obvious and legitimate heirs to this tradition (R. M. Lumiansky and Donaldson), I note as an amusing extreme of the Kittredgean Dryden a recent misreading of the word *comedy*—a word put into Dryden's mouth by Kittredge and now subject to what threatens to be a traditional misconstrual. It should not be necessary to point out in a literary-historical context that the word *comedy* in classical English criticism is only indirectly related to such terms as *stand-up comic,* and that *comedians* are only recently people who deliver one-liners. Nor should it be necessary to note that the combination of terms *humor* and *comedy* in classical English criticism does not refer to such jokers and one-linerers. But the recent anthology by Jean E. Jost proves otherwise.[13] "The concept of comedy is complicated and multi-faceted. The most obvious definition and recognizable characteristic, no doubt includes the humorous and funny" (Introduction, [understandably anonymous], xxxiv). The referent of Dryden and Kittredge's language, or its metaphoric basis if you will, is consistently missed in this anthology, even when authorities are cited who specifically address this relation.[14]

Yet whether comedy in Kittredge's sense is correctly taken to mean drama or carelessly associated with anything that happens to claim to be funny, whether humor is taken to be a defining attribute of a character or as just another-thing-that-is-funny, the effect of this line of criticism initiated by Dryden and Kittredge is the same: it acts to "unbook" Chaucer—to remove individual tales from their context (in a collection!) and to place them in new context: to Dryden, a different collection, to Kittredge, a psychological or novelistic one. Chaucer is taken out of the book and placed on the stage. A metaphoric stage to be sure, but one where the notion of character dominates. Chaucer is placed there in part because of a virtually inaccessible book. To Dryden, the book was obsolete. For Kittredge's original listeners, of course, the book is in their hands, I assume in the form of the Globe Chaucer by Pollard. But for the most extensive of Kittredge's audience—his readers—the book is at best an abstraction. Somewhat surprisingly, there is not a single reference in Kittredge's lectures to the particular text he uses.[15]

Donaldson and the Chaucerian Persona

In the mid-1950s, two major revivals of Kittredge took place. One was due to Lumiansky, whose *Of Sondry Folk* systematized in a scholarly monograph what Kittredge had outlined in 1915. A second, more interesting and finally more influential variant was Donaldson's "Chaucer the Pilgrim" (1954).[16] As in the Kittredge lectures, here we have a major Chaucerian scholar adopting, now almost perversely, a lecture style in which normal scholarly apparatus is ignored. This is all the more surprising for Donaldson, since the article appeared first in the organ of mainstream American literary scholarship, *PMLA*. At the heart of this article is a Chaucer who is now divorced from the book in which he had been constituted.

Donaldson's article has clear and explicit roots in Kittredge's objection to the notion of a naive Chaucer: "a naïf Collector of Customs would be a paradoxical monster," one of the few critical references in Donaldson's article (2; quoting Kittredge, *Chaucer and his Poetry*, 45). I have discussed this article elsewhere, and I am here interested only in particular aspects of its reception, particularly the reception of Donaldson's "multiple Chaucers" and the dramatic implications of his argument.

On the first issue, as Howard claimed in 1976: "Everyone knows about Chaucer the Man and Chaucer the Pilgrim" (Howard, *Idea of the Canterbury Tales*, 279). Chaucerian narrative presumably distinguishes a narrator from a poet, and this sort of thing, even by the mid-1970s, was old hat. This double Chaucer is well-documented both by Donaldson's followers and by his detractors. Ruggiers in 1965 spoke of multiple Chaucers, but implied that these were reducible to two:

> If one 'Geffrey' is on pilgrimage as one of the 'wel nyne and twenty,' it should be possible to define the range of his double nature, no less than that of his fellows on the journey. The doubleness on which I have chosen to focus here is that of the man, conscious of the salvation of his soul, and that of the artist, concerned about the integrity of his poem.[17]

A decade later, Howard also assumed a double Chaucer:

> All the double truths we must accept are present in this passage: the voice addressing us is at once the poet who writes and the narrator who rehearses; the narrator is at once teller and performer; the pilgrims are at once being performed and performing; we the audience are at once hearers and readers; and we are free to choose but told how to react.
> (Howard, *Idea of the Canterbury Tales*, 83)

Donaldson's second point concerned drama. Again, the reference is obviously Kittredge and his notion of a Human Comedy. The essence of Chaucerian irony, to Donaldson, was to be found in the oral nature of Chaucer's text—the supposed fact that Chaucer read this text before his audience, acting out the role of the naive narrator who was distinct from Chaucer himself. Donaldson could hardly be more explicit about the dramatic implications of his argument:

> [T]he several Chaucers must have inhabited one body, and in that sense the fictional first person is no fiction at all. . . . One can imagine also the delight of the audience which heard the Prologue read in this way, and which was aware of the similarities and dissimilarities between Chaucer, the man before them, and Chaucer the pilgrim, both of whom they could see with simultaneous vision. ("Chaucer the Pilgrim," 10)

I have never completely understood Donaldson here, and I think he (and perhaps Kittredge as well) are somewhat disingenuous in their arguments. If the historical records are accurate, and Chaucer managed to maintain his political position through the late fourteenth century, his feigned naiveté, however obvious to twentieth-century Chaucerians, must, according to these same critics, have been an extremely effective façade. But how then could it have been a part of his performed text, causing all kinds of mirth and admiration? In other words, did his immediate audience recognize him for the shrewd calculating charlatan he was, even though that charlatanry could cost them nothing? And did his employers, forking over their daily tuns of wine, fail to see this? That a literary critic should be able to penetrate the façade of naiveté that remained opaque to his political employers seems itself a myth of literary criticism, a projection of the modern university where those who pay (donors and students) can hardly claim to understand Chaucer as well as those who share his jokes and sometimes reap the profits (professors).

The notion of a performing Chaucer is of a book-less Chaucer. But in the original objections to this notion of a Chaucerian performance, the book is also cast as the villain. In 1940, Bertrand H. Bronson had already raised many issues found in Donaldson's article; in 1960, perhaps after a careful scrutiny of Donaldson's footnotes revealed the absence of any reference to his 1940 work, Bronson's rhetoric was much stronger. The problem he saw with the arguments by Kittredge and Donaldson was that they ignored the implications of drama and once again relied on the book. Their "schizoid notion of two Chaucers" was simply wrong. "It is wrong because it was conceived in and of the world of printed books."[18] Donaldson's article, couched in the language of drama and relying on the notion of a dramatic performance of the text by Chaucer the historical being, is, according to Bronson, indebted rather to readings of a bookish Swift (a reference that itself comes from Donaldson's own text; (see Donaldson, "Chaucer the Pilgrim," 8).

The early reception of Donaldson is peculiar in many ways. First, Donaldson's own myth of originality seems to have been accepted, as the notion of multiple Chaucers becomes Donaldson's rather than Kittredge's. Second, the word *persona* becomes Donaldson's, even though nowhere in that article does Donaldson explicitly identify Chaucer the Pilgrim with the *persona*. The word *persona* appears only twice in the essay; it is defined simply as a "device" ("Chaucer the Pilgrim," 9). Third, the notion that Donaldson defines two Chaucers is itself erroneous. Donaldson never limits his discussion to two Chaucers. Rather, he speaks of three Chaucers: Chaucer the Man, Chaucer the Poet, and Chaucer the Pilgrim. "But the third entity, Chaucer the poet, operates in a realm which is above and subsumes those in which Chaucer the man and Chaucer the pilgrim have their being" ("Chaucer the Pilgrim," 11). And finally, the notion of drama, essential to Donaldson's argument, is used to refute it. In each step, a "more dramatic than thou" attitude is adopted—an attitude still found among Chaucerians, although blessedly one largely confined to conference workshops.[19]

Recent Voices I: Voice as Poet

The various denunciations and restatements of Donaldson thus have proceeded in two lines and are easily visible in contemporary Chaucer criticism. The first is New-Critical. The second involves the word *dramatic*. Both arguments retextualize what is called voice or drama and in so doing reintroduce into their arguments the very targets of polemic.

The most familiar denunciation of Donaldson is a New-Critical one, although its proponents might not wish to be so classified. I am thinking here of work by Jesse M. Gellrich, H. Marshall Leicester, Jr., Barbara Nolan, and to some extent work by Robert Jordan and Lee Patterson. These studies attempt to circumvent the mark of the Dryden-Kittredge drama—the notion of character—and to do so by recovering the notion of text through voice.[20] Leicester's often-cited 1980 article had as an apparent target Howard, and is a good example of the power of Donaldson's assumptions. Leicester argued, through use of the word *voice*, against Donaldson's multiple narrators. Voices do not require speakers ("Art of Impersonation," 217). In 1990, Leicester claimed to go beyond this position, moving from self, to society, to institutions. His guiding claim is the same—that speakers' texts are forms of activity (activity that is socially determined) rather than indications of particular psychological selves.[21] Yet in both cases, as soon as Leicester rids us of the notion of speaker, he reintroduces it in a new *persona*. In 1980, Leicester's multiple narrators yielded to a single narrator—Kittredge's "great poet" (*Chaucer and his Poetry*, 5) in a New-Critical guise:

> The proper method is to ascribe the entire narration in all its details to a *single* speaker . . . and to use it as evidence in constructing that speaker's consciousness, keeping the question of the speaker's "identity" open until the analysis is complete. ("Art of Impersonation," 218)

This conclusion, interestingly enough, is identical to that of Bronson in 1960: "We are not involved in *them* [his characters] but in *him* [Chaucer]. For he is almost the only figure in his 'drama' who is fully realized psychologically, and who truly matters to us" (Bronson, *In Search of Chaucer*, 67).

Leicester in 1980 and again in 1990 is trapped within the conventions of an author-centered article or monograph. Chaucer must take credit for the object-texts Leicester studies: anything less than that leads to the charge of "irrelevance," "digressiveness," etc. Whether Chaucer actually wrote these texts is not a major concern: it is rather an assumption required by the genre in which Leicester writes. And so must Leicester take credit for his own words (themselves the result of particular discourses within twentieth-century English Departments).

There are many recent variants of Leicester's argument. Jordan, for example, speaks of Chaucer's "conspicuous textuality" and follows

Leicester in describing the Pardoner as a "textual construct" (Jordan, *Poetics*, 122, 136). Compare Leicester, *Disenchanted Self*, 63, where the Pardoner is characterized as representing "not an entity but an activity." But text leads to poet. "The ultimate and only subject is the absent poet. He alone enjoys privileged status outside the language of the text" (Jordan, *Poetics*, 148). Patterson makes similar claims:

> This [that the author is not mere subject and the text object] may seem a perverse assumption to apply to a writer who typically conceals himself within a mask, whether of a narratorial persona or a pilgrim. But it is not Chaucer's personality that is the object of scrutiny: it is Chaucer's self-constitution as a poet. (*Chaucer and the Subject of History*, 45)

Nolan argues that Chaucer in the General Prologue projects "three major authorial voices." Nolan claims not to be interested in the personality of Chaucer, but rather in "the problem of being a poet in the late fourteenth century" ("A Poet Ther Was," 155).[22] But I don't see the difference between Leicester's "speaker's consciousness" and Nolan's "essentially rhetorical, ideologically oriented character of the poet's presentation" (ibid, 155).

Whether we call the new focus the author, the *persona*, the person, we see only a displacement. As long as the Dryden-Kittredge Human Comedy informs these arguments, there remains a psychological center for aspects of the text: either an author or, in a common technique of New Criticism, a personified text, with its appropriate, Drydenesque dress.[23]

Recent Voices II: Drama as Text

I have already noted some of the peculiarities in the reception of the Kittredgean notion of comedy. But efforts to revive his dramatic metaphors remain. As in the above studies, these attempt to do away with the psychological entity of character; equally important, they do away with the material entity of the book in favor of the abstract one of the text and in favor of historical events (real and imagined) of performance.

In C. David Benson's definition (introduced somewhat portentously as "beyond dramatic theory"), drama is textual (as it had been of course for both Dryden and Kittredge, and even Lumiansky). But

Benson tries to strip it of characters as well. "Our attention should not be on the man, but on his words" (44)—the same conclusion reached by any number of New Critics.[24] The words "play" and "theatricality" also have achieved a vogue among Chaucerians. The most interesting of these is John Ganim, who in 1990, attempted to strip from this language the heritage of Kittredge and Donaldson.[25] But the major force of Kittredge-Donaldson line of criticism in American Chaucerianism remains in Ganim, who privileges interpretative readings as well as tensions and conflicts "neither synthesized nor neutralized nor transcended" (*Chaucerian Theatricality*, 16). The apparent rejection of Kittredge and Donaldson leads to a classical New-Critical position. Ganim's rejection of tradition is his embracing of it.

The defining characteristic of this entire tradition is the metaphoric use of dramatic language—metaphors that have the effect of denigrating the bookish foundation to which they inevitably return. If we take the dramatic language literally, we can move beyond Kittredge's pure metaphor, and even beyond Donaldson's notion of a performing Chaucer, to a different Chaucer—one less bound to our academic traditions, but also a culmination of those traditions. We simply dramatize in fact, rather than in theory, by giving over Chaucer's text (however defined) to some paid hack actor to read in public. This has dangerous implications for Chaucerians; the best Middle English accent would be simply the most intelligible one, and the best Chaucerian would be the best actor (Gr. *hypocrites*). An authorial death with these implications is a significant one: an *actor* takes over from the *auctor*, who no longer requires a professional critic or historian as an interpreter. This line of criticism might move far from the book of Chaucer, which would function only as a libretto or promptbook. But if such critical experiments seem valuable and interesting in theory, they have not proved to be so in fact. Studies actually published in this vein have exhibited only the most banal forms of critical self-indulgence.[26]

H. Lüdeke and the Drama of the Chaucerian Critic

Henri Lüdeke's 1928 monograph *Die Funktionen des Erzählers in Chaucers epischer Dichtung* is a work of mainstream Chaucer studies, complete with dutiful references to Kittredge.[27] It is a work in which we find the twentieth-century history of the Chaucerian *persona* and its relation to the Chaucerian enacted. Although little noted in English Chaucer studies, it was cited by Muscatine in 1957, and shows the lineage of modern American Chaucer studies in its identification of a critical tradition leading directly to German romanticism.[28]

Lüdeke begins by distinguishing the *Verfasser* (the implied author) from the *Erzähler* (narrator) found only in epics (or narratives). The early chapters provide what to readers with the benefit of Ernst Robert Curtius's 1948 work might seem a familiar and pedestrian catalogue of various authorial *topoi*. The most interesting chapter is chap. 4: "Gestaltende Funktionen des Erzählers" (*Funktionen*, 77ff.). Here, Lüdeke speaks of the "sovereign freedom" which the writer (*Dichter*) enjoys in the role of narrator, and the "absolute separation" of this role from the bonds of the everyday in which the writer lives (*Funktionen*, 77). This separation is a variant of romantic irony ("dieser 'ironische' Abstand des Erzählers von seinem Stoff," ibid, 78) and is underscored by oral delivery. The doubleness of teller and tale leads to the impression of an independent teller who develops "a unique personality" (97), a personality distinct from the personality of the reading poet.

In this suggestive chapter, Lüdeke describes the artist's use of the notion of a narrator as a liberation from the constraints of artistic materials. But what we see at the same time is a critic's attempted self-liberation from the constraints of the academic monograph.

> Whenever his teller presents himself as a pedant, Chaucer is usually playing a joke, and through his irony shows only more clearly his independence of the narrative. . . . From the standpoint of the role of the teller, such irony is one among many means to free the person of the teller from his representation and to validate that teller apart from it. (*Funktionen*, 110)

The sovereignty of the *Erzähler* over narrative (115) is Chaucer's own sovereignty over the *Erzähler*.

Lüdeke's monograph thus enacts the critical story that is its subject matter. Each figure (including Lüdeke) is struggling for personal autonomy.

> The narrator is not established only as a mouthpiece, a link between the writer and the tale; rather, he gains also his own characteristics,

that have their very reason for being in him. It is the logical conclusion of the various degrees of participation in the narration. The narrator presents his own opinions—opinions that reveal not the elements of the narrative but rather himself. He confers on himself characteristics that reveal his own being. (*Funktionen*, 119)

Chaucer finds his own freedom in (or sacrifices it for) the freedom of his narrator (*Funktionen*, 144-46). But how can a narrator enjoy freedom? The narrator's freedom is a critical hypothesis that could only be realized in a real critic.

It is no wonder Muscatine recognizes a kindred spirit here. And in his later work, *Poetry and Crisis* (and even to some extent in his 1963 history of Chaucer editions), we can see Muscatine struggling to free himself from the insularity and textual constraints of the very New Criticism he popularized.[29]

The period from the late nineteenth century to 1940 saw the production of many critical editions of Chaucer—those from the Chaucer Society, Skeat, Robinson, Manly-Rickert. By contrast, during the hey-day of New Criticism, the production of new editions was relatively casual—a seeming paradox in view of the New Critics' emphasis on the text. Yet in the past two decades, when New Criticism has come into question, when voice is privileged over text, we find a renewed, almost obsessive interest in the production of Chaucerian texts and editions.[30] The Chaucerian book thus appears to regain its vitality within a tradition often intent on its condemnation.

Chapter 9

PROBLEMS OF EVIDENCE IN MODERN CHAUCER EDITIONS

The two sections of the following chapter deal with what Chaucer scholars of the past century understand as evidence, particularly the evidence regarding such central questions as canon and authorship. The first section considers the authority that is embedded in the book; the subject is the amusing and overly violent reaction of W. W. Skeat to an earlier single-volume Chaucer edition published by Moxon. Why would a convenient and serviceable edition such as this have caused Skeat any concern? The second deals with the variable definitions of internal and external evidence and how those definitions are brought to bear on traditional topics such as canon and authorship; a central figure here is again Skeat. The history of these terms since Skeat, however, reveals a growing institutional uncertainty over what constitutes the Chaucerian's proper objects of study.

I. SKEAT'S MOXON AND THE AUTHORITY OF THE BOOK

One of the most popular Chaucer editions of the nineteenth century was *The Poetical Works of Geoffrey Chaucer* (London: Edward Moxon, 1843). In terms of its text, the edition is less interesting than competing nineteenth-century editions and it has received little attention in the past century. In terms of format, however, the Moxon Chaucer is exceptional. The Chalmers edition (1810), the Chiswick Chaucer (1822), the Aldine edition (1845 and later reprints), the Bell edition (1854-56), and the edition by Wright (1847-51)—all are small-format, multi-volume sets, and all are part of a series (Wright's is part of the Percy Society publications). Moxon's edition is the only single-volume complete works of Chaucer until Skeat's *Student Edition* of 1895 and Alfred G. Pollard's Globe edition of 1898, and it is the first single-volume complete works of Chaucer in a format smaller than folio.[1]

In her description of this book, Hammond notes that "the misleading title page of this edition is corrected by Skeat, I:30 note" (*Manual*, 139); and it is the nature and the ferocity of Skeat's correction that I will examine here. Hammond's reference here is to volume 1 of Skeat's first Chaucer edition (1894), where Skeat had spoken of the "disastrous results" of Moxon's title page. Skeat had written a more heated note in 1889 (*Notes and Queries*), responding to an unidentified "F.N." who had criticized him for his admission a year earlier that he had once been deceived by this page. Skeat's language was, as Hammond notes, "very strong"; the Moxon title page, according to Skeat, is "a cruel fraud and ought to brand the perpetrator of it with indelible disgrace."[2] Why this reaction (or overreaction) to the Moxon edition? What is the cruel fraud? And what are the disasters? First, let us consider that pernicious title page itself (fig. 19). The last line of the title page of Moxon states in capitals: "BY THOMAS TYRWHITT." There is potentially an ambiguity here, since it is not clear what Tyrwhitt is being credited with: the "Essay on Language and Versification," the "Introductory Discourse," the notes and glossary, or the entire book, containing text and commentary. In his comment of 1894, quoted in full below, Skeat calls the period preceding the final line a "slight unintentional misprint" that produces a "startling" change in sense: Tyrwhitt is credited on this title page with the entire editorial project.

Whether many readers other than Skeat read the title page with this care can't be known. But what Skeat calls a misprint is clearly no misprint at all. It is simply the convention by which Moxon printed his title pages, as the "List of Books recently published by Edward Moxon" included in the edition makes clear:

BEAUMONT AND FLETCHER. | WITH AN INTRODUCTION. | By George Darley. In two volumes, 8vo, with Portraits and vignettes, price 32s. cloth.
SHAKESPEARE. | WITH REMARKS ON HIS LIFE AND WRITINGS. | By Thomas Campell.
BEN JONSON. | WITH A MEMOIR. | By William Gifford.

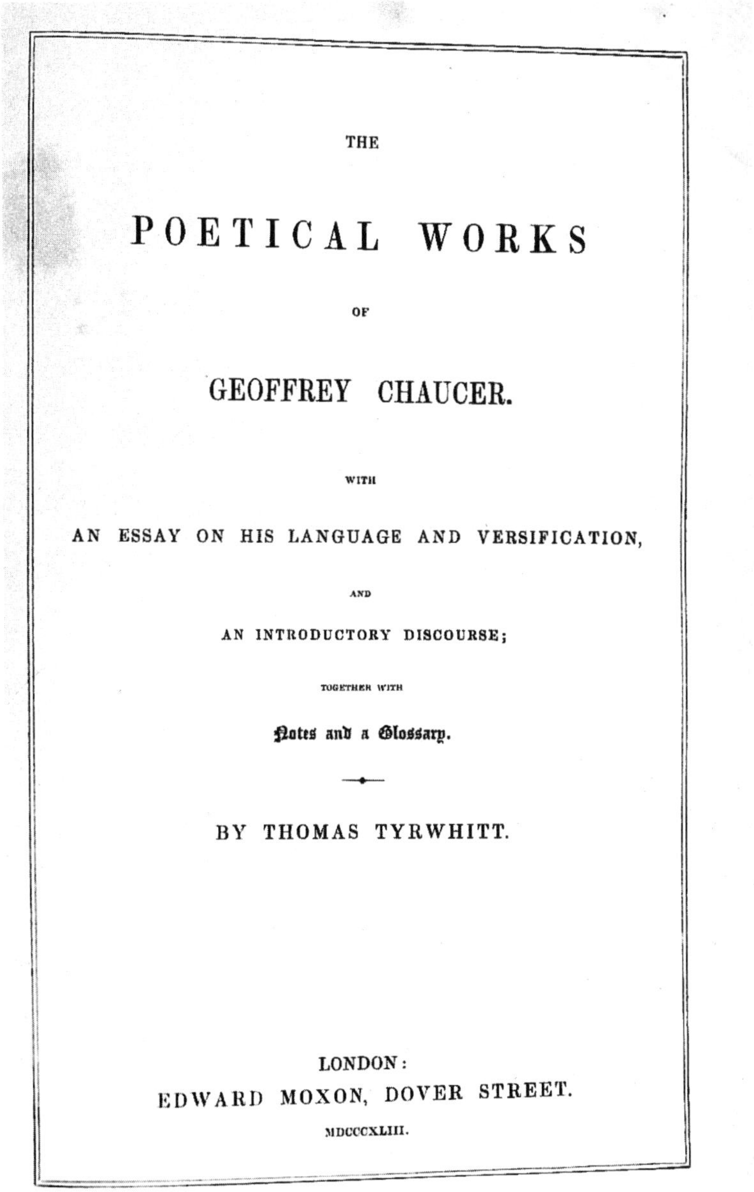

THE

POETICAL WORKS

OF

GEOFFREY CHAUCER.

WITH

AN ESSAY ON HIS LANGUAGE AND VERSIFICATION,

AND

AN INTRODUCTORY DISCOURSE;

TOGETHER WITH

Notes and a Glossary.

———◆———

BY THOMAS TYRWHITT.

LONDON:

EDWARD MOXON, DOVER STREET.

MDCCCXLIII.

Figure 19. Chaucer, *Poetical Works* (London, 1843).

MASSINGER AND FORD. | WITH AN INTRODUCTION. | By Hartley Coleridge.
WYCHERLEY, CONGREVE, VANBRUGH, AND FARQUHAR. | With BIOGRAPHICAL AND CRITICAL NOTICES | By LEIGH HUNT.

Among the many books listed in these pages, only one entry includes the name of the editor: "SHELLEY'S POETICAL WORKS. | Edited by MRS. SHELLEY." In Moxon's productions, editors were invisible. The author was presented directly to the reader, with the sole mediation that of the writer of introductory material. Only in the case where the editor's mediation might be thought to have value in and of itself (perhaps marketing value) was that editor named (thus "Mrs. Shelley").

Skeat, of course, could not be expected to know the conventions of Moxon publications of the early 1840s. Nor am I certain that these conventions still applied to the 1850s when the Chaucer was reprinted. But he should have known the general history of Chaucer editing well enough not to have been misled by a publisher's blurb.

Tyrwhitt's edition of Chaucer came out in 1774-78 in five volumes, and was reprinted in two large quarto volumes in 1798. In the early nineteenth century, it was often pirated and reprinted. Yet the only text that Tyrwhitt had edited and that was included in these editions was the *Canterbury Tales*. Later Chaucer editors who used Tyrwhitt's text, as Moxon, simply filled out their editions with texts from the Urry edition or from blackletter editions. Generally, this was openly acknowledged in introductions, as in the Anderson edition of 1793 or the Chiswick Chaucer of 1822.[3] It is this second context—the process of canon-formation that takes place in the often accidental history of the book—that seems responsible for the intensity of Skeat's anger.

Skeat referred to the title page of the Moxon edition in a series of notes: first in his 1888 edition of Chaucer's *Minor Poems*; next in a *Notes and Queries* article responding to an early note in the same journal by "F.N.," and finally and most extensively in his multi-volume Chaucer edition of 1894. In his 1888 edition of Chaucer's *Minor Poems*, Skeat states the following:

> I have often made use of a handy edition with the following title-page:
> 'The Poetical Works of Geoffrey Chaucer with an Essay on his Language and Versification and an Introductory Discourse together with Notes

and a Glossary, By Thomas Tyrwhitt. London, Edward Moxon, Dover Street, 1855.' I cannot but think that this title-page may have misled others, as it for a long time misled myself. As a fact, Tyrwhitt never edited anything beyond the Canterbury Tales, though he has left us some useful notes upon the Minor Poems, and his Glossary covers the whole ground. The Minor Poems in this edition are merely reprinted from the black-letter editions. (Minor Poems, xviii, n. 2)[4]

This is a perfectly reasonable note. Skeat treats the Moxon edition for what it is: a "handy edition." Apparently, Skeat is using a reprint, although the 1843 edition is even today as common as dirt. It "may have misled others" as it once did Skeat; but Chaucerians such as Skeat had better things to do than to research the date of the edition or even to seek other copies.

What galled Skeat was the suggestion by F.N. that no reasonable person could be misled by this title page. Skeat's rejoinder in *Notes and Queries* (1889) is tart, and begins with the proper bibliographical data for Moxon (a book he has probably never seen):

With reference to the remark by F.N., that 'it is strange that any one pretending to know anything about Chaucer should ever have been deceived by the dishonest title-page' of Moxon's 'Chaucer,' I have to confess, with shame and confusion, that it was really some time before the truth about this title-page dawned upon me.

Skeat then quotes the passage (above) from his *Minor Poems* edition and continues:

I beg leave to say that I have probably instructed more pupils in Chaucer than any one else; and I never yet met with any one who had not, at the outset, been deceived. To every young student the revelation has been a surprise.

The reason is simple, viz., that the unsophisticated reader is quite ready to believe that what a respectable publisher says is really true; though I can quite understand that booksellers and publishers may know better. I think this title-page is a cruel fraud, and ought to brand the perpetrator of it with indelible disgrace. I would fain hope that cases of equal enormity are uncommon.

If few of the world's enormities were of this magnitude, the Rev. Skeat would have been a happy man; and had his note ended here, it would have to be considered ironic. However, Skeat continues, noting the "artful way in which the 'Minor Poems' are introduced between portions of Trywhitt's genuine work" and the precise details that make "the deception . . . so clever and so complete."

I know of nowhere else in Skeat's major work where he cites the opinions of his students as evidence. The ordinary reader does not care much who edits a text; scholars can find out; and beginning students are not in a position to pronounce upon such things. Any student who knows enough about the history of English literature to care who edited Chaucer should know also that Tyrwhitt edited only the *Canterbury Tales.*

Skeat returned to the problem twice more in his *Complete Works of Chaucer,* once in a note in vol. 1 (p. 30) noting the error on the title page, and again in an extensive discussion in vol. 5 (p. xiii):

> In 1845 [*sic*] appeared the edition in which modern critics, till quite recently, put all their trust; and no student will ever understand what is really meant by 'the canon of Chaucer's Works' until he examines this edition with something like common care. It bears this remarkable title: —'The Poetical Works of Geoffrey Chaucer. With an Essay on his Language and Versification, and an Introductory Discourse; together with Notes and a Glossary. By Thomas Tyrwhitt. London: Edward Moxon, Dover Street, 1855.'[5] In this title, which must be most carefully scanned, there is one very slight unintentional misprint, which alters its whole character. The stop after the word 'Glossary' should have been a comma only. The difference in sense is something startling. The title-page was meant to convey that the volume contains, (1) The Poetical Works of Geoffrey Chaucer (comprising Tyrwhitt's text of the Canterbury Tales, *the remaining poems being anonymously re-edited*); and that it *also* contains, (2) an Essay, a Discourse, Notes, and a Glossary, all by Thomas Tyrwhitt. Such are the facts; and such would have been the (possible) sense of the title-page, if the comma after 'Glossary' had not been misprinted as a full stop. But as the title actually appears, even serious students have fallen into the error of supposing that Tyrwhitt edited these Poetical Works; an error of the first magnitude, which has produced disastrous results. . . . It is here that we find no less than twenty-five poems *which he never edited* reprinted (inexactly) from the old black-letter editions or from Chalmers. (*Works of Chaucer,* 5:xiii-xiv)

Skeat's tone is subdued here, but he makes up for that with the extent of his comment. Obviously, his reading of the title page is simply in error. It contradicts the history of Chaucer editing, and, as I have shown, it contradicts as well the conventions of the Moxon title pages themselves. Then what are the disastrous results Skeat speaks of here, if not simply (1) the fact of his own deception and (2) the fact that he has been transmitting false information about Chaucer to his students at the same time that he has been promoted as the leading Chaucerian in the world? Skeat's own justification is as follows:

> This somewhat tedious account is absolutely necessary, every word of it, in order to enable the reader to understand what has always been meant (since 1845) by critics who talk about some works as being 'attributed to Chaucer.'

And finally:

> The chief value of the anonymous edition in 1845 is, that it gave practical expression to Tyrwhitt's views. The later editions by Bell and Morris were, in some respects, retrogressive. (*Works of Chaucer,* 5: xv)

These statements are quite contradictory. The first implies that the Moxon edition, which is the very embodiment of Tyrwhitt's views on the canon, is the basis for what a critical statement "attributed to Chaucer" means. The second, however, shows that Tyrwhitt's views on the canon were largely ignored by editions competing with that of Moxon. In fact, understanding the nuances of Moxon's title page will give the student no handle whatsoever on what critics mean by "attributed to Chaucer" in the mid-century. But it might give the student some idea of what Skeat means by "attributed to Chaucer."

The myth of the modernity of Tyrwhitt is one I have already noted. This myth was created very early, and found expression in many of the earliest editions that pirated his text. What Moxon did, as Skeat rightly notes, was to give "practical expression" to Tyrwhitt's views on the canon in the context of an edition. The modernity of Tyrwhitt, however, had little to do with the text. In terms of the text itself, Urry's edition was far more radical and broke more radically with past tradition. Where Tyrwhitt's edition was pivotal in Chaucer studies was in the matter of canon, proceeding not by the process of addition

(Thynne's "diuers workes neuer in print before") but rather on the basis of exclusion. And the reason Skeat has such a stake in this tradition is that it is his own edition that gives scholarly support to Tyrwhitt's views—where Moxon gave material support.[6]

Tyrwhitt claimed to base his canonical decisions on style (internal evidence), and rejected all those poems added to the canon in Stow's edition of 1561. Tyrwhitt's list of works in turn became a "received canon"—analogous to the *textus receptus* that was the basis for the editing of individual works in earlier editions.[7] And it is this canon (Tyrwhitt's) to which Skeat applies his rules for internal evidence. Not only does Tyrwhitt provide the list of works, he also defines what would constitute evidence, as well as the texts that serve as the foundation for evidence (the *Ormulum*).[8]

Skeat describes his scholarship and his argument here in a characteristic manner:

> After the preceding somewhat tedious, but necessary discussion of the contents of the black-letter and other editions (in many of which poems were as recklessly attributed to Chaucer as medieval proverbs used to be to King Solomon), it is some relief to turn to the manuscripts, which usually afford much better texts, and are altogether more trustworthy. (*Minor Poems*, xxxvii)

Skeat's self-proclaimed love of manuscript detail was, as Hammond points out, somewhat disingenuous. In fact, Skeat's descriptions of these manuscripts, to which he claims to turn with relief, are perfunctory. Why is this the case?

To Skeat, the difference between the book and the text remained paramount. The text was an abstraction embodied in manuscripts. Thus he speaks of Furnivall's work, whose "excellent, careful, and exact reproduction in print of the various MSS. leaves nothing to be desired." But as was the case with the tradition of editors before him, the question of authorship was one determined by the book. To the early eighteenth-century Chaucerians, the omission of the Retraction from the folio editions was tantamount to its being a monkish forgery. The book provided the decisive evidence. Skeat has gone no further. The foundation of canon is the printed book, not the manuscript. And what constitutes legitimate internal evidence is that which supports the external evidence of this book.

Skeat was surely aware that his own ideas of canon had been *previously embodied in a book*. And a cheap one at that. The cruel fraud and disastrous results Skeat imagines are that the physical nature of the book has proved to be a more important factor in later theories of canon (his own) than the actual arguments (Tyrwhitt's) that that physical book only embodies. Despite Skeat's protests, Moxon's Chaucer was Chaucer's Book—and such a thing not only contained evidence but in and of itself constituted evidence.

II. THE NOTION OF EXTERNAL EVIDENCE IN CHAUCER STUDIES

Throughout this study, I have made reference to the question of evidence, external and internal. In most cases, the distinction is one of convenience, distinguishing an object of study from statements or material that bear on that object. But these terms are far from stable, and the history of these terms in relation to Chaucer studies shows an uncertainty that itself reflects the modern uncertainty of what might be called the Chaucerian object of study. Is it Chaucer? The material embodiment of Chaucer (his book)? Or the cultural institutions in which this is embedded?

In his notes to the *Romaunt of the Rose* in the *Riverside Chaucer,* Alfred David takes up the authorship question and claims the following:

> Lydgate's testimony could well be based entirely on what is said in [*Legend of Good Women*], but the God of Love's remarks cannot be taken as external evidence about Chaucer's translation since he is a character in a work of fiction, and Chaucer's defense of himself is part of the fictional situation. (*Riverside Chaucer,* 1103)

What interests me here is not the question of authorship per se, but rather David's definition of the evidence that bears on that question (by implication, the definition promoted by this edition) and the way that definition has arisen in Chaucer studies in the late twentieth century.

David is referring to the *Legend of Good Women,* lines 331-31. (The same lines appear in Gg; I quote the text called the F text):

Thou maist yt nat denye,
For in pleyn text, withouten nede of glose,
Thou has translated the Romaunce of the Rose,
That is an heresye ayeins my lawe,
And makest wise folk fro me withdrawe
                    (lines 327-31)

The *Legend* claims that Chaucer translated the *Roman de la Rose*.
However obvious or preposterous that claim, it concerns the text in
question, and ought to have the status as external evidence.

So far, my case is stronger than David's. Yet even to make this simple argument, I have had to personify the poem and use the name
Chaucer to refer to what post-Dryden critics might call his various *personae* or voices. I assume these are the kinds of logical shenanigans
that David is quite rightly guarding against. Yet why the appeal to
types of evidence? How does the particular warning issued by David
(a legitimate warning directed to the authorship question) have bearing on the history within Chaucer studies and medieval studies of the
terms "external" and "internal" evidence?

My purpose is not to argue that David is wrong here. However
eccentric, this variation of a common distinction between evidence
types is itself a product of the opposition charted in the preceding
chapter between modern Chaucerian critics in the tradition of
Dryden and Kittredge, and the more conservative (now more radical)
historians, textual scholars, and codicologists who find themselves in
an uneasy alliance opposing them.

No absolute definition of the distinction between internal and
external evidence is possible, and its meaning and utility depend on
the application. The terms are used in a variety of fields, and the very
invocation of the distinction often identifies the principal objects of
concern.[9] In literary studies, the distinction has been traditionally
used in questions of authorship and canon; by identifying internal
and external evidence, a scholar defines the first as evidence contained within the object text itself, the second as any evidence apart
from the abstract, reproducible text. Examples are easy to find;[10] and
the terms have a long history in medieval English studies. In the area
of drama (an area where questions of authorship are largely inapplicable) the distinction has even been embodied in an institutional
product—the Records of Early English Drama series.[11] What I am

concerned with in the discussion below is how a distinction between types of evidence becomes one between the relative value of types of evidence. For modern Chaucerians, the most important revaluation of these terms occurred in discussion associated with New Criticism.

New-Critical Variants

The traditional distinction was revived at mid-century in America under the influence of New Criticism. There are two marks of what I will call the New-Critical use of the distinction. First, the distinction is applied primarily to matters of interpretation. And second, these two categories of evidence are defined in terms of value. What was originally a distinction between types of evidence became suddenly a distinction between qualities of evidence. Even when the problem was the classical one of historical attribution, a New-Critical influence created a new understanding (often a polemical one) of the matter at issue.

A popular anthology of the 1960s was *Evidence for Authorship*, edited by David V. Erdman and Ephim G. Fogel—an anthology originating in an English Institute conference of 1958 that dealt with the problem of internal evidence and attribution. The subject under discussion is attribution. Erdman found precedent in a statement by Coleridge:

> Any work which claims to be held authentic must have had witnesses, and competent witnesses; this is external evidence. Or it may be its own competent witness; this is called internal evidence.[12]

The claim of Coleridgean origins is itself New-Critical (even Chaucerians preceded Coleridge in their use of the distinction). But the most markedly New-Critical stance was that adopted by Arthur Sherbo to lead off the conference. Sherbo asked, somewhat mischievously I think: "How many would quarrel with the statement that internal evidence deals with essentials while external evidence deals with accidentals?"[13] In one sense, Sherbo seemed right. In classical terms, the difference between essence and accident is almost precisely that suggested by the literary-critical use of internal and external. But the implication of value in this neutral philosophical language got the better of his colleagues—none was willing to accept the denigration of external evidence that the analogy entailed.

The papers in this conference are clearly products of American
New Criticism, and under its influence, the application of the terms
internal/external and intrinsic/extrinsic was widened, with the implication that one type of evidence (however defined or applied) was
superior to the other. In 1991, Cleanth Brooks himself offered a summary:

> In 1947 I published a book called *The Well Wrought Urn.* I wrote it to
> show how much intrinsic evidence—what is provided by a careful con-
> sideration of the internal structure of the poem, the use of diction, fig-
> urative language, tonal shadings, rhythms, and so forth—could reveal
> about what actually got 'said' in the poem as compared with extrinsic
> evidence, as that provided by the author's life, the historical epoch in
> which he lived, and so on.
>
> Thus, in *The Well Wrought Urn* I deliberately played down the rele-
> vance of extrinsic evidence. Of course, it would be difficult to eliminate
> it in its entirety. If you do no more than name the author or date his
> poem, you have begun to furnish extrinsic evidence. Actually, *The Well
> Wrought Urn* contains more than a modicum of such evidence, but I
> had been so restrained in my use of it as to make many a reader believe
> that I had dismissed all extrinsic evidence. To such readers, I seemed to
> be saying that the dominant graduate school program for literature was
> irrelevant to literary criticism.[14]

Brooks claims to have derived the terms from René Wellek and
Austin Warren, *Theory of Literature* (1942), and their distinction
between intrinsic and extrinsic approaches to literature itself.[15] The
distinction used by Wellek and Warren is slightly different in that the
object of their study is an institution, not a particular work (see, for
example, the chapter headings under "Extrinsic Approaches":
Literature and Biography; Literature and Psychology; Literature and
Society; Literature and Ideas; Literature and the Other Arts).[16] Yet
Brooks is undoubtedly correct here in conflating these distinctions.
The terms internal/external—what one might call sleepy philological
terms dealing with sleepy philological problems (who wrote what)—
suddenly acquired new meaning by being defined as central to the
entire institution of literary study. What could once distinguish a
rhyme from a colophon was now a distinction between two apparently
diametrically opposed methodologies and could also apply to what

was becoming the basic activity of the American academic literary scholar—the interpretation of a text. Within the context of the institution of New Criticism (however accurately or speciously defined), examples would be easy to multiply.[17]

Since the presumed demise of New Criticism, the application of the distinction to questions of literary interpretation has become rare. The difference between a critic of the 1980s and one of the 1960s can be seen in the one reference to evidence types I found searching the MLA CD-ROM Bibliography—an article by Richard Levin on Shakespeare's *Lucrece*. Levin's article is directed against a classic position of New Criticism, and criticizes what Levin sees as overly high value placed on internal evidence. Scholars have recently interpreted Shakespeare's attitude toward Lucrece as ambivalent, as if his praise of her were not to be taken at face value. What external evidence is there that this ironic reading is correct? Levin simply gathers contemporary allusions to Lucrece and all those in other Shakespeare's plays. They are unanimous. The external evidence is that "all statements about Lucrece contemporary with Shakespeare praise her." From this, one must conclude: (1) that *Lucrece* is not ironic; or (2) that it is uniquely ironic; or (3) that all statements in praise of Lucrece are ironic.[18]

Classification of Evidence in Chaucer and Langland Studies:
Thomas Tyrwhitt and W. W. Skeat

The earliest use of the distinction in Chaucer studies I find is in Tyrwhitt's "Introductory Discourse to the Canterbury Tales" (vol. 4 of his 1774 edition). Tyrwhitt's distinction between internal and external evidence is explicit. It is the same distinction seen later in Coleridge and refers to what Coleridge would call "competent witnesses":

> After the *Tale of the Manciple* the common Editions, since 1542, place what is called *the Plowmans Tale;* but, as I cannot understand that there is the least ground of evidence, either external or internal, for believing it to be a work of Chaucer's, I have not admitted it into this Edition. (*Canterbury Tales*, 4:184-86)

Tyrwhitt's note 32 reads:

We can therefore only judge of it by the internal evidence, and upon
that I have no scruple to declare my own opinion, that it has not the
least resemblance to Chaucer's manner, either of writing or thinking.
(*Canterbury Tales*, 4: 184-85 n. 32)

Tyrwhitt referred again to such distinctions in his final volume of
1778, containing both his Glossary and his brief "An Account of the
Works of Chaucer to which this Glossary is Adapted and of those
other Pieces which have been improperly intermixed with his in the
Editions":

> *The Court of Love* was first printed among the additions made to
> Chaucer's works by John Stowe, in the Edition of 1561. One might rea-
> sonably have expected to find it mentioned in L.G.W. *loc. cit.* but
> notwithstanding the want of that testimony in its favour, I am induced
> by the internal evidence to consider it as one of Chaucer's genuine
> productions. I have never heard of any MS. of this poem. (*Canterbury
> Tales*, 5: viii)

On the *Parlement of Foules*, Tyrwhitt notes that it is mentioned by
Chaucer in *Legend of Good Women*, line 419, then adds: "I have found
no reason to retract the suspicion there intimated as to the date of
this poem; nor can I confirm it by any external evidence" (5: ix-x).
And in his final paragraph:

> The anonymous compositions, which have been from time to time
> added to Chaucer's in the severall Editt. seem to have been received,
> for the most part, without any external evidence whatever, and in
> direct contradiction to the strongest internal evidence. Of this sort are
> "*The Plowman's tale*," first printed in 1542 . . . "*The Story of Gamelyn*" and
> "*The Continuation of the Canterbury Tales*," first printed in Mr. Urry's edi-
> tion; "*Jack Upland*" first produced by Mr. Speght in 1602. I have
> declared my suspicion, [in the Gloss. v. *Origenes.*] that the "*Lamentation
> of Marie Magdalene*" was not written by Chaucer; and I am still clearer
> that the "*Assemblee of ladies*," "*A Praise of Women*," and the "*Remedie of
> love*," ought not to be imputed to him. It would be a waste of time to sift
> accurately the heap of rubbish, which was added, by John Stowe, to the
> Edit. of 1561. (5:xxii)

To Tyrwhitt, the inclusion of a piece within a certain manuscript or collection might constitute a type of external evidence, but it is clear from this paragraph that negligible external evidence is tantamount to no external evidence. The fact that the Tale of Gamelyn, for example, appears in a number of manuscripts of the *Canterbury Tales* constitutes no evidence—no more than the fact that a poem might be included among the "heap of rubbish" added by Stow.

Tyrwhitt's language seems to be followed directly by Anderson (1793), in one of the many early reprints of Tyrwhitt's text:

> The present edition of the Canterbury Tales is from Tyrwhitt's incomparable edition. The Plowman's Tale, Tale of Gamelyn, Adventure, and Merchant's Second Tale, omitted by Tyrwhitt, have been retained, though all evidence, internal and external, is against the supposition of their being the production of Chaucer.[19]

The same language appears in the opening sentence to the introduction of Bell's edition of 1854.[20] It was subsequently adopted by Skeat, in part through the influence of Henry Bradshaw, and from there, found its way into the vocabulary of a number of Chaucerians.[21]

Skeat's edition of the *Kingis Quair* in 1884 initiated serious discussion of such evidence types. The paramount question was one of authorship. Skeat invokes the distinction in his edition, although he does not develop it systematically:

> The question of the authorship of Peebles to the Play has been discussed almost ad nauseam; but the internal evidence ought to decide the matter. There is no resemblance to the Kingis Quair discoverable; whereas there is a marked dissimilarity in the tone, in the vocabulary, and in the metre.[22]

In returning to this question in 1896, J. L. T. Brown extends the implications of Skeat's discussion and organizes his entire argument around these terms with chapter headings "The External Evidence" (5-20) and "The Internal Evidence" (21-60). Brown, with reference to Skeat, defines these as follows: "Historical or External evidence, viz. (a) the Bodleian Manuscript, and (b) the testimony of Historians; and, second, with the Internal evidence, viz. (a) the Dialect, (b) the Court of Love, and (c) the Autobiography in the poem."[23]

Skeat uses the terminology in relation to Chaucer in his discussion of *Romaunt of the Rose* and the Minor Poems in the first volume of his 1894 edition; as in the *Kingis Quair*, the primary scholarly concern here is one of attribution.

> A critical examination of the internal evidence at once shews that by far the larger part of 'the translation' cannot possibly be Chaucer's; for the language of it contradicts most of his habits, and presents peculiarities such as we never find in his genuine poems. (*Works of Chaucer*, 1:2)

The section includes discussion of dialect, rimes, and the relation of three fragments, gaps in text. On pp. 11ff., Skeat heads sec. 21 "The External Evidence":

> In what has preceded, we have drawn our conclusions from the most helpful form of evidence—the internal evidence. It remains to look at the external form of the poem, and to enquire how it has come down to us. (ibid, 1:11)

The parallel is not perfect here, since the opposition seems to be between "form of evidence" (internal evidence) and "external form of the poem." The word *form* is thus somewhat misleading, for by external form, Skeat means the material embodiment of the poem in Thynne's edition and the Glasgow manuscript. To Skeat, Chaucer's book is itself the external evidence for Chaucer's text and, in the case of the *Romaunt*, resemblances between forms of these books is also a matter of external evidence.

Skeat returns to the question of internal and external evidence in his section on the Minor Poems (*Works*, 1:20ff.): "We will therefore consider, in the first place, the external evidence generally." Skeat's headings include the following: Testimony of Chaucer regarding his works; Lydgate's list of Chaucer's Poems; Testimony of John Shirley; Testimony of Scribes of the MSS.; Testimony of Caxton; Early Editions of Chaucer's Works; Table of Contents of Stowe's Edition (1561); Additions by John Stowe; Discussion of the Poems in Part I. of Ed. 1561; Poems added in Speght's Editions of 1598 and 1602; Pieces added in Morris's Edition, 1866; Description of the MSS; Remarks on Some of the MSS. Cambridge MSS; Oxford MSS. Discussion of individual poems follows. As far as I can determine, there is no discussion of internal evidence whatsoever.

Skeat's use of the distinction here is related to two different problems. Although the central question is Chaucer attribution generally, the attribution of the *Romaunt* involves a second problem: the relation of the parts to each other—and here nearly all is a matter of internal evidence. There is no comparable problem (to Skeat) for the other minor poems. Thus here the bulk of evidence fits easily into the category of external evidence; for Skeat, the inclusion of a poem within a manuscript containing other Chaucer items was external evidence (Tyrwhitt had placed less weight on such evidence).

Skeat seems to have become more concerned with the problem in his later work, and his *Chaucer Canon* of 1900 uses the terminology often. Here, he acknowledges his reliance on Tyrwhitt, citing Tyrwhitt's Introductory Discourse, sec. xl (on the Plowman's Tale—the passage from Tyrwhitt quoted above). It is interesting that in this work Skeat repeatedly speaks of internal evidence (rhyme and grammar) as "tests" of external evidence, even though more properly it is this internal evidence that determines questions of canon. All such arguments, however, proceed from a foundation of incontrovertible "external evidence," without which there can be no conclusions to be drawn from internal evidence. See for example his introductory statements: when we understand peculiarities of the *Canterbury Tales*, "it becomes an easy matter to see whether such peculiarities are equally well represented in such poems as are known to be his *from external evidence*" (*Chaucer Canon*, 2-3).

When Brusendorff takes up the same problem in 1925, his categories come directly from Skeat. Brusendorff distinguishes External from Internal Evidence, with further subcategories direct and indirect, absolute and relative. Direct external evidence (Brusendorff's "Ia") consists of notes of authorship due to the poet himself or added by the early scribes; indirect external evidence ("Ib") consists of allusions to the poet's works made by himself or his contemporaries. Brusendorff's category IIa is "absolute internal evidence," which consists of such matters as Chaucer's allusion to his office work in the *House of Fame*, line 652; "relative internal evidence" (IIb) consists of "verbal reminiscences of his known writings" and other parallels (*Chaucer Tradition*, 50ff.).

Brusendorff differs from the main tradition of Chaucerians in claiming "no trust can be put in those tests which lately have been in so much favour: compliance with certain grammatical and metrical rules, deduced from a number of the author's known works" (50-51). He also denies (arguing against Skeat) that the inclusion of a work in a manuscript with other Chaucer pieces is a conclusive test of authorship, although such a "test" is of course "based on external evidence" (51).[24]

George Kane and Piers Plowman

The notion of external and internal evidence in medieval studies might have languished in Brusendorff, but for two factors: first, of course, the promotion of intrinsic approaches to literary interpretation by New Criticism. And second, the revival of classical uses of the term by George Kane in relation to *Piers Plowman.*

The *Piers Plowman* controversy arose during the late nineteenth century and involved not only authorship, but also the relation of the three versions defined by Skeat. The parallels with Chaucer's *Romaunt of the Rose* are obvious. In either case, internal evidence could consist of parallels within the three object texts. That is, internal evidence for authorship of B might well include the words of A. I am somewhat surprised to find that although Skeat used the distinction frequently in his work on Chaucer, this seems not to be the case in his work on Langland.[25] Nor do the essays printed in the EETS volume responding to Skeat's edition use the terminology.[26]

Kane's *Piers Plowman: The Evidence for Authorship* (1965) discusses in detail the problems of applying this terminology to *Piers* and specifically addresses the grey area between external and internal. His initial definitions are as follows:

> In a case of ascription the character of external evidence is that it exists absolutely, in some determinable way independent of the text which it concerns. It may be bad; its accuracy can be questioned, but its existence cannot. It is a kind of physical fact. Internal evidence, by contrast, is a critical postulate. It has a contingent character, depending for its existence on being identified as such by someone, and for its validity upon, first, the correctness of the identification, and second, the quality of the reasoning applied to it. (5)[27]

Kane denies the superiority of external evidence (6), and a good part of his most influential work on *Piers* has focused entirely on internal evidence (for example, the difference between scribal and authorial usage).

After discussing these two kinds of evidence, he raises the question of "Signatures" (chap. IV pp. 52ff.), the apparent naming of the poet within the poem:

> If this assessment is to be complete it must include one further consideration: the implications of the fact that the first-person narrator in each of the three versions of *Piers Plowman* is called Will. This consideration has not been admitted to preceding discussions because the occurrences of the name are by my classification neither external evidence of authorship, since the name is an element of the text, nor internal evidence, since its existence is absolute, not contingent on identification by the critical faculty. (52)

The grey area that Kane defines here is that area on which his concentration is focused—that area of the text that names the author. The evidence cannot be classified here without circularity. If the word *Will refers to* an authorial person (whether accurately or inaccurately), it is external evidence; if it does not, it is internal evidence. And although Kane is very careful to distinguish the classification of evidence from the evaluation of evidence (see p. 6), in this case, to classify that evidence is the same as evaluating it.

Conclusion

To editors, the question of authorship retains the centrality it had to Tyrwhitt and Skeat, even though the understanding of authorship has changed radically in literary-critical work that is not editorial.[28] And the inevitable reaction against the New-Critical value placed on what could be described as "internal" has made itself felt. In 1951, Robert A. Pratt could oppose the "internal evidence" that determined the Chaucerian order of tales to the less authoritative "manuscript evidence" that determined only the post-Chaucerian 1400 order. Thirty years later, in a 1982 article dealing with the same subject, Larry D. Benson catches Furnivall associating "internal evidence, probability, or presumption," and claims by contrast to base his own work on the more solid evidence of manuscripts.[29]

It is this climate that leads to David's analysis of evidence in the *Romaunt of the Rose*. David's argument is *ex post facto*. Questions of canon for the *Riverside Chaucer* were settled (or finessed) in large part through the authority of the earlier Robinson edition. The validity of whatever evidence an individual editor would find was thus predetermined, since decisions of canonicity had effectively been made before individual editors were called upon to write their textual notes: the *Romaunt of the Rose* would indeed appear in the edition, and that was that. But David implies that the only legitimate support for such a decision is what can be called external evidence:

> The God of Love's remarks cannot be taken as external evidence about Chaucer's translation since he is a character in a work of fiction, and Chaucer's defense of himself is part of the fictional situation. (*Riverside Chaucer*, 1103)

As this survey has shown, this is at odds with earlier definitions of types of evidence. A reference to a particular poem, whether by Chaucer or by one of his contemporaries, is what Brusendorff calls "direct external evidence." David's statement reflects the intellectual background of Chaucerians, especially American Chaucerians, in the mid century—Chaucerians who had been reminded over and over again that Chaucer the Man and Chaucer the Persona were two different entities. The New-Critical emphasis on the internal or the intrinsic here finds a late variant. Sherbo's challenge to his colleagues of the 1960s had been to make the internal and the intrinsic all-important. Here, the internal, itself disparaged, becomes at the same time greatly extended in scope, encompassing and making suspect all texts that imply speakers who are potentially unreliable, ironic, fictional. The anti-scholarly tradition of Dryden here controls the editorial one.

With the reaction against a somewhat caricatured version of New Criticism (denounced even by Brooks) comes the promotion of the historical, however defined. To late twentieth-century Chaucerians, the external or historical has value in and of itself; evidence must "deserve the name" of external evidence, as if inaccurate historical evidence and misleading external evidence were somehow more valuable than the abstract text that ultimately holds all this evidence together.

Chapter 10

SCRIBES AS CRITICS

T he following chapter concerns recent variants on the question of the status of the Chaucer editor in relation to Chaucer criticism generally. The thesis I examine below arises from editorial work: that early Chaucer readers, in particular early scribes, are early Chaucer critics; that is, the earliest editor (and by extension the latest one) not only provides a foundation for criticism but provides as well a central example of it. The thesis has been presented in a series of important articles by Paul Strohm, Lee Patterson, B. A. Windeatt, and Seth Lerer.[1] The studies arise from the tradition of Dryden discussed in an earlier chapter and represent an extension of criticism into the fields of bibliography and textual criticism.

These studies challenge the distinction assumed by turn-of-century Chaucerians, that "criticism" and "scholarship" are two different things. Lerer has articulated this challenge directly:

Chaucer *criticism* may seem, to both the participant and the observer, almost willfully omnivorous. Approaches grounded in feminism, psychoanalysis, sociology, and deconstruction have produced a range of readings that align the poet with the broader interest of the modern academy. On the other hand, Chaucer *scholarship* seems to be moving away from the sheer amassment of historical, biographical, and literary information on the poet and his sources and toward an appreciation of the contexts that disseminated his texts.[2]

The distinction is, in Lerer's opinion, on the verge of collapse.

The articles under discussion here, arguing that editorial activities and critical ones are indistinguishable, are in one sense symptomatic of the recent blurring of once accepted distinctions. What distinguishes these articles is the projection of this modern sense of collapse onto the earliest period of Chaucer studies—the period of the constitution of both the Chaucerian text and the Chaucerian book. The modern Chaucerian crisis is written here by imagining an analog in the earliest history of Chaucerianism.

A sense of crisis is a recurring element in the history of editing, one of the more famous examples in English literary history being Samuel Johnson's defense in his Preface to Shakespeare of what Pope had characterized as the "dull duty of the editor."[3] But the nature of the crisis has changed. For Johnson, the fundamental relation in editing was that between the great poet and his successors in a belletristic tradition—successors such as Pope, Rowe, Warburton, and himself; scribes and printers were largely irrelevant. In classical textual criticism, scribes are mere obstacles; they are studied only to determine the nature of the thing that stands between author and editor.[4] To a classicist, the rehabilitation of these scribes would make little sense: why would anyone be much interested in how a Byzantine professional "read" a classical poet? For medievalists, the possibility of a near contemporary (the scribe) involved in the production of a text is a different matter. By providing us with the first transcription of Chaucer, they provide as well a "reading" in the broad use of the word accepted by literary critics. Scribes are thus the "first critics" of Chaucer. The textual-critical notion of a scribal *usus scribendi*, developed in part to define an authorial *usus* by denigrating the *usus* of scribes, has paradoxically given birth to those same scribes as artistic and critical personalities.

There is, of course, something paradoxical about this attitude. On the one hand, scribes are rescued from their early modern detractors, real and imagined. But on the other hand, they are rescued only at the cost of becoming proto-critics. They thus take their place (deservedly) at the head of a critical tradition—we depend on them absolutely. But they have lost all power over that tradition. Whereas the earlier detractors of scribes acknowledged, with some annoyance, the power of scribes to alter the nature of literature, here, their activity is infantilized: rather than professional scribes, they are amateur critics.

Principles of Inclusion: The Corpus and Canon of Early Criticism

The studies in question here depend on an assumption concerning a field of evidence. Evidence of fifteenth-century readings has been available since the 1598 and 1602 editions of Chaucer began to include the comments of Lydgate, Hoccleve, and Douglas. But recent studies claim to be uncovering material of a different quality altogether—not allusions to Chaucer, but criticism of Chaucer such as has been hitherto unknown and unavailable.

These readings are presumably not to be found in the extensive references in Spurgeon's *Five Hundred Years of Chaucer Criticism and Allusion*. The studies in question do not present themselves as followers of Spurgeon, and they do not characterize their evidence as mere addenda to her materials. The newly-discovered early criticism of Chaucer must, by definition, be un-Spurgeon-like and thus depends for its definition on the occasionally fluid bounds of this early twentieth-century work. The exclusion is defined variously:

> References by fellow poets to Chaucer as "flour of eloquence" and "rose of rethoris" and so on remind us that he wrote in a larger poetical and rhetorical tradition, but are finally disappointing in their impersonality. [ref. to Spurgeon] But if responses from Chaucer's immediate audience are wanting, the personal responses of one member of Chaucer's early fifteenth century reading public do survive, known to textual critics but few others. (Strohm, "Jean of Angoulême," 69)

The references Strohm finds are "personal" rather than rhetorical and impersonal (what is presumably found in Spurgeon). Patterson's version of this definition is similar: Spurgeon provides a mere catalog of contemporary "likes and dislikes" (a phrase I think taken from Strohm); Patterson's newly-discovered critic, by contrast, provides a view of the "medieval experience":

> Although we can infer what qualities his fellow poets admired in his work, the common reader was content to leave at most a list of likes and dislikes. [ref. to Spurgeon and Strohm]. In this paper I shall offer evidence from a little known and perhaps unlikely source that can help us to reconstruct something like the medieval experience of reading *Troilus and Criseyde*. (Patterson, "Ambiguity and Interpretation," 297)

To Windeatt, these readers "respond to the difficulties of the text" and to its texture (120); those in Spurgeon's catalogue do not:

> While there is no doubt of the appreciation of Chaucer as poet among his contemporaries and immediate successors, the precise nature of that appreciation is more elusive because of the terms used by the poet's admirers . . . [ref. to Skeat and Strohm]. But such comments give an overall impression of Chaucer's poetic rather than analyzing what was so special in it for his contemporaries. Their comments summarize, but do not aim to recreate a detailed response to the texture of the poetry which would approximate more to modern critical analysis. Yet the behaviour of the scribes in mss of Chaucer's works offers line-by-line a contemporary response to his poetry. (Windeatt, "Scribes," 121)[5]

These comments occur on the opening pages of each article. References to Spurgeon are usually explicit. Each begins with an act of exclusion: the materials gathered by Spurgeon are inadequate, although the reasons for that inadequacy are variously defined. They are "impersonal," or consist only of "likes and dislikes," or are the opinions of a mere "common reader."

The rejection of Spurgeon, however, is a rejection of an oversimplified perception of Spurgeon's work. Spurgeon's work is presented here, in its very rejection, as an unanalyzed or naively analyzed corpus of material. There is no critique in any of these articles of the history of criticism contained in Spurgeon's volume 1, nor of the organizing categories of her index. Ignoring this leaves a chronological listing of Chaucer citations, perhaps in the genre of Spurgeon's Renaissance work on imagery, or in the genre of source and analogue criticism.

The import of these articles, then, is quite different from the apparent working assumption: the stated concern is to present newly-discovered criticism; the actual concern is to re-analyze known material under more recent critical assumptions, particularly the assumption that each piece of evidence, whether a poem, statement, or historical document, can be subjected to close reading. The implied rejection of Spurgeon leads to a new reception, both of Chaucerianism and of Spurgeon. Rather than simply adding to the (incomplete) corpus of material in Spurgeon, the articles here promote a program that would allow a re-reading of each of the citations in Spurgeon, thus increasing the field of early criticism in direct proportion to the increase in the production of modern contemporary criticism.

Chaucerian Critics, Ancient and Modern: Paul Strohm and Jean of Angoulême

Strohm's 1971 article is one of the first of many important contributions he has made on Chaucer's fourteenth- and fifteenth-century audiences. It is a brief note, with no pretensions to presenting new material; the material from Jean, although not included in Spurgeon, had been readily available since 1940 in Manly-Rickert's *Text of the Canterbury Tales*, 1:402-4.[6] The article is a seminal one, and the assumptions that underlie it are more easily visible than the modified versions of those same assumptions found in more recent work.

In the case of the Paris manuscript, both scribe and owner are known and named. Strohm assumes (as later scholars in this tradition might not) that the details of the manuscript are attributable to its owner, Jean, whose opinions the scribe (known as Duxworth) reproduces precisely (70). Strohm judges Jean's comments in terms of modern criticism, as his conclusions make clear:

> Examination of Jean's and Shirley's literary views is not a particularly heartening experience for the modern reader. Their approach to Chaucer is broadly inclusive with respect to questions of quality, educational value, good sense, and the like, but . . . not necessarily tolerant. The response is more likely to be expressed in flat value judgments of individual tales than in appreciation of structure, of characterization, of stylistic texture, of tone, and other qualities for which modern readers value Chaucer's works. . . . in Jean we do glimpse the tone and style of some of the more limited and dogmatic members of Chaucer's immediate audience. (76)

Obviously Strohm would not characterize either Jean or Shirley in this fashion today. But the critical language by which Jean is made to be limited is revealing: "structure, characterization, stylistic texture, tone"—the language of various schools of American criticism (New Criticism, Chicago School Criticism). Strohm assumes, then, that Jean d'Angoulême and John Shirley were doing roughly what he and his colleagues in 1971 were doing; they simply were not doing it as well.

Strohm's discussion of Jean has several foci: Strohm's own evaluation of authorial *compilatio*, Jean's selection of tales, particular phrases
that appear in Jean's brief comments. In the heading to the Man of
Law's Prologue, Jean refers to Chaucer as a "compiler": "sequntur
[sic] verba Galfridi Chauncers compilatoris libri." And Strohm
assumes a general, universal understanding of this term, citing
Chaucer's own *Astrolabe*: "I n'am but a lewd compilator of olde
astrologiens" (quoted 71). Strohm sees the reference in *Astrolabe* as a
note of humility; a commentator using this epithet would use it in the
same denigrating sense: "anyone calling Chaucer a compilator probably valued him more for his organizational abilities than his originality" (71). According to Strohm, we are therefore surprised to see this
word used by Chaucer's admirer-critic, Jean d'Angoulême.

Strohm is judging the term *compiler* before the now classic discussions of the medieval concept of *compilatio* by Parkes and by Minnis.[7]
Therefore, his pretended surprise at seeing this word is itself a function of the negative value the word has in classical aesthetics: how
could this early critic of Chaucer fail to recognize in Chaucer the
qualities that make him great by mid-twentieth-century aesthetics?

The Paris manuscript does not contain all of the *Canterbury Tales*
and Strohm interprets these omissions as acts of criticism, criticism
with which he himself is rarely in sympathy. Strohm expresses baffle-
ment over "the silent omission of Melibee and the Parson's Tale" (71
n.2). On the omission of the Tale of Sir Thopas, Strohm is more
direct: "The silent omission of ll. 1920-2018 of Sir Thopas probably
argues an inability to respond to the kind of humor the tale offers"
(72).

The first of these issues is not worth Strohm's pretended surprise,
since the only critical faculty required to classify Melibee and the
Parson's Tale together is the ability to distinguish verse from prose:
the same judgment was responsible for the misbinding of the
Hengwrt manuscript, where these two tales appear together at the
end.[8] The aesthetic speculations of Strohm (71-72) are superfluous,
since the reasons for the omissions are material or economic.[9]

The most detailed readings Strohm offers are on the three occur-
rences of the phrases "valde bona" and "valde absurda": (1) Jean's
comments on the Knight's Tale are partially quoted in Manly-Rickert.
Strohm quotes the sentence in its entirety: "explicit fabula militis
valde bona." (2) Strohm says both the Squire's Tale and the Canon

Yeoman's Tale are labeled "extremely absurd." The complete quotations are as follows: "Ista fabula est valde absurda in terminis et ideo ad presens pretermittatur nec ulterius de ea procedatur"; "maior pars istius fabule est pretermissa usque huc quia termini sunt valde absurdi." (3) On the Monk's Tale: "non plus de ista fabula quia est valde dolorosa."

Strohm's own reading of these fragments is not accurate.[10] In the second above, Jean does not label these tales themselves "absurd," but rather the *termini*. Strohm states: "*Termini* might refer to the larger outlines or forms of the two tales, but probably refers to the words or terms in which they are written" (72-73). Clearly the latter is the case; only the critical and aesthetic assumptions Strohm accepts in 1971 could cast doubt on this.

The discussions of the more problematic terms "valde absurda" and "valde dolorosa" follow the same pattern:

> Jean probably admired the KNT for its avoidances of extremes of solace and sentence. Remember his rejection of Sir Thopas, a literary parody without evident sentence. Remember too, his apparent agreement with the Knight and Harry Bailly that the Monk's Tale deserved to lose its audience for offering sentence without solace. (74)

Strohm then confirms his reading by interpreting Shirley in the same way. Shirley defines Chaucer's audience as one that reads for pleasure: "to kepe yow frome ydelnesse and slowthe in escheuing other folies" (75).

To Strohm, critical comments must be put within the categories *sentence* and *solas*. The correct Chaucer reader is one who does not read strictly for *sentence* (the Robertsonian reader), or for *solas* (a New-Critical reader), but one who reads as a neo-Aristotelian moderate.[11]

But the terms will not state this in any convincing fashion: the Tale of Sir Thopas and the Canon Yeoman's Tale are criticized not, as Strohm suggests, because they are absurd, and not because their structure is inadequate (a rhetorical suggestion Strohm makes only to reject), but rather because the language is meaningless and difficult: there are too many absurd terms. The Monk's Tale is rejected by Jean simply because it is sad. These are not related in any systematic way, nor opposed in the way that tales of *sentence* and *solas* are opposed in discussions of Chaucer in the 1960s.

Strohm, then, is trying to interpret these comments (these extra-Spurgeon comments) within a neo-Aristotelian framework, one consistent with some of the statements by critics associated with the Chicago School. Jean's comments and apparent decisions must have to do with such things as form, structure, tone. If they do not say anything of substance about these topics, they are critically inferior to those that do.

Strohm recreates the mentality of this early annotator in his own image. While pretending to promote these comments and to give them a measure of critical respect, Strohm actually has a different agenda altogether. His own critical prejudices of the late 1960s are being given a pedigree, legitimized by discovering ancestors. Somewhat paradoxically, these ancestors are then criticized for being less noble than ourselves.

Lee Patterson and an Anonymous Fifteenth-Century Reader

Patterson's 1979 article, "Ambiguity and Interpretation," begins with Strohm's assumption: that most medieval readers (meaning those fifteenth-century readers catalogued in Spurgeon) knew only what they liked and what they did not: "the common reader was content to leave at most a list of likes and dislikes" (297). Patterson's contribution, although potentially no more than an addition to Spurgeon, offers the evidence enabling us "to reconstruct something like the medieval experience of reading *Troilus and Criseyde*" (279). This is found in a fifteenth-century treatise for women (a translation of a thirteenth-century treatise by David of Augsburg), in which "a key stanza" of *Troilus* is quoted.[12] The *Troilus* stanza is the second of three quotations, cited under "the first token of carnal love." The first is from Ovid's *Ars amatoria* (with Middle English translation): "Nescio quid sit amor nec amoris cencio nodum / Set scio si quis amat nescit habere modum." The third is a French proverb: "De chiens, d'oseaux, d'armes, d'amours, / Pour un plaisir quatre dolours." The *Troilus* stanza is a stanza from "Canticus Troili," cited in this manuscript as by "another poet": "If no love is O god what fele I so . . ." (*Troilus and Criseyde* 1:400-6) ("Ambiguity and Interpretation," 304). The question Patterson asks is "What were the interpretive assumptions and procedures that led our fifteenth-century reader to apply David of Augsburg's account of the seven tokens of love to *Troilus and*

Criseyde?" (307) To answer this question, Patterson first analyzes David of Augsburg's theories of love, ending with the notion that medieval readers are engaged in modern critical enterprises:

> This decoding is also a demystification. If medieval readers were capable of anticipating the modern taste for ambiguity, the temptation of misreading was also available to them. And as we might expect of a culture of the book, medieval misprision brought with it little but anxiety. (309)

He then explains why this was applied to Chaucer:

> [The compiler] saw *Troilus and Criseyde* as in fact fulfilling the monastic requirements for spiritual reading. . . . By applying David's categories to Chaucer's poem the compiler allows the reader to moralize *Troilus and Criseyde*, to render it not only harmless but instructive. (322-323)
>
> By locating *Troilus and Criseyde* within the context of *amor* and *amicitia* our fifteenth-century reader provides a stance from which disambiguating can take place. But as his affectionate regard for the poem's texture shows, the inevitable reductions of interpretation are not for him a primary task. They are instead a potentiality that enables a fully responsive reading. (329)

Patterson is clearly talking about his own reading of *Troilus and Criseyde* and his own procedures (the use of medieval categories as a "potentiality" to enable a "fully responsive reading"). For the appearance of the stanza within the treatise constitutes not a reading, but a non-reading. The most important piece of information for the entire discussion is left in a footnote: the Chaucer stanza circulated independently of the poem.[13] Consistently (and I assume intentionally) Patterson reverses the question. The compiler does not locate *Troilus and Criseyde* within a new context, nor are David of Augsburg's categories applied to the poem. Rather, the compiler locates these categories within a decontextualized stanza, one that could be from any medieval poem.[14]

The appearance of a passage in a florilegium and the subsequent use of that passage does not imply an interpretation of the original context. Quite the reverse. The original context is specifically denied, as the appearance of this passage independent of *Troilus* in other manuscripts proves (the passage from Ovid, by contrast, is fully attributed to both poet and work). And as long as a passage occurs without reference to its context, it cannot even be said to provide directives for a reading of that context. There is no context to be read.

Patterson is quite right that this work does offer a fifteenth-century response to *Troilus and Criseyde* and an important one. But the nature of that response may be different from the one he implies: *Troilus and Criseyde* was viewed, as this evidence proves, as a convenient source of moral *flores*. Patterson's argument requires an appeal to a very uncommon reader, one different from the "common readers" whose responses Patterson sees as catalogued in Spurgeon. But this uncommon reader seems unlikely to represent "the medieval experience" nor is he likely to have been able to instill that in others.[15]

Neither Patterson nor Strohm encounter readings; they rather create them out of allusions to works, borrowings from works, and notes on works. To late twentieth-century professional literary scholars, this is the very stuff of professional readings—illustrative passages, footnotes, authorities. The citation of a work is part of a reading—the way both Strohm and Patterson were trained to deal with literature, and a background against which both seem to be reacting as their work proceeds.

B. A. Windeatt and Early Scribes

In discussing Jean d'Angoulême, Strohm makes a passing reference to his scribe, an English scribe who names himself "Duxworth." Yet Strohm dismisses any role this scribe might have had: the words written are all attributable to Jean (70), and only Jean, not Duxworth, receives credit for being a proto-critic. Windeatt will take this argument much further. Not only are the book-owners and compilers to be seen as critics, so are those engaged in copying. Ruggiers would define the tradition of Chaucer editors as a "Great Tradition"; to Windeatt, our admiration should be directed toward the scribes as well:

> But most admirers of Chaucer do not come to his work as editors, and
> it is possible that they can use the means offered by the scribes to
> rather different ends. The scribal responses to Chaucer's poetry, which
> are implicit in the variants offered by the mss for any work, are not to

be despised as the equivalent of mere printing errors. . . . When the work of individual scribes is examined, their achievements in response to the difficulties of a text are sometimes (but not, of course, always!) impressive and arresting. ("Scribes," 120)

In medieval studies, Dragonetti many years ago raised the errors and slips of scribes to authorial status; Windeatt here grants those same slips critical status.[16] Windeatt's argument is itself part of a larger movement, involving the shift from the so-called Old to New Bibliography, the rejection of classical textual-critical stemmatics, and a reevaluation of what constitutes authorship. For the Old Bibliographers and classical textual critics, the facts of production were of importance only so that they could be transcended. The New Bibliography, beginning with McKerrow and extending in a line to the textual-critical theories of McGann, has clearly shifted the emphasis.

Windeatt's work as an editor and a textual critic of medieval literature has placed him in direct conflict with classical theories of textual criticism, in particular, the assumption that the business of the textual critic is to erase the damaging work of scribes to recover the text of the original author.

But classical textual-critical theory focuses on a special kind of literature, where texts are culturally remote from the documents that represent them. In this sense, the medieval author is in the camp of the moderns rather than the ancients. And the medieval manuscript has much the same theoretical status as do the early editions of a modern writer such as Byron: it is nearly contemporary with the supposed generating text, and thus has legitimate status as an historical document, a status equal to that of the text it represents. That a medieval scholar should have been one of the first to object to classical method follows from the unique nature of medieval studies: the manuscript situation seems to mirror the manuscript tradition of classical studies. But the medieval poet, having assumed no stature equal to that of Ovid or Horace, is in no real need of preservation. Joseph Bédier's exasperation at textual-critical method and his inability to carry it out led to a privileging of the single manuscript—and his work has become (oddly) a classic statement of single-text editing. The result is a shift in status, here, from poet to scribe—the same shift one will find in McGann, emphasizing the Byron edition over Byron himself, and the same shift one will find in McGannites, who may find the Rossetti archives finally of more interest than what is archived there.[17]

The scribe under the Bédierian method of despair has become the hero: Chrétien's Guiot as read by Dragonetti, the Chaucerian's Hg/El scribe. Windeatt and following him Lerer are interested not in rehabilitating scholarship and criticism—modernizing criticism and purging it of such antiquities as Spurgeon—but rather in continuing the rehabilitation of the scribe, a scribe who is both the object of serious study and serious attack in the editorial projects of Kane.

Windeatt's Troilus and Criseyde

In editing *Troilus*, Windeatt ran immediately into the "three version" theory—a theory for *Troilus* with its counterpart in the reception of Gower and Langland. Although the available economic resources apparently permitted a multi-column edition (he is able to print Boccaccio's *Filostrato* alongside Chaucer), Windeatt rejects what could be known in classical bibliographical terms as "issues" or "versions" of Chaucer (*Troilus and Criseyde*, 36).

Windeatt's rejection of versions is also a rejection of the grandiose claims of recension editions:

> The *TC* MSS produce evidence within themselves of certain groups of relatedness between MSS, but modern advances in textual criticism have modified the confidence of editors of ME texts both in traditional methods of recension and in other alternatives. (37)

Windeatt rejects theories that would align *Troilus and Criseyde* with *Piers Plowman* through the notion of a "linear progression of authorial revision" (39).

> There is no cohesive, consistent manuscript support for the independent entity of an earlier version of the text. . . . The evidence for a sustainedly distinct version or state of [Chaucer's text], earlier and close line by line to the Italian source, does not exist. (40-43)

Despite some "spot survivals" of canceled stanzas, agreement among manuscripts (for example, the Ph group) represents only that—a manuscript family, not a "version" of the text (45).

Windeatt's polemic is so far marshaled in service of a classical entity: the abstract, but printable, text. A text which, in the modern edition, concretizes the idea (or ideal) of the text. Whether such a text had material existence in the Middle Ages, it is surely an economic desideratum of any book publisher.

But Windeatt takes this argument further. He finds "fascinating readings" or "an equally authentic line" (43). In order to justify his interest in these and other readings—readings that once had been sufficient to produce different texts altogether (the various "versions" of *Troilus and Criseyde*)—he lends them not only possible status as Chaucer's own (they are traces of the compositional process) but also declares them important as original critical readings of Chaucer's text. Scribal variation, under Windeatt's very radical program, is not something to be studied in order to transcend (the purpose governing Kane's notion of *usus scribendi*); it is something of critical value in its own right. Note, in the following quotation, how the word *reading* provides a transition from textual-critical issues (the notion of 'variant reading') to literary ones (the notion of 'critical reading'):

> The form of this edition presents the text of TC in the context of the corpus of variants, or "readings", from the extant MSS, not only because those variants can be of editorial value in helping to establish the text, but also because they are held to be of a positive literary value, to embody in themselves a form of commentary, recording the responses of near-contemporary readers of the poetry. (25)

This to me is the most radical statement of a textual critic and in the work discussed below, Lerer is quite right to seize on it. But in the context of the history of textual criticism, what does it mean?[18]

In a pure recension edition, the groupings of readings would record (somewhat disingenuously perhaps) the textual critic's own process of reconstructing the text. Windeatt is committed to the notion of a single *Troilus and Criseyde*, not a three-version one, and offers what is in effect a base-text/best-text method for producing that version; such a method renders variant readings and groups editorially irrelevant. Windeatt then rehabilitates these textual irrelevancies as proto-literary criticism.

Windeatt's examples of scribal participation are noted on pp. 27ff. Although *Troilus* scribes are not involved in "controversial material" (as are the scribes of *Piers Plowman*), they are involved stylistically:

> And when Pandarus advises Troilus on letter-writing style ("I woot thow nylt it dygneliche endite," II, 1024) one scribe alters to *papally* (R), another suggests *clergaly* (H4), another *clerkissly* (J), and yet others write *dignellche ne mystileche* (GgH5). This range of substitution in a line *about writing* reflects the scribes' relation to their texts in TC, which is not generally a topical response but often a response to what they find distinctive in the poem's diction and syntax. (27)

Windeatt advances two arguments here: (1) that scribes react to content about their own activity (somehow, they see letter-writing as akin to professional copying); (2) they react to "distinctive features" in poet's style. The variants for this line that Windeatt prints on 205 are as follows:

> it dygneliche] d.i. AH2PhS2. / dygneliche] d. ne mystileche GgH5; clergaly H4; clerkissly J; papally R; clerkly Cx; deyneliche H3Th.

To me, these indicate less involvement with the subject than confusion: H3 and Th misread one word; H4, J, R, and Cx misread another; Gg and H5 add a gloss.

Another example noted by Windeatt is Book 3, lines 1566-67, where a scribe (R again) "improves" the line from "Trowe I, quod she," to "Traytour quod she"; (see also H5: "Ho wolde leve yow"). Other examples lead Windeatt to claim "The scribes have entered into the context of complaint and lament, and generally scribes can be observed to participate by emphasizing events in the narrative or by rephrasing direct speech" (27). This argument could be reversed: the scribes have merely hit upon the traditional cliches with which they are familiar. Similarly Book 5, line 1051: "My name of trouthe in loue for evero mo," and Gg's variant "I[n] mene of trouth for now and euer mo." This looks very much like a mechanical error involving n/m.

In his apparatus (p. 503), Windeatt notes that Gg's "In" is corrected to "I." This correction is significant, since it constitutes what Windeatt claims to be an example of scribal literary criticism. But this reading is not a scribal version of a Chaucerian text; it is rather Windeatt's problematic representation of that scribal text. What Windeatt prints as Gg is an ideal: "I mene"; this is a reading (desperately?) correcting the first reading in MS Gg ("In mene of trouth"), not a reading of the supposed original: "My name."[19]

In the next section, Windeatt modifies his suggestion: here scribal errors (or changes) are seen as reactions to Chaucer's "unusual and difficult" diction (28). The scribal actions are "glossing and substitution." And "the TC scribes can be observed pervasively engaged in so registering their sense of the figurative force of Ch's poetic language" (30).[20]

Windeatt's examples are not clear and occasionally deteriorate into triviality.[21] In the absence of convincing statistics, we would only interpret trivial stylistic variations as reactions to a specific style if we know what style is. On p. 30, Windeatt notes that some of the variants he cites simplify, others embellish. Yet these are the same categories used by Kane as examples of ordinary scribal habits found indiscriminately in scribal situations. Windeatt claims their "tendency to the more obvious and familiar associations of words can suggest the freshness of Ch's own uses of diction" (30). But he himself characterizes these as "scribal cliches."

> But Ch's style can also be full, and here scribes may skip the lines in copying. The numerous variations of these types recurring in the MSS are little problem editorially, and individually of little interest, except in that they collectively illustrate an aspect of Ch's style which his scribal readers find unusual. (32)

The abstract nature of Windeatt's diction here is telling. I have no idea how a full style might be defined. The lines Windeatt cites in his notes to this section seem examples of something quite different; see for example Windeatt's own note supporting the statement above (p. 35n. 17):

> Cf. I, 294: seen] haue sen A; to seen had H4. II, 1090: that he shette] whan he hadde it schette Gg; that he beforn hadde shett H5. II, 1079: And that she sholde] Besechyng hir H5; And preyde hir S1. Ch's conditional clauses are often emended; e.g. II, 1393: Al han men] All if men DgS2; Thouh men haue H4.

Even if such changes are not considered ordinary and uninteresting, Windeatt's argument is circular in its own terms. He assumes the importance of scribes for criticism (on matters of style), but is unable to demonstrate a single instance that does not assume knowledge of Chaucer's style.

Windeatt's article differs from Strohm's and Patterson's in several ways. Strohm and Patterson were content to find individual readers; Windeatt ignores individual readers in favor of his assumption of institutional scribal criticism. Thus, despite the number of times the scribes of H5 and Gg appear in his examples, he makes no attempt to describe their personal *usus scribendi*—a personalizing of these scribes that would have the paradoxical effect of making their differences from Chaucer's text less significant. But that is precisely the analysis that is necessary. These scribes are imposing their own style on that of their text; they are not reacting as a group to the style of the text.

Windeatt's discussion involves three distinct institutions: (1) the scribal institution (economic and historical); (2) the textual-critical institution (a modern institution with the scribal institution as its object); (3) the critical institution, in which scholars like Windeatt now function. Whereas criticism following the lead of McGann might conflate the second and third of these, here we have the conflation of the first and the third.

Seth Lerer

None of the particular arguments of Strohm, Patterson, or Windeatt will stand scrutiny in its details. But the reason for that may well be that these scholars are unwilling to admit what their arguments entail, or to give up the foundation of such arguments—that is, the notion of Chaucer as a major author. A similar study of scribal variation of Lydgate, for example, would be unlikely to get a hearing.[22]

In two articles, Seth Lerer has noted the implications of this. The New Chaucerianism, in the form outlined above, must eventually be willing to do without Chaucer. The issue of all such works, Lerer implies, is the entire "cult of authorship" on which Chaucerians depend ("Textual Criticism and Literary Theory," 337).

From the famous passages in Books 2, 3, and 5 of *Troilus and Criseyde*, from the *Thopas-Melibee* Link . . . modern critics have abstracted

Chaucer's views on what we would now label textual criticism and literary theory—views which center on the relationship of "sentence" to poetic form, on the primacy of authorial "intente," and on the mediations of that intent by historical change, linguistic instability, or human misinterpretation. At such moments, Chaucer thematizes the problems of reading and reception, and among the questions that I wish to raise here are how Chaucer's reflections on the reader's engagement with the text shape the responses of his later, fifteenth-century transmitters. ("Textual Criticism and Literary Theory," 329-30, with reference to Windeatt, Patterson, and John Bowers)

Lerer's language conflates the two poles without analyzing the differences; his purpose is "to recover the critical vocabulary of the age and to re-situate its terms in the historical environments of literary making and reception" (330). Lerer also mediates the gap between the individual critic (Strohm, Patterson) and the notion of the scribal institution in his study of particular manuscript variants:

The notion that these manuscripts "simplify" Chaucer's poetry affiliates my work with recent critiques of Chaucerian reception . . . While the scribes of HM 140 and Helmingham differ in their editorial procedures, both, in the end, more firmly align their [versions of the *Canterbury Tales*] to certain fifteenth-century expectations of form or meaning. In this, they perform what Lee Patterson has called "disambiguating," a process of determining a moral reading of a text according to the demands of a new audience and the purposes of a new manuscript environment. ("Rewriting Chaucer," 322)[23]

The question is whether this "new audience" is in the position to make demands: Patterson's text indicates only the demands made on a new audience.

Although Lerer implies we can do without a cult of authorship, this does not mean we can do without a personality: the figure of Chaucer (a poet) is replaced by the figure of John Shirley, who "offers himself as a compiler and an editor, a scribe and a critic" ("Textual Criticism and Literary Theory," 342)—and perhaps a theorist as well.[24] It is clear how far this argument has come since Strohm's denial that Chaucer could be anything as lowly as a mere compiler.

What Lerer argues, and what is not specifically addressed by others, is that the conflation of the terms "scribe" and "critic" entails (and may justify) a further conflation. If the scribe and critic are indistinguishable, then neither can assume a role distinct from the author: all conspire in the creation of the text itself, which in turn creates the illusion of the autonomous author. For Strohm, Patterson, and Windeatt, the critic/scribe was a product of the author; for Lerer, the situation is the reverse: "For Shirley, works have authors and authors have names" (337).[25]

What might be called the bad conscience of all involved in this creation of authorship is found in Chaucer's "Adam Scriveyn." Lerer avoids the question of whether the poem is by Chaucer (a question that assumes the "cult of authorship"), and seeks rather "to assess its place in Shirley's own critical enterprise" (338).

> By enacting the dynamic between scribe and author, by encapsulating the scope of Chaucerian creation, and by finding itself couched in the characteristic tone of Chaucer's poetic persona, the stanza offers the quintessence of the Chaucerian, and the Shirleyan, project. (341)[26]

Conclusion

In the 1970s and early 1980s, Harold Bloom and Geoffrey Hartmann claimed that the work of the critic was indistinguishable from that of the poet: critics deserved the same status as poets. That argument implied that the best poets were proto-critics and parodists.[27] The arguments I have discussed here extend the claims of Hartmann and Bloom, by denying as well the traditional distinctions scholar/critic and finally poet/scribe.

The argument that Chaucer's early scribes, publishers, and collectors can be seen as early literary critics is one that rewrites ordinary histories of literary criticism. This revision of history is itself a reaction to several factors: (1) the critical uncertainty of the distinction between scholars and critics, and the lack of any institutional support for such distinctions; (2) the denigration of pure aesthetic criticism, and the flight of literary critics into more meaningful areas, once "hard" areas: history (and its -icisms); psychoanalysis; cultural history; (3) the search for roots, that is, the attempt of modern academic literary criticism to historicize its own modern decisions and directions, and the projection of itself onto its historical objects. The new respect for early scribes, seems to be a variant of the respect literary criticism demands for its own activities.[28]

CONCLUSION: CHAUCERUS NOSTER AND THE FINE PRESS CHAUCER

My conclusion concerns the collection of Chauceriana at the William Andrews Clark Memorial Library of Los Angeles. Chaucer was never specified as a major area of concern in the history of the library (the case was clearly different at the nearby Huntington). Yet the collection there today, unsystematically developed, has much to say about what constitutes Chauceriana and about the relation of these materials to what is now the institution of Chaucer studies.

A consistent feature of the modern history of Chaucer studies has been the gap between Chaucer scholars and amateurs. One result of this gap is that Chaucer materials, as understood by Chaucerians, are unstable—both in respect to their availability and in respect to their very definition. Particular Chaucer books and manuscripts are absorbed by and circulate within the rare book trade. They subsequently either escape through the avenue of the large public and semi-public library, or, as is the case with the numerous Caxtons untraced in De Ricci's *Census*, simply disappear. Yet while a few major libraries now hold most of the rarest materials, the very definition of what constitutes primary material for Chaucer studies has broadened, and it has done so in direct proportion to the increased holdings at American and English university libraries generally and the British Library in particular. Chaucerians will always be able to purchase cheaply primary source material, but the nature of the primary material available changes due to the interest in Chauceriana by the book trade. The Chaucerian must settle for increasingly marginal primary material, or must redefine as primary material entities increasingly abstract and finally reproducible. By defining the text, rather than the book, as the primary object of concern, modern Chaucerians have all but freed themselves from the economics of the book trade.

I have alluded many times in this study to the marked increase in the production of primary materials during the eighteenth century. No one knows how many copies of blackletter editions were produced; but it is clear that they were produced while the rare book trade exerted little influence on book production, and as a result, many of these copies have been lost. The catalog of Harley's library, however, shows the serious change that occurred in the eighteenth century: Harley's library contains copies of Caxton's *Book of Fame* and *Troilus and Criseyde;* an undated Chaucer in blackletter (the implication seems to be that this precedes the Thynne edition, and if so, it is Pynson's of 1526); two copies of the 1532 edition, single copies of the editions of 1550, 1561, 1602, and 1687. Harley's library could have been supplemented by a 1542 edition (well-known) and a 1598 edition (Sloane owned a copy), and clearly would have been had these been available. Harley's library also contained three copies of the 1721 edition: one on ordinary copy, one on large paper, another on Royal paper.[1]

As the Chaucer book became rarefied, the Chaucer text became modernized and popularized. Tyrwhitt's small-format edition, as well as the numerous translations and modernizations of the eighteenth century that shared this format, embody what most Chaucerians have come to speak of as the "modernization" of Chaucer editing in particular and Chaucer studies in general. This modernization is in essence a textualization—a wresting of Chaucer away from the expensive Chaucer book. One of the clear goals of the Chaucer Society in the nineteenth century was to make materials available—that is, to textualize manuscripts through the production of diplomatic editions. Facsimile editions and electronic editions seem the next steps in this progression.[2] Yet here, the book trade again asserts itself: with the advent of electronic editions, the target audience of facsimiles has shifted from the academic (the Pilgrim Press black-and-white facsimiles) to the book trade (the expensive Ellesmere facsimile recently published by the Huntington Library Press).[3]

When Chaucer scholars list the editions produced in the last hundred years, they generally list these in a familiar series: the Globe edition, the Oxford edition of Skeat, the Riverside editions, the Variorum and the list of cheap facsimiles that support it. All are generally affordable editions, to be used by students and professional Chaucerians. But there are many alternative series: translations such as those by Dryden, and more recently, by such notable Chaucerians as J. S. P. Tatlock, Lumiansky, and Nevill Coghill; bowdlerizations and vulgarizations, most notably Charles Cowden Clarke's *Riches of Chaucer;*[4] and the series of twentieth-century Fine Press editions, this last completely neglected in Chaucer studies. There is, to my knowledge, no systematic bibliography of such editions and no interest in them by Chaucerians.

The Clark Library has well-known collections in Oscar Wilde, Dryden, and Restoration literature, yet its Chaucer holdings, although incidental to the central areas of concern in the development of the library, are impressive. All major Chaucer folio editions and principal variants from 1532-1687 are represented. Also in the Clark are such supplementary items as Brathwait's commentary on the Wife of Bath's Tale and the Miller's Tale and Kynaston's Latin translation of *Troilus and Criseyde.* Accession records show that these were purchased from 1918 to 1927 as part of Clark's plan to form what was considered a "representative" collection of early English editions.[5] Clark ended with what was the fourth-ranking collection of Shakespeare quartos in the U.S. There are no comparable figures on his Chaucer holdings, but for Chaucer materials of the sixteenth to eighteenth century, I believe a ranking would be comparable.

The Library developed this collection further through the area of fine printing. And since Clark's death in 1934, the Library has added some dozen Fine Press Chaucers, beginning with the Golden Cockerel Press *Canterbury Tales* with engravings by Eric Gill, purchased in 1945 (fig. 20). I list these below (in order of date of publication) followed by the date of acquisition when available. Note in the list, the indifference to the normal scholarly hierarchy of canon:

The Works of Geoffrey Chaucer (Hammersmith: Kelmscott Press 1896) (acquired 1921)

The Floure and the Leafe, and the boke of Cupide (Hammersmith: Kelmscott press 1896) (acquired before 1934)

The Flower and the Leaf (London: E. Arnold, 1902) (acquired 1960)

Troilus and Criseyde . . . engravings by Eric Gill (Waltham Saint Lawrence, Berkshire: The Golden Cockerel Press, 1927) (acquired 1956)

The Canterbury Tales . . . with engravings by Eric Gill (Waltham Saint Lawrence, Berkshire: The Golden Cockerel Press, 1929-31) (copy 1: acquired 1945; copy 2: acquired before 1934)

And on his knowes bare he sette him doun,
And in his raving seyde his orisoun.
For verray wo out of his wit he breyde.
He niste what he spak, but thus he seyde;
With pitous herte his pleynt hath he bigonne
Unto the goddes, and first unto the sonne:
He seyde, 'Appollo, god and governour
Of every plaunte, herbe, tree and flour,
That yevest, after thy declinacioun,
To ech of hem his tyme and his sesoun,
As thyn herberwe chaungeth lowe or hye,
Lord Phebus, cast thy merciable ye
On wrecche Aurelie, which that am but lorn.
Lo, lord! my lady hath my deeth ysworn
Withoute gilt, but thy benignitee
Upon my dedly herte have som pitee!
For wel I woot, lord Phebus, if yow lest,
Ye may me helpen, save my lady, best.
Now voucheth sauf that I may yow devyse
How that I may been holpe and in what wyse.
Your blisful suster, Lucina the shene,
That of the see is chief goddesse and quene,
Though Neptunus have deitee in the see,
Yet emperesse aboven him is she:
Ye knowen wel, lord, that right as hir desyr
Is to be quiked and lightned of your fyr,
For which she folweth yow ful bisily,
Right so the see desyreth naturelly
To folwen hir, as she that is goddesse
Bothe in the see and riveres more and lesse.

37

Figure 20. Chaucer, *Canterbury Tales* (Golden Cockerel Press, 1929-31), 2:37.
Reproduced by permission of the William Andrews Clark Memorial Library.

The Frankeleyns Tale (Pittsburgh: Bentley Press, 1931) (acquired 1947)

Troilus and Cressida, tr. George Philip Krapp, with engravings by Gill (New York: Literary Guild, 1932) (acquired 1948)

A.B.C. (Birmingham: Birmingham School of Printing, 1933)

Canterbury Tales: The Knights Tale: A William Morris Broadside (San Francisco: The Grabhorn Press, 1934) (acquired before 1934)

The Canterbury Tale of the Miller (San Francisco: Lawton R. Kennedy, 1939) (acquired 1971)

Troilus and Cressida, tr. Krapp. (London: Limited Editions Club, 1939) (acquired 1948)

The Canterbury Tales, tr. Frank Ernest Hill (Birmingham: City of Birmingham School of Printing, 1949)

The Booke of the Duchesse (Lexington, Ky.: Anvill Press, 1954) (acquired 1954)

A.B.C. called La Priere de Nostre Dame (San Francisco: Grahborn-Hoyem, 1967) (acquired 1967)

The Prologue to the Canterbury tales (Los Angeles: Plantin Press, 1975) (acquired 1975)

Possible inclusions to this list might be the catalogues of the Golden Cockerel Press of 1936 and 1943, entitled respectively *Chanticleer* and *Pertelote.*[6]

Clark's own interests in fine printing were with Doves, Kelmscott and Ashendene Presses; among his Morris books is included, of course, the Kelmscott Chaucer.[7] It is from these books that the collection grew both forward (with a large boost in California presses after the library came into the hands of the University of California in 1934) and backwards, defining a tradition of fine printing that extends back through eighteenth-century printers such as Baskerville and includes a few earlier typographical monuments such as *Poliphili Hypnerotomachia.*[8] The history of printing, thus, is a back-formation of sorts from the field of fine printing. It is not a history considered (as it might well be in a modern academic library) a natural part of literary studies. Archer, in his 1946 report on recent Clark acquisitions, apparently feels that some justification was required for the interest in books as mere "artifacts" and his tone seems often apologetic.[9]

What results from these varied interests is a rather striking alternative Chaucer—a Chaucer collected more by accident than plan, and produced in part by the printers themselves as a tribute to the tastes of Morris. The Chaucers listed above supplement the editions I have discussed in the preceding chapters as well as numerous seventeenth- and eighteenth-century modernizations and vulgarizations. Together, these show clearly what the smooth narrative of scholarly history written by Chaucerians often only implies and sometimes completely obscures: an almost unbridgeable gap from the mid-nineteenth century to the early sixteenth century. There simply is no Chaucer worth having in this period—none by Baskerville, none by the Sheldon Theatre, none even by Cambridge University Press or by the prolific London printer Tonson. None, that is, until the seventeenth-century editions of Chaucer gain value by virtue of age alone.[10]

But is it Chaucer?

An account of such alternative Chaucers as that represented by the Clark's holdings of Fine Press editions will not be found in most modern Chaucer bibliographies (Hammond's is an exception here); without explicitly stating so, what now-standard bibliographies consider editions are those designed for academics. Thus, a student edition based largely on Skeat or Robinson has a better chance of inclusion within such bibliographical surveys than any of those listed here.[11]

In part, this may be due to Hammond's own *Manual*—the one bibliography that made some effort at inclusiveness. Hammond distinguished various categories of editions: Editions, Partial Editions, Editions of Portions for School Use, and Modernizations and Translations. The Kelmscott Chaucer appears under Editions, between Skeat's Student Chaucer of 1895 and Pollard's Globe Chaucer of 1898.[12] Hammond had no reason to define a special category of Fine Press Chaucers since in 1908, that tradition did not exist; the Kelmscott was included in the list of editions because it had presumably been "edited," by F. S. Ellis.[13] Modern bibliographers of Chaucer seem to have accepted the categories defined by Hammond and refined her list further, ending with the smooth, coherent, and thoroughly academic list of editions one finds in the Variorum Chaucer. The Kelmscott Chaucer (a Chaucer whose appearance is probably more familiar to modern readers than that of any other Chaucer edition) is now omitted, and with that is omitted as well the many Fine Press Chaucers that were produced as a tribute to it.

Hammond's criteria for classifying editions were based on the type of text these editions contained. While useful and inclusive earlier this century, these criteria are inadequate today; for the Fine Press tradition now has its own autonomy and constitutes its own genre apart from whether the text is edited, translated, or modernized. Like mainstream Chaucer editions, it has developed its own subgenres—complete works, partial works, and even its own vulgarization. The cheap 1930s reprints of the Golden Cockerel Press *Troilus and Creseida* translated by George Krapp with illustrative erotica by Gill (cf. the *Canterbury Tales* illustration above, fig. 20) are books more readers have likely to have seen than, say, Robert K. Root's edition. And it has as well its own negligibilities: I once ran into a *Canterbury Tales* packaged in a foot-high replica of a highly-stylized and unspecified cathedral (this may be a well-known edition, but I neglected to record the proper bibliographical information).[14]

With the exception of a few references to Morris's Kelmscott Chaucer, this final series has no part in Chaucer studies: the books are neither cited nor discussed, nor are they considered part of the editorial history of Chaucer. To the mainstream institution of Chaucerians, of paramount interest is the text of Chaucer, not the artifact that contains it. Yet nearly all the books routinely used in the history of Chaucer editing exist as artifacts, not as texts, as the bindings of these books in collections such as the Clark collection attest.

The exclusion of these books from Chaucer scholarship, the disappearance of many Caxtons into unrecorded private libraries, the physical locking up of some of them away from the hands of Chaucerians and their replacement by facsimiles, photographic and electronic—all are manifestations of the sometimes inadvertent rejection of the book that has characterized Chaucer studies since Dryden and continues today in the renewed interest in textual-critical theories and in the production of editions attempting to represent these theories. As professional Chaucerians develop an increasingly esoteric textual Chaucer, other Chaucerians continue about their business, reading the most absurd editions, naively repeating what decades ago where the prevailing scholarly cliches, and occasionally (like William Andrews Clark, Jr.) squandering substantial amounts of money on Chaucer artifacts. Nearly all professional Chaucerians and the vast majority of amateur ones will at some point pass through our classes; I suspect that in spite of our efforts (or in some cases because of these same efforts), they will continue to have little to do with each other.

NOTES

INTRODUCTION

1. See the introductory comments in Derek Pearsall, *The Life of Geoffrey Chaucer: A Critical Biography* (Oxford: Blackwell, 1992), where Pearsall speculates that a revisionist biographer might do well to avoid this by defining a Chaucer as everything we dislike.

2. William Thynne, ed., *The Workes of Geffray Chaucer newly printed . . .* (London: Godfray, 1532) (STC 5068); John Urry et al., *The Works of Geoffrey Chaucer, compared with the Former Editions, and many valuable MSS* (London: Lintot, 1721); Thomas Tyrwhitt, ed., *The Canterbury Tales of Chaucer to which are added An Essay upon his Language and Versification; an Introductory Discourse; and Notes*, 5 vols. (London: T. Payne, 1775-78).

3. William L. Alderson and Arnold C. Henderson, *Chaucer and Augustan Scholarship* (Berkeley and Los Angeles: University of California Press, 1970); W. W. Greg, "The Early Printed Editions of the *Canterbury Tales*," *PMLA* 39 (1924): 737-61; Eleanor Prescott Hammond, *Chaucer: A Bibliographical Manual* (New York: Macmillan, 1908); John R. Hetherington, *Chaucer, 1532-1602: Notes and Facsimile Texts* (Birmingham, privately printed, 1964; rev. 1967); Charles Muscatine, *The Book of Geoffrey Chaucer* (San Francisco: The Book Club of California, 1963). See also the chapters in Paul G. Ruggiers, ed., *Editing Chaucer: The Great Tradition* (Norman, Okla.: University of Oklahoma Press, 1984) and the reservations I have expressed in *Huntington Library Quarterly* 48 (1985): 172-79. Still of value is the earlier account by Thomas R. Lounsbury, *Studies in Chaucer*, 3 vols. (New York: Harper, 1892), 1: 261-353.

4. Walter W. Skeat, ed., *The Works of Geoffrey Chaucer and Others, being a reproduction in facsimile of the first collected edition 1532 from the copy in the British Museum* (London: Oxford University Press, 1905), "Introduction," xiii; see further xvi-xxi, describing the editions of 1532-1561.

5. Skeat, ed., *Chaucer Facsimile, 1532,* from a British Museum copy, and from a copy in Clare College, D. S. Brewer, ed., *Geoffrey Chaucer: The Works, 1532 with Supplementary material from the Editions of 1542, 1561, 1598 and 1602* (London: Scolar Press, 1974).

6. John Leland, *Commentarii de Scriptoribus Britannicis,* ed. Anthony Hall (Oxford: Sheldon Theatre, 1709), 423; rpt. accurately by Hammond, *Manual,* 1-6. I discuss the statement in greater detail below, chap. 2.

7. Alfred W. Pollard and G. R. Redgrave et al., *A Short-Title Catalogue of Books Printed in England, Scotland, and Ireland, and of English Books Printed Abroad,* 2d rev. ed., 3 vols. (London: Bibliographical Society, 1976-91) [hereafter STC]. Slightly different definitions are given in Fredson Bowers, *Principles of Bibliographical Description* (1949), new ed., with introduction by G. Thomas Tanselle (New Castle: Oak Knoll Press, 1994), esp. 35-123, where any "consciously planned unit" is considered an issue. So also the first edition of STC (London: The Bibliographical Society, 1926).

8. So Hammond, *Manual,* and Hetherington, *Chaucer: Notes and Facsimile Texts.*

9. The decimal point and number are of no significance as to the classification itself.

10. Reproductions of the two title-pages are readily available in Muscatine, *Book of Chaucer,* 27. Compare these or the STC transcriptions with the transcription in the Sotheby's catalogue, "The Aldenham Library: Catalogue of the Famous Library, the Property of the Rt. Honourable Lord Aldenham" (22 March 1937), p. 42, lot 106: "Chaucer (G.) Workes . . . with diuers additions. With the Siege and Destrvction of the worthie Citie of Thebes . . ."

11. In all likelihood, a version with woodcuts would be more valuable, *all things being equal;* see Hammond, *Manual,* 120, citing Quaritch prices earlier this century.

12. See my critique of the prefatory matter to the Scolar Press facsimile of the 1532 edition in "On 'Correctness': A Note on Some Press Variants in Thynne's 1532 Edition of Chaucer," *The Library* ser. 6, 17 (1995): 156-67, and for a more detailed discussion, "Perfect Order and Perfected Order: The Evidence from Press-Variants in Early Seventeenth-Century Quartos," *Papers of the Bibliographical Society of America* 90 (1996): 272-320. See also, the classic essay by D. F. McKenzie, "Printers of the Mind: Some Notes on Bibliographical Theories and Printing-House Practices," *Studies in Bibliography* 22 (1969): 1-75. Anne Hudson, in collating the various issues of the 1542 and 1550 Chaucer to determine the copytext for the Stow edition, mistakenly assumes that press variants will be distributed systematically among issues; "John Stow (1525? - 1605)," in Ruggiers, ed., *Editing Chaucer,* 53-70. Issue concerns only resetting of individual sheets (in this case, preliminaries and colophon) and is unrelated to ordinary press-variation that will be found in the majority of sheets.

13. One of the best representatives of these new approaches to late medieval English studies is the anthology edited by Jeremy Griffiths and Derek

Pearsall, *Book Production and Publishing in Britain 1375-1476* (Cambridge: Cambridge University Press, 1989). See also the essays now collected in Ralph Hanna III, *Pursuing History: Middle English Manuscripts and Their Texts* (Stanford: Stanford University Press, 1996); Hanna combines the best of the various (and often competing) bibliographical and codicological schools, and his consistently understated tone masks the often radical nature of his concerns.

14. "The Importance of Importance," *Huntington Library Quarterly* 56 (1993): 307-17.

CHAPTER ONE

1. The present consensus that Chaucer is there as a reward for his professional rather than his poetic activities is itself an affront to the myth of Poet's Corner. See Martin M. Crow and Clair C. Olson, *Chaucer Life-Records* (Oxford: Oxford University Press, 1966), 535-40, and the concluding statements of Martin M. Crow and Virginia E. Leland, "Chaucer's Life," in Larry D. Benson, ed., *The Riverside Chaucer* (Boston: Houghton Mifflin, 1987), xxvi. That Chaucer's interment was itself a political act, directed against monastic control of the abbey, was argued by E. P. Kuhl, "Chaucer and Westminster Abbey," *JEGP* 45 (1946): 340-43. Kuhl's emphasis on the political implications of Chaucer's poetry anticipates the working assumptions of such studies as John H. Fisher, *The Importance of Chaucer* (Carbondale: Southern Illinois University Press, 1992).

2. [Thomas Speght], *The Workes of our Antient and Learned English Poet, Geffrey Chaucer . . .* (London: Bishop, 1598); *The Workes . . .* (London: Islip, 1602). For the tomb itself and its inscriptions, John W. Hales, "The Grave of Chaucer," *Athenaeum*, 9 August 1902, 189-90, offers one of the more concise accounts. Most of the relevant bibliography is cited in Crow and Olson, *Life-Records*, superseding the earlier material collected by the Chaucer society.

3. William Caxton, *Boethius: The Consolacion of Philosophie* (1478) (Huntington Library copy, sig. m6v); the second *u* in "tumulatus" is inverted. The epilogue is available in W. J. B. Crotch, *The Prologues and Epilogues of William Caxton*, EETS 176 (London: Oxford University Press, 1928), 37; he omits the lines by Surigone. On Surigone, see N. F. Blake, "Caxton and Chaucer," *Leeds Studies in English*, n.s. 1 (1967): 19-36, rpt. N. F. Blake, *William Caxton and English Literary Culture* (London: Hambledon Press, 1991), 149-65 (page references below are to the reprint); Blake modifies the basic accounts in R. Weiss, "Humanism in Oxford," *Times Literary Supplement*, 9 January 1937, p. 28, elaborated further in R. Weiss, *Humanism in England During the Fifteenth Century* (1941; 3rd ed. Oxford: Blackwell, 1967), 138-39. Surigone's poem is reprinted on the last page of the first complete works of Chaucer by William Thynne (1532), following the colophon; *Workes*, 1532, fol. 383. The richest and most intriguing reading of Caxton's print of this epitaph is Seth

Lerer, *Chaucer and His Readers* (Princeton: Princeton University Press, 1993), chap. 5: "At Chaucer's Tomb: Laureation and Paternity in Caxton's Criticism," 147-75 and notes 266-73.

4. For Brigham, see James Alsop, "Nicholas Brigham (d. 1558), Scholar, Antiquary, and Crown Servant," *Sixteenth Century Journal* 12 (1981): 49-67. The physical monument may have been purchased cheaply by Brigham following the destruction of the graves and tombs of Grey Friars in 1547, hundreds of which may have been available for sale; see M. H. Bloxam, "On Chaucer's Monument in Westminster Abbey," *Archaeological Journal* 38 (1881): 361-64 and Hales, "The Grave of Chaucer." This suggestion has met with some resistance; see the excellent discussion by Charlotte C. Stokes, "The Grave of Chaucer," *Athenaeum*, 25 October 1902, 552 and Katherine A. Esdaile, in *Times Literary Supplement*, 28 February 1929, 163, who calls this suggestion "heresy."

5. "Our Weekly Gossip," *Athenaeum*, 10 July 1850, 768:

> An examination . . . of the tomb itself by competent authorities has proven this objection to be unfounded: inasmuch as there can exist no doubt, we hear, from the difference of workmanship, material, &c., that the altar tomb is the original tomb of Geoffrey Chaucer. . . . So that sympathy of Chaucer's admirers is now invited to the restoration of what till now was really not known to exist—*the original tomb* of the Poet.

The author, I assume, is the Samuel Shepherd referred to by Henry Poole, "Westminster Abbey: A Study on Poets' Corner," *The Antiquary* 4 (October 1881): 139. According to Poole, "the proposition was, happily, abandoned" (139). Some restorations may have made in 1868, when the stained glass window in Chaucer's honor was opened directly above the monument. This window features iconography from "The Flower and the Leaf," a poem declared spurious by the same Chaucerians who celebrated the window. See, e.g., F. J. Furnivall, *A Temporary Preface to the Six-text Edition of Chaucer's Canterbury Tales*, Chaucer Society Publ., ser. 2, pt. 3 (London: Trübner, 1868), 107-10 and Appendix III: "The Chaucer Window in Westminster Abbey," 133.

6. Henry Troutbeck, in *The Nineteenth Century* 42 (August 1897): 336: "I calculated that his height must have been about 5 feet 6 inches." I know of no scholar who has registered the slightest skepticism concerning this report.

7. The earliest use I find of the phrase "ii old verses" is in Foxe's *Actes and Monuments* (1570); see Caroline F. E. Spurgeon, *Five Hundred Years of Chaucer Criticism and Allusion (1357-1900)*, 5 pts. (1908-17), 3 vol. reprint (Cambridge: Cambridge University Press, 1925), 1:107 (citations below are to part and page). Leland, before quoting Surigone's poem, singles out these two verses, but refers to them only as "hoc disticho . . . Hi duo versus"; Leland, *Commentarii*, ed. Hall (1709), 425, very accurately transcribed by Hammond, *Manual*, 6-7.

8. The documentation for Surigone's activities in England at some time between 1454 and 1471 is presented in the one-column correspondence of R. Weiss, "Humanism in Oxford," 28. Weiss extends this in *Humanism in England*, 138-39; although more information is added in his appendix (Weiss's text is unchanged in later editions) Weiss's discussion in 1941 is a reinterpretation of the evidence presented in 1937. For further references on Surigone, see Lerer, *Chaucer and his Readers*, 271n. 34.

9. Blake's article is generated by the discussion in William Blades, *The Life and Typography of William Caxton, England's First Printer*, 2 vols. (London: Joseph Lilly, 1861), 2:67: "Caxton . . . raised a public monument to [Chaucer's] memory before St. Benet's Chapel, in Westminster Abbey, in the shape of a pillar supporting a tablet upon which the above 'Epitaphye' was written." Blake denies further that the final four lines ("Post obitum . . .") were ever inscribed on this tablet, although it is unclear to me that Blades ever directly claims that.

10. Lounsbury, *Studies in Chaucer*, 1:133-42, parts of Lounsbury's translation have been reprinted in Derek Brewer, *Chaucer: The Critical Heritage*, 2 vols. (London: Routledge & Kegan Paul, 1978), 1: 91-96. Brewer's anthology, however useful, is unreliable. Among the errors in this particular section is the assertion, after a discussion of Foxe, that the inscription on the tomb is no longer extant: "This inscription [by Brigham], no longer extant, describes Chaucer as 'Anglorum vates ter maximus olim' . . ." (1: 109); surely this should refer to the verses about the ledge.

11. See the references in Charlton T. Lewis and Charles Short, *A Latin Dictionary* (Oxford: Clarendon Press, 1907), s.v. *tabella*, II. A.1 and 2 (plural). See also, Robert Copland's "Lenvoy of R Coplande boke prynter" in de Worde's 1530 edition of Chaucer's *Assemble of Foules* (STC 5092); Copland speaks of a printer of having preserved a boke "In snowes wyte paper"; Percy Simpson, *Proof-Reading in the Sixteenth, Seventeenth and Eighteenth Centuries* (Oxford: Oxford University Press, 1935), 222.

12. Examples I discuss below include Elias Ashmole, *Theatrum Chemicum Britannicum, containing severall poeticall pieces of our famous English Philosophers, who have written the Hermetique Mysteries in their owne Ancient Language,* (London: Brooks, 1652); Urry et al., *Works of Chaucer*, 1721; John Dart, *Westmonasterium or The History and Antiquities of the Abbey Church of St. Peters Westminster . . . 1723*, 2 vols. (London: J. Cole, [1723]); William Camden, *Reges, Reginae, Nobiles, et Alij in Ecclesia Collegiata B. Petri Westmonasterij Sepulti* (London: Bollifantus, 1600); John Weever, *Ancient Funerall Monuments within the United Monarchie* (London: Harper, 1631).

13. Pearsall, *Life of Geoffrey Chaucer*, 276. Pearsall elaborates in "Chaucer's Tomb: The Politics of Reburial," *Medium Aevum* 64 (1995): 51-73. Pearsall's prefatory reference to the *HLQ* version of the present chapter states that I register no skepticism on any of the details of the traditions surrounding the tomb (67); I should state here, without any irony whatsoever, that that is the reverse of my intent.

14. I thank Prof. Anthony Kemp and Giovanna Pompele of University of Southern California for these reports, which are perfectly consistent with the various publicity card packs and "Official Guide" (rev. ed. 1988) provided by Westminster Abbey. See also, the early twentieth-century photos in Spurgeon, *Chaucer Criticism*, Pl. 10, facing 1: 94 (before 1917) and in the Royal Commission of Historical Monuments (England), *An Inventory of the Historical Monuments in London*, vol. 1: *Westminster Abbey* (London: Stationer's Office, 1924), 1: 51 and Pl. 95. Not much of the inscription is legible in these photos, beyond the placement of the arms, the placement of lines, and some faded capitals, among them "uit Anglor. . . quae tibi cuncta not . . ./ Octobris . . . / . 5.6" All of these photos are based on restorations, most notably the one by Poole in 1881, who restored several letters; Poole, "Poet's Corner," 139, quoted in the concluding section of this chapter.

15. Henry J. Todd, *Illustrations of the Lives and Writings of Gower and Chaucer. Collected from Authentick Documents* (London: Rivington, et al., 1810), plate facing 143 (for the conventional depiction of text, see n. 33 below). Only two pictorial illustrations are contained in Todd, the other of Gower's tomb. J. P. Neale and E. W. Brayley, *History and Antiquities of the Abbey Church of St. Peter, Westminster* (1818-23), 2: 235, describe the inscription as "now almost obliterated." Earlier, Brayley described Chaucer's monument as "now much defaced, and . . . only very slightly glanced at." [E. W. Brayley], *The Beauties of England and Wales*, vol. 10, pt. 3: *London and Middlesex*, vol. 3, pt. 2: *Containing the History and Description of the City and Liberty of Westminster* (London: Harris, 1815), 99. Cf. William Godwin, *Life of Geoffrey Chaucer the Early English Poet*, 2 vols. (London: T. Davison, 1803), 1:2; Godwin claims that the inscription "may, with some little trouble, be deciphered at the present day."

16. The date 1606 is of Camden's third edition; it is so given by Hammond and repeated in Crow and Olson's *Chaucer Life-Records*. The date of the report should be given as 1600, the date of the first edition, as it is in Spurgeon, *Chaucer Criticism*, 1:163. The 1606 edition may have been used for convenience of citation; the two earlier editions are unpaginated.

17. For the source of the material in Stow, see John Stowe, *A Survey of London* (1598), ed. C. L. Kingsford (Oxford: Clarendon Press, 1908), 2:110-11, and Lounsbury, *Studies in Chaucer*, 1: 154. Certainly Francis Thynne regarded Speght as the editor and author of the Life: Francis Thynne, *Animadversions uppon the Annotacions and Corrections of some imperfections of impressiones of Chaucers workes* . . . , (1598), ed. G. H. Kingsley, rev. J. F. Furnivall, EETS (London: Trübner, 1875), 12-27. The 1598 Life is readily available in the transcription of Hammond, *Manual*, 19-35, or in facsimile among the supplementary material included in Brewer, *Chaucer: Works 1532*. For discussion of the edition, see Derek Pearsall, "Thomas Speght (ca. 1550-?)," in Ruggiers, ed., *Editing Chaucer*, 71-92.

18. *Maternae haec* is the reading of Caxton and the one followed by most other authorities with the exception of the antiquarians John Weever

(*Ancient Funerall Monuments*, 1631), who gives *Materna hac*, and Jodocus Crull, who gives *haec* in his 1711 monument survey, altered to the standard *hac* in the subsequent edition of 1722. The change is based on material already in the 1598 edition, where Surigone's 30-line poem is quoted in its entirety, its final line reading: "Maternae hac sacra sum timulatus humo" (*Works*, 1598, sig. c3r; the error "timulatus" remains in the 1602 print of this poem).

19. Hammond, *Manual*, 35-36 reads *whiche* and *cleane* (cf. fig. 1 above). Hammond is generally extremely reliable in her transcriptions and there may well be a copy of Speght with these spellings.

20. Walter W. Skeat, *The Complete Works of Geoffrey Chaucer*, vol. 1 (1894) (Oxford: Oxford University Press, 1899). I quote the Nicolas text from a re-issue of the second edition, *The Poetical Works of Geoffrey Chaucer*, ed. Richard Morris, with Memoir by Sir Harris Nicolas, vol. 1 (London: Bell, 1891), 43. For the text of the inscription in Dart's Life of Chaucer in the 1721 edition, see *Works*, 1721, sig. e2r (Dart cites both Speght and Weever). Nicolas cites Weever in detail in his discussion of the tomb (42) but does not use the variants characteristic of Weever in his transcription. For the inscription itself, he seems to rely on the title page of Urry's 1721 edition (the ungrammatical *nota* is corrected; see 43n.15, citing as well Dart, Weever, and Neale and Brayley). Skeat acknowledges his quotation of Nicolas on 1:xlvi, but in all copies of Skeat I have seen, the quotation is not closed: it extends through the discussion of the epitaph and the verses "on the ledge." The differences between Nicolas and Skeat are merely formal: Nicolas's inscriptions are each surrounded by quotation marks and given in small capitals (with the exception of the large capitals for the poet's name). Skeat's text eliminates the capitals—thus an odd lower case *d* for *domini* appears. The text of the verses "about the ledge" agrees with that of 1602 (fig. 2). Nicolas then quotes the "ii old verses" from the edition of Speght; Skeat omits these, but quotes the four lines Caxton adds to Surigone's poem.

21. Cf. the discussion of the legend of Chaucer's death date by R. J. Yeager, "British Library Additional MS. 5141: An Unnoticed Chaucer *Vita*," *Journal of Medieval and Renaissance Studies* 14 (1984): 273-76; Yeager implies that the "opportunity" to view the tomb inscription is significant in the transmission of the statements on that inscription.

22. John Pits, *Relationum Historicarum de Rebus Anglicis . . . Libri* (Paris: Thierry, 1619), 575, accurately transcribed in Hammond, *Manual*, 17. Pits's text of the inscription is identical to Camden's with the exception of the form *notent* for Camden's *notant*, and his omission of the line referring to Brigham.

23. See Speght's alternate readings: *rogites, eram* and *negat* (fig. 1). Camden's reading *fueram* will not scan, and is corrected to *eram* in all other texts I have seen. The word *fueram* is probably an error originating in the line "Unica quae fueram proles spesque alma parentum" in the epitaph on Rachael Brigham (presumably the daughter of Nicholas Brigham, d.

1557), which Camden quotes after an entry on Robert Haule. The rather striking statement in the Westminster Abbey "Official Guide" that Nicholas Brigham is "said to have been buried near Chaucer" (93) must have its origin here. Hammond implies that Camden's reference to the burial site of Rachael Brigham appears as a "note" at the bottom of p. 67. That position is an accident of the 1606 format; the section on Rachael Brigham in 1600 is clearly another entry (see sigs. I1r-v).

24. Henry Keepe, *Monumenta Westmonasteriensa: Or a Historical Account of the Original Increase, and Present State of St. Peter's, or the Abby Church of Westminster . . .* (London: Wilkinson, 1683), 21. [Jodocus Crull], *The Antiquities of St. Peter's, or the Abbey Church of Westminster* (London: J.N., 1711), 230; *The Antiquities of St. Peter's or, the Abby-Church of Westminster . . .*, 3d ed., 2 vols. (London: Bell, 1722), 2:32. Few of the engravings in Crull have inscriptions; Dryden's is one of the exceptions.

25. Included are Norton's "The Ordinal of Alchemy," Dee's "Testament," Gower on the Philosopher's stone, Lydgate's "Hermes Bird." Ashmole MS 766 contains a 1576 "Discourse uppon the Philosophers Armes" by Thynne, where Chaucer is mentioned as an alchemist among many that Ashmole includes (ref. in Spurgeon, *Chaucer Criticism*, 1: 113); for text, see Thynne, *Animadversions*, 135-36. Among those mentioned are "the good britishe Riplye . . . Sir Geffray Chaucer . . . the morall Gower . . . Norton"—all represented in *Theatrum Chemicum Britannicum.* For the traditional association of Chaucer and alchemy, see the detailed discussion of Robert M. Schuler, "The Renaissance Chaucer as Alchemist," *Viator* 15 (1984): 305-33.

26. See Arthur M. Hind, *Engraving in England in the Sixteenth and Seventeenth Centuries: A Descriptive Catalogue with Introduction*, vol. 3: "The Reign of Charles I" (by Margery Corbett and Michael Norton) (Cambridge: Cambridge University Press, 1964), 66-67. I cannot find in the references cited by Corbett and Norton the precise evidence that "special drawings were made from the original in Westminster Abbey" (66). For the brief reference in Ashmole's diary, see *Memoirs of the Life of that Learned Antiquary, Elias Ashmole, Esq, drawn up by himself by way of Diary*, publ. Charles Burman (London: J. Roberts, 1771), 25 (entry for 22 Sept. 1651). Corbett and Norton note that Ashmole has substituted a book for the rosary beads in Hoccleve's drawing. For discussion of the portrait itself, see e.g., David R. Carlson, "Thomas Hoccleve and the Chaucer Portrait," *Huntington Library Quarterly* 54 (1991): 283-300, and Pearsall, *Life of Chaucer*, Appendix I: "The Chaucer Portraits," 285-305. Pearsall suggests that the phrase "worthy Schollar Tho. Occleve" shows that Ashmole is using as a model the image on "the progeny page" of the Speght edition (1598 and 1602), the inscription of which identifies Hoccleve as Chaucer's "scholar" (*Life of Chaucer*, 296).

27. Cf. the engraving of Cole, fig. 4 below, which ignores the precise placement of the arms, but gives the text in capitals. See also, the engravings of Vaughan reproduced in Hind, *Engraving in England*, vol. 3, Plates 25-

      38, where all forms of print are used, including roman capitals inscribed on a tomb (Pl. 37a, title page to Sir Richard Fanshawe's *La Fida Pastora,* 1658).

28. In Ashmole's transcription of the verses about the ledge and the old verses on p. 472, all variants are those of Speght, with the exception of *Materna,* shared only by Weever and possibly Ashmole's correction. Although Ashmole used Speght for his prefatory material and for glossary (he calls the Life a "commendable account," 470), his Canon's Yeoman's Tale text is not from Speght, but from the 1532 edition (Ashmole's annotated 1532 edition is now MS Ashmole 1095); see Schuler, "Chaucer as Alchemist," 326, n. 34, and any number of Ashmole variants, e.g., "He con the werke" (a possible variant of 1532 "he couthe werke," but not derivable from 1602: "he couth werke"). Cf. the reported MSS readings *koude*; John M. Manly and Edith Rickert, *The Text of the Canterbury Tales,* 8 vols. (Chicago: University of Chicago Press, 1940), 4:310 and 8:605.

29. Dart himself later claims that the Life has been significantly altered, although he himself has never seen the edition "except on a Bookseller's shelf" (Dart, *Westmonasterium,* 87, and discussion below, chapter 4). Dart is instead satisfied with his old edition "with my own written Notes."

30. Dart does not quote the inscription in his accompanying text, nor does he quote Surigone's verses. He does quote the verses on the ledge with the variants *rogitas, eram, neget.*

31. W. R. Lethaby, "Chaucer's Tomb," *Times Literary Supplement,* 21 Feb. 1929, 137.

32. Dart, *Westmonasterium,* 86, describes this portrait of Chaucer as "exactly like the Painting of *Ocklefe,* printed before the old Edition, and . . . remaining in Mr. Ashmole's Time, who in one of his treatises, has given us the Monument."

33. Crull, *Antiquities,* (1722), 2, facing 32. The plate is clearly not a tracing of Ashmole. R. Ackermann, *The History of the Abbey Church of St. Peter's Westminster, its Antiquities and Monuments,* 2 vols. (London: Ackermann, 1832), 91-92, and Plate F, facing 98 (color engraving by J. Bluck). Nearly all engravings of this collection represent inscriptions by a wavy line.

34. STC lists 1563, 1570, 1576, 1583, 1596, and 1610. References below are to the 1576 edition, the first to print proper names as well as text in blackletter. John Foxe, *The First volume of the Ecclesiastical History, contayning the Actes & Monumentes of thinges passed in every Kinges time . . .* (London: John Day, 1576). The text of the 1570 edition is substantially the same.

35. See e.g. *Foxe, Actes and Monuments . . .* (London: John Daye, 1583), 839: *one M. Brickham*; variants *nota, notent,* and *25. Octob. Anno. 1400.* The 1596 edition (London: Peter Short, 1596), 767, spells *Brickham*; in the epitaph, the error *nota* is corrected to *notae.* The 1610 edition seems to be a line-for-line reprint of the 1596 edition.

36. F. J. Furnivall, "Chaucer's Tomb in Westminster Abbey," *Notes and Queries* ser. 10, 1 (1904): 28.

37. Unique among early witnesses, Commaunder uses the *e* spelling for the ligature *ae* in the words *quaeras, notae,* and *quae.*
38. Foxe's comments entered the traditions concerning Chaucer's tomb very early. Hales, fairly reliable, suggests that Stow himself adopted an error from Foxe, that Chaucer was first buried in the cloister; Hales, "The Grave of Chaucer," 190. The text of "Jack Upland," printed with Chaucer's Works by Speght in 1602, is also taken from Foxe; see Pearsall, "Thomas Speght," 88.
39. Neale and Brayley, (*History and Antiquities* 2: 235). I assume the curious date "1550" is a misprint, although it may be due to a misreading of Dart's engraving.
40. Poole, "Westminster Abbey," 139. The date 1558 appears twice in this article; the date 1556 once.
41. Speght's reading *Gaufredus* is simply his conventional Latin spelling of the name, one which conveniently scans; his *Anno domini 1400, die mensis Octob. 25* functions as do his italics—it is a conventional way of expressing what is on the tomb in somewhat different form. As for the variant *vitae/mortis,* neither is entirely satisfactory and thus either could have given rise to the other.

CHAPTER TWO

1. The edition has been the object of several studies: James E. Blodgett, *William Thynne and His 1532 Edition of Chaucer* (diss. University of Indiana, 1975) and "William Thynne (d. 1546)," in Ruggiers, ed., *Editing Chaucer,* 35-52; and the study on the Chaucer canon by Yeager, discussed in detail below.
2. Paul Needham, *The Printer and the Pardoner: An Unrecoded Indulgence printed by William Caxton for the Hospital of St. Mary Runceval, Charing Cross* (Washington: Library of Congress, 1986), 18-19.
3. The *Testament* was inserted on three unfoliated leaves in the middle of a quire (sig. 2Q) between the end of *Troilus and Criseyde* and *Legend of Good Woman,* after the outer bifolia of the quire (sig. 2Q) had been set and foliated. The Beinecke copy includes the original concluding page to *Troilus and Criseyde* as a cancelland. See Alice S. Miskimin, *The Renaissance Chaucer* (New Haven: Yale University Press, 1975), 208, and extensive discussion by Denton Fox, ed., *Robert Henryson: The Testament of Cresseid* (London: Nelson, 1968), 9-10.
4. See, for example, H. S. Bennett, *English Books and Readers, 1475 to 1557: Being a Study in the History of the Book Trade from Caxton to the Incorporation of the Stationers' Company,* 2d ed. (Cambridge: University Press, 1969), chap. 4 "Patronage," 40-53.
5. Lounsbury is the only Chaucerian I know of who has acknowledged the strangeness of Thynne's preface: "It is little more than a jungle of sentences through which it requires a patient and practised student of

language to make his way. Unfortunately, after he has succeeded, he is usually no better off than when he began" (*Studies in Chaucer,* 1: 267).

6. Compare the punctuation in the following:

> But of all speeches, those which most approach to the *Latine* be the *Italian* and *Spanish* tongues; of whome the one by corruption of the *Gothes* and *Longobardes* had her beginning, as *Latine* spoken by strangers of a barbare understanding: The other, being also Latine, was by Vandales, Gothes, Moores, Saracens and other so many times blemished, as marveile it is to see now unto what perfection these two formed out of the Latine and Barbares speeches be reduced. (sig. g2v)

7. The 1598 Speght edition, in an unacknowledged paraphrase, also evades the syntactical difficulties of its source: "who in most unlearned times and greatest ignorance, being much esteemed, cannot in these our daies, wherin Learning and riper iudgement so much flourisheth, but be had in great reuerence, vnlesse it bee of such as for want of wit and learning, were neuer yet able to iudge what wit or Learning meaneth" ("To the Readers").

8. Crotch, *Prologues and Epilogues of Caxton,* 91. For discussion, see in particular Lerer, *Chaucer and his Readers,* 164-68. On these early editions, see section below and notes 18 and 19.

9. Tim William Machan, *Textual Criticism and Middle English Texts* (Charlottesville: University Press of Virginia, 1994), 15-19. I have argued specifically against this notion in "The Myth of Print Culture," New Chaucer Society, Los Angeles, California, 27 July 1996.

10. See Todd, *Illustrations of the Lives of Chaucer and Gower* (1810). The history of these manuscripts and the curious absence of them from early Chaucer scholarship has not been written, even by some who have been commissioned specifically to address the question, for example, Alfred David, "The Ownership and Use of the Ellesmere Manuscript," in Daniel Woodward and Martin Stevens, eds., *Ellesmere Chaucer: Essays in Interpretation* (San Marino: Huntington Library Press, 1995), 307-26. Contrast this indifference with the opening paragraphs by N. F. Blake in the same volume, "The Ellesmere Text in the Light of the Hengwrt Manuscript," 205-24; and Ralph Hanna III and A. S. G. Edwards, "Rotheley, the De Vere Circle, and the Ellesmere Chaucer," *Huntington Library Quarterly* 58 (1996): 11-35.

11. For the notion of the sovereign as reader, see Seth Lerer, *Literacy and Power in Anglo-Saxon Literature* (Omaha: University of Nebraska Press, 1991), chap. 2: "The Beautiful Letters: Authority and Authorship in Asser and King Alfred," 61-96.

12. For Hearne's ambivalence on Leland's authority, see chap. 5 below.

13. The implied relation between Godfray and Berthelet seems borne out by typographical evidence; see my discussion in "Bibliographical History versus Bibliographical Evidence: The Plowman's Tale and Early Chaucer

Editions," *Bulletin of the John Rylands University Library of Manchester* 78 (1996): 47-61 and chap. 3, n. 17, below. Nonetheless, what Leland states here constitutes not the claim of a relation, but may be more accurately described as a confusion of the work of the two printers. A page earlier in Leland's account he claims that his own hendecasyllables were written at the behest of Berthelet.

14. Cf. John H. Fisher, *John Gower: Moral Philosopher and Friend of Chaucer* (New York: New York University Press, 1964), 16-17 and n. at 323: "The interrelationships suggest that Berthelette, Thynne, and Leland were in communication while these two editions and Leland's Commentaries were being prepared." Fisher's statement is cited by David Carlson, "The Writings and Manuscript Collections of the Elizabethan Alchemist, Antiquary, and Herald Francis Thynne," *Huntington Library Quarterly* 52 (1989): 203-72, and more recently by Tim William Machan, "Thomas Berthelette and Gower's *Confessio*," *Studies in the Age of Chaucer* 18 (1996): 153n. 26. The "interrelations" Fisher invokes here are restricted to those between Godfray and Berthelet. He offers no evidence that there are relations between either of these printers and Leland other than the words of Leland's obviously inaccurate account.

15. I believe Leland's authority controls many of Pearsall's arguments in his recent "Chaucer's Tomb: The Politics of Reburial." Nonetheless, since Pearsall has misread my intentions in an earlier version of chap. 1, I am willing to concede that I may be misreading his as well (see above, chap. 1, n. 13).

16. To accept Leland does not necessarily entail accepting Tuke as author of preface. In the Urry edition, Thomas identifies the Preface in the 1532 edition as Tuke's, but in the Testimonies, this is identified as "Mr. William Thynne's Epistle Dedicatory to King Henry the Eighte before Chaucer's Works." Thomas's opinions are of no documentary merit; but they do show that there is a perfectly logical explanation that accounts for all material evidence. It is clear that Thomas does not believe that Tuke wrote this particular preface, but rather that he wrote some other preface which is missing from the 1532 edition he has (one he believes is possibly Berthelet's).

17. James E. Blodgett, "Some Printer's Copy for William Thynne's 1532 Edition of Chaucer," *The Library* ser. 6, 1 (1979): 97-113; see also Ralph Hanna III and Traugott Lawler, Textual Notes to *Boece, Riverside Chaucer,* 1151. The use of Caxton texts as copytexts is surveyed by N. F. Blake, "Aftermath: Manuscript to Print," in Griffiths and Pearsall, eds., *Book Production*, 403-32, esp., Appendix A: Caxton Prints for which a copy-text survives or which were used as copy," 419-25.

18. De Worde in 1498 uses the same woodcuts found in Caxton's second edition, as does Thynne in 1532. Pynson's woodcuts of 1492 are recut and many of these are reused in 1526. Edward Hodnett, *English Woodcuts, 1480-1535,* 2d ed. (Oxford: University Press, 1973), 128-30, 363-67. An extensive study of these woodcuts is by David R. Carlson, "Woodcut

Illustrations of the Canterbury Tales, 1483-1602," *The Library*, ser. 6, 19 (1997): 25-67.

19. Greg claims that Pynson 1526 is "clearly printed" from Pynson 1492—a copy corrected from Caxton's second edition (not the same copy used in 1492) ("Early Editions," 755 and n. 9). I do not find Greg any too clear here. But the preface in 1526 is definitely not a copy of nor is it set from the version of 1492; a few variants suggest that it may be set from the same copy of Caxton used in 1492, but this requires further study. See further, Blodgett, "William Thynne," 42-47, for notes on the copytexts for these early editions and the history of speculation regarding them. Donald C. Baker, "William Thynne's Printing of the *Squire's Tale*: Manuscript and Printer's Copy," *Studies in Bibliography* 39 (1986): 125-32, has some additional notes, but the evidence is not clearly presented and could support a number of conclusions other than the one he seems to prefer.

20. Whereas Caxton, de Worde, and Pynson in 1526 asked readers to "remember the soule of the sayd Geffrey Chaucer," in 1492 Pynson associated the well-being of Chaucer's soul with the actual ability of readers, who "may so take & vnderstond the gode and vertuous tales that it may so profitte to the helth of oure soules. and inespecial of the soule of the seid Geffrey Chaucer." See further Stanley Howard Johnston, Jr., "A Study of the Career and Literary Publications of Richard Pynson" (diss. University of Western Ontario, 1977), 232-34.

21. Walter W. Skeat, *The Chaucer Canon, with a discussion of the works associated with the name of Geoffrey Chaucer* (Oxford: Clarendon Press, 1900), 117; and most recently Bradford Y. Fletcher, "Printer's Copy for Stow's *Chaucer*," *Studies in Bibliography* 31 (1978): 184-201.

22. Descriptive tables of contents are readily available in Brewer's facsimile. There are two title pages for the 1561 edition, but the wording varies only in the spelling; see reproductions in Muscatine, *Book of Geoffrey Chaucer*, 27, and discussion in Introduction above. Cf. the 1598 title: "The Workes of our Antient and Learned English Poet, Geffrey Chaucer, newly Printed. In this impression you shall find these additions: [portraiture, life, notes] . . . Two Bookes of his, neuer before Printed." The two poems are *Chaucer's Dream* and the *Flour and the Leaf.*

23. So also Hammond, *Manual*, 117-19.

24. Robert F. Yeager, "Literary Theory at the Close of the Middle Ages: William Caxton and William Thynne," *Studies in the Age of Chaucer* 6 (1984): 135-64.

25. See Skeat, *Works of Chaucer*, 5: x. "Thynne neither attempted to draw up a lists of Chaucer's genuine works, nor to exclude such works as were not his. He merely printed such things as came to hand. . . . The mere repetition of this collection, in various reprints, did not confer on it any fresh authority. Stow indeed, in 1561, added more pieces to the collection, but he suppressed nothing. Neither did he himself exercise much principle of selection; see vol. 1, p. 56." Skeat's reference here is to his own discus-

sion of MS Trinity College, R.3.19, used by Stow. See also, *Canon,* 117ff., on Stow's edition.

26. Although Yeager concedes "we have no idea exactly what [Thynne] looked at" (149), he also argues that Thynne made decisions based on extra-textual evidence of previous editions. See, e.g., 149n. 37, on Pynson's edition, where "Thynne's selectivity is arresting." Yeager here shows Thynne acting as a scholar, attributing texts to Chaucer on the basis of colophons and ascriptions. Caxton in 1478 attributes the Proverbs to Christine. Thynne omits "Letter of Dido" "as having no specific claim made for it by Pynson in a heading or colophon." "Mary Magdalene" alone would have been included for literary-critical reasons. See, however, Blodgett, "Printer's Copy," a work ignored by Yeager.

27. "If Thynne, as perhaps Caxton, envisioned Chaucer as the poet of multiple narrative voices, the consummately skillful creator of personae, might he not have suspected that Chaucer wrote 'In Praise of Peace' disguised, so to speak, as Gower?" (157). The language here is straight from H. Marshall Leicester, Jr., "The Art of Impersonation: A General Prologue to the *Canterbury Tales*," *PMLA* 95 (1980): 213-24; see chap. 8 below.

CHAPTER THREE

1. Pollard and Redgrave gave each of the three parts a separate STC number in 1926 but added a note to STC 5086: "This, with nos. 5088, and 5096 may be called the first edition of Chaucer's works" (Pollard and Redgrave, 1926). I believe the implications of this note as printed in the revised STC are different, with the capitalization of "Chaucer's Works" although this claimed edition receives no separate entry.

2. Hammond, *Manual,* 132-36. The first small-format edition is arguably the three-volume edition of modernizations by Ogle: *The Canterbury Tales of Chaucer, Modernis'd by Several Hands* (London, 1741). On the partial edition in octavo by Morell of 1737, see chap. 6 below.

3. Hetherington, *Chaucer: Notes and Facsimile Texts,* 1. Contrast Hammond's largely textual history of editions (Hammond, *Manual,* 114-49). It would be almost impossible to use Hammond's manual to identify a sixteenth-century Chaucer one had in hand. Muscatine, in a recent letter that I hope he will not mind my citing, considered his book so "rare" that he was astonished I knew of it. Yet despite Muscatine's self-effacement, his book is basic to any history of Chaucer editions.

4. Wytze and Lotte Hellinga, *The Fifteenth-Century Printing Types of the Low Countries,* 2 vols. (Amsterdam: Hertzberger, 1966), 1:17-21, 67 (on relations between Veldener and Caxton) and 2: plates 185-88 (for Veldener's types); H. D. L. Vervliet, *Sixteenth-Century Printing Types of the Low Countries* (Amsterdam: Hertzberger, 1968), 42-43 (on de Worde); George D. Painter, *William Caxton: A Quincentenary Biography of England's First Printer* (London: Chatto and Windus, 1976), 182.

5. The importance of de Worde was recognized in one of the first treatises on English type; see Edward Rowe Mores, *A Dissertation upon English Typographical Founders and Founderies (1778)*, ed. Harry Carter and Christopher Ricks (Oxford: Oxford Bibliographical Society, 1961), 4-5. De Worde's type finally became the model used by Caslon in the eighteenth century. A. J. Johnson, *Type Designs: Their History and Development* (1934) (3rd ed. Norwich: Andre Deutsch 1966), chap. 1, 5-36; Stanley Morison, with assistance of Harry Carter, *John Fell: The University Press and the 'Fell' Types: The punches and matrices designed for printing in the Greek, Latin, English and Oriental Languages bequeathed in 1686 to the University of Oxford by John Fell, D.D.* (Oxford: Clarendon Press, 1967), 113-14.

6. Talbot Baines Reed, *A History of the Old English Letter Foundries*, rev. ed. A. F. Johnson (London: Faber and Faber, 1952), chap. 9: "The Later Founders of the Seventeenth Century," 185-205. See also: Stanley Morison, "Introduction: Bibliography and Typography," in W. Turner Berry and A. F. Johnson, eds. *Catalogue of Specimens of Printing Types by English and Scottish Printers and Founders, 1665-1830* (London: Oxford University Press, 1935), esp. xxxiii-xxxiv; Derek Nuttall, "English Printers and their Typefaces, 1600-1700," in Robin Myers and Michael Harris, eds., *Aspects of Printing from 1600* (Oxford: Oxford Polytechnic Press, 1987).

7. On the efforts by John Fell of Oxford to obtain continental materials, see Morison and Carter, *John Fell*, chap. VI, 59-65; Horace Hart, *Notes on a Century of Typography at the University Press Oxford, 1693-1794* (1900), ed. Harry Carter (Oxford: Clarendon Press, 1970), App. II, pt. 2, 161-72.

8. Joseph Moxon, *Mechanick Exercises on the Whole Art of Printing*, ed. Herbert Davis and Harry Carter, 2d ed. (London: Oxford University Press, 1962), 123 (sec. 14).

9. A. F. Johnson, "The Classification of Gothic Types" (1929) and "Notes on Some Seventeenth-Century English Types and Type Specimens" (1938), in A. F. Johnson, *Selected Essays in Books and Printing*, ed. Percy H. Muir (London: Routledge, 1970), 1-17, 305-12. An attempted solution is the use of capitals in the 1532 Gower (see fig. 13).

10. [Richard Brathwait], *A Comment upon the Two Tales of our Ancient, Renowned, and Ever Living Poet Sir Jefray Chaucer, Knight . . .* (London, 1665); Fr. Kynaston, *Amorum Troili et Creseide Libri duo priores Anglico-Latini* (Oxford: Lichfield, 1635). Cf. Machan, *Textual Criticism and Middle English Texts*, 41-46: "In printing an English version in outdated black letter type, [Kynaston] responds to what Edwards calls 'the need to retrieve and preserve the text' by offering the reader Chaucer's words in a format that stresses their antiquity" (46). The sentence is ambiguous, but I don't think it is accurate to claim that blackletter was outdated in the early seventeenth century for these texts. Machan first made this argument in "Kynaston's *Troilus*, Textual Criticism, and the Renaissance Reading of Chaucer," *Exemplaria* 5 (1993): 161-83.

11. Frank Isaac, *English and Scottish Printing Types, 1501-35, 1508-41* (London: Oxford University Press, 1930). See also the final volume of Robert

Proctor, *An Index of Early Books in the British Museum*, pt. 2, sec. 2-3 (1938); Isaac was responsible for introducing to the *Index* the descriptive system used by Stanley Morison to measure type, and the system was in turn adopted by the *British Museum Catalog of Fifteenth-Century Books*.

12. Compare the system designed solely for identification purposes by Konrad Haebler, *Typenrepertorium der Wiegendrucke*, 5 vols. (Leipzig, 1905-24; rpt. Nendeln: Krauss, 1968), and summary discussion in Konrad Haebler, *The Study of Incunabula* (1925), tr. Lucy Eugenia Osborne (New York: The Grolier Club, 1933), 104ff. *The British Museum Catalog of Fifteenth-Century Books*, having committed in general to Isaac's system over Proctor's, provides no generic classification for the earliest types.

13. The large texturas used for Missals is one of the more obvious examples of the relation of size to genre.

14. "And as I am and always have been studious to promote the Honour of my Native Country, so I soon resolv'd to put their Merits to the Trial, by turning some of the *Canterbury Tales* into our language, as it is now refin'd." Both Ovid and Chaucer are dressed "in the same English Habit" and may be compared by the reader "without obtruding my Opinion on him"; John Dryden, *Fables Ancient and Modern; translated into Verse, from Homer, Ovid, Boccace, & Chaucer* (London: Tonson, 1700), Preface, sig. A1.

15. *The Plough-man's Tale, Shewing by the doctrine and lives of the Romish Clergie, that the Pope is Antichrist and they his Ministers. Written by Sir Geffrey Chaucer, Knight, amongst his Canterburie tales* (London: Macham and Cooke, 1606). Muscatine's history omits both the 1606 book and Godfray's earlier version, and thus defines the history of Chaucer's printing as the history of the printing of texts now thought to be by Chaucer.

16. Occasionally, the same is claimed for the Speght edition, but no convincing cases of this have been cited; see Pearsall, "Speght," 87; Derek Pearsall, ed., *The Nun's Priest's Tale*, Variorum Chaucer, II, 9 (Norman, Okla.: University of Oklahoma Press, 1984), 114.

17. "His press seems in some mysterious way to have been connected with that of Berthelet and some have gone so far as to assert that Godfray was not a printer at all and that the books with his name were printed by Berthelet"; E. Gordon Duff, *A Century of the English Book Trade . . . 1457-1557* (London: The Bibliographical Society, 1948), 56. See also, my "Bibliographical History versus Bibliographical Evidence," 55, notes 16 and 17, and Andrew N. Wawn, "Chaucer, The Plowman's Tale and Reformation Propaganda: The Testimonies of Thomas Godfray and *I Playne Piers*," *Bulletin of the John Rylands Library* 56 (1973): 174-92, at 177-78 with ref. to R. B. McKerrow and F. S. Ferguson, *Title-page Borders used in England and Scotland, 1485-1640* (1932), pp. 13 and 16 (nos. 16 and 19). The transference of such woodcuts was discussed as early as Alfred W. Pollard, "The Transference of Woodcuts in the Fifteenth and Sixteenth Centuries," *Bibliographica* 2 (London: Kegan Paul, Trench, 1890): 343-69.

18. The folio in 6s is unknown in Caxton's works. There are a few examples in de Worde, and the format becomes common in Pynson. For de Worde and Pynson, see E. Gordon Duff, *Fifteenth Century English Books: A Bibliography of Books and Documents Printed in England and of Books for the English Market Printed Abroad* (London: Bibliographical Society, 1917), 24-26. Somewhat less specific information is given in E. G. Duff, W. W. Greg et al., *Hand-lists of Books Printed by London Printers, 1501-1556* (London: Oxford University Press, 1913).

19. See W. Craig Ferguson, *Pica Roman Type in Elizabethan England* (London: Scolar Press, 1989), 3-4. Isaac refers to the problem with specific reference to the Godfray Chaucer in Frank Isaac, *English Printers' Types of the Sixteenth Century* (Oxford, Bibliographical Society, 1936), p. 15 and Plate 30. See further, my "On Correctness." The mixture of various capitals with this font can be seen also in the history of Pynson's type 2; see Duff, *Fifteenth Century English Books*.

20. Elyot, *Boke of the Governour* (1531). For Heywood's plays printed in bâtard; see n. 30 below. Berthelet used two rotundas (87, with variant, and 54) as well as two bâtards (5 and 72; 72 is used for Latin in Gower). For the significance of Berthelet's use of a bâtard similar to that used by Godfray in the 1532 Chaucer, see Johnson, *Type Design*, 23: Berthelet is the only printer who used it for general publications.

21. See the many references and discussion in Spurgeon, *Chaucer Criticism*, 1: lxxiii-lxxiv.

22. The only author now considered canonical with a publication record comparable to that of Chaucer and Gower is Malory, printed in folio by Caxton in 1485 (STC 801) and reprinted twice in folio by de Worde (1498 and 1529) (STC 802, 803). Malory's publication stops abruptly with the quarto edition of 1634 (STC 806); he was not reprinted again until the nineteenth century.

23. One noteworthy folio in 6s is Godfray's Plowman's Tale (1535, STC 5099.5); on textual grounds, this has been related to other *Piers* pamphlets of mid-sixteenth century. I have shown that these textual relations are misleading, since the Plowman's Tale was circulated only as a folio book—(with Chaucer's works or in the independent print by Godfray). The putative relations to such things as the Pilgrim's Tale and small *Piers* pamphlets could only be made once the tale was circulated (in fact or second hand) as a text rather than a book. See my "Bibliographical History versus Bibliographical Evidence."

24. Leland, *Commentarii*, 422.

25. Cf. Richard Helgerson, *Forms of Nationhood: The Elizabethan Writing of England* (Chicago: University of Chicago, 1992), whose many reproductions of title-pages imply, erroneously I think, that an appropriate representation does exist.

26. That Caxton himself recast Type 2 to produce 2* was claimed by William Blades, *The Biography and Typography of William Caxton* (2nd ed. New York: Scribner, 1882), 113-14, repeating discussion in *The Life and Typography of*

William Caxton, 2: xxvi and xxxii. This has been denied by Robin Myers, "William Blades's Debt to Henry Bradshaw and G. I. F. Tupper in his Caxton Studies: A Further Look at Unpublished Documents," *The Library* ser. 5, 33 (1978): 281, with reference to Painter, *Caxton*, 95. See, however, Lotte Hellinga, *Caxton in Focus* (London: British Library, 1982), 75-76, arguing that Caxton owned the matrices for Type 2, and Witze and Lotte Hellinga, *Fifteenth-Century Printing Types*, 1:17ff.

27. Daniel Berkeley Updike, *Printing Types: Their History, Forms, and Use: A Study in Survivals*, 2 vols., 2d ed. (Cambridge: Harvard University Press, 1937), chap. xiv: "French Types: 1500-1800," 1:188-276; A. Claudin, *Histoire de l'imprimerie en France au XVe et au XVIe siècle* (Paris: Imprimerie Nationale, 1900), vol. 1, and the convenient collection of illustrations in *Harvard College Library, Dept. of Printing and Graphic Arts, Catalogue of French Sixteenth Century Books*, 2 vols. (Cambridge: Belknapp Press, 1964).

28. M. A. Screech, *Rabelais* (Ithaca: Cornell University Press, 1979), 223. For the typographical history of Rabelais, see Pierre-Paul Plan, *Les Editions de Rabelais de 1532 à 1711: Catalogue raisonné*, (1904; rpt. New York, 1970); Stephen Rawles and M. A. Screech, *A New Rabelais Bibliography: Editions of Rabelais before 1626, Etudes Rabelaissiennes*, 20 (Geneva: Droz, 1987), and Stephen Rawles, "Les Typographie de Rabelais: Réflexions bibliographiques sur les éditions faussement attribuées," *Etudes Rabelaisiennes* 21 (1988): 37-48.

29. "Typi sunt alij ab ijs qui in ceteris, quas vidi, Edd. habentur. In una parte libra haec verba constat W. Thynne leguntur"; *Remarks and Collections of Thomas Hearne*, 11 vols., ed. C. E. Doble, D. W. Rannie et al. (Oxford: Oxford Historical Society, 1885-1921), 4: 42, quoted Spurgeon, *Chaucer Criticism*, 1: 321. See further, chap. 5 below.

30. Heywood's plays printed by Rastell include *A mery Play betwene the Pardoner and the Frere* (1533, STC 13299), *A Mery Play betwene Johan Iohan the husande, Tyb his wyfe, & syr Jhan the preest* (1533, 13298), *Play of the Wether* (1533, STC 13305), *A Play of Love* (1534, STC 13303); Rastell also printed Henry Medwall, *A goodly interlude of Nature* (1530-34, STC 17779). Of these all but *Play of the Wether* and *Play of Love* are printed in bâtard (102B). On Rastell, see the early discussion by Henry R. Plomer, "John Rastel and his Contemporaries," *Bibliographica* 2 (1890): 437-51.

31. Annie S. Irvine, "A Manuscript Copy of *The Plowman's Tale*," *University of Texas Studies in English* 12 (1932): 37. See my "Bibliographical History versus Bibliographical Evidence," n. 27.

32. For recent discussion of the 1532 Gower, see Machan, "Thomas Berthelette and Gower's *Confessio*," 143-66; Machan's discussion is useful, but the description of format on p. 145 is not accurate.

CHAPTER FOUR

1. See, most recently, David R. Carlson, "Chaucer's Boethius and Thomas Usk's *Testament of Love*: Politics and Love in the Chaucerian Tradition," in

Robert A. Taylor et al., eds., *The Centre and Its Compass: Studies in Medieval Literature in Honor of Professor John Leyerle* (Kalamazoo: Western Michigan University, 1993), 29-70.

2. Skeat actually had three categories: Chaucer works; spurious works (contained in his Supplement); and finally, works that apparently do not require inclusion. Skeat does not explain why *Testament of Love* and *Testament of Criseyde* fall into the second category, while the *Siege of Thebes* and Tale of Beryn apparently fall into the third.

3. See chap. 1, n. 34 above.

4. The 1548 Plowmans Tale (by Hyll) (STC 5100) is printed directly from the text of the Plowmans Tale in the 1542 Chaucer (a text inserted at the end of the *Canterbury Tales*) and even copies its colophon.

5 See further, P. L. Heyworth, *Jack Upland, Friar Daw's Reply and Upland's Rejoinder* (London: Oxford University Press, 1968), 5-6, 29; Pearsall, "Thomas Speght (ca. 1550-?)," 88.

6. I have silently expanded abbreviations. The passage concludes both versions; see text in Skeat, *Works of Chaucer*, 7:144-45.

7. Skeat emends "ne ought to loke thinges" (the text that would result from his rearrangement) to "nat to loke, ne thinges."

8. The problem of the text's incoherence was not faced until Bradley. Earlier readers were presented with a text that editors implied was clear. In the 1721 edition, a summary in large type is inserted between the Prologue and the first Boke, which states that it is in two Parts; in the first, Love "bequeaths to all them that follow her Instructions, the knowledge of Truth from Error . . . In the second Part she teacheth the Knowledge of one very God our Creator, as also the State of Grace, and the State of Glory; all which good things are figur'd by a Margarite Pearl" (*Works*, 1721, 479).

9. "Testimonies of Learned Men concerning Chaucer and his Works"; *Works*, 1721, sig. h1v, printed in full from "I marvel to consider this . . ." Quoted here from Foxe, 1570, 2:965; see further Spurgeon, *Chaucer Criticism*, 1:105-6.

10. "Provided allso that all bokes in Englishe printed before the yere of our Lorde a thousande fyve hundred and fourtie intytled the Kings Hieghnes proclamacions iniunctions, translacions of the Pater noster, the Aue Maria and the Crede, the psalters prymers prayer statutes and lawes of the Realms, Cronycles Canterburye tales, Chaucers bokes Gowers bokes and stories of mennes lieues, shall not be comprehended in the prohibision of this acte" (Spurgeon, *Chaucer Criticism*, 1: 34).

11. According to Francis Thynne's version of the origin of the Plowman's Tale, the Bishops were not in the least blinded to the meaning of the Plowman's Tale, and caused it to be suppressed from the 1532 edition (*Animadversions*, 7-10).

12. Even earliest editions were available; Hearne is surprised that a correspondent claims that the 1570 edition is rare: "If John Fox's commentaries be a book that is scarce, 'tis grown so of late. For some few years

ago it was very common and very cheap"; Hearne, *Remarks and Collections,*
letter 18 Feb. 1724/5; on the 1563 edition, see 21 Feb. 1726/7. Having had
need of the 1570 edition in several locales, I side with the correspondent.

13. Thomas's handwritten notes in the British Library copy claim: "This Life
was very uncorrectly drawn up by Mr Dart, and corrected and enlarged by
W.T. especially in that part which gives an account of the Author's Works
. . ." See further below.

14. The section proceeds to discussion of the Pilgrim's Tale:

> Mr. *Speght* in his Life . . . 1602, mentions a Tale in Mr. *William
> Thynne's* first printed Book of Chaucer's Works, more odious to
> the Clergy than the Speech of the *Plowman,* which began thus;

>> In Lincolneshire fast be a Fenne
>> Standeth a religious house, who doth it kenne, &c.

> The Argument of which Tale, as also the occasion thereof, and
> the cause why it was left out of *Chaucer's* Works, he promised
> should be shewed in Mr. *Francis Thynne's* Comment upon *Chaucer;*
> but neither the one nor the other have been since published"
> (*Works,* 1721, sig. f2r).

15. Dart, *Westmonasterium,* 87, claims that he has never seen the 1721 edition
except on a bookseller's shelf and that he is satisfied with his old one
"with my own written Notes."

16. The skepticism registered by Nicolas in his biography centers only on the
obscurity of the text: "of which it is equally difficult to comprehend the
meaning or the purport" ("Life," 33). On the slow rejection of Chaucer's
authorship in mid-century, see Lounsbury, *Studies in Chaucer,* 1:201 and
Skeat, *Canon,* 97-98.

17. Skeat, *Works of Chaucer,* 5: xii n. 2. The note ends with a reference to *The
Academy,* 11 March, 1893; p. 222. To form this anagram, Skeat has in a
few cases redefined the paragraphs indicated by ornamented capitals in
Thynne's edition—something he discusses more explicitly in his 1905
Chaucer 1532, xl.

18. "Thomas Usk: The 'Testament of Love,'" *Athenaeum,* 6 February 1897,
184, rpt. *The Collected Papers of Henry Bradley* (Oxford: Clarendon Press,
1928), 229-32.

19. Skeat, *Chaucer 1532,* xxxviii-lx.

20. The phrase is Bradshaw's in a letter to Furnivall; see Paul Needham, *The
Bradshaw Method: Henry Bradshaw's Contribution to Bibliography* (Chapel
Hill, N.C.: Hanes Foundation, 1988), 8-12. Bradshaw had himself much
earlier doubted Chaucer's authorship of the *Testament of Love,* see his letter to Payne Collier of 1869, responding to Collier's own *Athenaeum* article on the subject: "I have been so constantly, for the last six years,
dinning into the ears of all whom I come across—Mr Furnivall and Mr R.
Morris among the number—the total want of trustworthy evidence in
favour of attributing to Chaucer any of the following pieces . . ."; G. W.

Prothero, *A Memoir of Henry Bradshaw* (London: Kegan Paul, Trench, 1888), 355.

21. See, e.g., Paul Saenger, *A Catalogue of the Pre-1500 Western Manuscript Books at the Newberry Library* (Chicago: University of Chicago Press, 1989); Barbara A. Shailor, *Catalogue of Medieval and Renaissance Manuscripts in the Beinecke Rare Book and Manuscript Library, Yale University*, 3 vols. (Binghamton: MRTS, 1984), see MS 228, "Dives and Pauper," a manuscript from Portugal written by a scribe trained in England.

22. Paul Strohm, "Politics and Poetics: Usk and Chaucer in the 1380s," in Lee Patterson, ed., *Literary Practice and Social Change in Britain, 1380-1530* (Berkeley and Los Angeles: University of California, 1990), 83-112.

CHAPTER FIVE

1. See Douglas Wurtele, "The Penitence of Geoffrey Chaucer," *Viator* 11 (1980): 335-59, and discussion in Jameela Lares, "Chaucer's *Retractions*: A 'Verray Parfit Penitence,'" *Cithara* 34 (1994): 18-33.

2. J. F. Royster, additions to Richmond P. Bond, "Some Eighteenth Century Chaucer Allusions," *Studies in Philology* 25 (1928): 316-39, at p. 336; Hearne claims to have seen this in February (Spurgeon, *Chaucer Criticism*, 1:331). The most convenient short biography of Hearne is by David C. Douglas, *English Scholars* (London: Jonathan Cape, 1939), 226-48. See also the early life of Hearne by William Huddesford in *The Lives of those Eminent Antiquaries John Leland, Thomas Hearne and Anthony à Wood*, ed. Thomas Warton and William Huddesford, 2 vols. (Oxford: Clarendon Press, 1772). For his relation to the press, see Harry Carter, *A History of Oxford University Press*, vol. 1: "To the Year 1780" (Oxford: Clarendon Press, 1975), esp. 263-69.

3. The first page is reproduced in Muscatine, *Book of Geoffrey Chaucer*, 42; see Spurgeon, *Chaucer Criticism*, 1:344-45.

4. Hearne, *Remarks and Collections*, 6 (1902): 95-6 (entry 5 Oct. 1717): "It is printing at Lond., in the white Letter, contrary to Mr. Urry's mind, who was resolved upon the black Letter and would not hear of the white. Mr. Urry went to London on purpose to concert Matters about a black Letter, and 'twas then that he got his Indisposition, wch carry'd him off. Mr. Thomas Rawlinson tells me yt the sd Ed. of Chaucer in the white Letter will be a very bad one. Mr. Thomas himself is displeas'd at ye white Letter. The Bp of Rochester, Dr. Atterbury, declared expressly agt the white Letter, when I saw him at Islip." See also, Alderson *Chaucer and Augustan Scholarship*, 69ff.

5. Letter to Rawlinson, in *Letters written by Eminent Persons* (1813), 2:97-98; Spurgeon, *Chaucer Criticism*, 1:376.

6. Thomas Hearne, ed., *Robert of Gloucester's Chronicle*, 2 vols. (Oxford: Sheldon Theatre, 1724). The edition contains the often-cited "A Letter to Mr. Bagford, containing some Remarks upon Geffray Chaucer and his Writings," 2:596-606.

7. Reed, *A History of the Old English Letter Foundries*, 185-228; see above, chap. 3, nn. 6-7.

8. Morison and Carter, *John Fell*, 114-15; Fell's blackletter was first used in George Hickes, *Institutiones grammatticae Anglo-Saxonicae et Moeso-Gothicae* (1689).

9. On Lintot's control of expenses, see the figures given in John Nichols, *Literary Anecdotes*, "Lintot and his Authors," 203-5, enumerating copies purchased by Lintot; Chauceriana includes Betterton's modernization of the Miller's Tale (1712) and Pope's *Temple of Fame* (1715). The arrangement with Urry is one of the few to cost Lintot nothing beyond the projected expenses of paper, print, copper plates and all incidental expenses.

10. Compare the average seventeenth-century English book with even run-of-the-mill publications by Tonson in the early eighteenth century. Tonson himself was dependent on Dutch matrices; Reed, *History*, 229.

11. Spurgeon, *Chaucer Criticism*, 1:94; the entry is given under Brigham's own name, and dated 1556 (see above, chap. 1). Generally, Spurgeon is careful to reproduce the typographical conventions of her sources.

12. Clear as these conventions are, they were garbled in later editions. See *The Works of Thomas Hearne, M.A.* (London: for Samuel Bagster, 1810), a reprint of Hearne's edition of Robert of Gloucester, complete with its appended Letter to Bagford. This claims to be a page for page reprint of the 1724 edition, but what appears in blackletter in the original is represented, oddly, by small roman (p. 601) or by italics (602-3).

13. The decision to omit the Retraction could have been similar to the decision to include "Eight Goodly Questions" following the Table of Contents. The 1532 edition had printed it there, apparently to fill up the nearby leaf (sig. A4) that would otherwise have been nearly blank, recto and verso; the Table of Contents ends halfway through the first column of the recto (sig. A3ra). The quire itself contains only five leaves, the fifth being the woodcut title-page for the *Canterbury Tales*.

14. Preface, sig. k2r: "With these helps Mr. *Urry* made several Corrections throughout the greatest part of *Chaucer's* Works, and had prepared a fair Copy for the Press, written partly in his own hand and partly by Mr. *Ainsworth*, to the end of the *Frankelein's* Tale." Ainsworth, according to the Proposals, then completed the text from Urry's notes (see further Alderson, *Chaucer and Augustan Scholarship*, 97-98).

15. See Alderson, *Chaucer and Augustan Scholarship*, 98, and Manly-Rickert, *Text of the Canterbury Tales*, 1:115. A copy of Stow exists with Urry's collations and a later collation of the Cholmondeley MS (now Delamere) by T. Thomas; these are identified by Thomas's note on fol. lii (quoted by Manly-Rickert, ibid).

16. On the Plowman's Tale, see my "Bibliographical History versus Bibliographical Evidence."

17. See Hammond, *Manual*, 130, and the excellent discussion in Alderson, *Chaucer and Augustan Scholarship*, 106-18.

18. Tanner's books were later bequeathed to the Bodleian; see Ian Philip, *The Bodleian Library in the Seventeenth and Eighteenth Centuries* (Oxford: Clarendon Press, 1983), 80-83. The first to use one of these books was Rawlinson in 1750; in 1781, Warton complains that they are still not catalogued. There is no Caxton *Canterbury Tales* at the Bodleian; see *Catalogus Librorum Impressorum Bibliothecae Bodleianae*, 3 vols. (Oxford: Typographeo Academico, 1843), listing early Chaucer editions of 1561, 1598, 1602, 1687 and 1721 and one Pynson edition; for copies outside the Bodleian, see Dennis E. Rhodes, *A Catalogue of Incunabula in all the Libraries of Oxford University outside the Bodleian* (Oxford: Clarendon Press, 1982), 102-03: the copy at Merton college was given in 1630; the copy at St. Johns is of the second edition. Sloane gave some 1,400 books, but these were duplicates and the Caxton was not among them; see William Dunn Macray, *Annals of the Bodleian Library, Oxford* (Oxford: Clarendon Press, 1890), 169 and 164f. The first Caxtons Macray lists were given in 1657 and 1680 (a composite volume). None other was given until 1736. They were not exceptionally valuable. Charles J. Sawyer and F. J. Harvey Darnton, *English Books 1475-1900: A Signpost for Collectors* (New York: Sawyer, 1927), 45-46, note that not until 1753 (the year Parliament agreed to purchase the Sloane Museum and the Harleian and Cottonian Libraries) were Caxtons even priced in pounds. The "leap in price" occurs in 1812. The price of a volume in 1496 is 6s; in 1678, three sold for 7s 10d.

19. Alderson speaks of only two copies—owned by Sloane and by Bagford. And these copies are now easily identifiable. See Seymour de Ricci, *A Census of Caxtons*, Bibliographical Society Monographs, 15 (Oxford University Press, 1909); the Bagford copy is a copy of Caxton's first edition, number 14 of the 30 copies recorded by de Ricci but untraced by de Ricci. This Caxton was imperfect and was among the books in the Harley collection before acquired by Ames in 1749. See Joseph Ames, *Typographical Antiquities: Being an Historical Account of Printing in England with some Memoirs of our Antient Printers, and A Register of the Books printed by them from the year MCCCCLXXI to the Year MDC* (London: W. Faden, 1749), 54: "This very early first edition of them is a pretty thick folio, . . . near 400 leaves, in my possession." Ames's note a states that the copy was obtained from Harley's library "after whose decease I bought it. Great industry has been used to compleat it, but without success." Ames also has a copy of the second edition: "[The copy of the first edition] wants a small matter at the beginning and end, has the tales disposed somewhat different from the second edition, which is complete in quarto, bound with some other of his works, at St. John's College, Oxon, communicated to me by that hopeful young man, Mr. Abr. Jos. Rudd, which I shall now give some account of, because it will give light to both" (54-55). This second edition is de Ricci, 23, copy 1. Sloane's Chaucer is de Ricci, 23, copy 2, now B.L. IB 55095 (the second edition, although Bagford seems to have thought it was the first). Margaret Nickson, "Bagford and Sloane," *The British Library Journal* 9 (1983): 51-55. It is also imperfect, missing all

text before sig. mii and after sig. K (see collations in de Ricci, *Census*). Other copies that may have been available include Pepys's copy of the second edition (this contains the Retraction) (de Ricci, 23, copy 5 = N. A. Smith, *Catalogue of the Pepys Library at Magdalene College, Cambridge* I: *Printed Books* [Cambridge: D. S. Brewer, 1978], item 2053). Rawlinson seems to have owned two Caxtons, a first edition (imperfect) (de Ricci, 22, copy 13), a second edition (de Ricci, 23, copy 12), missing the Retraction. In all, there are perhaps six relevant copies. Four lack the Retraction, including one that was unquestionably in Hearne's hands. Two include the Retraction, one of which Hearne knows about and speaks about directly (as including Retraction).

20. Bagford's projected history was never written but served as the basis for others, for example, by Joseph Ames. See esp. Milton McC. Gatch, "John Bagford, Bookseller and Antiquary," *The British Library Journal* 12 (1986): 150-71; "John Bagford's Manuscript Fragments," *The Library* ser. 6, 7 (1985): 95-114; and Bagford's "An Essay on the Invention of Printing, by Mr. John Bagford; with an Account of his Collections for the same by Mr. Humfrey Wanley," Royal Society, *Philosophical Transactions* 25 (1706-7): 237-410.

21. Hearne, *Remarks and Collections* 2 (1886): 188; Spurgeon, *Chaucer Criticism*, 1:297-98.

22. "Letter to Bagford," 597; Spurgeon, *Chaucer Criticism*, 1:303-4; see also, *Remarks and Collections*, 6: 199, quoted below.

23. "Gulielmum Caxodunum . . . quem constat primum *Londini* artem exercuisse typographicam, *Chauceri* opera, quotquot vel pretio vel precibus comparare potuit, in unum volumen collegisse" (Leland, *Commentarii*, 423).

24. On the modern function of this codicological notion of "booklet," see below, chap. 7.

25. *Remarks and Collections*, 6:199, quoted also Spurgeon, *Chaucer Criticism*, 1: 301; the idea is repeated in a letter of the same year (*Remarks and Collections*, 6:597; Spurgeon, *Chaucer Criticism*, 1:303).

26. Hearne generally gives credence to Leland. He accepts Leland's account of Berthelet's involvement in the 1532 Chaucer (which may be accurate) and uses it to claim that the Thynne edition must have been published later, in 1540 "not in 1532 as Mr. Wood insinuates (Athenae Oxon 1:53)." The lack of a complete copy of the 1532 edition, with its unambiguous colophon, was clearly a problem, and what are now considered the most basic facts concerning its publication were not settled even by the date of the Urry edition (1721). T. A. Birrell, "Anthony Wood, John Bagford and Thomas Hearne as Bibliographers," in Robin Myers and Michael Harris, ed., *Pioneers of Bibliography* (Winchester, Hampshire: St. Paul's Bibliographies, 1988), 25-39, is overly enthusiastic in picturing Hearne as "collating every manuscript and printed text of Chaucer that he could lay his hands on" (34).

27. See, most conveniently, Duff, *Fifteenth Century English Books*, nos. 86-90, pp. 24-25. See further, 1709 Diary extracts (Hearne, *Remarks and*

Collections, 6:195; Spurgeon, *Chaucer Criticism*, 1:298) on MS Arch Seld. B 30: "The Conclusion conteyning Chaucer's acknowlegement of his Faults &c. not in the Print." I cannot match the "Edition of his Poems with Mr. *Tanner*" with any of the Caxtons in de Ricci's *Census*. On Tanner's books, see above, n. 18. Copies of de Worde remained rare, and Dibdin in 1825 doubted its existence: "The sober critic will, I apprehend, conclude, that the notion of an early-printed edition of the Canterbury Tales, by Wynkyn de Worde, is purely *romantic*. Certain it is, that the supposed edition of 1495 has no foundation in truth; and probably it is, that the early impression of the Canterbury Tales by Pynson, deterred Wynkyn de Worde from the attempt of republication . . ."; T. F. Dibdin, *The Library Companion: or, the Young Man's guide, and the old man's comfort in the choice of a library,* (2d ed. (London: Harding, Triphook and Lepard, 1825), 675-82 (note at 679).

28. Diary entry, 9 June 1712; quoted Spurgeon, *Chaucer Criticism*, 1:321.

29. See Nickson, "Bagford and Sloane." The losses in this copy are extensive; see the complete collation in de Ricci, *Census*, 23, copy 2. The copy is missing 105 leaves. Collations were given as early as Blades, *Life and Typography of William Caxton* (1861-63), 2:162-64 (no. 57) (there is a typographical error in Blades's description: "wanting all sig. m. ij; before m iiij and 5" should be transposed "wanting all before sig. m ij; m. iiij and 5").

30. See Hearne's letter of November 1712 and Sloane's thanks (included in Spurgeon, *Chaucer Criticism*, 1:336, 342-43). Hearne says he is looking for three items: P. 150, MS 378 and MS 324 (*Astrolabe*). P. 150 is a 1598 edition (p. 342). An additional Caxton is also mentioned by Hearne; in a diary entry of Nov. 1713: "Mr Bagford tells me that Caxton printed Chaucer's Fragments in 4to without Date which are not taken into his Ed. of the Tales. This is now in the Hands of the Bishop of Ely who had it of Mr. Bagford. Dr. Tanner hath seen this Book. And 'tis certainly a Treasure." This is probably de Ricci 24 and 25—a volume with several Caxtons bound together including *Anelida and Arcite*, and *Parlement of Foules*. In Skeat's account, the copy seems to have been rediscovered by Bradshaw (*Minor Poems*, 1894, xv).

31. Nov 20, 1715, Hearne to Brome, relaying a message from Bagford: "Mr. Hearne, I would have you to demand my Chaucer's Canterbury Tales, printed by William Caxton, lent to Mr. Urry sometimes since" (Spurgeon, *Chaucer Criticism*, 1:337); the book was received in February (1:342).

32. In *Robert of Gloucester*, 603. Hearne says he has found the revocation in a Bodleian manuscript, and also in a manuscript of Selden.

33. Hammond's generally reliable *Manual* seems to claim that Hearne changed his mind on these matters, a change of mind due to a simple misprint by Hammond's printers. "Hearne, in his Remarks and Collections II: 200, says that he believes the Revocation genuine; in his Letter to Bagford he says: 'I begin to think the Revocation is not genuine, but that it was made by the monks'" (Hammond, *Manual*, 321). Hearne's

actual passage is as follows: "I believe the Revocation annex'd to the Parson's Tale in some Copies of Chaucer not to be genuine, but made by the Monks" (*Remarks and Collections*, 2:200). Hearne may, however, have waffled; see note above referring to the Selden MS containing "Chaucer's acknowlegement of his Faults &c." (n. 27 and Spurgeon, *Chaucer Criticism*, 1:298).

34. See Hearne's comments on the 1606 edition of the Plowman's Tale, quoting with approval, the "Author of ye Notes (wch are very good): 'In the former Editions of Chawcer this Tale is made the last, but in the latter, set out by Mr. Spight's advise, and commendable paines, it is the last saving the parson's Tale, I doubt not but this change is warranted by some olde coppies written, as ye corrections also of divers words: and it seems to be most reasonable, that the Parson's Tale should bee the conclusion of their morning werke. . .'" (Diary entry 1709, Hearne, *Remarks and Collections*, 6:199, noted, but not quoted in Spurgeon, *Chaucer Criticism*, 1:301).

35. Thomas, Preface, sig. k1r, notes that Urry left no notes of what printed editions he used. Alderson, *Chaucer and Augustan Scholarship*, 93, notes that Urry obtained a 1550(?) edition from Harley through Atterbury. See Spurgeon, *Chaucer Criticism*, 1:319 (4 Jan. 1712): "An old Geffrey Chaucer in Mr. Urry's Hands (belonging to my Ld. Harley) printed by Rich. Rele [*sic*] dwellyng in Lombard Street." For Urry's borrowings from Sloane, see above, n. 30.

36. Bagford's Caxton is among these, since Wanley had obtained his books for Harley, much to the dismay of Hearne.

37. C. E. Wright and Ruth C. Wright, The *Diary of Humfrey Wanley 1715-1726*, 2 vols. (London: The Bibliographical Society, 1966), see xvii n. 1. Harley's printed books were dispersed and are recorded only in the catalog of Osborne, *Catalogus Bibliothecae Harleianae*, 4 vols. (London: Thomas Osborne, 1743-45); see esp. the section "English Poetry and Romances" (3: 237ff.). At this point, only two Caxton Chaucers remained in the library, *Troilus and Criseyde* (item 3543) and *Book of Fame* (item 3542). This part of Library was used by Michael Maittaire, *Annales Typographici* (vol. 2 dedicated to Edw. Harley).

38. Thomas is as accurate as Ames on editions after 1532. Ames, *Typographical Antiquities*, 127-8, 130. Revisions of Ames, through Dibdin's of 1812, are the basis for history of editions now in STC. *Typographical Antiquities, or the History of Printing in England Scotland and Ireland containing Memoirs of our Ancient Printers . . . begun by the late Joseph Ames. . .* , ed. Thomas Frognall Dibdin, 4 vols. (London: Miller, 1810-).

39. I assume that the Caxtons include Bagford's copy returned in 1715 and Sloane's. On the rarity of de Worde editions, see Dibdin, *Library Companion,* 679, quoted above n. 27. Between the initial collection of materials for the Urry and the handwritten notes in the printed copy, the Thomases had access to the Caxtons collected in Harley's library: "Caxton also printed Chaucer's Book of Fame in the same form and with

the same types as he used in the Second Edition of his Works" (*Works*, 1721, British Library copy, sig. ll, on Caxton; reference is made to the Earl of Oxford's book and Ames, *Typographical Antiquities*, pp. 60, 61.)

40. A handwritten sidenote in the B.L. Urry changes this: "Ames says 1495, p. 84."

41. The parenthetical statement is corrected by hand to "which was the first time it was printed." This is probably corrected to accord with the inaccurate printed statement a few sentences later that the 1532 edition had also contained the Retraction; this statement also has been corrected by hand, and the contradiction, as well as the error on Pynson, remain.

42. Note is to "Mr. Bagford in his collections." Bagford died in 1716. Thomas is referring perhaps to an introductory note in the Testimonies included in this edition: sig. g2r on some lines by Leland: "This was written by Leland, at the request of *Thomas Berthelet*, a diligent and learned Printer, who first printed *Chaucer's* Works, put out by Mr. *Thynne*" (ref. is to Leland's biography of Chaucer).

43. Diary entry 26 Dec. 1712, Hearne, *Remarks and Collections*, 4:42; Spurgeon, *Chaucer Criticism*, 1:321.

44. See the Harley catalog, which notes two copies. The Chaucers noted in Osborne's catalog include Caxton editions of the *Book of Fame* and *Troilus and Criseyde*, one without date identified only as "Works black letter" (Pynson?); two copies of the 1532 edition; and single copies of 1550 (Toye), 1561 (Kynaston), 1602, and 1687, along with three copies on various paper of the 1721 edition; see *Catalogus Bibliothecae Harleianae*, vol. 3, items 3542-66.

45. On the sixteenth-century folios, Thomas is more accurate, identifying two 1542 variants (STC 5070 and 5071); two by Kele and Toye dated 1555 (there are two additional variants, by Bonham and Petit; STC 5071, 5072, 5073, 5074) ; one by Stow (of STC 5075, 5076, and 5076.3); two issues of the 1598 edition by Islip and Bishop (STC 5077 and 5078) although he claims that the first is reprinted by Kele. He is also aware of most of the seventeenth-century partial texts, the 1606 Plowman's Tale, the partial editions by Kynaston, Brathwait, Ashmole, and Dryden.

46. The reference at sig. l2v, note g to "Lord Harley's library" is probably due to William Thomas, in Harley's employ. But it does not appear that either made serious use of the available materials until after the edition was printed (the collations in the B.L. copy are entirely additions of Harley manuscripts; Hammond, *Manual*, 329, quoting note in Harley catalogue on Harley 3943, for *Troilus and Criseyde:* "colated by Wm. Thomas, Esq").

CHAPTER SIX

1. Pearsall, ed., *Nun's Priest's Tale*, "General Editors' Preface" by Paul G. Ruggiers and Donald C. Baker, xii (this Preface varies in various fascicles).

2. Benson, *Riverside Chaucer* (1987), ix.

3. An extreme example of this is Donald C. Baker, ed., *The Squire's Tale*, Variorum Chaucer, II, 12 (Norman: University of Oklahoma Press, 1990), whose edition seems solely designed for the production of new readings. See my review in *Envoi* 2 (1990): 292-99.

4. George Kane and E. Talbot Donaldson, eds., *Piers Plowman: The B Version* (London: Athlone, 1975). The Kane-Donaldson edition is the locus for much textual theory on medieval literature, most notably Lee Patterson, "The Logic of Textual Criticism and the Way of Genius: The Kane-Donaldson *Piers Plowman* in Historical Perspective," in Jerome J. McGann, ed., *Textual Criticism and Literary Interpretation* (Chicago: University of Chicago Press, 1985), 55-91. Patterson has come under attack by Robert Adams, "Editing Piers Plowman B: The Imperatives of an Intermittently Critical Edition," *Studies in Bibliography* 45 (1992): 31-68, esp. 41n. 16.

5. Thomas Morell, *The Canterbury Tales of Chaucer* (London, 1737). The fundamental work on Urry and Morell is Alderson and Henderson, *Chaucer and Augustan Scholarship*. See also: Hammond, *Manual*, esp. 128-31, 204-11; Alice Miskimin, "The Illustrated Eighteenth-Century Chaucer," *Modern Philology* 77 (1979): 26-55; Muscatine, *Book of Geoffrey Chaucer*; B. A. Windeatt, "Thomas Tyrwhitt (1730-1786)," in Ruggiers, ed., *Editing Chaucer*, 117-43. The excellent account of eighteenth-century English editing by Simon Jarvis, *Scholars and Gentlemen: Shakespearian Textual Criticism and Representations of Scholarly Labour, 1725-1765* (Oxford: Clarendon Press, 1995) presents the Urry edition as an exception to what Jarvis sees as the prevailing view in the early century that vernacular editing was "laughable" (48-49); see also, John H. Middendorf, "Eighteenth-Century English Literature," in D. C. Greetham, ed., *Scholarly Editing: A Guide to Research* (New York: MLA, 1995), 283-307.

6. Thomas W. Ross, ed., *The Miller's Tale*, Variorum Chaucer, II, 3 (Norman: University of Oklahoma Press, 1983), 49; Donald C. Baker, "Introduction: The Relation of the Hengwrt Manuscript to the Variorum Chaucer Text," in Paul G. Ruggiers, ed., *Geoffrey Chaucer: The Canterbury Tales: A Facsimile and Transcription of the Hengwrt Manuscript* (Norman: University of Oklahoma Press, 1979), xviii; see also Editor's Preface in the same volume: "The editors . . . made the important decision to adopt the Hengwrt Manuscript . . . as base text for the *Variorum Chaucer*. They further decided that the Hengwrt text would be utilized as a 'best' text. . . . This text . . . is as close as well will come to Chaucer's own intentions. And . . . the best-text method, modified for our purposes, provides a neutral text of the *Canterbury Tales* to which the commentary may be appended and referred" (xii). See Ralph Hanna III, review of Pearsall, *Nun's Priest's Tale*, *Analytical and Enumerative Bibliography* 8 (1984): esp. 187-88.

7. Preface to the 1532 edition, ed. Thynne. See also chap. 2 above. I have addressed such language in "Copy-Text and Its Variants in Some Recent Chaucer Editions," *Studies in Bibliography* 44 (1991): 163-83.

8. John Entick published proposals for an edition in 1736, initiating a public letter-writing polemic with Morell. The letters are printed as an appendix

in Alderson and Henderson, "The Morell-Entick Controversy," *Chaucer and Augustan Scholarship*, 165-88 (quotation on 180). Entick's 1736 proposal sheet is reprinted in Muscatine, *Book of Geoffrey Chaucer*, 46. The table of contents in this proposal suggest that Entick planned to include everything in Urry (including the Tale of Beryn) as well as the *Siege of Thebes*.

9. Tyrwhitt, *Canterbury Tales*, Appendix to Preface, 1:xx; Advertisement to Glossary, 5:vi.

10. Nichols, *Literary Anecdotes;* ed. Clair, 376.

11. Ross's phrase "condemned out of hand" is taken from Alderson, to whom Ross refers here. But Alderson is criticizing modern scholars of the edition, not characterizing its eighteenth-century contemporaries, and says that since the preface by the Thomas brothers "few men have felt it necessary to study the edition before condemning it out of hand" (*Chaucer and Augustan Scholarship*, 102).

12. Donald C. Baker, ed., *The Manciple's Tale*, Variorum Chaucer, II, 10 (Norman: University of Oklahoma Press, 1984), 69; George B. Pace, "The Printed Editions," in George B. Pace and Alfred David, eds., *The Minor Poems*, Part One, Variorum Chaucer, V (Norman: University of Oklahoma Press, 1982), 33 and n. 10. Baker says nothing about the supposed eccentricity of Urry in his lengthy second description of it in *Squire's Tale*, 108-10.

13. Preface by Thomas. See Tyrwhitt, "An Essay on the Language and Versification of Chaucer," *Canterbury Tales*, 4: 95, n. 68, on Urry's spelling. Tyrwhitt's own suggestion is for the use of an apostrophe, e.g., "shoure's" for Urry's "shouris."

14. See, e.g, the same passage in the 1532 edition:
    Our hoste sawe that he was dronken of ale
    And sayd abyde Robyn leue brother
    Some better man shal tel us first an other
    Abyde/ and let us wirche thriftely
    By goddes soule (quod he) that wol not I
    For I wol speke /or els go my way.

15. See Robinson, *Works* (1957), Textual Notes to *Parliament of Fowls*, 902; E. Talbot Donaldson, *Chaucer's Poetry: An Anthology for the Modern Reader* (New York: Ronald Press, 1958); W. W. Greg, "The Rationale of Copy-Text," *Studies in Bibliography* 3 (1950-51): 19-36. See further, my "Copy-Text and its Variants" and a rejoinder by Machan, *Textual Criticism and Middle English Texts*, 35 and 201n. 89. Note that Urry's respelling was not confined to the text but extended to the Testimonies as well; see the spelling changes introduced into the passage from Thynne's Preface (quoted above, chap. 2).

16. Morell comments: "I am persuaded he [Thomas] would have done it better, had he never seen Mr. Urry's design at all" (xxiii).

17. The handwritten notes in the British Library copy (presumably by William Thomas) imply that some effort was to be made to tone down these objections.

18. See also, the illustration preceding the Tale of Gamelyn, which Urry claims is appropriate to Squire's Yeoman. "And because I think there is not any one that would fit him so well as this, I have ventur'd to place his Picture before this Tale, tho' I leave the Cook in Possession of the Title" (36; noted by Alderson, *Chaucer and Augustan Scholarship*, 116).

19. Manly-Rickert, "Early and Revised Versions," *Text of the Canterbury Tales*, 2: 495-518; Manly's comments appear on 511-14.

20. Some of these problems have been cleared up in the textual notes to the *Riverside Edition*. But there is still some uncertainty over whether this is a new edition, or a revision of Robinson's earlier editions. See John M. Flyer, on *House of Fame:* "I have made only a few changes in Robinson's text, usually to restore manuscript readings where he and other editors have emended for metrical reasons" (1139); see also the remarks by Vincent J. Dimarco on the *Parliament of Fowls*, 1147. For a judicious statement, see Ralph Hanna II, Textual Notes on the *Canterbury Tales*, 1118-22.

21. After the subscribers received their copies, the remaining ones went to the printer, Urry's executor, and to Christ Church, which required each entering study to purpose one. See Alderson, chap. 5. For Dart's comments, see *Westmonasterium*, 87.

22. Windeatt, "Thomas Tyrwhitt," in Ruggiers, ed., *Editing Chaucer*, 118-19. Cf. Pearsall, who emphasizes Tyrwhitt's "typically old-fashioned" method: "[Tyrwhitt's] attitude to his task as an editor is not fundamentally different from that of his predecessors" (*Nun's Priest's Tale*, 118, 120); see also Hammond, *Manual*, 209.

23. "so complete, correct, and satisfactory, that it were difficult perhaps to mention any other CLASSIC, ancient or modern, which has received more copious and curious illustration. It is a model of editorship; and may fully rank on a par with the Lucian of Hemsterhusius, the Athenaeus of Schweighaeuser, and the Virgil and Homer and Pindar of Heyne. . . . What exquisite learning and taste . . . had the Editor of this incomparable work"; Dibdin, *The Library Companion*, 682-83 and note.

24. Thomas Wright, *Anecdota Literaria*, 23 (quoted Spurgeon, *Chaucer Criticism*, 1:158). See also, Thomas Wright, ed., *The Canterbury Tales of Geoffrey Chaucer: A New Text with Illustrative Notes*, 3 vols. (London: Percy Society, 1847-51), 1:31-42. On Wright's attitude toward Tyrwhitt, see Lounsbury, *Studies in Chaucer*, 1:319-21, and for Tyrwhitt's early reviews, not all favorable, Hammond, *Manual*, 206-7.

25. Skeat's praise is tempered by his remark two lines later on Tyrwhitt's "imperfect knowledge of ME grammar."

26. Ross, ed., *Miller's Tale*, 109; Pearsall, ed., *Nun's Priest's Tale*, 118; Beverly Boyd, ed., *The Prioress's Tale*, Variorum Chaucer, II, 20 (Norman: University of Oklahoma Press, 1987), 105. Atcheson L. Hench, "Printer's Copy for Tyrwhitt's Chaucer," *Studies in Bibliography* 3 (1950): 265-66. In 1946, Pace examined the notes on a page of Speght's Chaucer and concluded they were not by T. Thomas as previously thought, but by Tyrwhitt. For a facsimile, see Muscatine, *Book of Geoffrey Chaucer*, 48.

27. The clearest example of this is in the Ruggiers volume in which Windeatt's essay appears; see my review "On Greatness in Editing."

28. Tyrwhitt, *Canterbury Tales*, 1:ii-iii (note). Tyrwhitt is referring to the first section of his "An Essay on the Language and Versification of Chaucer," 4:46-73.

29. For Tyrwhitt's activities as a classicist, see J. E. Sandys, *A History of Classical Scholarship* (Cambridge: Cambridge University Press, 1980), 2:419-20; M. L. Clarke, *Greek Studies in England (1700-1830)* (Cambridge: Cambridge University Press, 1945), 57-59; Rudolf Pfeiffer, *History of Classical Scholarship from 1300-1850* (Oxford: Oxford University Press 1975), 161-62. Tyrwhitt's edition of Aristotle appeared in 1794. Its notes ("Tyrwhitti Animadversiones") are extremely polemical, suggesting that the more subdued notes of his Chaucer are less the product of his personality than a product of the genre—antiquarian rather than scholarly: see *Aristotle: Poetics*, ed. Thomas Tyrwhitt 3d ed. (Oxford: Oxford University Press, 1806), 141.

30. For a list of these editions, see Hammond, *Manual*, 132-41. The Bell edition of *The Poets of Great Britain* in 1782 pirated Tyrwhitt's text. Other series using the Tyrwhitt, text were by Anderson (1795); Chalmers (1810); Chiswick (1822); and the first Aldine edition of 1845. The Chalmers edition is the first to repudiate Urry, by using Tyrwhitt in combination with blackletter editions, although it does use Urry for spurious tales: The Tale of Beryn, Gamelyn, the Plowman's Tale, and Merchant's Second Tale; *The Works of the English Poets from Chaucer to Cowper* (London, 1810), vol. 1: *Chaucer*, xv.

31. For the available translations, see Hammond, *Manual*, 220-28. The first to appear after Tyrwhitt's edition is an expurgated version by Lipscomb in 1795, a version which prints the tales in Tyrwhitt's order.

32. Karl Kiralis, "William Blake as an Intellectual and Spiritual Guide to Chaucer's *Canterbury Tales*," *Blake Studies* 1 (1969): 139-90, Appendix A, 167-74; G. E. Bentley, "Comment Upon the Illustrated Eighteenth-Century Chaucer," *Modern Philology* 78 (1981): 398; Alexander S. Gourlay, "What was Blake's Chaucer?" *Studies in Bibliography* 42 (1989): 272-83. Betsy Bowden, "The Artistic and Interpretive Context of Blake's *Canterbury Tales*," *Blake: An Illustrated Quarterly* 13 (1980): 164-73, offers Urry as a guess. Lamb considered Blake's "Sir Jeffery Chaucer and the nine and twenty Pilgrims" (1809) "the finest criticism he had ever read of Chaucer's poem" (Spurgeon, *Chaucer Criticism*, 2:49).

33. I thank Jerome J. McGann for his skepticism regarding my hopes for definitive statements on any of these matters. For Keats, see *The Poetical Works and Other Writings of John Keats*, ed., H. Buxton Forman, rev. Maurice Buxton Forman, 4 (1939; New York: Phaeton, 1970), 40-42. For the 1782 edition by Bell, see Hammond, *Manual*, 132. A facsimile of Keats's poem is in Spurgeon, *Chaucer Criticism*, 2:91-92. Keats is probably as much inspired by Dryden's version of this poem as by Chaucer's. See further Beth Lau, "Keats's Markings in Chaucer's *Troilus and Criseyde*," *Keats-Shelley Journal* 43 (1994): 39-55.

34. Spurgeon, *Chaucer Criticism*, 2:27 (to Lamb); 2:35 quoting Prol. to *Legend of Good Women* (1807). Wordsworth claims in 1814 that he "became first familiar with Chaucer" through Anderson (Spurgeon, *Chaucer Criticism*, 1: 68). On Anderson's edition, see Hammond, *Manual*, 134-35; Anderson's *Canterbury Tales* is from Tyrwhitt, the rest from Urry. I assume Anderson's Chaucer is referred to in 1801 (Spurgeon, *Chaucer Criticism*, 2:2-3, 14). Dorothy Wordsworth seems to be quoting from memory (and occasionally inaccurately); see Journals 1801 and 1820 (Spurgeon, *Chaucer Criticism*, 2:14, 130). By 1822, Lamb has acquired a blackletter Chaucer, but claims "it is painful to read"; Frank N. Owings, Jr., "Keats, Lamb, and a Black-letter Chaucer," *Papers of the Bibliographical Society of America* 75 (1981): 147-55.

35. See James Engell and W. Jackson Bate, eds., *Samuel Taylor Coleridge: Biographia Literaria*, 2 vols. (Princeton: Princeton University Press, 1983), 2:92 and n. 1. The text referred to but not quoted by Spurgeon in *Literary Remains*, "Notes of Lectures" (1818), is Tyrwhitt's. William Hazlitt, *Lectures on the English Poets* (1818) (*Collected Works*, ed. Waller and Glover, 1902-6), 5:19ff. (see Spurgeon, *Chaucer Criticism*, 2:93-105). Leigh Hunt, "Preface to the Story of Rimini" (Spurgeon, *Chaucer Criticism*, 2:82) (the text is Tyrwhitt's, but line references suggest a later reprint). George Frederick Nott, "Of Chaucer's Versification," in *The Works of Henry Howard Earl of Surry and of Sir Thomas Wyatt the Elder*; Spurgeon, *Chaucer Criticism*, 2:73-76. For Scott, see ref. in Spurgeon, *Chaucer Criticism*, 2:17 (correcting Chatterton's misreading; Scott's text is close to Tyrwhitt's). The text used in "Chivalry" (Spurgeon, *Chaucer Criticism*, 2:107-8) is inconsistent—at times it is a modernization. Scott undoubtedly used Tyrwhitt, but not with any great reverence. I thank Clare Simmons of Ohio State University for her notes on Scott.

36. Thomas Warton, *The History of English Poetry from the Close of the Eleventh to the Commencement of the Eighteenth Century*, 3 vols. (London: Dodsley, 1775-78); rev. Richard Price, 4 vols. (London: T. Tegg, 1824) (additions by Ritson, Ashby, Douce and Park); rev. Richard Taylor, 3 vols. (London: T. Tegg, 1840) (additions by Madden, Thorpe, Kemble, Wright); ed. W. Carew Hazlitt, 4 vols. (London: Reeves and Turner, 1871) (additions by Skeat, Morris, and Furnivall).

37. See Morris's 1866 Preface: "In this edition of Chaucer's poetical works Tyrwhitt's text has been replaced by one based upon manuscripts where such are known to exist . . . No better manuscript of the Canterbury Tales could be found than the Harleian MS, 7334, which is far more uniform and accurate than any other I have examined; it has, therefore, been selected, and faithfully adhered to throughout as the text of the present edition." Richard Morris, ed., *The Poetical Works of Geoffrey Chaucer* (1866; new ed. London: Bell, n. d.). Morris does not cite Wright, but the editorial principle articulated here is the same. This edition went through four reprints until superseded by Skeat's 1894 edition; see Hammond, *Manual*, 140-41.

38. This note was in vol. 2 of the first edition (1778), "Emendations and Additions," 458: "The ingenious editor of the *Canterbury Tales* treats the notion, that Chaucer imitated the Provençal poets, as totally void of foundation." Even though Warton and Tyrwhitt were in correspondence, Tyrwhitt only became "the ingenious editor" between volumes 1 and 2 of Warton's *History*.

39. Tyrwhitt's printer was T. Payne, involved in the consortium that produced the British Poets series in 1790 (with prefaces by Johnson)—a series that was a competitor for the Bell series, which had pirated Tyrwhitt's text.

40. The pirated edition of Bell (1782) printed Tyrwhitt's notes on the bottom of each page. The Chalmers edition omitted them altogether.

41. Discussion of Morell is not included in the excerpts from Alderson printed in Ruggiers, ed., *Editing Chaucer*, 93-115; the edition receives some mention by Muscatine, *Book of Geoffrey Chaucer*, 45.

42. See e.g. Thomas Morell, ed., *Euripidis Hecuba, Orestes, et Phoenissae, cum Scholiis antiquis: ac Versione, Notisque Johannis King, ferè integris, curante Thoma Morell qui Alcestin adjecit*, 2 vols. (London, 1748). The volume is a school edition, "In Usum Scholae Etonensis." A typical layout places the Greek text on the left, Latin translation on the right. Beneath the Greek text is a Greek paraphrase and Greek notes—notes which continue beneath the Latin text (fig. 17). On Morell's editions, see Clarke, *Greek Studies in England*, 60-61.

43. Noted by Henderson, in *Chaucer and Augustan Scholarship*. I exclude tales included in collections such as Ashmole's *Theatrum Chemicum Britannicum*.

44. On the question of Tyrwhitt's use of Morell, see Henderson's judicious remarks, *Chaucer and Augustan Scholarship*, 159-61. Henderson says Tyrwhitt cites Morell for two readings, but gives no references. In line 53, Tyrwhitt refers to Morell with the curt "All the Edd. (except M.)."

45. The sentiment seems lifted from the preface of Speght, "To the Readers," *Workes* (1598).

46. Tyrwhitt's notes were freely borrowed by Skeat; in the Variorum Chaucer volumes by Ross and Pearsall, I found only four of some fifty notes by Tyrwhitt omitted.

47. Hearne, diary entry 16 Nov. 1711; *Remarks and Collections*, 3:164.

48. Iolo A. Williams, "English Book-Illustration, 1700-1775," *The Library* ser. 4, 17 (1937): 1-21. On Vertue and his reputation, see Nichols, *Literary Anecdotes*, 376-81. On Nicholas Pigné (born 1700, and active in both Paris and London), see the brief entry in Hans Vollmer, *Allgemeines Lexikon der bildenden Künstler von der Antike bis zur Gegenwart, Thieme-Becker Künstler-Lexicon*, vol. 27 (Leipzig: E. A. Seemann, 1933), 35.

49. Pope's *Iliad*, 6 vols. (London, 1771), indeed has a double engraving, with a full-page engraving of Pope facing another full-page engraving, not of Homer, but of a bust of Homer.

50. Special Collections, Bowdoin College, Brunswick, Maine. I thank the staff for their cooperation.
51. *The Works of Alexander Pope Esq. . . . with the commentaries and notes of Mr. Warburton,* 9 vols. (London: Knapton, 1751), Plate I. Margery Corbett and Ronald Lightbown, *The Comeley Frontispiece: The Emblematic Title-Page in England, 1550-1600* (London: Routledge, 1979) is based almost entirely on Alfred Forbes Johnson, *A Catalogue of Engraved and Etched English Title-Pages down to the Death of William Faithorne, 1691,* Bibliographical Society, Facsimiles and Illustrations, no. IV (Oxford University Press, 1934).
52. These include Tomlinson's translation of Lomazzo; Chapman's *Homer,* and Harington's *Ariosto.* These are far outnumbered by the translations with engraved title pages containing only the author.

CHAPTER SEVEN

1. John Norton-Smith, ed., *Bodleian Library MS Fairfax 16* (London: Scolar Press, 1979), vii, where the certainty of Norton-Smith's description of such booklets fades in a series of heavily qualified terms and inverted commas; Ralph Hanna, "The Hengwrt Manuscript and the Canon of *The Canterbury Tales*" (1989), in *Pursuing History,* 142-43.
2. See further:
> For worthy Chaucer in that same boke
> In goodly termes / and in ioly verse
> Compyled hath his cares who wyl loke
> To breke my slepe another queare I toke
> In which I founde the fatal desteny
> Of fayre Creseyde / whiche ended wretchedly
>   (sig. 2Q3v)

On the addition of Henryson in Beinecke copy, see Miskimin, *Renaissance Chaucer,* and above, chap. 2. For other early references to quires in late medieval English, see Julia Boffey and John J. Thompson, "Anthologies and Miscellanies: Production and Choice of Texts," in Griffiths and Pearsall, eds., *Book Production and Publishing in Britain, 1375-1475,* 279-315, in particular 308n. 63.
3. M. B. Parkes, "The Influence of the Concepts of *Ordinatio* and *Compilatio* on the Development of the Book," in J. J. G. Alexander and M. T. Gibson, eds., *Medieval Learning and Literature: Essays Presented to R. W. Hunt* (Oxford: Clarendon Press, 1976); A. J. Minnis, *Medieval Theory of Authorship,* 2d ed. (1984; 2nd ed. Philadelphia: University of Pennsylvania Press, 1988). See further John J. Thompson, "The Compiler in Action: Robert Thornton and the 'Thornton Romances' in Lincoln Cathedral MS 91," in Pearsall, ed., *Manuscripts and Readers,* 113-24, esp. 114 n. 3, where Thompson (here in 1981) claims to extend what he characterizes as the "specialized" notion from Minnis to encompass in this case the owner of the manuscript.

4. See Boffey and. Thompson, "Anthologies and Miscellanies," 279-315, esp. n. 111.
5. The basic opposition here is between those now somewhat creaking studies by McLuhan and Elizabeth L. Eisenstein, *The Printing Press as an Agent of Change: Communication and Cultural Transformations in Early-Modern Europe*, 2 vols. (Cambridge: Cambridge University Press, 1979) and the more modern approaches, seeking the relation of printing to earlier production modes. See for example the essays in Sandra L. Hindman, ed., *Printing the Written Word: The Social History of Books, circa 1450-1520* (Ithaca: Cornell University Press, 1991), and those in Griffiths and Pearsall, eds., *Book Production*.
6. See the discussion in Siegfried Wenzel, *Macaronic Sermons; Bilingualism and Preaching in Late-Medieval England* (Ann Arbor: University of Michigan Press, 1994), "The Manuscripts," 30-64.
7. Jean Destrez, *La Pecia dans les manuscrits universitaires du xiiie et du xive siècle* (Paris: Jacques Vautrain, 1935); for its influence, see Mary A. Rouse and Richard H. Rouse, "Book Production: Stationers and Peciae," in *Authentic Witnesses: Approaches to Medieval Texts and Manuscripts* (Notre Dame: University of Notre Dame, 1991), 257-318; Pearsall, "Introduction," in Griffiths and Pearsall, eds., *Book Production*, 3-4, with clear reference to Destrez. Pearsall's discussion extends to such matters as presentation copies by Christine de Pisan and even Jankyn's book in the Wife of Bath's Prologue.
8. Destrez's terminology is refined by L. E. Boyle, "Peciae, Apopeciae, and a Toronto MS. of the Sententia Libri Ethicorum of Aquinas," in Peter Ganz, ed., *The Role of the Book in Medieval Culture*, 2 vols., Bibliologia, 3 (Turnhout: Brepols, 1986), 71-82, with reference to Destrez and G. Pollard, "The Pecia System in the Medieval Universities," in M. B. Parkes and A. G. Watson, eds., *Medieval Scribes, Manuscripts and Libraries: Essays presented to N. R. Ker* (London: Scholar Press, 1978), 145-61. Three types of manuscript need to be distinguished, which Boyle calls peciae, epipeciae, and apopeciae: "an epipeciae MS. is that exemplar, whatever its origin, upon which the stationer's peciae are based, while apopeciae MSS. are MSS. based on those peciae of the stationer" (73). Material evidence exists for only the latter two.
9. Destrez's notes indicate that he had identified as many as 82 exemplaria; see J. Destrez and M. D. Chenu, "Exemplaria universitaires des xiiie et xive siècles," *Scriptorium* 7 (1953): 6-80, and Boyle, "Peciae, Apopeciae," 73.
10. Boyle emphasizes this as well, although Pollard suggests the possibility of amateur copying within a professionally organized system.
11. Cf. Boyle, "Peciae, Apopeciae," 75, discussing editions of St. Thomas, *Liber de causis*. H. D. Saffrey's edition (1954) shows two distinct sets of peciae. Later editions ("leonine" edition, 1969) show evidence of three sets. Stationers apparently used these sets interchangeably.
12. G. Pollard, "The Pecia System," 145-61. Pollard suggests that the system was dying out in Oxford (and in northern Europe generally) in the

fourteenth century (149). It was not used for any arts texts in Oxford, but did appear to be used for some Parisian preaching manuals. Pollard made an additional modification to Destrez by placing its invention in Bologna in 1200 rather than in Paris.

13. P. R. Robinson, "Self-contained Units in Composite MSS of the Anglo-Saxon Period," *Anglo-Saxon England* 7 (1978): 231-38; "The Booklet: A Self-Contained Unit in Composite Manuscripts," *Codicologica* 3 (1980): 46-69. Robinson claimed "The practice of assembling booklets into compilations was already well established in the Anglo-Saxon period" ("Self-Contained Units," 234). Destrez had placed the practice nearly as early, but had not sought evidence for it.

14. Ralph Hanna III, "Booklets in Medieval Manuscripts: Further Considerations," *Studies in Bibliography* 39 (1986): 100-11. In what strikes me as a slyly casual note, Hanna places the "vendor" in the first category rather than the second, thus implying that the vendor is part of the consumption rather than production process. Hanna's article is reprinted as the lead chapter in his *Pursuing History*, as the first of three articles discussing booklet production.

15. In the revisions of his article in *Pursuing History*, 21, Hanna clearly associates this definition with Robinson; that this is Robinson's definition is less clear in "Booklets," 100-1.

16. See C. W. Dutschke, *Guide to Medieval and Renaissance Manuscripts in the Huntington Library*, 2 vols. (San Marino: Huntington Library Press, 1989), 1:150-52 and 197-203.

17. See also, Boffey and Thompson, "Anthologies and Miscellanies," 315, n. 111 and references.

18. Yet see his critique of Owen for not placing enough emphasis on codicology; review of Charles A. Owen Jr., *The Manuscripts of the Canterbury Tales* (Cambridge: D. S. Brewer, 1991), in *Studies in the Age of Chaucer* 15 (1993): 247-51.

19. Pearsall claims that this book will focus on entrepreneurial production, but the studies in this book that have the most bearing on Chaucer (by Harris, Meale, Edwards and Pearsall, Boffey and Thompson, and Blake) do not. Furthermore, the collection of essays promotes a theory that combines all three forms of publication Pearsall is at pains to distinguish: a form of publication or "book-production" that takes place by the booklet, rather than the book. Meale concerns "home-made" miscellanies; Carol M. Meale, "Patrons, Buyers and Owners: Book Production and Social Status," 201-17. What may be the most influential article, by Boffey and Thompson, "Anthologies and Miscellanies," defines the basic unit as the "collection" (280).

20. Reference to A. I. Doyle and M. B. Parkes, "The Production of Copies of the *Canterbury Tales* and the *Confessio Amantis* in the Early Fifteenth Century," in Parkes and Watson, eds., *Medieval Scribes, Manuscripts and Libraries*, 163-210.

21. The reference by Edwards and Pearsall to monastic scriptoria is to George Haven Putnam, *Books and their Makers During the Middle Ages,* 2d ed. (New York: Putnam, 1896-97), 65-67.

22. The only text rejected from previous editions by Urry was Lydgate's *Siege of Thebes.* In Entick's 1737 proposals, even that text was promised to subscribers; see above, chap. 6, n. 8. Aage Brusendorff, *The Chaucer Tradition* (Oxford: Clarendon Press, 1925), 45-50, summarizes the history of the canonization of Tyrwhitt's list. The editions of Bell (1782) and Anderson (1795) print most of what Tyrwhitt rejected. Chalmers (1810), relegates the texts Tyrwhitt rejected to an Appendix. The Chiswick edition (1822), Moxon edition(1843), the Aldine edition (1845) and Bell (1854), generally follow Tyrwhitt's list. See also, the list of late editions in Hammond, *Manual,* 132-49.

23. For the notion of a "canonical apocrypha," I am indebted to Kathleen Forni, "Studies in the Chaucerian Apocrypha" (diss. University of Southern California, 1995). In addition to the texts in vol. 7., the Tale of Gamelyn appears in Skeat's *Canterbury Tales* volume. The egregiously spurious, such as the Tale of Beryn and *Siege of Thebes,* have no place in Skeat whatsoever.

24. Brusendorff, *Chaucer Tradition* (1925). In addition to Hammond's *Manual,* see: "MS. Pepys 2006—A Chaucerian Codex," *MLN* 19 (1904): 196-98; "Omissions from the Editions of Chaucer," *MLN* 19 (1904): 35-38; " MS. Longleat 258—A Chaucerian Codex," *MLN* 20 (1905): 77-79; "Two British Museum Manuscripts (Harley 2251 and Adds. 34360): A Contribution to the Bibliography of John Lydgate," *Anglia* 28 (1905): 1-28; "Ashmole 59 and other Shirley Manuscripts," *Anglia* 30 (1907): 320-48; "On the Editing of Chaucer's Minor Poems," *MLN* 23 (1908), 20-21; *English Verse Between Chaucer and Surrey* (Durham, NC.: Duke University Press, 1927); and "A Scribe of Chaucer," *Modern Philology* 27 (1929): 26-33. I am grateful to Seth Lerer for insisting on many occasions on the importance of these two scholars.

25. Hammond's notion of Shirley as the owner of commercial shops has been challenged by A. I Doyle, "More Light on John Shirley," *Medium Aevum* 30 (1961): 93-101 and Richard F. Green, *Poets and Princepleasures: Literature and the English Court in the Late Middle Ages* (Toronto: University of Toronto Press, 1980), 130-33; see also the numerous references to Shirley in Lerer, *Chaucer and his Readers.* Brusendorff's concern with the authorship of the *Romaunt of the Rose* no longer is a central question to Chaucer studies; cf. the space devoted to the question a century ago by Lounsbury, *Studies in Chaucer,* 2:1-165.

26. Reference is to Flügel, "List of the Manuscripts of the Minor Poems," *Anglia* 22 (1899): 510; Flügel singled out Skeat's treatment of Pepys 2006, but Skeat's carelessness may be defensible. Hammond in 1904 had complained about the lack of a proper catalogue for this collection; manuscripts were available only grudgingly and transcription was forbidden (Hammond, "Pepys 2006," 196). Duff in 1905 called the collection

"almost inaccessible"; E. Gordon Duff, *William Caxton* (1905; rpt. New York: Burt Franklin, 1970), 76.

27. Such classifications were the norm, although both Brusendorff and Hammond often point out the irrelevance of present location. Skeat had based his textual-critical studies on the findings of Chaucer Society, and in the Chaucer Society, there was a legitimate concern that major library collections be represented. This was expressly stated as a factor in the choices of texts for what are known as the Six and Eight Text editions, as the locations of key manuscripts suggests: Cp (Oxford), Hg (Wales), Gg (Cambridge), La (British Museum), El, Pw (private).

28. See also her judgment of Pepys 2006: Bilderbeck's "censure of its LGW as containing blunders 'many and outrageous' is a fairer average estimate of the textual value of the MS. than is implied by Prof. Skeat" ("Pepys 2006," 198).

29. "On the Editing of Chaucer's Minor Poems," (1908), 21. Hammond claims the "lost Fairfax-Bodley codex [can be] reconstructed with clearness, and its texts of the Minor Poems established." The manuscript "two degrees nearer Chaucer" in the above quotation is the "lost ancestor Oxford, containing at least 11 entries" (20).

30. See in particular *Canon of Chaucer* (1900), 110 and 139 where the same "authoress" is claimed for both. Another (unstated) reason for rejection of "Flower and the Leaf" is the fact that it appeared first in the Speght edition of 1598 (the "Assembly of Ladies" had appeared in the edition of 1532). Although Skeat never states this as a principle, the later a work appeared under Chaucer's name, the less claim he felt it had on the canon. On the reception of this text, see Kathleen R. Forni, "The Swindling of Chaucerians and the Critical Fate of the *Flower and the Leaf*," *Chaucer Review* 31 (1997): 379-400.

31. See the somewhat schematic summary of Brusendorff's classifications in Pace and David, eds., *Minor Poems*, 18-19.

32. See Julia Boffey, "The Reputation and Circulation of Chaucer's Lyrics in the Fifteenth Century," *Chaucer Review* 28 (1993): 23-40. Boffey notes, citing Brusendorff, that Chaucer "registered" poems singly, and often inserted them into longer poems; such fugitive copies were collected later by fifteenth-century anthologists (33-35).

33. So Hammond, "Omissions from the Editions of Chaucer," 35.

34. Hammond, "Two British Museum Manuscripts," 26: "May we not therefore assume a lost Shirley volume, four leaves of which remain bound into the scrapbook now called Harley 78, as the archetype of our two manuscripts in much of this portion?"

35. So also the notion of "hidden booklets" proposed by Hanna, "Booklets in Medieval Manuscripts"; see discussion above.

36. Brusendorff, *Chaucer Tradition*, 186n. 4: "There is no evidence at all for Miss Hammond's view of the MS. as written for the original owner by his private scribe" (ref. to Hammond, 53). I assume the reference is to the

discussion in Hammond, *Manual,* 52-53; Hammond's views as stated here are much more qualified than Brusendorff implies.

37. Brusendorff cites Skeat, *Works of Chaucer,* 1:80 and 88, with further reference to Skeat's remarks in *Acad.* 2 (1894): 67f. Skeat, 1:80, concerns "Merciles Beaute": "It is the last poem in the MS., and is in excellent company, as it immediately follows several other of Chaucer's genuine poems"; 1:88 concerns "Against Women Unconstaunt": "Again, the poem is only found in company with other poems by Chaucer. Such collocation frequently means nothing, but those who actually consult MSS. Ct. and Ha. will see how close is its association with the Chaucerian poems in those MSS." Skeat's note 2 at 80 reads: "The critics who rush aside such a statement as this should learn to look at MSS. for themselves." At 88, Skeat's vigor increases: "It would be decent, on the part of such critics as do not examine the MSS., to speak of my opinions in a less contemptuous tone."

38. Robinson's primary reference seems to be to Skeat and to a lesser extent Brusendorff; see *Works,* 1933, 1034ff.

39. See Hanna's clear statement of this situation in notes to *Canterbury Tales,* and my "Copy-Text and its Variants." Criticism of Robinson's editorial methods can be tempered by consideration of the context in which this edition was produced and the multiple purposes it was intended to serve; see George F. Reinecke, "F. N. Robinson (1872-1967)," in Ruggiers, ed., *Editing Chaucer,* 231-51. The latest Riverside, however, might be more accurately called the third Robinson edition rather than the third Riverside edition.

40. See my "The Presumed Influence of Skeat's *Student's Chaucer* on Manly and Rickert's *Text of the Canterbury Tales," Analytical and Enumerative Bibliography* 7 (1993): 18-27.

41. See the purely decorative reference to Brusendorff: "Much useful information on manuscripts may be gained from Brusendorff (1925) if searched for" (27); although this occurs in a section signed by Pace, the next paragraph refers to him and I assume the comment is David's.

42. All Variorum volumes provide detailed descriptions of printed editions, even at the expense of the obvious repetition this entails. See my review, *Envoi* 1 (1988): 324-30; a similar criticism is made by A. S. G. Edwards in a series of reviews; see most recently, *Studies in the Age of Chaucer* 17 (1995): 157-60.

43. Pilgrim Books has produced Tanner 346, Pepys 2006, Bodley 638, and Trinity R.3.19 (all produced after the Pace-David edition). Fairfax 16 has been edited by Norton-Smith, (1979); Gg by M. B. Parkes & Richard Beadle, *Geoffrey Chaucer: Poetical Works, a Facsimile of Cambridge University Library MS Gg. 4.27* (Norman, Okla.: Pilgrim Books, 1980).

44. I have argued this specifically with reference to Shakespeare facsimiles: "'Ideal Copy' versus 'Ideal Texts': The Application of Bibliographical Description to Facsimiles," *Papers of the Bibliographical Society of Canada* 33 (1995): 31-50; see also T. H. Howard-Hill, *Review of English Studies* 43

(1992): 420-22, review of Michael Warren, *The Complete King Lear (1608-1623)* (Berkeley and Los Angeles: University of California Press, 1989). See also, Ralph Hanna III, Introduction, *The Ellesmere Manuscript of Chaucer's Canterbury Tales: A Working Facsimile* (Cambridge: D. S. Brewer, 1989), 4-11, on the modifications made in the El MS format by the 1911 facsimile, of which facsimile this is in turn another facsimile.

45. These problems are noted by Linda L. Brownrigg in *Medieval Book Production: Assessing the Evidence* (Los Altos: Anderson-Lovelace, 1990), Introduction, xiv-xv: "it is unfortunately true today that the greater the interest in the early book, the more the evidence is going to be removed from study. Manuscripts are fragile artifacts and those who study them are often necessarily restricted in access to their material." (The unintended ambiguity in "their" implies that scholars *own* the manuscript material!).

46. Daniel Woodward and Martin Stevens, eds., *The Canterbury Tales (ca. 1410): The New Ellesmere Chaucer Facsimile* (San Marino, Calif.: Huntington Library Press, 1995).

47. The various essays in Norman Blake and Peter Robinson, ed., *The Canterbury Tales Project: Occasional Papers*, vol. 1 (Oxford: Office for Humanities Communication, 1993) are reserved on this; see Blake, "Editing the *Canterbury Tales*," 14-16; but the freedom of individual readers to determine such basic issues as tale order has been asserted in earlier editions: see Hanna, "Presenting Chaucer as Author," *Pursuing History*, 180, with reference to Derek Pearsall.

48. Richard Beadle and Jeremy Griffiths, ed., *St. John's College, Cambridge, Manuscript L. 1, Troilus and Criseyde: A Facsimile* (Norman: Pilgrim Books, 1983), xi.

49. Norton-Smith, ed., *MS Fairfax 16*, vii. Cf. Paula Robinson, ed., *MS Bodley 638* (Norman, Okla.: Pilgrim Books, 1982), Introduction, and A. S. G. Edwards, ed., *MS Pepys 2006: A Facsimile* (Norman, Okla.: Pilgrim Books, 1985), xvi., who claims only that these manuscripts "suggest the broadening of the audience for Chaucer's works." By contrast, the justification for these facsimiles by the general editors of the facsimile series is entirely textual-critical; Donald M. Rose and Paul G. Ruggiers, Preface, *Bodley 638*, xii. Shirley volumes are somewhat paradoxically unavailable in facsimile, despite clear evidence of circulation and intended circulation; see Hammond, *English Verse*, 196-97.

50. Jerome J. McGann, *A Critique of Modern Textual Criticism* (Chicago: University of Chicago Press, 1983), 84.

51. Hanna and Edwards, "Rotheley, the De Vere Circle, and the Ellesmere Chaucer."

52. See recent work on *Roman de la Rose* by Huot and Hult, and some of the rhetoric in the two decades old work on *Beowulf* manuscript. Sylvia Huot, *From Song to Book: The Poetics of Writing in Old French Lyric and Lyrical Narrative Poetry* (Ithaca: Cornell University Press, 1987); *The Romance of the Rose and its Medieval Readers: Interpretation, Reception, Manuscript*

Transmission (Cambridge: Cambridge University Press, 1993); David F. Hult, *Self-Fulfilling Prophecies: Readership and Authority in the First "Roman de la Rose"* (Cambridge: Cambridge University Press, 1986).

CHAPTER EIGHT

1. Warton, *History of English Poetry*, 1:209. Warton does not identify these antiquaries, but there is a reference to Humphrey Wanley on 206, and to Thomas Hearne in the preceding chapter. Warton's citations in this chapter to Chaucer are to the Urry edition of 1721.

2. "It is in an enlightened age only that subjects of scripture history would be supported with proper dignity. But then an enlightened age would not have chosen such subjects for theatrical exhibition. It is certain that our ancestors intended no sort of impiety by these monstrous and unnatural mixtures. . . . They had no idea of decorum, consequently but little sense of the ridiculous"; *History of English Poetry*, 1:242-43. Cf. the more limited definition implied in his discussion of the Squire's Tale: "To this young man the poet, with great observance of decorum gives the tale of Cambuscan, the next in knightly dignity to that of Palamon and Arcite" (1:450).

3. Lee Patterson, *Negotiating the Past: The Historical Understanding of Medieval Literature* (Madison: University of Wisconsin Press, 1987), chap. 1: "Historical Criticism and the Development of Chaucer Studies," 3-39; Patterson defines the American institution of Chaucerianism as one opposing Donaldson and Robertson. See further David Aers's critique of New Historicists for having revived Robertson's romantic and nostalgic view of the Middle Ages; David Aers, "A Whisper in the Ear of Early Modernists: or, Reflections on Literary Critics Writing the 'History of the Subject,'" in David Aers, ed., *Culture and History (1350-1600): Essays on English Communities, Identities and Writing* (Detroit: Wayne State University Pres, 1992), 177-202. Howard's most important work consists of two books: Donald R. Howard, *The Three Temptations: Medieval Man in search of the World* (Princeton: Princeton University Press, 1966); *The Idea of the Canterbury Tales* (Berkeley and Los Angeles: University of California Press, 1976). For the apparent continuation of the legacy of Howard, see the *PMLA* "Cluster on Chaucer," ed. Seth Lerer, *PMLA* 107 (1992): 1139-80, and my review, "The Importance of Importance," *Huntington Library Quarterly* 56 (1993): 307-17.

4. See the critique of this notion by Elaine Tuttle Hansen, *Chaucer and the Fictions of Gender* (Berkeley and Los Angeles: University of California Press, 1992), esp. 11-25, arguing that the projection of modern political views onto a medieval author is simply a new form of the "adulation of the author."

5. See the work of Bernard Cerquiglini and its reception in recent English studies: Bernard Cerquiglini, *Eloge de la variante: Histoire critique de la philologie* (Paris: Seuil, 1989); introduction to the special issue of *Speculum*

entitled "The New Philology" by Stephen G. Nichols, "Introduction: Philology in a Manuscript Culture," *Speculum* 65 (1990): 1-10. I have compared Cerquiglini's criticism to that of Paul Zumthor, whose career shows a similar movement away from what he calls "texte"; see my "The Lure of Oral Theory in Medieval Criticism: From Editing 'Text' to Critical 'Work,'" *TEXT* 7 (1992): 145-60.

6. John Dryden, *Fables Ancient and Modern; Translated into Verse, from Homer, Ovid, Boccace, & Chaucer: with Original Poems* (London: Tonson, 1700).

7. Alderson, *Chaucer and Augustan Scholarship*, chap. 4, 53-68.

8. Reference is to Rymer, "A Short View of Tragedy" (1692); Rymer mentions Provençal, but only in such phrases as "Provençal, French or Latin," etc. Excerpts from Rymer and from Dryden's Preface are included as the final entries on the last page of Testimonies of the 1721 edition (*Works*, 1721, sig. ilv).

9. See Patterson, "Chaucer Studies," 21, noting the importance of character to twentieth-century Chaucer studies.

10. Dryden's insistence on dramatic propriety has an analogue in late nineteenth-century notions of textual propriety, whereby the central narrative of the *Canterbury Tales* is seen to be the "links," and the order of the fragments adjusted to make topographical references coherent. Furnivall, *A Temporary Preface to the Six-Text Edition*, sec. 3: "Arrangement of the Tales and their Component Parts," 9-43, is heavily indebted to Henry Bradshaw, "The Skeleton of Chaucer's Canterbury Tales" (1868), in *Collected Papers of Henry Bradshaw* (Cambridge: University Press, 1889), 102-48, and to later correspondence; see Prothero, *A Memoir of Henry Bradshaw*, 346-59. The topic has been studied by Daniel P. Terkla, "The Centrality of the Peripheral: Illuminating Borders and the Topography of Space in Medieval Narrative and Art, 1066-1400" (diss. University of Southern California, 1993), chap. 4. See also the table of contents of Tyrwhitt's "Introductory Discourse," summarizing his sec. 1: "The Dramatic form of Novel-writing invented by Boccace. The Decameron a species of Comedy" (Tyrwhitt, *Canterbury Tales*, 4:112); Tyrwhitt's discussion moves from "The Fable" to "Characters" at 4:118.

11. "*Virgil* was of a quiet, sedate Temper; *Homer* was violent, impetuous, and full of Fire" (sig. A2v); Homer is "cholerick and sanguin"; Virgil is "phlegmatick and Melancholick" (sig. B1r).

12. George Lyman Kittredge, *Chaucer and his Poetry* (Cambridge: Harvard University Press, 1915).

13. Jean E. Jost, ed., *Chaucer's Humor: Critical Essays* (New York: Garland, 1994). The essay by Ruggiers, "A Vocabulary for Chaucerian Comedy: A Preliminary Sketch," 41-77 (from 1976) is one of few in this anthology that at least addresses issues of plot and character.

14. Jost's essay on humor, "The Voice of the Past," 3-21, quotes Godwin and Lamb, but misreads their obvious and explicit allusions to stage drama as references to things-that-are-funny. See my comments on humor in "The Myth of Chaucerian Irony," *Papers on Language and Literature* 24 (1988):

115-33; rpt. *The Critical Mythology of Irony* (Athens: University of Georgia, 1991), 135-45, and the review of Jost by Roy C. Pearcy, *Studies in the Age of Chaucer* 18 (1996): 227-31.

15. Amusingly enough, in the page for page reprint of *Chaucer and his Poetry* edited by B. J. Whiting (Cambridge: Harvard University Press, 1970), the quotations are changed, with the effect that Kittredge of 1915 cites the Robinson text of 1957; see the Introduction by B. J. Whiting, n. 1. The same bizarre treatment was accorded Warton in later editions of his *History of English Poetry*; see above, chap. 6.

16. E. Talbot Donaldson, "Chaucer the Pilgrim," (1954), rpt. *Speaking of Chaucer* (New York: Norton, 1970); Robert M. Lumiansky, *Of Sondry Folk: The Dramatic Principle in the Canterbury Tales* (Austin: University of Texas Press, 1955).

17. Paul G. Ruggiers, *The Art of the Canterbury Tales* (Madison: University of Wisconsin Press, 1965), 17.

18. Bertrand H. Bronson, *In Search of Chaucer* (Toronto: University of Toronto Press, 1960), 29, 25; Bronson's earlier "Chaucer's Art in Relation to His Audience," in *Five Studies in Literatutre,* University of California Publications in English 8 (1940), articulates precisely the issues raised by Donaldson fifteen years later: "Besides the interplay . . . of characters within the framework of the plots he invented, there was always present the possibility of a dramatic use of the immediate physical situation, the relationship between himself and the persons in front of him" (21); "The 'I' in his poetry never means anyone else than Geoffrey Chaucer, then and there visibly present" (37).

19. See, however, n. 26 below. An exception to the general twentieth-century critical elevation of the term is Robertson's denigration of what he calls "dramatic" approaches and his implicit association of the word with what he feels to be forms of romanticism; D.W. Robertson, Jr., *Preface to Chaucer: Studies in Medieval Perspectives* (Princeton: Princeton University Press, 1962) 32-37.

20. Jesse M. Gellrich, *The Idea of the Book in the Middle Ages: Language Theory, Mythology, and Fiction* (Ithaca: Cornell University Press, 1985); Robert M. Jordan, *Chaucer's Poetics and the Modern Reader* (Berkeley and Los Angeles: University of California Press, 1987); Leicester, "The Art of Impersonation: A General Prologue to the *Canterbury Tales*"; Barbara Nolan, "'A Poet Ther Was': Chaucer's Voices in the General Prologue to the *Canterbury Tales,*" *PMLA* 101 (1986): 154-69; Lee Patterson, *Chaucer and the Subject of History* (Madison: University of Wisconsin Press, 1991). See also Leonard Michael Koff, *Chaucer and the Art of Storytelling* (Berkeley and Los Angeles: University of California Press, 1987), 160ff.

21. H. Marshall Leicester, Jr., *The Disenchanted Self: Representing the Subject in the Canterbury Tales* (Berkeley and Los Angeles: University of California Press, 1990), 29.

22. Nolan's reading can be seen as the literary-critical variation of Middleton's argument of 1978, one that attempts to avoid the complexities of narrative

personae by focusing on audience. For Middleton, the problem of the *persona* "disappears if we take these voices seriously, as expressions . . . of the social and ethical ideals of the work itself" (102); Anne Middleton, "The Idea of Public Poetry in the Reign of Richard II," *Speculum* 53 (1978): 94-114.

23. "The text is not a screen of personality through which the reader seeks to perceive the author, Chaucer the poet. . . . The 'voice' of such utterance properly belongs not to the speaker but to the text" (Gellrich, *Idea of the Book*, 226); "voices emanate from language that the narrator does not fully control" (233). See also, the language in R. A. Shoaf, *Dante, Chaucer, and the Currency of the Word: Money, Images and Reference in Late Medieval Poetry* (Norman: University of Oklahoma Press, 1983), 15, 209. The technique is the New-Critical one of personifying the text through a simple metonymy: "The poem . . . is detached from the author at birth and goes about the world beyond his power to intend about it or control it. The poem belongs to the public. It is embodied in language"; W. K. Wimsatt, Jr., with Monroe C. Beardsley, "The Intentional Fallacy," in *The Verbal Icon: Studies in the Meaning of Poetry* (Louisville: University of Kentucky Press, 1954), 5.

24. C. David Benson, *Chaucer's Drama of Style: Poetic Variety and Contrast in the Canterbury Tales* (Chapel Hill: University of North Carolina Press, 1986), see chap. 1: "Beyond the Dramatic Theory," where the phrase "dramatic theory" means specifically Kittredge's *Chaucer and his Poetry*.

25. Laura Kendrick, *Chaucerian Play: Comedy and Control in the Canterbury Tales* (Berkeley and Los Angeles: University of California, 1988); John M. Ganim, *Chaucerian Theatricality* (Princeton: Princeton University Press, 1990), 5: "My definition of theatricality is then primarily stylistic rather than sociological." See Ganim's opening chapter, "Introduction: Critical Metaphors and Chaucerian Performance." See also Robert R. Edwards, *The Dream of Chaucer: Representation and Reflection in the Early Narratives* (Durham: Duke University Press, 1989), where drama is defined as Chaucer's dramatization of his poetic office "making that dramatization an essential part of his work" (17); the narrator "enacts the drama of imagination and memory" (41).

26. A number of studies have recently claimed that contemporary performances are worthy objects of study, the most egregious of these being Betsy Bowden, *Chaucer Aloud: The Varieties of Textual Interpretation* (Philadelphia: University of Pennsylvania Press, 1987). A number of others are reviewed by Alan T. Gaylord, "Imagining Voices: Chaucer on Cassette," *Studies in the Age of Chaucer* 12 (1990): 215-38. See further Helen Cooper, *The Canterbury Tales: Oxford Guides to Chaucer* (Oxford: Clarendon Press, 1988), 104: "Line for line, the Miller's Tale reads aloud at almost twice the rate of the knight's—an astonishingly large differential . . ."; here the supposed reading rate is regarded as a more legitimate piece of evidence than the objective number of lines. See also William A. Quinn, *Chaucer's Rehersynges: The Performability of The Legend of Good Women*

(Washington, D. C.: Catholic University Press, 1994), 7: "an attempt to assess Chaucer's role as the reciter of *The Legend of Good Woman*"; Quinn rejects historical evidence in favor of "more positive [!] and accessible tonal features of Chaucer's oral performance" (ibid). V. A. Kolve, *Chaucer and the Imagery of Narrative: The First Five Canterbury Tales* (Stanford: Stanford University Press, 1984), 59, speaks of "our modern privilege to be readers" (59).

27. Henri Lüdeke, *Die Funktionen des Erzählers in Chaucers epischer Dichtung* (Halle: Niemeyer, 1928), refs. to Kittredge at 65, 68, 74.

28. Charles Muscatine, *Chaucer and the French Tradition: A Study in Style and Meaning* (Berkeley and Los Angeles: University of California Press, 1957). The relation to German romanticism of American New Criticism and its heir deconstruction can be seen throughout the work of Wimsatt, Abrams, de Man. I have discussed one aspect of this in *Critical Mythology of Irony,* chaps. 10 and 12 (149ff.).

29. Charles Muscatine, *Poetry and Crisis in the Age of Chaucer* (Notre Dame: University of Notre Dame Press, 1972).

30. Windeatt's *Troilus,* the new Robinson by Benson, the Oklahoma Variorum, and Blake's *Canterbury Tales* all appeared in the last decade, and the electronic Chaucer is clearly designed to render them all obsolete; see Blake and Robinson, eds., *The Canterbury Tales Project: Occasional Papers.* A major exception to the above statement concerning the lack of editions from 1940-80 is Donaldson's *Chaucer's Poetry* (1958), an edition that has received less serious study than it deserves.

CHAPTER NINE

1. Hammond, *Manual,* 131-41. According to Hammond, and seconded by the NCSTC, the Moxon edition was reprinted in 1851 and 1855, and in 1860 and 1874 by Routledge, with a different title page.

2. Walter W. Skeat, *Notes and Queries* ser. 7, 8 (1889): 133; *Works of Chaucer,* 1:30; 5:xiii.

3. Chiswick Chaucer, 1822, note in vol. 5 (quoted Hammond, *Manual,* 137): "It is with this edition (1532) and that of 1542, which are in general very correctly printed, that the minor poems of Chaucer have been collated for the present impression, with the exception of a few which appeared for the first time in Speght's edition of 1597. 'The Flower and the Leaf' is given from Mr. Todd's collation of Speght and Urry, and the 'Canterbury Tales' are given from Mr. Tyrwhitt's edition." Anderson, 1793, (quoted Hammond, *Manual,* 134): "The present edition of the Canterbury Tales is from Tyrwhitt's incomparable edition. . . . The genuine miscellaneous piecs of Chaucer are printed from Urry's edition."

4. Walter W. Skeat, *Chaucer: The Minor Poems* (Oxford: Clarendon Press, 1888). I quote from the second edition of 1896.

5. I assume the 1843 date correctly given at the head of the *Notes and Queries* article came from Skeat's editors, not from Skeat himself. Skeat's n. 1 to

the passage quoted here (5:xiii) reads: "Originally (I understand) 1845. I have only a copy with a reprinted title-page and an altered date."

6. Hammond is one of the few scholars to note this: "Of the 18th century Tyrwhitt still remains, the age of cautious and thorough annotation, of eager search in original and recondite sources, of painstaking and enormous labor,—but not of modern critical method. And secondly, after we have justified his procedure historically, let us remember how little Chaucer scholars have passed beyond him. The edition of Skeat in 1894 is still an edition of the 18th-century type" (*Manual*, 209).

7. The process by which Tyrwhitt's list of canonical works is itself canonized is discussed by Brusendorff, *Chaucer Tradition*, 45-50: the editions of Bell (1782) and Anderson (1793-95) print most of what Tyrwhitt rejected, even though Tyrwhitt's text is used for the *Canterbury Tales*; the Chiswick edition (1822), Aldine edition (1845) and Bell edition (1854), generally follow Tyrwhitt's list.

8. Skeat, *Chaucer Canon*, v, on the importance on the *Ormulum*, with ref. to Tyrwhitt.

9. An example of the ideological underpinnings of the distinction in the field of linguistics has been pointed out to me by Bernard Comrie of University of Southern California, and occurs in the work on historical linguistics by Hans Eggers, for whom the "internal history" of a language refers to social and cultural history, while "external history" refers to grammatical matters of phonology and morphology. This is precisely the opposite of how most linguists would understand these terms. Hans Eggers, *Deutsche Sprachgeschichte* (Reinbek bei Hamburg: Rowolt, 1963-77).

10. On Homer, see e.g. George Melville Bolling, *The External Evidence for Interpolation in Homer* (Oxford: Clarendon Press, 1925), where the distinction (left undefined) is used as a means of determining interpolations. In bibliographical and codicological studies, the term applies to evidence used in dating: see e.g. Seth Lerer, "British Library MS Harley 78 and the Manuscripts of John Shirley," *Notes and Queries* 235 (1990): 400-3, and ref. 402n. 2 to A. S. G. Edwards, "The Unity and Authenticity of *Anelida and Arcite*: The Evidence of the Manuscripts," *Studies in Bibliography* 41 (1988): 178.

11. Alexandra F. Johnston, "What if No Texts Survived? External Evidence for Early English Drama," in Marianne G. Brixcoe et al., eds., *Contexts for Early English Drama* (Bloomington: Indiana University Press, 1989), 1-19; the implication is that any manuscript containing a text is internal evidence, although in most applications, the physical manuscript or book constitute external evidence. See also Teresa Coletti, "Reading REED," in Lee Patterson, ed., *Literary Practice and Social Change in Britain, 1380-1530* (Berkeley and Los Angeles: University of California Press, 1990), 248-84.

12. Coleridge, "Intercepted Correspondence," *Morning Post* (3 Feb. 1800), quoted by David V. Erdman, "The Signature of Style" (1958), *Bulletin of the New York Public Library* 63 (1959): 88-109; rpt. David V. Erdman and Ephim G. Fogel, eds., *Evidence for Authorship: Essays on Problems of*

Attribution (Ithaca: Cornell University Press, 1966), 45-67. Coleridge was probably drawing on theological distinctions here; see Thomas McFarland, "Shoring up the Self: The Ragged Brilliance of Coleridge's Philosophy of Religion" *Times Literary Supplement,* 17 June 1994, 3 on "Aids to Reflection": "It was intended to convey 'a compleat System of internal evidences' of Christianity (as opposed to the external evidences of Paley), with 'no essential Article of Faith omitted'."

13. Arthur Sherbo, "The Uses and Abuses of Internal Evidence" (1958), rpt. Erdman and Fogel, ed., *Evidence for Authorship,* 7.

14. Cleanth Brooks, "A Summarizing Epilogue," in *Historical Evidence and the Reading of Seventeenth-Century Poetry* (Columbia: University of Missouri Press, 1991), 155.

15. René Wellek and Austin Warren, *Theory of Literature,* 3d ed. 1942; (New York: Harcourt, Brace and World, 1962).

16. See also, *Theory of Literature,* 71, where for all but contemporary periods, the terms "extrinsic" and "historical" are equivalent.

17. Wayne C. Booth, *The Rhetoric of Fiction* (Chicago: University of Chicago Press, 1961), 369-70, and 330:

> If we felt that the question of Joyce's precise attitude toward Stephen's vocation, his aesthetics, and his villanelle were irrelevant, we would hardly dispute with each other about them . . . Like most modern critics, I would prefer to settle such disputes by using internal rather than external evidence. But the experts themselves give me little hope of finding answers to my three problems by re-reading *Portrait* one more time.

Wimsatt and Beardsley also speak of evidence "outside the poem" with full awareness of how difficult this would be to define; Wimsatt and Beardsley, "The Intentional Fallacy" in *The Verbal Icon,* 4. In medieval literary studies, the most important work to base interpretive questions on types of evidence is that of D. W. Robertson, Jr., although I am not certain whether he formulates his approach in these terms. In the 1950s and 1960s, Robertson's almost exclusive reliance on evidence external to the text seemed a radical departure from New Criticism, and clearly this is the target of his introduction in *Preface to Chaucer* , "Introduction," esp. the language of the conclusion, 51.

18. Richard Levin, "The Ironic Reading of the Rape of Lucrece and the Problem of External Evidence," *Shakespeare Survey* 34 (1981): 85-92. Levin addresses here the same problem that David treats in his notes to the *Riverside Chaucer,* noting that these allusions (considered here as external evidence) are in the mouths of "characters and may not be Shakespeare's own words."

19. Robert Anderson, ed., *The Works of the British Poets, with prefaces, biographical and critical,* (Edinburgh, 1793), vol. 1; from Life of Chaucer, quoted Hammond, *Manual,* 134.

20. Robert Bell, ed., *Poetical Works of Geoffrey Chaucer*, (1854; rpt. London: Griffin, n. d.), iii: "This edition of Chaucer's works includes all the poems which appear entitled, from internal or external evidence, to be considered genuine."

21. For Bradshaw's use of the distinction, see the letter to Collier in Prothero, *Memoir*, 355, and for Skeat's debt to Bradshaw, 358. Lounsbury does not use the term in his discussions of types of evidence (*Studies in Chaucer*, 1:367ff. and 2:3ff.), although the distinction is implied in his classifications of evidence: the import of rhyme, vocabulary, dialect, grammar, fidelity of translation, style and expression, relation to other Chaucer's works is discussed on 1:158; manuscript and printing history is discussed on 160ff.

22. Walter W. Skeat, ed., *The Kingis Quair: Together with A Ballad of Good Counsel*, The Scottish Text Society (Edinburgh: Blackwood, 1884), xx-xxi; repeated in 2nd edition, xix.

23. J. L. T. Brown, *The Authorship of the Kingis Quair: A New Criticism* (Glascow: James Maclehose, 1896; New York: Macmillan). The distinction is clear, although blurred somewhat in 2(b), where Brown considers stylistic resemblance between the "Kingis Quair" and the "Court of Love."

24. It is inaccurate to claim that Brusendorff relies entirely on external evidence; instead, Brusendorff denies the validity of what in 1925 was considered the principle form of internal evidence—the rhyme tests associated with Bradshaw and Skeat. Cf. the discussion of Brusendorff in Erdman and Fogel, *Evidence for Authorship*, Appendix.

25. The only reference I find is in vol. 2 of the three-volume EETS edition, containing many prefatory essays. Walter W. Skeat, ed., *Langland's Vision of Piers Plowman*, 3 vols. EETS 17-19 (London: Trubner, 1867-85); see vol. 2 "The Whitaker Text; or Text C" (1873) on "Date of the C-Text": "On this point the internal evidence is most conclusive; given the B-text, it is not difficult to see how the C-text was formed from it, by various omissions, additions, transpositions, and corrections . . ." (xi).

26. John Matthews Manly, *Piers the Plowman and its Sequence*, EETS O.S., extra issue 135b (London: Henry Frowde, 1908), includes reprints of Manly, "The Lost Leaf of Piers the Plowman" (1906) and Henry Bradley, "The Misplaced Leaf of *Piers the Plowman*," *Athenaeum* (21 April 1906); see also, *The Piers Plowman Controversy*, EETS O.S., extra issue 139 b, c, d, e (London: Kegan Paul, 1910), with articles by Jusserand, Manly, and R. W. Chambers. The Chambers article here is "The Authorship of Piers Plowman" from *MLR* (1910), and Chambers does not use the distinction. Chambers does refer to the notion of external evidence in a later article, "The Three Texts of 'Piers Plowman,' and Their Grammatical Forms," *MLR* 14 (1919): 129-51, reprinted in part in Erdman and Fogel.

27. George Kane, *Piers Plowman: The Evidence for Authorship* (London: The Athlone Press, 1965); Kane's target here is D. C. Fowler, *Piers the Plowman: Literary Relations of the A and B Texts* (Seattle: University of Washington

Press, 1961). See also, E. T. Donaldson, "The Texts of Piers Plowman: Scribes and Poets," *Modern Philology* 50 (1953): 269-73.

28. For medieval studies, the classic work is Minnis, *Medieval Theory of Authorship*. See also: Jack Stillinger, *Multiple Authorship and the Myth of Solitary Genius* (New York: Oxford University Press, 1991); Peter Shillingsburg, "The Autonomous Author, the Sociology of Texts, and the Polemics of Textual Criticism," in Philip Cohen, ed., *Devils and Angels: Textual Editing and Literary Theory* (Charlottesville: University of Virginia Press, 1991), 22-43; and the essays in Martha Woodmansee and Peter Jaszi, eds., *The Construction of Authorship: Textual Appropriation in Law and Literature* (Durham: Duke University Press, 1994).

29. Robert A. Pratt, "The Order of the *Canterbury Tales*," *PMLA* 66 (1951): 1141-67, esp. 1165; Larry D. Benson, "The Order of *The Canterbury Tales*," *Studies in the Age of Chaucer* 3 (1981): 79. A similar devaluation of internal evidence is apparent in the edition of the *Canterbury Tales* by N. F. Blake, where the Canon Yeoman's Tale is omitted because of its absence in Hg; N. F. Blake, *The Canterbury Tales by Geoffrey Chaucer, edited from the Hengwrt Manuscript* (London: Arnold, 1980). Blake moderated his position in *The Textual Tradition of the Canterbury Tales* (London: Edward Arnold, 1985); see esp. the closing statements at 202.

CHAPTER TEN

1. Paul Strohm, "Jean of Angoulême: A Fifteenth Century Reader of Chaucer," *Neuphilologische Mitteilungen* 72 (1971): 69-76; Lee W. Patterson, "Ambiguity and Interpretation: a Fifteenth-Century Reading of *Troilus and Criseyde*," *Speculum* 54 (1979): 297-330, rpt. in *Negotiating the Past*, 115-56; B. A. Windeatt, "The Scribes as Chaucer's Early Critics," *Studies in the Age of Chaucer* 1 (1979): 119-41; "The Scribal Medium," in *Geoffrey Chaucer: Troilus & Criseyde: A New Edition of 'The Book of Troilus'* (London: Longman, 1984), 25-35; Seth Lerer, "Rewriting Chaucer: Two Fifteenth-Century Readings of the *Canterbury Tales*," *Viator* 19 (1988): 311-26; "Textual Criticism and Literary Theory: Chaucer and his Readers," *Exemplaria* 2 (1990): 329-45. Others have participated in this debate: William McClennan, "The Transcription of the 'Clerk's Tale' in MS HM 140: Interpreting Textual Effects," *Studies in Bibliography* 47 (1994): 89-102, with specific reference to Lerer, "Rewriting Chaucer"; Derek Pearsall, "Editing Medieval Texts," in McGann, ed., *Textual Criticism and Literary Interpretation*; and in a strong rebuttal directed largely against Windeatt and Pearsall, George Kane, "'Good' and 'Bad' Manuscripts: Texts and Critics," (1986), rpt. George Kane, *Chaucer and Langland: Historical and Textual Approaches* (Berkeley and Los Angeles: University of California Press, 1989), 206-27.

2. Seth Lerer, "Introduction," to "Cluster on Chaucer," *PMLA* 107 (1992): 1139-42 (quotation on 1140). A similar distinction appears in Skeat, in his specific rejection of what he calls "aesthetic criticism" (Skeat, *Works*, 6: xxiii); see my *Critical Mythology of Irony*, 140.

3. See the somewhat different characterization of the competing forces in eighteenth-century vernacular English editing in Jarvis, *Scholars and Gentlemen*, esp. 159-81 on Johnson.

4. Of modern editors, Kane is most squarely within this classical tradition. For classicists, see the rhetoric of James Willis, *Latin Textual Criticism* (Urbana: University of Illinois Press, 1972).

5. Cf. Lerer, who makes no such claims: "A manuscript of a given work can represent, potentially, a critical reading of that work, and in manuscripts which are considered textually unreliable we may find evidence for the critical interpretation of Chaucer's poetry" (Lerer, "Rewriting Chaucer," 311). Yeager's definition of criticism as "making choices" is untenably broad: "medieval writers and readers must have thought a good deal about what today gets called literary theory" ("Literary Theory," 135; see chap. 2 above).

6. It is so cited by Strohm, "Jean of Angoulême," 70n. 1; see also Martin Crow, "John of Angoulême and his Chaucer Manuscript," *Speculum* 17 (1942): 86-99. More recent discussion of the MS can be found in Owen, *Manuscripts*, 27-28.

7. Parkes, *"Ordinatio* and *Compilatio"*; Minnis, *Medieval Theory of Authorship*.

8. Manly-Rickert, *Text of the Canterbury Tales*, 1:403 note further that the Tale of Melibee was to be added, and that room was left for it. On Hengwrt, see the Introduction by Doyle in the Variorum *Hengwrt Facsimile*.

9. Strohm's explanation for the omission of the Tale of Sir Thopas is anachronistic. The notion that the tale is a parody or burlesque, a form of meta-literature, is not to be found before the eighteenth century; see my "Genre and Authority: The Eighteenth-Century Creation of Chaucerian Burlesque," *Huntington Library Quarterly* 48 (1985): 345-62.

10. The reading of the phrase "valde bona" is repeated, with reference to Strohm, by Boffey, *Manuscripts*, 1 and 2n. 2.

11. The classic article stating these assumptions is Alan T. Gaylord, "Sentence and Solaas in Fragment VII of the *Canterbury Tales*: Harry Bailly as Horseback Editor," *PMLA* 82 (1967): 226-35.

12. Patterson does not note how he made this discovery, whether through an article by Wager (1939), where the passage is quoted, or through the reference to Wager in Howard's *Three Temptations* (both cited and discussed, 297n. 2).

13. The stanza appears in Camb. MS Gg 4.12 and Cotton Otho A.xviii; George B. Pace, "Otho A. XVIII," *Speculum* 26 (1951): 306-08. See Patterson's n. 3 for citation to Pace.

14. See Windeatt, *Troilus and Criseyde*, 113, who notes that Chaucer here has inserted as Troilus's song Petrarch's Sonnet 132. See further Daniel S. Silvia, "Some Fifteenth-Century Manuscripts of the *Canterbury Tales*," in Beryl Rowland, ed., *Chaucer and Middle English Studies in Honour of Rossell Hope Robbins* (Kent: Kent State University Press, 1974), 153-63, on the individual tales of the *Canterbury Tales* that circulated independently.

These are predominantly moral tales and not representative of the work as a whole.

15. That a florilegium quotation could bring with it its context is implied by the opening of the Wife of Bath's Prologue, and may be part of the joke in the frivolous citations in the opening of the Nun's Priest's Tale.

16. Roger Dragonetti, *La Vie de la lettre au Moyen Age (Le Conte du Graal)* (Paris: Seuil, 1980).

17. An excellent account of the background for Bédier's theories is Mary B. Speer, "Old French Literature," in Greetham, ed., *Scholarly Editing*, 382-416. Among the many interpretations of the importance of Bédier, see Sebastiano Timpanaro, *La Genesi de metodo del Lachmann* (Padua: Liviana, 1981), 123-27; David F. Hult, "Reading It Right: The Ideology of Text Editing," in Marina S. Brownlee et al., eds., *The New Medievalism* (Baltimore: Johns Hopkins University Press, 1991), 113-30; Bédier's work was brought to the fore in Chaucer studies by the introductory discussion in Manly-Rickert, *Text of the Canterbury Tales*, 2: 12-14. On single-text editing in relation to Chaucer studies, see Ralph Hanna, "Problems of 'Best Text' Editing and the Hengwrt Manuscript of *The Canterbury Tales*," in Derek Pearsall, ed., *Manuscripts and Texts* (Cambridge: D. S. Brewer, 1987), 87-94.

18. Despite the radical nature of Windeatt's claims, the edition he produces is quite ordinary looking—nothing, for example, to compare with the Kane-Donaldson B version of *Piers Plowman*. A corpus of variants, clearly catalogued, appears on the same page, along with a facing column of Boccaccio (perhaps imported from a different genre of scholarship altogether—that of the parallel text edition).

19. The case is parallel to the idealized text G distinct from the manuscript Gg that results in what I consider the mirage of two authorial prologues of *Legend of Good Women*; see my "The Notions of Text and Variant in the Prologue to Chaucer's *Legend of Good Women*," *Papers of the Bibliographical Society of America* 84 (1993): 65-80.

20. On scribal variation as an index of authorial style, Kane agrees, "scribal variation can direct an editor with alert literary sensibility toward the stylistically notable features of his text" ("'Good' and 'Bad' Manuscripts," 208). Such analysis recalls much-earlier work by Riffaterre defining "stylistic devices" through a study of the text's reception; Michael Riffaterre, "Criteria for Style Analysis," *Word* 15 (1959): 154-74, and in Jacques Ehrmann, ed., "Describing Poetic Structures: Two Approaches to Baudelaire's 'Les Chats,'" in *Structuralism* (1966; Garden City, N.Y.: Anchor Books, 1970), 188-230. Strohm I think misreads Windeatt in claiming "Evidence of early reception suggests that Chaucer was probably regarded as a somewhat difficult poet"; Paul Strohm, *Social Chaucer* (Cambridge: Harvard University Press, 1989), 62. Windeatt's readers are scribes, and many of their ordinary changes result in a *lectio facilior*.

21. E.g., 3: 1415, "But whan the cok comune astrologer." Windeatt claims Gg "bungles" this line to "the cok come aftyr longere." The reasons for such

a change are obviously mechanical; there is no strange diction involved. Other variants Windeatt lists here include the following: And fynde a tyme] A. f. a leyser (1:1034); thriftily] discretly (3:211); entreparten] take a part of (1:592); red] conseill; yet thought] imagined yet (4:542) (Windeatt, *Troilus and Criseyde,* 30). None strikes me as noteworthy.

22. So Kane, "'Good' and 'Bad' MSS"; but see Peter Nicholson, "Poet and Scribe in the Manuscripts of Gower's *Confessio Amantis,*" in Pearsall, ed., *Manuscripts and Texts,* 130-42.

23. McClennan, "Transcription of the 'Clerk's Tale' in MS HM 140," criticizes Lerer because "the scribe's or editor's intentions" are impossible to determine (101). McClennan in making his own case refers without comment to *ordinatio* as the "intentional structure of the MS" (96).

24. See further on Shirley, Lerer, "British Library MS Harley 78 and the Manuscripts of John Shirley," and references indexed in *Chaucer and His Readers.*

25. Lerer is arguing against the notion that Shirley's peculiarities are due to his familiarity with the authors themselves. This is implicitly a challenge to what has become a general reliance among Chaucerians on Shirley's attributions; see above, chap. 7.

26. Lerer, citing A. C. Spearing, *Medieval to Renaissance in English Poetry* (Cambridge: Cambridge University Press, 1985), 105-6, calls this process a "de-authorization" but attributes it to Chaucer, moving the *Canterbury Tales* from "work" to a "text" (free from paternity and authorship). Cf. my own discussion of these terms, in "The Lure of Oral Theory," (doubtless, albeit unwittingly, inspired by Lerer).

27. Harold Bloom, *Agon: Towards a Theory of Revisionism* (New York: Oxford University Press, 1982), 16; Geoffrey H. Hartman, *Criticism in the Wilderness: The Study of Literature Today* (New Haven: Yale University Press, 1980).

28. Cf. Lynn Staley Johnson, "The Trope of the Scribe and the Question of Literary Authority in the Works of Julian of Norwich and Margery Kempe," *Speculum* 66 (1991): 820-38, who sees "scribe" as a metaphor for the author, that is, under authorial control; I believe this is the reverse of the argument advanced by the Chaucerians under review here.

CONCLUSION

1. *Catalogus Bibliothecae Harleianae,* 3: 237ff.

2. See Blake and Robinson, ed., *The Canterbury Tales Project: Occasional Papers,* and the excellent review by Tim William Machan, *Studies in the Age of Chaucer* 17 (1995): 175-78. See more generally Peter Shillingsburg, "Polymorphic, Polysemic, Protean, Reliable, Electronic Texts," in George Bornstein and Ralph G. Williams, ed., *Palimpsest: Editorial Theory in the Humanities* (Ann Arbor: University of Michigan Press, 1993), 29-43.

3. Woodward and Stevens, eds., *The New Ellesmere Chaucer Facsimile* (1995); prices for this range from $7,000 to $15,000; a cheaper black-and-white

version is now available; cf. the black-and-white facsimile designed for scholarly research, Hanna, ed., *The Ellesmere Manuscript of Chaucer's Canterbury Tales: A Working Facsimile* (1989), a facsimile of the earlier 1911 facsimile.

4. Clarles Cowden Clarke, *The Riches of Chaucer, in which his impurities have been expunged* . . . (London, 1835), many reprintings. See Hammond, *Manual,* 229.

5. See esp. Cora Edgerton Sanders, "The Beginnings of the Library," and Hugh G. Dick, "The English Drama to 1700," in *The William Andrews Clark Memorial Library: Report of the First Decade 1934-1944* (Berkeley and Los Angeles: University of California Press, 1946), 13-17, 26-33. An unpublished paper by Sanford M. Dorbin, "The Origin and Development of the Library of William Andrews Clark, Junior, During His Lifetime" (1965), offers a corrective to some of the statements of Sanders and Dick, arguing on the basis of accession records that the "outline of the total diversity of the collection was remarkably complete by 1920" (71). I thank Suzanne Tatian of the Clark Library for making accession records available to me.

6. Neither the Clark collection nor any collection could possibly be considered complete, nor could any reasonable definition of completeness in this area be fashioned. Among the more notable absences, however, is the Ashendene Press *Prologue and Canterbury Tales,* printed in 1897, the third year of operation. This was printed in roman type, interspersed with woodcuts from Caxton and a text by Skeat; see *A Descriptive Bibliography of the Books Printed at the Ashendene Press, 1895-1935* (Chelsea: Shelley House, 1935).

7. H. Richard Archer, "Fine Printing," *Clark Library Report: First Decade,* 67-78 and esp. Everett T. Moore, "Fine Printing," *William Andrews Clark Library: Report of the Third Decade* (Berkeley and Los Angeles: University of California Press, 1966), 46-63. (The 1956 Report is not useful.) See also, Robert Ernest Cowan, Cora Edgerton Sanders and Harrison Post, *The Library of William Andrews Clark, Jr.: The Kelmscott and Doves Presses* (San Francisco: J. H. Nash, 1921), with introduction by A. W. Pollard—part of the twenty-volume printed Clark catalog.

8. At the time the first report was written in 1946, Archer notes that the library still lacks, but is seeking, what now seem rather basic volumes in printing history: T. B. Reed's *History of Old English Type Foundries* (1887), and Moxon's *Mechanick Exercises.*

9. Archer, "Fine Printing," 67.

10. I have suggested in earlier chapters that the 1532 Chaucer might be a legitimate member of the series of fine press Chaucers; its value, however, depends largely on its date and rarity. The later Chaucer folios collected by Clark are only moderately priced; see Dorbin, "Origin and Development," 25-75.

11. *Riverside Chaucer,* 772, lists only Thynne, Tyrwhitt, and Skeat among the category "Editions of Chaucer" (there are 11 entries under the category

"Courtly Love"). Under the category "Modern Editions" found in the Variorum Chaucer volumes, the listed editions are Skeat, Robinson, Manly-Rickert, Pratt and occasionally, Fisher. Baker's edition of the Squire's Tale adds Betherum, Blake and the Riverside (Baker, *Squire's Tale*, 113).

12. Hammond, *Manual*, 147-48.

13. The Kelmscott Chaucer is in large part a reprint of Skeat's 1894 edition, and the copy marked by Ellis and Morris is now at the Beinecke Library; see William S. Peterson, *The Kelmscott Press: A History of William Morris's Typographical Adventure* (Berkeley and Los Angeles: University of California Press, 1991), 235-39.

14. This may be a concretion of Burne-Jones's remark that the Kelmscott Chaucer will itself be "a little like a pocket cathedral"; quoted Duncan Robinson, *William Morris, Edward Burne-Jones, and the Kelmscott Chaucer* (London: Gordon Fraser, 1982), 36.

WORKS CITED

Ackermann, R. *The History of the Abbey Church of St. Peter's Westminster, its Antiquities and Monuments.* 2 vols. London: Ackermann, 1832.

Adams, Robert. "Editing *Piers Plowman* B: The Imperatives of an Intermittently Critical Edition." *Studies in Bibliography* 45 (1992): 31-68.

Aers, David. "A Whisper in the Ear of Early Modernists: or, Reflections on Literary Critics writing the *History of the Subject.*" In David Aers, ed. *Culture and History (1350-1600): Essays on English Communities, Identities and Writing.* Detroit: Wayne State University Press, 1992. Pp. 177-202.

Alderson, William L., and Arnold C. Henderson. *Chaucer and Augustan Scholarship.* Berkeley and Los Angeles: University of California Press, 1970.

Alsop, James. "Nicholas Brigham (d. 1558), Scholar, Antiquary, and Crown Servant." *Sixteenth Century Journal* 12 (1981): 49-67.

Ames, Joseph. *Typographical Antiquities: Being an Historical Account of Printing in England with some Memoirs of our Antient Printers, and A Register of the Books printed by them from the year MCCCCLXXI to the Year MDC.* London: W. Faden, 1749.

Andrew, Malcolm et al., eds. See Chaucer.

Archer, H. Richard. "Fine Printing." In *The William Andrews Clark Memorial Library: Report of the First Decade 1934-1944.* Berkeley and Los Angeles: University of California Press, 1946. Pp. 67-78.

Ashmole, Elias. *Theatrum Chemicum Britannicum, containing severall poeticall pieces of our famous English Philosophers, who have written the*

Hermetique Mysteries *in their owne Ancient Language.* London: Brooks, 1652.

———. *Memoirs of the Life of that Learned Antiquary, Elias Ashmole, Esq, drawn up by himself by way of Diary.* Publ. Charles Burman. London: J. Roberts, 1771.

Bagford, John. "An Essay on the Invention of Printing, by Mr. John Bagford; with an Account of his Collections for the same by Mr. Humfrey Wanley . . ." Royal Society, *Philosophical Transactions* 25 (1706-7): 237-410.

Baker, Donald C. "William Thynne's Printing of the *Squire's Tale*: Manuscript and Printer's Copy." *Studies in Bibliography* 39 (1986): 125-32.

———, ed. See Chaucer.

Beadle, Richard, and Jeremy Griffiths, ed. *St. John's College, Cambridge, Manuscript L. 1, Troilus and Criseyde: A Facsimile.* Norman: Pilgrim Books, 1983.

Bennett, H. S. *English Books and Readers, 1475 to 1557: Being a Study in the History of the Book Trade from Caxton to the Incorporation of the Stationers' Company.* 2nd ed. Cambridge: University Press, 1969.

Benson, C. David. *Chaucer's Drama of Style: Poetic Variety and Contrast in the* Canterbury Tales. Chapel Hill: University of North Carolina Press, 1986.

Benson, Larry D. "The Order of the *Canterbury Tales.*" *Studies in the Age of Chaucer* 3 (1981): 77-120.

Bentley, G. E. "Comment Upon the Illustrated Eighteenth-Century Chaucer." *Modern Philology* 78 (1981): 398.

Birrell, T. A. "Anthony Wood, John Bagford and Thomas Hearne as Bibliographers." In Robin Myers and Michael Harris, ed. *Pioneers of Bibliography.* Winchester, Hampshire: St. Paul's Bibliographies, 1988. Pp. 25-39.

Blades, William. *The Biography and Typography of William Caxton.* 2d ed. New York: Scribner, 1882.

———. *The Life and Typography of William Caxton, England's First Printer.* 2 vols. London: Joseph Lilly, 1861.

Blake, N. F. "Aftermath: Manuscript to Print." In Pearsall and Griffiths, eds. *Book Production and Publishing in Britain.* Pp. 403-32.

———. "Caxton and Chaucer." *Leeds Studies in English,* n.s. 1 (1967): 19-36. Rpt. N. F. Blake. *William Caxton and English Literary Culture.* London: Hambledon Press, 1991. Pp. 149-65.

————. "The Ellesmere Text in the Light of the Hengwrt Manuscript." In Woodward and Stevens, ed. *Ellesmere Chaucer: Essays in Interpretation.* Pp. 205-24.

————. *The Textual Tradition of the* Canterbury Tales. London: Edward Arnold, 1985.

————, ed. See Chaucer.

Blake, Norman, and Peter Robinson, eds. *The Canterbury Tales Project: Occasional Papers.* Vol. 1. Oxford: Office for Humanities Communication, 1993.

Blodgett, James E. "Some Printer's Copy for William Thynne's 1532 Edition of Chaucer." *The Library* ser. 6, 1 (1979): 97-113.

————. "William Thynne and His 1532 Edition of Chaucer." Diss. University of Indiana, 1975.

————. "William Thynne (d. 1546)." In Ruggiers, ed. *Editing Chaucer.* Pp. 35-52.

Bloom, Harold. *Agon: Towards a Theory of Revisionism.* New York: Oxford University Press, 1982.

Bloxam, M. H. "On Chaucer's Monument in Westminster Abbey." *Archaeological Journal* 38 (1881): 361-64.

Boffey, Julia. *Manuscripts of English Courtly Love Lyrics in the Later Middle Ages.* London: D. S. Brewer, 1985.

————. "The Reputation and Circulation of Chaucer's Lyrics in the Fifteenth Century." *Chaucer Review* 28 (1993): 23-40.

————, and John J. Thompson. "Anthologies and Miscellanies: Production and Choice of Texts." In Pearsall and Griffiths, eds. *Book Production and Publishing in Britain.* Pp. 279-315.

Bolling, George Melville. *The External Evidence for Interpolation in Homer.* Oxford: Clarendon Press, 1925.

Bond, Richmond P. "Some Eighteenth Century Chaucer Allusions." *Studies in Philology* 25 (1928): 316-39.

Booth, Wayne C. *The Rhetoric of Fiction.* Chicago: University of Chicago Press, 1961.

Bowden, Betsy. "The Artistic and Interpretive Context of Blake's *Canterbury Tales.*" *Blake: An Illustrated Quarterly* 13 (1980): 164-73.

————. *Chaucer Aloud: The Varieties of Textual Interpretation.* Philadelphia: University of Pennsylvania Press, 1987.

Bowers, Fredson. *Principles of Bibliographical Description.* 1949. New ed., with introduction by G. Thomas Tanselle. New Castle: Oak Knoll Press, 1994.

Bowers, John. "*The Tale of Beryn* and *The Siege of Thebes*: Alternative Ideas of *The Canterbury Tales*." *Studies in the Age of Chaucer* 7 (1985): 23-50.

Boyle, L. E., "Peciae, Apopeciae, and a Toronto MS. of the Sententia Libri Ethicorum of Aquinas." In Peter Ganz, ed. *The Role of the Book in Medieval Culture*. 2 vols. Turnhout: Brepols, 1986.

Bradley, Henry. *The Collected Papers of Henry Bradley*. Oxford: Clarendon Press, 1928.

Bradshaw, Henry. *Collected Papers of Henry Bradshaw*. Cambridge: University Press, 1889.

[Brathwait, Richard]. *A Comment upon the Two Tales of our Ancient, Renowned, and Ever Living Poet Sr Jefray Chaucer, Knight* . . . London, 1665.

[Brayley, E. W.] *The Beauties of England and Wales*, vol. 10, pt. 3: *London and Middlesex*, vol. 3, pt. 2: *Containing the History and Description of the City and Liberty of Westminster*. London: Harris, 1815.

Brewer, Derek. *Chaucer: The Critical Heritage*. 2 vols. London: Routledge & Kegan Paul, 1978.

Bronson, Bertrand H. "Chaucer's Art in Relation to His Audience." in *Five Studies in Literature*. University of California Publications in English 8, 1. Berkeley and Los Angeles: University of California Press, 1940. Pp. 1-54.

———. *In Search of Chaucer*. Toronto: University of Toronto Press, 1960.

Brooks, Cleanth. *Historical Evidence and the Reading of Seventeenth-Century Poetry*. Columbia: University of Missouri Press, 1991.

Brown, J. L. T. *The Authorship of the* Kingis Quair: *A New Criticism*. Glascow: James Maclehose, 1896.

Brownrigg, Linda L., ed. *Medieval Book Production: Assessing the Evidence*. Los Altos: Anderson-Lovelace, 1990.

Brusendorff, Aage. *The Chaucer Tradition*. Oxford: Clarendon Press, 1925.

Carlson, David R. "Chaucer's *Boethius* and Thomas Usk's *Testament of Love*: Politics and Love in the Chaucerian Tradition." In Robert A. Taylor et al. ed. *The Centre and Its Compass: Studies in Medieval Literature in Honor of Professor John Leyerle*. Kalamazoo: Western Michigan University, Medieval Institute Publications, 1993. Pp. 29-70.

———. "Thomas Hoccleve and the Chaucer Portrait." *Huntington Library Quarterly* 54 (1991): 283-300.

———. "Woodcut Illustrations of the *Canterbury Tales*, 1483-1602." *The Library* ser. 6, 19 (1997): 25-67.

———. "The Writings and Manuscript Collections of the Elizabethan Alchemist, Antiquary, and Herald Francis Thynne." *Huntington Library Quarterly* 52 (1989): 203-72.

Carter, Harry. *A History of Oxford University Press*, vol. 1 *To the Year 1780*. Oxford: Clarendon Press, 1975.

Catalogus Bibliothecae Harleianae. 4 vols. London: Thomas Osborne, 1743-45.

Catalogus Librorum Impressorum Bibliothecae Bodleianae. 3 vols. Oxford: Typographeo Academico, 1843.

Cerquiglini, Bernard. *Eloge de la variante: Histoire critique de la philologie*. Paris: Seuil, 1989.

Chambers, R. W. "The Three Texts of *Piers Plowman*, and Their Grammatical Forms." *Modern Language Review* 14 (1919): 129-51.

Chaucer, Geoffrey. *The Canterbury Tales: A Facsimile and Transcription of the Hengwrt Manuscript*. Ed. Paul G. Ruggiers. Norman: University of Oklahoma Press, 1979.

———. *The Canterbury Tales by Geoffrey Chaucer, edited from the Hengwrt MS*. Ed. N. F. Blake. London: Arnold, 1980.

———. *The Canterbury Tales of Chaucer*. Ed. Thomas Morell. London, 1737.

———. *The Canterbury Tales of Chaucer to which are added An Essay upon his Language and Versification; an Introductory Discourse; and Notes*. Ed. [Thomas Tyrwhitt]. 5 vols. London: T. Payne, 1775-78.

———. *The Canterbury Tales of Geoffrey Chaucer: A New Text with Illustrative Notes*. Ed. Thomas Wright. 3 vols. London: Percy Society, 1847-51.

———. *The Complete Works of Geoffrey Chaucer*. Ed. Walter W. Skeat. 7 vols. Oxford: Oxford University Press, 1894–1899.

———. *The General Prologue*. Ed. Malcolm Andrew, Charles Moorman et al. *Variorum Chaucer*, II, 1A-B. Norman: University of Oklahoma Press, 1993.

———. *The Manciple's Tale*. Ed. Donald C. Baker. *Variorum Chaucer*, II, 10. Norman: University of Oklahoma Press, 1984.

———. *The Miller's Tale*. Ed. Thomas W. Ross. *Variorum Chaucer*, II, 3. Norman: University of Oklahoma Press, 1983.

———. *The Minor Poems.* Ed. Walter W. Skeat. Oxford: Clarendon Press, 1888.

———. *The Minor Poems.* Part One. Ed. George B. Pace and Alfred David. Variorum Chaucer, V. Norman: University of Oklahoma Press, 1982.

———. *The Nun's Priest's Tale.* Ed. Derek Pearsall. Variorum Chaucer, II, 9. Norman: University of Oklahoma Press, 1984.

———. *Poetical Works, a Facsimile of Cambridge University Library MS Gg. 4.27.* Ed. M. B. Parkes and Richard Beadle. Norman, Okla.: Pilgrim Books, 1980.

———. *Poetical Works of Geoffrey Chaucer.* Ed. Robert Bell. 8 vols. 1854-56; rpt. London: Griffin, [1870-71].

———. *The Poetical Works of Geoffrey Chaucer.* London: Edward Moxon, 1843.

———. *The Poetical Works of Geoffrey Chaucer.* Ed. Richard Morris. 1866; new ed. London: Bell, n. d.

———. *The Poetical Works of Geoffrey Chaucer.* Ed. Richard Morris, with Memoir by Sir Harris Nicolas. Vol. 1. London: Bell, 1891.

———. *The Riverside Chaucer.* Ed. Larry D. Benson. Boston: Houghton Mifflin, 1987.

———. *The Squire's Tale.* Ed. Donald C. Baker. Variorum Chaucer, II, 12. Norman: University of Oklahoma Press, 1990.

———. *Troilus & Criseyde: A New Edition of The Book of Troilus.* Ed. B. A. Windeatt. London: Longman, 1984.

———. *The Workes of Geffray Chaucer newly printed . . .* Ed. [William Thynne]. London: Godfray, 1532.

———. *The Workes of our Antient and Learned English Poet, Geffrey Chaucer.* Ed. [Thomas Speght]. London: Bishop, 1598.

———. *The Workes of our Antient and Learned English Poet, Geffrey Chaucer.* Ed. [Thomas Speght]. London: Islip, 1602.

———. *The Works, 1532 with Supplementary material from the Editions of 1542, 1561, 1598 and 1602.* Ed. D. S. Brewer. London: Scholar Press, 1974.

———. *The Works of Geoffrey Chaucer.* Ed. Alfred W. Pollard. The Globe Edition. London: Macmillan, 1898.

———. *The Works of Geoffrey Chaucer and Others, being a reproduction in facsimile of the first collected edition 1532 from the copy in the British Museum.* Ed. Walter W. Skeat. London: Oxford University Press, 1905.

————. *The Works of Geoffrey Chaucer, compared with the Former Editions, and many valuable MSS.* Ed. John Urry et al. London: Lintot, 1721.

Clarke, M. L. *Greek Studies in England (1700-1830).* Cambridge: Cambridge University Press, 1945.

Claudin, A. *Histoire de l'imprimerie en France au XVe et au XVIe siècle.* Paris: Imprimerie Nationale, 1900.

Coletti, Teresa. "Reading REED." In Lee Patterson, ed. *Literary Practice and Social Change in Britain, 1380-1530.* Berkeley and Los Angeles: University of California Press, 1990. Pp. 248-84.

Cooper, Helen. *The Canterbury Tales: Oxford Guides to Chaucer.* Oxford: Clarendon Press, 1988.

Corbett, Margery, and Ronald Lightbown. *The Comeley Frontispiece: The Emblematic Title-Page in England, 1550-1600.* London: Routledge, 1979.

Cowan, Robert Ernest, et al. *The Library of William Andrews Clark, Jr.: The Kelmscott and Doves Presses.* San Francisco: J. H. Nash, 1921.

Crotch, W. J. B. *The Prologues and Epilogues of William Caxton.* EETS 176. London: Oxford University Press, 1928.

Crow, Martin. "John of Angouleme and his Chaucer Manuscript." *Speculum* 17 (1942): 86-99.

————, and Clair C. Olson. *Chaucer Life-Records.* Oxford: Oxford University Press, 1966.

[Crull, Jodocus]. *The Antiquities of St. Peter's, or the Abbey Church of Westminster.* London: J.N., 1711. 3rd ed. 2 vols. London: Bell, 1722.

Curtius, Ernst Robert. *European Literature and the Latin Middle Ages.* 1948. Tr. Willard R. Trask. Princeton: Princeton University Press, 1953.

Dane, Joseph A. "Bibliographical History versus Bibliographical Evidence: *The Plowman's Tale* and Early Chaucer Editions." *Bulletin of the John Rylands University Library of Manchester* 78 (1996): 50-64.

————. "Copy-Text and Its Variants in Some Recent Chaucer Editions." *Studies in Bibliography* 44 (1991): 163-83.

————. *The Critical Mythology of Irony.* Athens: University of Georgia Press, 1991.

————. "Genre and Authority: The Eighteenth-Century Creation of Chaucerian Burlesque." *Huntington Library Quarterly* 48 (1985): 345-62.

————. "'Ideal Copy' versus 'Ideal Texts': The Application of Bibliographical Description to Facsimiles." *Papers of the Bibliographical Society of Canada* 33 (1995): 31-50.

————. "The Importance of Importance." *Huntington Library Quarterly* 56 (1993): 307-17.

————. "The Lure of Oral Theory in Medieval Criticism: From Edited 'Text' to Critical 'Work'." *TEXT* 7 (1992): 145-60.

————. "The Notions of Text and Variant in the Prologue to Chaucer's *Legend of Good Women*." *Papers of the Bibliographical Society of America* 84 (1993): 65-80.

————. "On 'Correctness': A Note on Some Press Variants in Thynne's 1532 Edition of Chaucer." *The Library* ser. 6, 17 (1995): 156-67.

————. "On Greatness in Editing." Review of Ruggiers, ed., *Editing Chaucer. Huntington Library Quarterly* 48 (1985): 172-79.

————. "The Presumed Influence of Skeat's *Student's Chaucer* on Manly and Rickert's *Text of the Canterbury Tales*." *Analytical and Enumerative Bibliography* 7 (1993): 18-27.

Dart, John. *Westmonasterium or The History and Antiquities of the Abbey Church of St. Peters Westminster . . . 1723.* 2 vols. London: J. Cole, [1723].

David, Alfred. "The Ownership and Use of the Ellesmere Manuscript." In Woodward and Stevens, ed. *Ellesmere Chaucer: Essays in Interpretation.* Pp. 307-26.

————, ed. See Chaucer.

De Ricci, Seymour. *A Census of Caxtons.* Bibliographical Society Monographs, no. 15. Oxford University Press, 1909.

A Descriptive Bibliography of the Books Printed at the Ashendene Press, 1895-1935. Chelsea: Shelley House, 1935.

Destrez, Jean. *La Pecia dans les manuscrits universitaires du xiiie et du xive siècle.* Paris: Jacques Vautrain, 1935.

————, and M. D. Chenu. "Exemplaria universitaires des xiiie et xive siècles." *Scriptorium* 7 (1953): 6-80.

Dibdin, T. F. *The Library Companion: or, the Young Man's guide, and the old man's comfort in the choice of a library.* 2nd ed. London: Harding, Triphook and Lepard, 1825.

————, ed. *Typographical Antiquities, or the History of Printing in England Scotland and Ireland containing Memoirs of our Ancient Printers . . . begun by the late Joseph Ames. . .* 4 vols. London: Miller, 1810.

Dick, Hugh G. "The English Drama to 1700." In *The William Andrews Clark Memorial Library: Report of the First Decade 1934-1944*. Berkeley and Los Angeles: University of California Press, 1946.

Donaldson, E. Talbot. *Chaucer's Poetry: An Anthology for the Modern Reader*. New York: Ronald Press, 1958.

———. "Chaucer the Pilgrim." 1954. Rpt. E. Talbot Donaldson. *Speaking of Chaucer*. New York: Norton, 1970.

———. "The Texts of *Piers Plowman*: Scribes and Poets." *Modern Philology* 50 (1953): 269-73.

Dorbin, Sanford M. "The Origin and Development of the Library of William Andrews Clark, Junior, During His Lifetime." Typescript, 1965.

Douglas, David C. *English Scholars*. London: Jonathan Cape, 1939.

Doyle, A. I. "More Light on John Shirley." *Medium Aevum* 30 (1961): 93-101.

———, and M. B. Parkes. "The Production of Copies of the *Canterbury Tales* and the *Confessio Amantis* in the Early Fifteenth Century." In M. B. Parkes and A. G. Watson, ed. *Medieval Scribes, Manuscripts and Libraries: Essays Presented to N. R. Ker*. London: Scolar Press, 1978. Pp. 163-210.

Dragonetti, Roger. *La Vie de la lettre au Moyen Age (Le Conte du Graal)*. Paris: Seuil, 1980.

Dryden, John. *Fables Ancient and Modern; translated into Verse, from Homer, Ovid, Boccace, & Chaucer*. London: Tonson, 1700.

Duff, E. Gordon. *A Century of the English Book Trade . . . 1457-1557*. London: Bibliographical Society, 1948.

———. *Fifteenth Century English Books: A Bibliography of Books and Documents Printed in England and of Books for the English Market Printed Abroad*. London: Bibliographical Society, 1917.

———. *William Caxton*. 1905; rpt. New York: Burt Franklin, 1970.

———, W. W. Greg, et al. *Hand-lists of Books Printed by London Printers, 1501-1556*. London: Oxford University Press, 1913.

Dutschke, C. W. *Guide to Medieval and Renaissance Manuscripts in the Huntington Library*. 2 vols. San Marino: Huntington Library Press, 1989.

Edwards, A. S. G. Review of *Chaucer: General Prologue*. Ed. Andrew, Moorman, and Ransom. Variorum Chaucer 2, 1. *Studies in the Age of Chaucer* 17 (1995): 157-60.

————, ed. *Manuscript Pepys 2006: A Facsimile.* Norman, Okla.: Pilgrim Books, 1985.

Edwards, Robert R. *The Dream of Chaucer: Representation and Reflection in the Early Narratives.* Durham: Duke University Press, 1989.

Eggers, Hans. *Deutsche Sprachgeschichte.* Reinbek bei Hamburg: Rowolt, 1963-77.

Eisenstein, Elizabeth L. *The Printing Press as an Agent of Change: Communication and Cultural Transformations in Early-Modern Europe.* 2 vols. Cambridge: Cambridge University Press, 1979.

Erdman, David V., and Ephim G. Fogel, eds. *Evidence for Authorship: Essays on Problems of Attribution.* Ithaca: Cornell University Press, 1966.

Esdaile, Katherine A. *Times Literary Supplement,* 28 February 1929. P. 163.

Ferguson, W. Craig. *Pica Roman Type in Elizabethan England.* London: Scolar Press, 1989.

Fisher, John H. *The Importance of Chaucer.* Carbondale: Southern Illinois University Press, 1992.

————. *John Gower: Moral Philosopher and Friend of Chaucer.* New York: New York University Press, 1964.

Fletcher, Bradford Y. "Printer's Copy for Stow's *Chaucer.*" *Studies in Bibliography* 31 (1978): 184-201.

Forni, Kathleen Rose. "Studies in the Chaucerian Apocrypha." Diss. University of Southern California, 1995.

————. "The Swindling of Chaucerians and the Critical Fate of the *Flower and the Leaf.*" *Chaucer Review* 31 (1997): 379-400.

Fowler, D. C. *Piers the Plowman: Literary Relations of the A and B Texts.* Seattle: University of Washington Press, 1961.

Fox, Denton, ed. *Robert Henryson: The Testament of Cresseid.* London: Nelson, 1968.

Foxe, John. *The First volume of the Ecclesiastical History, contayning the Actes & Monumentes of thinges passed in every Kinges time.* London: John Day, 1576.

Furnivall, F. J. "Chaucer's Tomb in Westminster Abbey." *Notes and Queries* ser. 10, 1 (1904): 28.

————. *A Temporary Preface to the Six-text Edition of Chaucer's Canterbury Tales.* Chaucer Society Publ., ser. 2, pt. 3. London: Trübner, 1868.

Ganim, John M. *Chaucerian Theatricality.* Princeton: Princeton University Press, 1990.

Gatch, Milton McC. "John Bagford, Bookseller and Antiquary." *The British Library Journal* 12 (1986): 150-71.

———. "John Bagford's Manuscript Fragments." *The Library* ser. 6 , 7 (1985): 95-114.

Gaylord, Alan T. "Imagining Voices: Chaucer on Cassette." *Studies in the Age of Chaucer* 12 (1990): 215-38.

———. "*Sentence* and *Solaas* in Fragment VII of the *Canterbury Tales*: Harry Bailly as Horseback Editor." *PMLA* 82 (1967): 226-35.

Gellrich, Jesse M. *The Idea of the Book in the Middle Ages: Language Theory, Mythology, and Fiction.* Ithaca: Cornell University Press, 1985.

Godwin, William. *Life of Geoffrey Chaucer the Early English Poet.* 2 vols. London: T. Davison, 1803.

Gourlay, Alexander S. "What was Blake's Chaucer?" *Studies in Bibliography* 42 (1989): 272-83.

Green, Richard F. *Poets and Princepleasures: Literature and the English Court in the Late Middle Ages.* Toronto: University of Toronto Press, 1980.

Greetham, D. C., ed. *Scholarly Editing: A Guide to Research.* New York: Modern Language Association, 1995.

Greg, W. W. "The Early Printed Editions of the *Canterbury Tales.*" *PMLA* 39 (1924): 737-61.

———. "The Rationale of Copy-Text." *Studies in Bibliography* 3 (1950-51): 19-36.

Griffiths, Jeremy, and Derek Pearsall, eds. *Book Production and Publishing in Britain 1375-1476.* Cambridge: Cambridge University Press, 1989.

Haebler, Konrad. *The Study of Incunabula.* 1925. Trans. Lucy Eugenia Osborne. New York: The Grolier Club, 1933.

———. *Typenrepertorium der Wiegendrucke.* 5 vols. Leipzig, 1905-24; rpt. Nendeln: Krauss, 1968.

Hales, John W. "The Grave of Chaucer." *Athenaeum,* 9 August 1902, 189-90.

Hammond, Eleanor Prescott. "Ashmole 59 and other Shirley Manuscripts." *Anglia* 30 (1907): 320-48.

———. *Chaucer: A Bibliographical Manual.* New York: Macmillan, 1908.

———. *English Verse Between Chaucer and Surrey.* Durham, N.C.: Duke University Press, 1927.

———. "MS. Longleat 258–A Chaucerian Codex." *Modern Language Notes* 20 (1905): 77-79.

————. "MS. Pepys 2006–A Chaucerian Codex." *Modern Language Notes* 19 (1904): 196-98.

————. "Omissions from the Editions of Chaucer." *Modern Language Notes* 19 (1904): 35-38.

————. "On the Editing of Chaucer's Minor Poems." *Modern Language Notes* 23 (1908), 20-21.

————. "A Scribe of Chaucer." *Modern Philology* 27 (1929): 26-33.

————. "Two British Museum Manuscripts (Harley 2251 and Adds. 34360): A Contribution to the Bibliography of John Lydgate." *Anglia* 28 (N.F. 16) (1905): 1-28.

Hanna, Ralph, III. "Booklets in Medieval Manuscripts: Further Considerations." *Studies in Bibliography* 39 (1986): 100-11.

————. "Introduction." In *The Ellesmere Manuscript of Chaucer's Canterbury Tales: A Working Facsimile.* Cambridge: D. S. Brewer, 1989.

————. "Problems of 'Best Text' Editing and the Hengwrt Manuscript of *The Canterbury Tales.*" In Derek Pearsall, ed. *Manuscripts and Texts.* Cambridge: D. S. Brewer, 1987. Pp. 87-94.

————. *Pursuing History: Middle English Manuscripts and Their Texts.* Stanford: Stanford University Press, 1996.

————. Review of Owen, *The Manuscripts of the Canterbury Tales. Studies in the Age of Chaucer* 15 (1993): 247-51.

————. Review of *Nun's Priest's Tale,* ed. Pearsall. *Analytical and Enumerative Bibliography* 8 (1984): 184-97.

————, and A. S. G. Edwards. "Rotheley, the De Vere Circle, and the Ellesmere Chaucer." *Huntington Library Quarterly* 58 (1996): 11-35.

Hansen, Elaine Tuttle. *Chaucer and the Fictions of Gender.* Berkeley and Los Angeles: University of California Press, 1992.

Hart, Horace. *Notes on a Century of Typography at the University Press Oxford, 1693-1794.* 1900. Ed. Harry Carter. Oxford: Clarendon Press, 1970.

Hartman, Geoffrey H. *Criticism in the Wilderness: The Study of Literature Today.* New Haven: Yale University Press, 1980.

Harvard College Library, Dept. of Printing and Graphic Arts, Catalogue of French Sixteenth Century Books. 2 vols. Cambridge, Mass.: Belknapp Press, 1964.

Hearne, Thomas. *Remarks and Collections of Thomas Hearne.* 11 vols. Ed. C. E. Doble, D. W. Rannie et al. Oxford: Oxford Historical Society, 1885-1921.

————. *The Works of Thomas Hearne, M.A.*. London: Samuel Bagster, 1810.

————, ed. *Robert of Gloucester's Chronicle*. 2 vols. Oxford: Sheldon Theatre, 1724.

Helgerson, Richard. *Forms of Nationhood: The Elizabethan Writing of England*. Chicago: University of Chicago, 1992.

Hellinga, Lotte. *Caxton in Focus: The Beginning of Printing in England*. London: The British Library, 1982.

Hellinga, Witze, and Lotte Hellinga. *The Fifteenth-Century Printing Types of the Low Countries*. 2 vols. Amsterdam: Hertzberger, 1966.

Hench, Atcheson L. "Printer's Copy for Tyrwhitt's Chaucer." *Studies in Bibliography* 3 (1950): 265-66.

Hetherington, John R. *Chaucer, 1532-1602: Notes and Facsimile Texts*. Birmingham, privately printed, 1964.

Heyworth, P. L., ed. *Jack Upland, Friar Daw's Reply and Upland's Rejoinder*. London: Oxford University Press, 1968.

Hind, Arthur M. *Engraving in England in the Sixteenth and Seventeenth Centuries: A Descriptive Catalogue with Introduction*. 3 vols. Cambridge: Cambridge University Press, 1964.

Hindman, Sandra L., ed. *Printing the Written Word: The Social History of Books, circa 1450-1520*. Ithaca: Cornell University Press, 1991.

Hodnett, Edward. *English Woodcuts, 1480-1535*. 2nd ed. Oxford: University Press, 1973.

Howard, Donald R. *The Idea of the* Canterbury Tales. Berkeley and Los Angeles: University of California Press, 1976.

————. *The Three Temptations: Medieval Man in Search of the World*. Princeton: Princeton University Press, 1966.

Howard-Hill, T. H, Review of Michael Warren, *The Complete King Lear (1608-1623)* (Berkeley and Los Angeles: University of California Press, 1989). *Review of English Studies* 43 (1992): 420-22.

Hudson, Anne. "John Stow (1525?-1605)." In Ruggiers, ed. *Editing Chaucer*. Pp. 53-70.

Hult, David F. "Reading It Right: The Ideology of Text Editing." In Marina S. Brownlee et al. *The New Medievalism*. Baltimore: Johns Hopkins University Press, 1991. Pp. 113-30.

————. *Self-Fulfilling Prophecies: Readership and Authority in the First Roman de la Rose*. Cambridge: Cambridge University Press, 1986.

Huot, Sylvia. *From Song to Book: The Poetics of Writing in Old French Lyric and Lyrical Narrative Poetry*. Ithaca: Cornell University Press, 1987.

————. *The Romance of the Rose and its Medieval Readers:
Interpretation, Reception, Manuscript Transmission.* Cambridge:
Cambridge University Press, 1993.

Irvine, Annie S. "A Manuscript Copy of *The Plowman's Tale.*" *University
of Texas Studies in English* 12 (1932): 27-56.

Isaac, Frank. *English and Scottish Printing Types, 1501-35, 1508-41.*
London: Oxford University Press, 1930.

————. *English Printers' Types of the Sixteenth Century.* Oxford:
Bibliographical Society, 1936.

Johnson, Alfred Forbes. *A Catalogue of Engraved and Etched English
Title-Pages down to the Death of William Faithorne, 1691.*
Bibliographical Society, Facsimiles and Illustrations, no. IV. Oxford
University Press, 1934.

————. *Selected Essays on Books and Printing.* Ed. Percy H. Muir.
London: Routledge, 1970.

————. *Type Designs: Their History and Development.* 1934. 3rd ed.
Norwich: Andre Deutsch, 1966.

Johnson, Lynn Staley. "The Trope of the Scribe and the Question of
Literary Authority in the Works of Julian of Norwich and Margery
Kempe." *Speculum* 66 (1991): 820-38.

Johnston, Alexandra F. "What if No Texts Survived? External
Evidence for Early English Drama." In Marianna G. Brixcoe et al.
eds. *Contexts for Early English Drama.* Bloomington: Indiana
University Press, 1989. Pp. 1-19.

Johnston, Stanley Howard, Jr. "A Study of the Career and Literary
Publications of Richard Pynson." Diss. University of Western
Ontario, 1977.

Jordan, Robert M. *Chaucer's Poetics and the Modern Reader.* Berkeley and
Los Angeles: University of California Press, 1987.

Jost, Jean E., ed. *Chaucer's Humor: Critical Essays.* New York: Garland,
1994.

Kane, George. "'Good' and 'Bad' Manuscripts: Texts and Critics."
1986. Rpt. *Chaucer and Langland: Historical and Textual Approaches.*
Berkeley and Los Angeles: University of California Press, 1989. Pp.
206-27.

————. *Piers Plowman: The Evidence for Authorship.* London: The
Athlone Press, 1965.

————, and E. Talbot Donaldson, ed. *Piers Plowman: The B Version.*
London: Athlone, 1975.

Keepe, Henry. *Monumenta Westmonasteriensa: Or a Historical Account of the Original Increase, and Present State of St. Peter's, or the Abby Church of Westminster.* London: Wilkinson, 1683.

Kendrick, Laura. *Chaucerian Play: Comedy and Control in the Canterbury Tales.* Berkeley and Los Angeles: University of California, 1988.

Kiralis, Karl. "William Blake as an Intellectual and Spiritual Guide to Chaucer's *Canterbury Tales.*" *Blake Studies* 1 (1969): 139-90.

Koff, Leonard Michael. *Chaucer and the Art of Storytelling.* Berkeley and Los Angeles: University of California Press, 1987.

Kolve, V. A. *Chaucer and the Imagery of Narrative: The First Five Canterbury Tales.* Stanford: Stanford University Press, 1984.

Kuhl, E. P. "Chaucer and Westminster Abbey." *Journal of English and Germanic Philology* 45 (1946): 340-43.

Kynaston, Francis. *Amorum Troili et Creseide Libri duo priores Anglico-Latini.* Oxford: Lichfield, 1635.

Lares, Jameela. "Chaucer's *Retraction*: A 'Verray Parfit Penitence'." *Cithara* 34 (1994): 18-33.

Lau, Beth. "Keats's Markings in Chaucer's *Troilus and Criseyde.*" *Keats-Shelley Journal* 43 (1994): 39-55.

Leicester, H. Marshall, Jr. "The Art of Impersonation: A General Prologue to *the Canterbury Tales.*" *PMLA* 95 (1980): 213-24.

———. *The Disenchanted Self: Representing the Subject in the Canterbury Tales.* Berkeley and Los Angeles: University of California Press, 1990.

Leland, John. *Commentarii de Scriptoribus Britannicis.* Ed. Anthony Hall. Oxford: Sheldon Theatre, 1709.

Lerer, Seth. "British Library MS Harley 78 and the Manuscripts of John Shirley." *Notes & Queries* 235 (1990): 400-03.

———. *Chaucer and His Readers.* Princeton: Princeton University Press, 1993.

———. *Literacy and Power in Anglo-Saxon Literature.* Omaha: University of Nebraska Press, 1991.

———. "Rewriting Chaucer: Two Fifteenth-Century Readings of *the Canterbury Tales.*" *Viator* 19 (1988): 311-26.

———. "Textual Criticism and Literary Theory: Chaucer and his Readers." *Exemplaria* 2 (1990): 329-45.

———, ed. "Cluster on Chaucer." *PMLA* 107 (1992): 1139-80.

———, ed. *Reading from the Margins: Textual Studies, Chaucer, and Medieval Literature. (Huntington Library Quarterly,* vol. 58, no. 1). San Marino, Ca.: Huntington Library Press, 1996.

Lethaby, W. R. "Chaucer's Tomb." *Times Literary Supplement*, 21 February 1929. P. 137.

Levin, Richard. "The Ironic Reading of the *Rape of Lucrece* and the Problem of External Evidence." *Shakespeare Survey* 34 (1981): 85-92.

Lewis, Charlton T., and Charles Short. *A Latin Dictionary.* Oxford: Clarendon Press, 1907.

Lounsbury, Thomas R. *Studies in Chaucer.* 3 vols. New York: Harper, 1892.

Lüdeke Henri. *Die Funktionen des Erzählers in Chaucers epischer Dichtung.* Halle: Niemeyer, 1928.

Lumiansky, Robert M. *Of Sondry Folk: The Dramatic Principle in The Canterbury Tales.* Austin: University of Texas Press, 1955.

Machan, Tim William. "Kynaston's *Troilus*, Textual Criticism, and the Renaissance Reading of Chaucer." *Exemplaria* 5 (1993): 161-83.

———. *Textual Criticism and Middle English Texts.* Charlottesville: University Press of Virginia, 1994.

———. "Thomas Berthelette and Gower's *Confessio*." *Studies in the Age of Chaucer* 18 (1966): 143-66.

———. Review of Blake and Robinson, *Canterbury Tales Project. Studies in the Age of Chaucer* 17 (1995): 175-78.

Macray, William Dunn. *Annals of the Bodleian Library, Oxford.* Oxford: Clarendon Press, 1890.

McClennan, William. "The Transcription of the 'Clerk's Tale' in MS HM 140: Interpreting Textual Effects." *Studies in Bibliography* 47 (1994): 89-102.

McFarland, Thomas. "Shoring up the Self: The Ragged Brilliance of Coleridge's Philosophy of Religion." *Times Literary Supplement*, 17 June 1994. P. 3.

McGann, Jerome J. *A Critique of Modern Textual Criticism.* Chicago: University of Chicago Press, 1983.

———, ed. *Textual Criticism and Literary Interpretation.* Chicago: University of Chicago Press, 1985.

McKenzie, D. F. "Printers of the Mind: Some Notes on Bibliographical Theories and Printing-House Practices." *Studies in Bibliography* 22 (1969): 1-75.

McKerrow, Ronald B. *An Introduction to Bibliography for Literary Students.* Oxford: Clarendon Press, 1927.

———, and F. S. Ferguson. *Title-page Borders used in England and Scotland, 1485-1640.* London: Bibliographical Society, 1932.

Manly, John Matthews. *Piers the Plowman and its Sequence.* EETS O.S., extra vol. 135b. London: Henry Frowde, 1908.

——, and Edith Rickert. *The Text of the Canterbury Tales.* 8 vols. Chicago: University of Chicago Press, 1940.

Middleton, Anne. "The Idea of Public Poetry in the Reign of Richard II." *Speculum* 53 (1978): 94-114.

Minnis, A. J. *Medieval Theory of Authorship.* 1984. 2nd ed. Philadelphia: University of Pennsylvania Press, 1988.

Miskimin, Alice S. "The Illustrated Eighteenth-Century Chaucer." *Modern Philology* 77 (1979): 26-55.

——. *The Renaissance Chaucer.* New Haven: Yale University Press, 1975.

Moore, Everett T. "Fine Printing." In *William Andrews Clark Library: Report of the Third Decade.* Berkeley and Los Angeles: University of California Press, 1966. Pp. 46-63.

Morell, Thomas, ed. *Euripidis Hecuba, Orestes, et Phoenissae, cum Scholiis antiquis: ac Versione, Notisque Johannis King, ferè integris, curante Thoma Morell qui Alcestin adjecit.* 2 vols. London, 1748.

——, ed. See Chaucer.

Mores, Edward Rowe. *A Dissertation upon English Typographical Founders and Founderies (1778).* Ed. Harry Carter and Christopher Ricks. Oxford: Oxford Bibliographical Society, 1961.

Morison, Stanley. "Introduction: Bibliography and Typography." In *Catalogue of Specimens of Printing Types by English and Scottish Printers and Founders, 1665-1830.* Ed. W. Turner Berry and A. F. Johnson. London: Oxford University Press, 1935.

——, and Harry Carter. *John Fell: The University Press and the 'Fell' Types: The punches and matrices designed for printing in the Greek, Latin, English and Oriental Languages bequeathed in 1686 to the University of Oxford by John Fell, D.D.* Oxford: Clarendon Press, 1967.

Moxon, Joseph. *Mechanick Exercises on the Whole Art of Printing.* Ed. Herbert Davis and Harry Carter. 2nd ed. London: Oxford University Press, 1962.

Muscatine, Charles. *The Book of Geoffrey Chaucer.* San Francisco: The Book Club of California, 1963.

——. *Chaucer and the French Tradition: A Study in Style and Meaning.* Berkeley and Los Angeles: University of California Press, 1957.

——. *Poetry and Crisis in the Age of Chaucer.* Notre Dame: University of Notre Dame Press, 1972.

Myers, Robin. "William Blades's Debt to Henry Bradshaw and G. I. F. Tupper in his Caxton Studies: A Further Look at Unpublished Documents." *The Library* ser. 5, 33 (1978): 265-83.

Neale, J. P., and E. W. Brayley. *History and Antiquities of the Abbey Church of St. Peter, Westminster*. London, 1818-23.

Needham, Paul. *The Bradshaw Method: Henry Bradshaw's Contribution to Bibliography*. Chapel Hill, N.C.: Hanes Foundation, 1988.

———. *The Printer and the Pardoner*. Washington, D. C.: Library of Congress, 1986.

Nichols, Stephen G. "Introduction: Philology in a Manuscript Culture." *Speculum* 65 (1990): 1-10.

Nicholson, Peter. "Poet and Scribe in the Manuscripts of Gower's *Confessio Amantis*." In Pearsall, ed. *Manuscripts and Texts*. Pp. 130-42.

Nickson, Margaret. "Bagford and Sloane." *The British Library Journal* 9 (1983): 51-55.

Nolan, Barbara. "'A Poet Ther Was': Chaucer's Voices in the General Prologue to the *Canterbury Tales*." *PMLA* 101 (1986): 154-69.

Norton-Smith, John, ed. *Bodleian Library MS Fairfax 16*. London: Scolar Press, 1979.

Nuttall, Derek. "English Printers and their Typefaces, 1600-1700." In Robin Myers and Michael Harris, ed. *Aspects of Printing from 1600*. Oxford: Oxford Polytechnic Press, 1987. Pp. 30-48.

Nykrog, Per. "A Warrior Scholar at the Collège de France." In R. Howard Bloch and Stephen G. Nichols, ed. *Medievalism and the Modernist Temper*. Baltimore: Johns Hopkins University Press, 1996. Pp. 286-307.

Owen, Charles A., Jr. *The Manuscripts of the Canterbury Tales*. Cambridge: D. S. Brewer, 1991.

Owings, Frank N., Jr. "Keats, Lamb, and a Black-letter Chaucer." *Papers of the Bibliographical Society of America* 75 (1981): 147-55.

Pace, George B. "Otho A. XVIII." *Speculum* 26 (1951): 306-08.

———, ed. See Chaucer.

Painter, George D. *William Caxton: A Quincentenary Biography of England's First Printer*. London: Chatto and Windus, 1976.

Parkes, M. B. "The Influence of the Concepts of *Ordinatio* and *Compilatio* on the Development of the Book." In J. J. G. Alexander and M. T. Gibson, ed. *Medieval Learning and Literature: Essays Presented to R. W. Hunt*. Oxford: Clarendon Press, 1976. Pp. 115-41.

———, and Richard Beadle, eds. See Chaucer.

Patterson, Lee W. "Ambiguity and Interpretation: A Fifteenth-Century Reading of *Troilus and Criseyde.*" *Speculum* 54 (1979): 297-330.

———. *Chaucer and the Subject of History.* Madison: University of Wisconsin Press, 1991.

———. "The Logic of Textual Criticism and the Way of Genius: The Kane-Donaldson *Piers Plowman* in Historical Perspective." In McGann, ed. *Textual Criticism and Literary Interpretation.* Pp. 55-91.

———. *Negotiating the Past: The Historical Understanding of Medieval Literature.* Madison: University of Wisconsin Press, 1987.

Pearsall, Derek. "Chaucer's Tomb: The Politics of Reburial." *Medium Aevum* 64 (1995): 51-73.

———. "Editing Medieval Texts: Some Developments and Some Problems." In McGann, ed. *Textual Criticism and Literary Interpretation.* Pp. 92-106.

———. *The Life of Geoffrey Chaucer: A Critical Biography.* Oxford: Blackwell, 1992.

———. "Thomas Speght (ca. 1550-?)." In Ruggiers, ed. *Editing Chaucer.* Pp. 71-92.

———, ed. See Chaucer.

Peterson, William S. *The Kelmscott Press: A History of William Morris's Typographical Adventure.* Berkeley and Los Angeles: University of California Press, 1991.

Pfeiffer, Rudolf. *History of Classical Scholarship from 1300-1850.* Oxford: Oxford University Press 1975.

Philip, Ian. *The Bodleian Library in the Seventeenth and Eighteenth Centuries.* Oxford: Clarendon Press, 1983.

The Piers Plowman Controversy. EETS O.S., extra issue 139 b, c, d, e. London: Kegan Paul, 1910.

Pits, John. *Relationum Historicarum de Rebus Anglicis . . . Libri.* Paris: Thierry, 1619.

Plan, Pierre-Paul. *Les Editions de Rabelais de 1532 à 1711: Catalogue raisonné.* 1904; rpt. New York, 1970.

Pollard, Alfred W., and G. R. Redgrave, et al. *A Short-Title Catalogue of Books Printed in England, Scotland, and Ireland, and of English Books Printed Abroad.* 2nd rev. ed. 3 vols. London: Bibliographical Society, 1976-91.

Pollard, G. "The Pecia System in the Medieval Universities." In M. B. Parkes and A. G. Watson, ed. *Medieval Scribes, Manuscripts and*

Libraries: Essays presented to N. R. Ker. London: Scolar Press, 1978. Pp. 145-61.

Poole, Henry. "Westminster Abbey: A Study on Poets' Corner." *The Antiquary* 4 (October 1881): 139.

Pratt, Robert A. "The Order of the *Canterbury Tales.*" *PMLA* 66 (1951): 1141-67.

Prothero, G. W. *A Memoir of Henry Bradshaw.* London: Kegan Paul, Trench, 1888.

Quinn, William A. *Chaucer's Rehersynges: The Performability of The Legend of Good Women.* Washington, D. C.: Catholic University Press, 1994.

Rawles, Stephen. "Les Typographie de Rabelais: Réflexions bibliographiques sur les éditions faussement attribuées." *Etudes Rabelaisiennes* 21 (1988): 37-48.

———, and M. A. Screech. *A New Rabelais Bibliography: Editions of Rabelais before 1626. Etudes Rabelaissiennes,* 20. Geneva: Droz, 1987.

Reed, Talbot Baines. *A History of the Old English Letter Foundries.* Rev. ed. A. F. Johnson. London: Faber and Faber, 1952.

Rhodes, Dennis E. *A Catalogue of Incunabula in all the Libraries of Oxford University outside the Bodleian.* Oxford: Clarendon Press, 1982.

Riffaterre, Michael. "Criteria for Style Analysis." *Word* 15 (1959): 154-74.

———. "Describing Poetic Structures: Two Approaches to Baudelaire's 'Les Chats'." In Jacques Ehrmann, ed. *Structuralism.* 1966. Rpt. Garden City, N.Y.: Anchor Books, 1970. Pp. 188-230.

Robertson, D. W., Jr. *Preface to Chaucer: Studies in Medieval Perspectives.* Princeton: Princeton University Press, 1962.

Robinson, Duncan. *William Morris, Edward Burne-Jones, and the Kelmscott Chaucer.* London: Gordon Fraser, 1982.

Robinson, P. R. "The Booklet: A Self-Contained Unit in Composite Manuscripts." *Codicologica* 3 (1980): 46-69.

———. "Self-contained Units in Composite MSS of the Anglo-Saxon Period." *Anglo-Saxon England* 7 (1978): 231-38.

———, ed. *MS Bodley 638.* Norman, Okla.: Pilgrim Books, 1982.

Ross, Thomas W., ed. See Chaucer.

Rouse, Mary A., and Richard H. Rouse. "Book Production: Stationers and Peciae." In *Authentic Witnesses: Approaches to Medieval Texts and Manuscripts.* Notre Dame: University of Notre Dame, 1991.

Royal Commission of Historical Monuments (England). *An Inventory of the Historical Monuments in London.* Vol. 1: *Westminster Abbey.* London: Stationer's Office, 1924.

Ruggiers, Paul G. *The Art of the Canterbury Tales.* Madison: University of Wisconsin Press, 1965.

———, ed. *Editing Chaucer: The Great Tradition.* Norman: University of Oklahoma Press, 1984.

Saenger, Paul. *A Catalogue of the Pre-1500 Western Manuscript Books at the Newberry Library.* Chicago: University of Chicago Press, 1989.

Sandys, J. E. *A History of Classical Scholarship.* Cambridge: Cambridge University Press, 1980.

Sawyer, Charles J., and F. J. Harvey Darnton. *English Books 1475-1900: A Signpost for Collectors.* New York: Sawyer, 1927.

Schuler, Robert M. "The Renaissance Chaucer as Alchemist." *Viator* 15 (1984): 305-33.

Screech, M. A. *Rabelais.* Ithaca: Cornell University Press, 1979.

Shailor, Barbara A. *Catalogue of Medieval and Renaissance Manuscripts in the Beinecke Rare Book and Manuscript Library, Yale University.* 3 vols. Binghamton: MRTS, 1984.

[Shephard, Samuel]. "Our Weekly Gossip." *Athenaeum,* 10 July 1850. P. 768.

Shillingsburg, Peter. "The Autonomous Author, the Sociology of Texts, and the Polemics of Textual Criticism." In Philip Cohen, ed. *Devils and Angels: Textual Editing and Literary Theory.* Charlottesville: University of Virginia Press, 1991. Pp. 22-43.

———. "Polymorphic, Polysemic, Protean, Reliable, Electronic Texts." In George Bornstein and Ralph G. Williams, ed. *Palimpsest: Editorial Theory in the Humanities.* Ann Arbor: University of Michigan Press, 1993. Pp. 29-43.

Shoaf, R. A. *Dante, Chaucer, and the Currency of the Word: Money, Images and Reference in Late Medieval Poetry.* Norman: University of Oklahoma Press, 1983.

Simpson, Percy. *Proof-Reading in the Sixteenth, Seventeenth and Eighteenth Centuries.* Oxford: Oxford University Press, 1935.

Silvia, Daniel S. "Some Fifteenth-Century Manuscripts of the Canterbury Tales." In Beryl Rowland, ed. *Chaucer and Middle English Studies in Honour of Rossell Hope Robbins.* Kent: Kent State University Press, 1974.

Skeat, Walter W. *The Chaucer Canon, with a discussion of the works associated with the name of Geoffrey Chaucer.* Oxford: Clarendon Press, 1900.

———. *Notes and Queries* ser. 7, 8 (1889): 133.

————, ed. *The* Kingis Quair*: Together with A Ballad of Good Counsel.*
The Scottish Text Society. Edinburgh: Blackwood, 1884.

————, ed. *Langland's Vision of* Piers Plowman. 3 vols. EETS 17-19.
London, Trubner, 1867-85.

————, ed. See Chaucer.

Smith, N. A. *Catalogue of the Pepys Library at Magdalene College,
Cambridge* I: *Printed Books.* Cambridge: D. S. Brewer, 1978.

Speer, Mary B. "Old French Literature." In D. C. Greetham, ed.
Scholarly Editing: A Guide to Research. New York: Modern Language
Association, 1995. Pp. 382-416.

Spurgeon, Caroline F. E. *Five Hundred Years of Chaucer Criticism and
Allusion (1357-1900).* 5 pts. 1908-17. Rpt. 3 vols. Cambridge:
Cambridge University Press, 1925.

Stillinger, Jack. *Multiple Authorship and the Myth of Solitary Genius.* New
York: Oxford University Press, 1991.

Stokes, Charlotte C. "The Grave of Chaucer." *Athenaeum,* 25 October
1902. P. 552.

Stowe, John. *A Survey of London.* 1598. Ed. C. L. Kingsford. Oxford:
Clarendon Press, 1908.

————, ed. See Chaucer.

Strohm, Paul. "Jean of Angoulême: A Fifteenth Century Reader of
Chaucer." *Neuphilologische Mitteilungen* 72 (1971): 69-76.

————. "Politics and Poetics: Usk and Chaucer in the 1380s." In Lee
Patterson, ed. *Literary Practice and Social Change in Britain, 1380-
1530.* Berkeley and Los Angeles: University of California, 1990. Pp.
83-112.

————. *Social Chaucer.* Cambridge: Harvard University Press, 1989.

Terkla, Daniel P. "The Centrality of the Peripheral: Illuminating
Borders and the Topography of Space in Medieval Narrative and
Art, 1066-1400." Diss. University of Southern California, 1993.

Thompson, John J. "The Compiler in Action: Robert Thornton and
the 'Thornton Romances' in Lincoln Cathedral MS 91." In
Pearsall, ed. *Manuscripts and Readers.* Pp. 113-24.

Thynne, Francis. *Animadversions uppon the Annotacions and Corrections
of some imperfections of impressiones of Chaucers workes.* 1598. Ed. G. H.
Kingsley. Rev. J. F. Furnivall. London: Trübner, 1875.

Timpanaro, Sebastiano. *La Genesi de metodo del Lachmann.* Padua:
Liviana, 1981.

Todd, Henry J. *Illustrations of the Lives and Writings of Gower and Chaucer. Collected from Authentick Documents.* London: Rivington, 1810.

Troutbeck, Henry. *The Nineteenth Century* 42 (August 1897): 336.

Tyrwhitt, Thomas, ed. *Aristotle: Poetics.* 3rd ed. Oxford: Oxford University Press, 1806.

———, ed. See Chaucer.

Updike, Daniel Berkeley. *Printing Types: Their History, Forms, and Use: A Study in Survivals.* 2 vols. 2nd ed. Cambridge: Harvard University Press, 1937.

Vervliet, H. D. L. *Sixteenth-Century Printing Types of the Low Countries.* With foreword by Harry Carter. Amsterdam: Hertzberger, 1968.

Warton, Thomas. *The History of English Poetry from the Close of the Eleventh to the Commencement of the Eighteenth Century.* 3 vols. London: Dodsley, 1775-78.

———, and William Huddesford, eds. *The Lives of those Eminent Antiquaries John Leland, Thomas Hearne and Anthony à Wood.* 2 vols. Oxford: Clarendon Press, 1772.

Wawn, Andrew N. "Chaucer, The Plowman's Tale and Reformation Propaganda: The Testimonies of Thomas Godfray and *I Playne Piers.*" *Bulletin of the John Rylands Library* 56 (1973): 174-92.

Weever, John. *Ancient Funerall Monuments within the United Monarchie.* London: Harper, 1631.

Weiss, R. *Humanism in England During the Fifteenth Century.* 1941. 3rd ed. Oxford: Blackwell, 1967.

———. "Humanism in Oxford." *Times Literary Supplement,* 9 January 1937. P. 28.

Wellek, René and Austin Warren. *Theory of Literature.* 1942. 3rd ed. New York: Harcourt, Brace and World, 1962.

Wenzel, Siegfried Wenzel. *Macaronic Sermons; Bilingualism and Preaching in Late-Medieval England.* Ann Arbor: University of Michigan Press, 1994.

Williams, Iolo A. "English Book-Illustration, 1700-1775." *The Library* ser. 4, 17 (1937): 1-21.

Willis, James. *Latin Textual Criticism.* Urbana: University of Illinois Press, 1972.

Wimsatt, W. K., Jr., and Monroe C. Beardsley. "The Intentional Fallacy." In *The Verbal Icon: Studies in the Meaning of Poetry.* Louisville: University of Kentucky Press, 1954.

Windeatt, B. A. "The Scribes as Chaucer's Early Critics." *Studies in the Age of Chaucer* 1 (1979): 119-41.

———. "Thomas Tyrwhitt (1730-1786)." In Ruggiers, ed. *Editing Chaucer*. Pp. 117-43.

———, ed. See Chaucer.

Woodmansee, Martha, and Peter Jaszi, eds. *The Construction of Authorship: Textual Appropriation in Law and Literature*. Durham: Duke University Press, 1994.

Woodward, Daniel, and Martin Stevens, eds. *The Canterbury Tales (ca. 1410): The New Ellesmere Chaucer Facsimile*. Tokyo: Yushodo, 1995; San Marino, Ca.: Huntington Library Press, 1995.

———, eds. *Ellesmere Chaucer: Essays in Interpretation*. San Marino: Huntington Library Press, 1995.

Wright, C. E., and Ruth C. Wright, eds. *The Diary of Humfrey Wanley 1715-1726*. 2 vols. London: The Bibliographical Society, 1966.

Wurtele, Douglas. "The Penitence of Geoffrey Chaucer." *Viator* 11 (1980): 335-59.

Yeager, Robert F. "British Library Additional MS. 5141: An Unnoticed Chaucer *Vita*." *Journal of Medieval and Renaissance Studies* 14 (1984): 273-76.

———. "Literary Theory at the Close of the Middle Ages: William Caxton and William Thynne." *Studies in the Age of Chaucer* 6 (1984): 135-64.

INDEX